The American Dream and Dreams Deferred

The American Dream and Dreams Deferred

A Dialectical Fairy Tale

Carlton D. Floyd and Thomas Ehrlich Reifer

LEXINGTON BOOKS
Lanham • Boulder • New York • London

Published by Lexington Books
An imprint of The Rowman & Littlefield Publishing Group, Inc.
4501 Forbes Boulevard, Suite 200, Lanham, Maryland 20706
www.rowman.com

86-90 Paul Street, London EC2A 4NE

British Library Cataloguing in Publication Information Available

Library of Congress Cataloging-in-Publication Data

Names: Floyd, Carlton D., author. | Reifer, Thomas Ehrlich, author.
Title: The American dream and dreams deferred : a dialectical fairy tale / Carlton D. Floyd and Thomas E. Reifer.
Description: Lanham : Lexington Books, [2022] | Includes bibliographical references and index.
Identifiers: LCCN 2022030016 (print) | LCCN 2022030017 (ebook) | ISBN 9781793634115 (cloth) | ISBN 9781793634139 (paper) | ISBN 9781793634122 (ebook)
Subjects: LCSH: American Dream in literature. | National characteristics, American, in literature. | United States—Civilization.
Classification: LCC PS169.A49 F55 2022 (print) | LCC PS169.A49 (ebook) | DDC 810.9/35873—dc23/eng/20220817
LC record available at https://lccn.loc.gov/2022030016
LC ebook record available at https://lccn.loc.gov/2022030017

Contents

Preface

This book is rooted in a friendship. We started at this university at roughly the same time but did not get acquainted until we both served on the President's Advisory Board on Inclusion and Diversity together. Over the years, and through the writing of this book, we suppose that we found in our friendship many of the truths we have tried to express here, about mutual interdependence and symbiosis, that we have found in each other, and in the larger world of which we are a part. No words can adequately express how much we have learned from each other, or our profound gratitude for what in many ways, has been our version of a blues and jazz improvisation. In many ways, our backgrounds are about as different as you can get, in tragicomic ironic ways, while simultaneously being closely related in terms of trauma, loss, and the challenges of moving from surviving to thriving in the context of the truth expressed by Lauren Olamina in Octavia Butler's *Parable of the Sower*, that "There is no end / To what a living world / Will demand of you." Happily, we have found through many trials and tribulations, that we are better working together, and that the lessons we have learned in the microcosms of our lives may be of value to others.

We also believe firmly that today's separation of disciplines impedes the kind of work necessary to productively approach issues of import that impact our world. We believe that bringing the insights of literature, the humanities, and the social and natural sciences together, as part of Immanuel Wallerstein's call to renew the search for the good, the true, and the beautiful, are necessary if we are to move to a world in which concern and care for others becomes part and parcel of our purpose. At this point, it is hard for us to even remember how we stumbled upon the question of the American Dream and dreams deferred, but having stumbled upon it, we have come to see how important the critique is for moving forward to a more hopeful future. Ultimately, it became clear to us that there was a story not being told about the American Dream. We wanted to tell that story, or at least some part of it, hoping that the voices we add will be considered, not only in work on the American Dream, but also in the formation and foundation of the Americas, the United States, and in its global implications. We realize that we have not been up to the task of incorporating all of the voices that could and should be heard, but we hope that we provide a start in a positive direction, and perhaps a frame within which further work of this nature may flourish. We look forward to continuing the conversation.

Acknowledgments

In memory of Sarah Lee Floyd. May you rest wrapped in love. And in memory of Kelly Marie Wells (1980–2010), and *Dear Freedom Writer* author, Alexi "Lexi" Emilia Rodriguez (2000–2022), and their California Dreams.

We offer our sincere thanks to the following people who worked with us under a Faculty Interdisciplinary Startup Grant Proposal, 2017–2018, *Another California, Another Country, Another World* from the Humanities Center at the University of San Diego, and whose thoughtful lines of inquiry helped form the basis of this book. Also, we offer our heartfelt apologies to anyone we may miss acknowledging here. Thank you, Cid Martinez (Sociology) and Leonora Simonovis (Spanish, Languages and Literatures), as well as our former students Hailey Brooks (Sociology), Cassandra Ortega (English and Sociology, McNair Scholar), Tiasha Rogers (Sociology and McNair Scholar), Dominique Shank (English, McNair Scholar), Hailey Trawick (English and Sociology), and Alexis Wiley (Sociology and Psychology). To Chris Nayve and the Mulvaney Center for Community Service-Learning, your support of our class on the American Dream by providing us with a Social Issues Grant, allowing us to formulate and provide a team-taught course on the American Dream, was invaluable to us. Finally, to the Departments of English and Sociology, we give thanks.

There are other colleagues and friends for whom we are eternally grateful. We consider them in many ways, members of our family. Their lives continue to enrich and support us. Our thanks to Erica Alcaraz, Marcy Alyn, Adina Batnitzky, Janet Biblin (Baggins), Sage Breslin, Roy Brooks, Noam and Valeria Chomsky, Christina Chopin, Catherine Coquery-Vidrovitch, Suzzanne Cromwell, Evelyn Cruz, Bahar Davary, Hilda Martinez, Mike Davis and Alessandra Moctezuma, all members of the Ehrlich and Reifer family, past and present, including Jane, Ray of Sunshine, Jill and Gus, Matthew, Miles and Jimmy, Dan and Patricia Ellsberg, Erin Gruwell and The

Freedom Writers, our friends in Ethnic Studies, Michelle Jacob, Judy Liu, Don Kelly, and Lisa Riccardi, Jessica Martinez, Moe Myers, Mychal Odom, Sister Dianna Ortiz, Kristen Parker, Gail Perez, Odilka Sabrina Santiago, Christina Shaheen, Laura Wakil, Jerry Rafiki Jenkins and Katie Sciurba, Adrian and Delia Arancibia and their daughters Esperanza and Victoria, Hassan Dhouti, Melisa and Rose Klimaszewski, the Floyd and Holmes Family, and particularly, Sarah Luese Banks, Elder Mae Thomas, Sophia Dell Holmes, Sharon Deleen Golden, Byron and Janis Mason, the faculty and staff at USD's Copley Library (especially Leslie Hovland), and the Legal Research Center (Library), and all our students and teachers over these many years. Too often we leave unacknowledged the staff at our university who make things run, and without whom, we would not have such a wonderful place to work. In particular, Milton Maples, from Public Safety, must be thanked, as his words of encouragement and support always gives us strength and purpose. We take all responsibility for any shortcomings evident in our work.

Introduction

The American Dream

A Dialectical Fairy Tale

Our purpose is to demonstrate how rival interpretations of the American Dream poignantly express conflict over its very meaning, and to elucidate the dialectical tension embedded therein. We intend to capture moments where the American Dream alternately appears possible, when it seems out of reach, and when it seems both possible and out of reach. We pay particular attention to these dialectically entwined moments. Our hope in exposing the gap between our imagined American Dream and equally stark historical realities is to help rouse people from their slumbers, to awaken from the dream. Herein, we present a synthesis of the Dream projecting alternative futures, simultaneously informed by the dystopian remembrance of sufferings past and present. In so doing, we invite readers to join us in making a new collective dream of a better future—on a socially just, enlarged, multicultural and ecologically sustainable social foundation—into a living reality.

Few dreams have been more discussed and debated than the American Dream, which has occupied our national and global attention now for nearly a century, if not more. Its prehistory, of course, goes back even further. And given the unique position of the United States in the world, this Dream has a global scale and scope arguably without equal in modern consciousness, as a model to be pursued and imitated.[1] In our usage, the Dream refers to the American Dream, in a national setting, that of the United States, but this makes it no less entwined with the dreams of the Americas as a whole.[2]

Our concerns about the state of the world, and the role of our home country, the United States in it, leads us to revisit the origins and development of the concept, its transformation over time, and its prehistory. We did not see such work being done among the numerous books and articles on the American Dream already published, as we read much of the literature, though there are certainly various texts, that inspired us. By and large, though, most books that deal with the American Dream take the concept for granted. We thought that

1

an exploration of this subject required greater investigation. For example, we are struck by how James Truslow Adams, who is credited with coining the term, argued that the Dream was not only or simply about personal advancement, but about a place where all members of society could rise above their current stations. At the same time, in a telling query, Adams asked whether the Dream was related to the harsh realities of continental processes of exploitation and conquest, fueled by dreams of wealth and power, taken as moral goods, without consideration of the human consequences, or a willingness to look these realities in the face.[3] Adams' words are eerily prescient. Dominant strains of thought about the Dream seem to reject and ignore these admonitions. Not only do they routinely ignore the scars our exploitation and conquest leaves on us, as Adams asserts, but they also ignore the ways in which such acts have scarred others, covered over as it were by the myth of perpetual progress. Indeed, permutations of the Dream have mutated across time to retain it's a willful blindness and ignorance about its "ugly scars."[4] Many who dream the American Dream insist on a focus almost entirely shaped by personal achievements or advancements, without any allusion to the power of collective memory or history, and to the triumphs *and* tragedies within it that a socially just society must acknowledge.

Thomas Piketty's *Capital in the Twenty-first Century* (2014) speaks to the historical contradictions of the American Dream. The book rocketed to the top of the bestsellers' list exactly because its focus on increasing inequalities in the US and across the globe challenged so many of the cherished myths associated with the concept. In a section of the book entitled "From Marx to Kuznets, or Apocalypse to Fairy Tale," Piketty writes: "we might say that economists' no doubt overly developed taste for apocalyptic predictions gave way to a similarly excessive fondness for fairy tales, or at any rate happy endings."[5] This fondness for "fairy tales" or "happy endings" was seen in the idea that a rising economic tide lifts all boats, increasingly at odds with the realities of the astronomical rise of inequality. Here, while an ever-smaller plutocracy shoots into outer space, both literally and in levels of wealth, those remaining, as on the Titanic, are sinking.

So how to explain this ever-widening gap between myth and historical reality? The multilayered answer to this question must begin with the recognition that the dominant version of the American Dream is based on a selective kind of memory and history, and on distorted intellectual understandings, obscuring from view those past events that mar the notions of our eternal forward progress, and mythic ideas of our increasing humanity.[6] In short, our preference for fairy tales or fantasy over reality, for myth over memory, for unidirectional notions of history and progress, offers a way to understand why the American Dream is so enduring, hard to critique, and hard to illuminate. And yet, such critiques have been done by individuals and groups, often deeply disenfranchised within and beyond the context of the United States that have been largely sidelined or ignored, and whose works and voices today are increasing being banned in schools and libraries across the country.[7]

In "The Explosion of US Inequality after 1980," Piketty notes that "income inequality has exploded in the United States. The upper decile's share increased from 30–35 percent of national income in the 1970s to 45–50 percent in the 2000s. . . . The shape of the curve is rather impressively steep . . . if change continues at the same pace . . . the upper decile will be raking in 60 percent of the national income by 2030." Moreover, Piketty argues that "it is possible to estimate that the upper decile's share slightly exceeded 50 percent of the national income on the eve of the financial crisis of 2008 and then again in the early 2010s."[8] This rising inequality has earlier antecedents.[9] As Piketty notes,

> In the United States . . . a (white) patrimonial middle class already existed in the nineteenth century. It suffered a setback during the Gilded Age, regained its health in the middle of the twentieth century, and then suffered another setback after 1980. . . . Hence the lost US paradise is associated with the country's beginnings: there is nostalgia for the era of the Boston Tea Party.[10]

This mythical idea—of creating or returning to paradise—represents one version of the American Dream, contrasted to egalitarian and solidaristic visions that will reappear herein.

We believe that a dialectical presentation of these questions and answers from authors rarely brought into interplay with each other can advance the dialogue and ongoing conversation and urgent need to act on these pressing challenges. While there are untold books written about the American Dream, none to our knowledge are framed via a combination of James Truslow Adams' original formulation of the concept, in 1931, and Langston Hughes' poetic reply in "Harlem, or Dream Deferred," from his larger work, *Montage of a Dream Deferred* (1951).[11] Combining and historicizing these voices allows for a unique exploration of the American Dream as "A Dialectical Fairy Tale," an homage to Walter Benjamin's monumental *Arcades Project* (1999), subtitled "A Dialectical Fairyland," and which was for him an exercise in "dream interpretation," preeminently a critique of the dream or myth of inexorable progress, the enchanted fairyland of capitalism as seen in the Paris Arcades, and its ruins.[12]

Like the work of one of Benjamin's favorite authors, Franz Kafka, the work of Hughes and Benjamin "may be thought of as having windows, windows that are at once lucent and opaque, which take in the light of interpretive minds and give back that light at an angle of refraction, since no single interpretation can penetrate. In *The Interpretation of Dreams*, Freud conceived of the dream as "'a window, through which to cast a glance into the interior of the mind.' Each dreamlike image . . . is such an opening through which to glimpse. . . . Yet no such window is entirely transparent. . . . And because each . . . has many windows, a glance at one will communicate with another. The windows catch one another's light; perspectives scintillate."[13] Through dream interpretation, then, Hughes and Benjamin offer powerful alternative retellings of modernity, and an important comparison and contrast with Max Weber's perhaps more famous "disenchantment of the world."[14]

Our subtitle, "A Dialectical Fairy Tale," also nods towards Thomas Piketty's reading of economists, among others, who graft on to the American Dream, the happily ever after ending deeply embedded in fairy tale traditions.[15] These perspectives are drawn together to critique the mythmaking that is part and parcel of the narrative of the American Dream, offering counter-narratives that allow the suffering, experience, striving and struggle of those often left out of the Dream into view. Edward Said reminded us in *Culture and Imperialism* (1994) that "nations themselves *are* narrations. The power to narrate, or to block other narratives from forming and emerging, is very important to culture and imperialism, and constitutes one of the main connections between them."[16] And in the American Century and beyond, America's preferred narrative self-representation has been and continues to be primarily through the ideology of the American Dream. It, too, is an imperial ideology, albeit one that presents itself as alternately anti-imperial, or that of a benevolent hegemony or empire.[17]

What are the consequences of the American Dream, and of the ruins of its imagined and unimagined better futures? This brings us to poet Langston Hughes' central line of inquiry in *Montage of a Dream Deferred* (1951), in his poem, alternately titled "Harlem (2)" or "Dream Deferred," "What happens to a dream deferred?" now interrogated from the vantage point of so many, indeed, perhaps, the majority, in terms of sheer numbers, and increasingly so arguably, living, and dying, in the ruins of the American Dream's deferment, or some would even say, and this is the dialectically entwined part, its partial realization.

Let us then revise Hughes' poem, asking whether the Dream *has* become desiccated. If we introspect, it does certainly seem to hold its allure, but its freshness must be questioned, and its sweetness is clearly tasted by an increasingly select few. No, the Dream hasn't dried up, but assuredly should be drying up, or revealed as a mirage given the water crisis, apocalyptic fires here and abroad, the socioeconomic state of many, and the ongoing march of violence, war, and displacement across the world. Given the numbers of people struggling, and the multiplicity of things they are struggling with, the Dream is certainly weighed down. The violence experienced largely by the impoverished, often people of color, but all "darkened," metaphorically, and through so-associated lived and living experiences, are curated in the context Hughes tentative ending for "Harlem," asking whether it has become too cumbersome or volatile.[18]

Since Hughes is asking questions about dreams, generally, and the American Dream, particularly, in the early 1950s, one might think that most have taken these questions to heart. Yet in our reading of contemporary discussions and debates, we still see their absence in significant parts of the public and scholarly consciousness. The global climate justice activist, who started the Friday for the Future Strikes among schoolchildren, Greta Thunberg, remarks upon this absence in her appearance before Congress on September 18th, 2019. In speaking concerning the global climate crisis, she implicitly conjures up James Truslow Adams, Langston Hughes and perhaps the most famous of all iterations of the American Dream, Martin Luther King Jr.:

> I am sixteen years old and I'm from Sweden. I am grateful for being with you here in the USA. A nation that, to many, is the country of dreams. I also have a dream . . .
>
> In fact I have many dreams. But this is the year 2019. This is not the time and place for dreams. This is the time to wake up. This is the moment in history when we need to be wide awake.
>
> And yes, we need dreams, we cannot live without dreams. But there's a time and place for everything. And dreams cannot stand in the way of telling it like it is.
>
> And yet, wherever I go I seem to be surrounded by fairytales. Business leaders, elected officials all across the political spectrum spending their time making up and telling bedtime stories that soothe us, that make us go back to sleep. These are "feel-good" stories about how we are going to fix everything. How wonderful everything is going to be when we have "solved" everything. But the problem we are facing is not that we lack the ability to dream, or to imagine a better world. The problem now is that we need to wake up. It's time to face the reality, the facts, the science.
>
> And the science . . . tells of unspoken human sufferings, which will get worse and worse the longer we delay action—unless we start to act now.[19]

Note that Thunberg, like Langston Hughes and Martin Luther King Jr. before her, insists on the centrality of hope and dreams, and, simultaneously, on the necessity of telling the truth, of laying out how things are, and how things must change if humanity and other sentient beings are to survive. At the same time, the reason why Langston Hughes, Greta Thunberg, and so many others deal with the question of the American Dream is because it is literally inescapable, and thus efforts to question, complicate, and change it must be given their due, as we seek to do here.

The authors, poets, and activists above are not alone in expressly challenging the ideas of social mobility and equal opportunity in the structure of global, and US capitalism, and the American Dream. Leading economist Raj Chetty noted the following in 2021:

> For kids born in the 1940s, it was a virtual guarantee—over 90%—that they would achieve the American Dream, meaning they would earn more over their lifetime than their parents.
>
>   Over time, this dream has faded. For kids born in the 1980s, only about 50% will achieve this metric. The notion that America is a land where, through hard work, anyone has a shot at being successful is unfortunately no longer the case. Instead, it comes down to a coin flip.[20]

Of course, one hastens to add here, that given the realities of racism, sexism, childism, and class inequities some parents were not making that much money in the first place, and many children were suffering as well, as the US is the only country in the world not to have ratified the UN Convention on the Rights of the Child, or act on its important recommendations.[21] Piketty's most recent book, *Capital and Ideology* (2020), brings the unfulfilled realities of the American Dream into stark focus. Piketty offers a telling comparison of the caste system in India, including the untouchables at the bottom of the system, and anti-Black racism and structural inequality in the US. Goran Therborn summarizes Piketty's findings as follows:

> In 1950 and 1960 the relative economic disadvantage of the former "untouchables" and Black Americans was almost the same, both possessing an income of half that of the rest of the respective populations. By the 2010s, African Americans, having risen to a peak of 60 percent of average US income in 1980, were back at their 1950 level, while the "Scheduled Castes and Tribes" had risen to about 75 per cent of the income of the rest of India.[22]

Tellingly, Isabel Wilkerson raises these exact issues in her recent book *Caste: The Origins of Our Discontents* (2020).[23] Wilkerson links caste systems in the US, India, and Nazi Germany. Here, the cruelty of caste, with its emphasis on some group being on the bottom rung, provides for hierarchical systems of domination that allow some to accrue wealth, cultural status, and power at the expense of others. In so doing, Wilkerson interrogates the destructive costs of such systems and their cultural legacies today in ways that animate a different way forward and cultivates hope for our common humanity.

This caste-like form of social stratification is a key feature of a now classic text from Ursula K. Le Guin, "The Ones Who Walk Away from Omelas" (1973), and N. K. Jemison's response to it more recently in "The Ones Who Stay and Fight," from her collection of short stories, *How Long 'Til Black*

Future Month? (2018).[24] At the heart of each story lies a child whose destitute condition is known to all, and upon which the success of the culture surrounding that child is built. All know of these children, of their condition and squalid situation. Many find justifications for this situation. Some, not finding such justifications adequate, walk away from Omelas; in Um-Helat, the city of Jemison's rendering, some stay and fight. In neither instantiation is the child's plight rendered in any way as to improve their life. In other words, the transformations in place, whether they consist of walking away or staying to fight, show a splintering of cultures around the child, rather than any productive or fruitful improvement of the child's condition, or any collective attempt to rise or improve their lives without hurting others.

Similarly, what we see is that the divisions in the US, and globally, threaten to further splinter human solidarity into a thousand shards, as scholar-activist Mike Davis expresses it, rather than bringing us together to overthrow the structures that maintain the ongoing destruction of our world and hopes of a better future.[25] In this splintering, more and more are seeing the American Dreams of a better life sinking, and this situation has produced a dramatic resurgence in scapegoating.[26] Another way of expressing this is that the American Dream, defined here economically, is now increasingly becoming as distant a possibility for the majority, as it has always been for the vast minority, which is to say persons of color, poor whites, and marginalized outsiders.

And with the decline of the common good, all sorts of malevolent symptoms are now proliferating. However limited, at least some facets of "Enlightenment" thought functioned on the premise that a socially just and politically valid, or so-called enlightened society, should reflect and promote the well-being of its citizens writ large, rather than select members among them. John-Jacques Rousseau and Thomas Jefferson both advocated for what one might call natural or human rights, represented in famous, or infamous, dicta, such as Rousseau's assertion in his *Discourse on Inequality* (1755), "Man was born free, but he is everywhere in chains," and Jefferson's (1776) "life, liberty, and the pursuit of happiness."[27]

Whereas some earlier iterations of the American Dream were animated by ideas of freedom, autonomy, and independence, and against both chattel slavery and wage slavery, these ideas were increasingly replaced by the embrace of the ideology of the consumer society in the last two centuries. For example, the rise of the Republican Party before the Civil War was animated by a hostility to both chattel and wage slavery and by ideas of autonomy and independence.[28] Of course, the Republican Party born in the 1850s, is a world away from that of the twenty-first century, whose leaders, former President Donald J. Trump first among them, hail the "lost cause" of the Civil War, paying tribute to those who seceded from the Union and fought to enshrine racist anti-Black slavery in the Confederacy. Yet as Eric Foner and many others have chronicled, during the middle of the 19th century, the Republican Party was part of the broad anti-slavery front, one that included arguably the world's most powerful abolitionist movement.[29]

As the dreams of expansive freedom for all in a multiracial democracy declined for roughly a hundred years with the defeat of Black Reconstruction, many Americans were reduced to neo slavery or wage slavery, and expectations were adjusted downward. Instead of the dream of autonomy and independence, where all could rise, Americans were encouraged to look away from freedom and autonomy in their working lives, and to seek these attributes in their ability to consume the increasing amount of goods the new industrial society produced. Such dreams were increasingly advertised not only at home but also abroad.[30] Tracy Chapman (1988) sung eloquently about this pernicious morphing of the ideology of the Dream in the song "Mountains of Things."[31] The price and costs of such transformations are an important part of our exploration.

As Eric Foner writes in his *Free Labor, Free Men: The Ideology of the Republican Party Before the Civil War* (1995),

> By the twentieth century, as the promise of economic abundance blunted hostility to the wage system, "slave wages" replaced "wage slavery" as a mark of servitude, and a family's level of consumption—the so-called American standard to living—came to define the essence of the American dream. The free American was the citizen able to consume some of the cornucopia of goods created by industrial capitalism. Here, we enter the realm of twentieth-century consumer culture, in which the focus of life shifted, over time, from work to leisure, production to consumption.[32]

The American Dream is often thought of as a dream of continuous progress. Things are getting better all the time, and all endings are happy endings. Langston Hughes and Walter Benjamin are two cultural critics who deftly critiqued notions of progress. Benjamin sought to do so in a series of works, including by looking at how narratives of modernity, and the emergence of capitalism, seen by many as coterminous with reason and progress, were enshrouded in myth, fairylands, fairy tales.

Walter Benjamin, of German-Jewish descent, preoccupied with literature and cultural criticism, shed light on the new worlds of visual culture and modernity in the early twentieth century. Here, Benjamin was part of those authors seeking to analyze the birth of the modern world, and the new features of capitalism, most especially the increasing rapidly of change, and the commodification of life. Benjamin sought to illuminate mass culture and its debris, through the study of "The Capital of the Nineteenth Century, Paris."[33] For Benjamin, the choice of Paris related to his understanding that the origins of modern consciousness lay especially in consumer culture, or dream worlds (in miniature) as he sometimes called them. Thus, Benjamin took the Parisian arcades, the glass malls originating in early nineteenth-century Paris, as point zero in his exploration. Although already in ruins, by the time he began his inquiry in 1927, Benjamin saw in the malls and its ruins the possibility of simultaneously representing and critiquing the bourgeois experience of the nineteenth century, unearthing the hopes and dreams of the nineteenth and twentieth centuries. In so doing, Benjamin hoped to conjure up an awakening of humanity in a way that approximated its stated or presumed desire for freedom, equality, peace, and justice. Benjamin never completed his project, but his monumental fragmentary *Arcades Project* survived, a message in a bottle for future generations, and has helped inspire our work.

There is another aspect of the work of Benjamin that deserves comment and that is on the American Dream in the age of increasingly visual media, and here we allude to both Benjamin's method, that of "literary montage," and his famous essay "The Work of Art in the Age of Its Technological Reproducibility."[34] What happens to history and historical understanding in an age where the written word is increasingly replaced by visual images that takes things out of their context, and repackages them for the corporations that control this medium? It is here, where the power of alternative images, perhaps the montage form, offers the possibility of remaking historical understanding.[35] Thus, what will be offered up here will be a combination of historical narratives, vignettes really, simultaneously with images that disrupt linear narratives of progress, of which the American Dream is arguably the most powerful.

Langston Hughes, of course, registered his refusal of the triumphal parade of American progress, and its penultimate expression, the American Dream, in his famous query, "What Happens to a Dream Deferred?" Hughes provided a powerful inquiry into the promissory note of the Dream in ways that have echoed throughout the course of US and global history. Like Benjamin's, Langston's inquiry also involves a city, yet instead of it being a consumer dream-world like Paris, it was the world-famous ghetto that gave rise to the Harlem Renaissance and later the Black Arts movements, part of the flowering of Black literary culture and artistic expression, registering the growing importance of visual culture, from photography to film.[36] In his emphasis on montage, Hughes has another elective affinity with Benjamin, taking things out of their original contexts, putting them in new ones, where their meaning could be revealed and depicted in radical ways, as did the incomparable African American artist Romare Bearden, and the Caribbean poet Derek

Walcott, whose book *White Egrets* (2010) also has affinities with Benjamin in its powerful meditations on the ruins of empires.[37]

Bearden was born in the South but raised "in the heart of the Harlem Renaissance," with family friends such as Langston Hughes and W.E.B. Du Bois. He worked with one of his first patrons, Duke Ellington, moving on to later work with other jazz artists, including adorning an album cover for Wynton Marsalis, whose brother Branford Marsalis devoted an album in turn to Bearden. Bearden's montage paintings and art, championed by Ralph Ellison, Derek Walcott, and others, in "working with fragments of the past, brought them into the now."[38] Of significant note here, is that Frederick Douglass was fascinated with the new medium of photography as well, wrote extensively about it, and was the most photographed American of the nineteenth century. Douglass sought to harness the means of communication, including the new medium of photography for the coming Jubilee, just as slave masters and others would harness these means to perpetuate what Douglass dubbed "the color line."[39]

Benjamin was primarily inspired by and concerned with print media and visual culture. Hughes was primarily inspired by and concerned with the blues, jazz, be-bop, and the like. Registered here as well were two radically alternative Diasporic trajectories: the African Diaspora, as part and parcel of what Ira Berlin calls the four great migrations, including the Great Black migration of the twentieth century, from the Mississippi Delta where the blues was born to the urban Black experience, and the Jewish Diaspora, which had its epicenter in Eastern Europe, but with important centers and offshoots elsewhere, including of course in Germany and Western Europe. These diasporas gave rise to an astonishing array of writers preoccupied with history and memory, freedom, and liberation from oppression, most especially through the biblical story of Exodus, and the search for the promised land.[40] The works of these authors we draw upon register multiple themes of ours, that of interconnection between what usually are viewed as separate and hermetically sealed histories, and what has been called the struggle of memory against forgetting. In our era of resurgent xenophobia, this is particularly important, for one of the key contemporary aspects of the period is what we call the war against historical memory.[41]

This preoccupation with memory, and the historical erasure of those memories which raises questions about the Dream, bring us back again to the work of Langston Hughes. For though unknown to many, Langston's query in *Montage of a Dream Deferred* (1951) was the second one of his two poems named after the city in which he long resided, namely Harlem. In the first iteration, part of *One-Way Ticket* (1949), Harlem is situated next to hell. Here we see the theme, as with Du Bois, of being in, or at the cusp of the inferno, for the border of hell is still, well, at least partially, hell. In this situated liminal space, one remembers the various ways and means used to postpone substantive change. One remembers the trite and yet nevertheless longstanding refrain, or some version of it, evident in the words, "These things take time," a phrase as meaningful only in its meaninglessness. What doesn't take time? The question is really how much time does it take? Sadly, the answer has been and remains, more time than thus far given. The Dream to which Hughes refers has not yet come to fruition. And again, revealed here is the deception, the secrecy and lies, surrounding this tragicomic experience. One is reminded of a set of comedic movies whose title plays off of the refrain one hears between children and parents on a long road trip. "Are we there yet?" the refrain goes, and the answer is generally, "Not yet! Now be quiet and look out the window or read your book." And this exchange repeats, until the destination is reached, except that as the poem highlights, it has not been reached yet. The more things change, in regard to the Dream, the more things stay the same. The call and response repeats, ad nauseam. To be sure, some things change, yet not so much the words uttered to the oppressed. And then we come once again to historical memory. We remember this exchange on the journey to a presumably better life. We remember the journey, and we hold on to what we can of this historical memory, in the face of its attempted erasure. This is part of the blues epistemology, or blues point of view, particular in its weight, yet universal in its scale and scope for those suffering. What changes? The cost of household goods or staples has gone up. We see Hughes, here, speaking directly to all those families then, and we could say again today, facing rising prices, stagnant wages, and increased taxation without any increase in representation. And here Hughes too echoes the reality of structural unemployment for Blacks, last hired and first fired, always last, at the bottom of the melting pot, as Toni Morrison would say. And once again, the omnipresence of the color line is expressed, with its jagged edges, the searing pain, often silently felt, and occasionally explosively expressed. And although we have traveled miles and miles, years after years, we are still standing on and in that liminal space, "On the edge of hell" from whence we began.

There are of course questions here, as Hughes articulates the notion of Harlem on the edge of hell, arguably a dialectical entwining of those without capital, working for those who do, with the only thing worse than exploitation being the recurrent processes of exclusion, exile, including in the land of one's birth after one's ancestors were stolen and kidnapped from Africa.

Here the question remains for the individual, the group, the question, what now, what to do, in the face of this recurrent storm, and the oft repeated answer to the question of when and even if one might reach the destination? The answer is of course to simply wait, these things take time, and when we remember just how much time and pain and agony this arduous journey has thus far taken, the wait morphs into the weight of the memories one carries.

The focus is yet still on memory, for in the presence of memory, the promise of the American Dream functions as a form of history, a history of old lies, old kicks, old and tiresome commands—Be Patient—for some a forthcoming fulfillment, albeit only for a select few, and even then, arguably, not in any truly fulfilling way. For even what some might call America's chosen people, those most closely within reach of the American Dream by virtue of religion, race, ethnicity, or class seem to be experiencing the sense that they might not be, if they ever were, the chosen ones these days.[42] Evoked here is the dilemma of having a shared history, yet no shared memory.[43] Harlem, in the personified form that Hughes gives it, stands next to hell, and thus hell becomes connected to the upper east and west sides immediately above Harlem, and to Central Park, Manhattan, and Wall Street below. This relationship between Harlem, largely Black and poor at the time, and Manhattan, largely white and wealthy, is the relationship Hughes draws between Harlem and Hell. This relationship is reiterated in the poems closing lines, with a twist. The personified place, Harlem, is replaced by the people there, standing on and in this liminal hellish place, as if to say that we not only stand with but also in this living, breathing, human entity, and that the question of what we will do, given what we remember, is a question for Harlem and the people standing with and in it.

The other Harlem poem in Hughes' book-length poetic project, *Montage of a Dream Deferred*, is, of course, "What Happens to a Dream Deferred?" The interrelationship of these poems leads us to assume that memories one easily forgets or knows what to do with. And yet these relationships, the asymmetric interactions they represent, are key to understanding the American Dream and its deferment, particularly considering the historic patterns in which they came to fruition. We draw on these insights to highlight the role of narratives of the American Dream that take the experience of the European American "white" immigrant settler majority as normative, and unchanging, with little to no understanding of the ongoing social and historical construction of color and its hierarchies.[44] The vast minority is simultaneously rendered invisible, even as these "minorities" are today becoming the numerical majority, albeit often of so-called mixed race and cultural backgrounds.[45] What in other accounts is rendered unseen or in the background is here brought into the foreground, the space through which we seek to enter, and, in so doing, to disrupt established narratives.[46]

We use Adams' epic narrative against Adams, looking at his own contradictions, as they are also those of the American Dream. Adams' inability to produce and sustain the Dream in the presence of what we have called the vast minority comes dramatically into view here. This effort on our part has elective affinities with the authors mentioned earlier, and with W.E.B. Du Bois whose work will be explored later. All these authors disrupt the nation as narration master narrative of James Truslow Adams, and his erasure of the racialized unequal social foundations upon which the American Dream is constructed. For W.E.B. Du Bois, in *Black Reconstruction* (1935), "That dark and vast sea of human labor" worldwide "and in the United States—that great majority . . . on whose bent and broken backs rest today the founding stones of modern industry—shares a common destiny; it is despised and rejected by race and color; paid a wage below the level of decent living; driven, beaten, prisoned and enslaved in all but name."[47] In *The Epic of America* (1935) Adams' discussion of the American Revolution instead depicts these realities as follows:

> The slaves in the South had been but little affected. Submerged at the bottom of society, the storm waves passed over them without being felt. Dependent upon their masters and not upon their own exertions, they worked, ate, and slept their existence away as usual. Apart from them, however, there was no one, rich or poor, whose existence has not been deeply influenced.[48]

For Du Bois, the vast despised minority are human beings, actors in the historical drama. For Adams, they are asleep and dramatic world-historical struggles in the name of human freedom and liberty, of which enslaved people could hardly be unaware of, were not even felt. Of course, empirically, Adams is totally wrong, as a host of books on the role of Blacks during the Age of Revolution have shown.

Adams' sins of omission go far beyond the historical erasure of the African American experience in the American Revolution. In fact, in *The Epic of America*, the only single Black person alluded to is Dred Scott, and this in the context of mentioning the *Dred Scott v. Sandford* Supreme Court case. Reading on, we soon find out why, in terms of where Adams' sympathies lie, which is basically with the Spanish, but especially the British Empire, of which he was an ardent admirer.[49] He sees little of any substance or value in any people beyond the white people who, in his words, conquered the Americas, locating the heart of Americanism, racially, and in terms of enslavement of other humans, referred to as enforced economic democracy, in the Mississippi Valley.[50]

Adams seems to refer to a whiteness of a different color, new immigrants that he thinks of as not really white, even though later they become considered as such, but at the time are clearly excluded from Adams' privileged heart of "Americanness," which is to say the Mississippi Valley and the South, with its white plantation holding oligarchy and enslaved Black humanity. As we can see, if one reads between the lines: The slave sleeps. The master exerts. Adams' Epilogue is telling as well, starting off as follows: "We have now traced, in very meagre outline but let us hope with a reasonable emphasis on essentials for our purpose, the course of our story from that dateless period when savages roamed over our continent, coming from we know not where."[51] Note the language: the savage roams over our continent; And what made it ours? Who are we? We are not told. It is inferred, just as for those others left out of the triumphal parade, the dream is deferred, as we walk upon their sleeping bodies, strange, given they were enslaved for the purpose of exploiting their labor.

At the time of that writing, we were amid the Great Depression, and Adams' book was perhaps an attempt to bolster the American spirit, albeit one radically skewed towards the middle and upper educated classes, the white patrimonial middle classes that Piketty writes of, on the invisible foundations of the darker masses of humanity. It should come as no surprise that fairy tales and fantasy are particularly evident components of Americana, displayed not only by Adams, Disney, and Horatio Alger, but more recently by the rise of "reality" television, a form that aided Donald Trump in his bid for the presidency.[52] The fairy tale was already represented soon after the founding of the U.S. in Benjamin Franklin's (1791) autobiography, which as one of his most prominent biographers noted, "gave us the definitive formulation of the American Dream," and is taken to be an earlier inspiration for the even more famous Horatio Alger stories. J.A. Leo Lemay co-edited with P. M. Zall, *Benjamin Franklin's Autobiography: A Norton Critical Edition* (1986), which includes a single-authored essay by Lemay titled "Franklin's Autobiography and the American Dream." In this essay, Lemay asks: "'What is the American Dream?' The simplest possible answer, as well as the most common general impression, is expressed by the standard cliche, the rise from rags to riches."[53] In a recent celebration of this narrative, Luigi Zingales writes: "In fact, they recount their protagonist's journey from rags to respectability, celebrating American capitalism and suggesting that the American Dream is within everyone's reach."[54]

Tellingly enough, one of the key authors from whom we take inspiration, Walter Benjamin, focuses not on riches and the dream of wealth, but instead on the rag-picker in his critiques, chooses the rags part of the equation, the refuse of society, those thrown away as Harlem-born rapper and poet of the streets 2Pac Shakur would later do. And thus, following Hughes, Benjamin, Tupac, and others, we focus on the often ignored "tired . . . poor . . . huddled masses yearning to breathe free, the wretched refuse of your teeming shore" that we once upon a time were thought to embrace. The general focus of our mythic tales is on the golden door to the land of opportunity (like Willie Wonka's golden ticket), and not on those that seek its embrace; it is on the rhetoric of riches, and not the stark realities of exploitation, exclusion, poverty, and displacement. Or, more precisely, in the Horatio Alger tales, and the fairy tales that follow, one's disenfranchisement is almost always brief and ultimately downplayed in the frame of the happily ever after ending.

The Horatio Alger stories were incredibly popular in the earlier moments of the twentieth century, although they have faded from public view recently, replaced, arguably, by the myriad rags-to-riches stories that populate our current cultural lives. Over 200 million copies of Horatio Alger stories have been sold.[55] The number of fairy tales consumed, since perhaps the horror movie, and fairy tale, *Birth of a Nation* (1915), and particularly since Disney entered the fairy tale business with *Snow White and the Seven Dwarfs* (1937), is too large to count. The plot of these fairy tales, in simplest form, is that someone finds themselves struggling, for reasons typically not of their own making; through hard work, perseverance, and industriousness, if male, or long-suffering devotion, purity, and obedience, if female, along with a little magical assistance, a fairy godmother, if female, or Adam Smith's invisible hand, if male, reach a place where all is alright, or at least better, ever after.

In this age of virtually unprecedented polarization between an ever-smaller rich minority, and ever larger impoverished majority, even our dreams of a vibrant democratic future are in jeopardy. Yet, democracy, at its best, presumably provides for the harnessing of the potential of people, including the ability to imagine or dream of better possible worlds. This iteration of dreams of democracy in the American Dream, has long animated hope for a better future, and yet it has also effaced the memory and history of its deferment. Hughes' query simultaneously illuminates the current state of the American Dream, and its history. Yet this view is not simply a tale of those at the margins; instead, they raise questions that go to the center, the heart of the American and modern experience.[56]

If the American Dream of the next millennium is best viewed from the ruins of its alternative futures, these futures themselves might be gleaned via a series of transformative historical moments. It became clear, over time, that claims upholding the American Dream as a potential reality could do so only in the absence of certain groups. The consistency by which this dark and darkening presence is elided stands out starkly. It might seem a paradox to go from invisibility to the dark teeming hordes threatening to overwhelm the perceived pristine whiteness of American shores, but this seeming antinomy, or paradox, is made clear in works such as Toni Morrison's *Playing in the Darkness: Whiteness and the Literary Imagination* (1993), and more recently in Erika Lee's *America for Americans: A History of Xenophobia in the United States* (2019) and *The Making of Asian-America: A History* (2021).[57] For our master narratives of America have historically constructed a kind of willful blindness to even the possibilities, not to mention the impending realities, of the presence of actual persons with their own dreams, and to the recurrent backlashes against them, once their presence is made visible, as well as to the historical antecedents that could have clarified possible paths to be taken to avert such moral panics about the presence of others. Here, the willful ignorance regarding earlier reactions to racial progress, namely the ongoing march of racist progress in reaction to such gains, as Ibram X. Kendi has argued, allows the fiction of what is essentially white progress to trump historical reality, predicated as these are on linear notions of the Dream taking us ever upward into a racially unbiased world (the fairy tale, in other words). The Orwellian underpinnings of such thinking will be explored later in the work of authors such as James Baldwin, Chester Himes, and others.[58]

While we interrogate the history, sociology, and literature of the dialectical and contested nature of the American Dream, we also offer a critical examination of the consistent backlash against those people deemed Other, in an increasingly heterogenous United States. Much of the historical literature on the subject leaves us ill-equipped to confront the present crisis. For the tendency to frame the American Dream in terms of individual social mobility, exemplifying the Dream as ideology, mystifies what lies before us. This tendency is seen in the edited collection by Sandra L. Hanson and John Kenneth White, *The American Dream in the 21st Century* (2011).[59] President Barack Obama looms large in the collection, but it is not largely about African Americans. Michael C. Kimmage highlights President Obama as the quintessential example of the Dream at work, and cites Obama's *Dreams of My Father* (1995), "its sober report on racial inequality balanced by its saga of triumphant individual will, as the book that launched Obama's career in national politics."[60] A loving nod to individual will is central to Kimmage's argument, as he feels compelled to assert that "it is the individual who dreams a nation's Dreams."[61] Well, yes, but it is also true that an individual, alone, does not dream a "nation's Dreams," but rather what some have called the dreaming collective, a collection of individuals who share this Dream as a collectivity. More importantly, what gets washed away in the current love for individuality, is the acknowledged but then ignored, "sober report on racial inequality," and related questions of social justice.

Jim Cullen's "Twilight's Gleaming: The American Dream & the Ends of Republics," in the same collection, justifies the exclusion of certain groups from the American Dream as necessary and legitimate when he tellingly comments:

> Some might go further and say that the American Dream itself is an imperial construct, a sense of possibility for some that necessarily depends on taking it away from others—in this case, Native Americans, African Americans, and Mexicans, among others.
> . . . As far as I can tell, *every* society has derived its legitimacy through some means of apportioning and distributing opportunity to its members, however

broadly or narrowly defined. . . . And that distribution has usually meant con-fiscating the resources of others. If we must shed our illusions about the Dream being a uniquely good thing, I think we should also recognize that it has not been uniquely bad.[62]

What a defense! The American Dream "has not been uniquely bad." And why, according to Cullen, is the dream "not . . . uniquely bad"? But the articulation of the ideology of the American Dream *is unique*, in that it posits, according to the Declaration of Independence and James Truslow Adams afterwards, that anyone can rise according to their abilities, and the possibilities for that actual realization, in what became the most powerful and richest society in the history of the world, as W.E.B. Du Bois powerfully argued in *Black Reconstruction* (1935). We hope that no one has ever mistaken the dreams of Nazi Germany as anything other than a racial hierarchy of the Master Race and those lower orders; but the idea of America, that has been broadcast, and often somehow believed, is that here is a nation with an imagined community truly for all, albeit belied of course, by the actual realities.

One of the few exceptions to the exclusion of the reality of others seen in *The American Dream in the 21st Century*, is the essay by the late James Loewen, focused primarily on the trajectory of Black and white relations in the American Dream framework and subsequent realities. The guiding adage for Loewen is: "Sociologists have long known that people's dreams are limited by their reality."[63] Our reality is one of an increasingly segregated and inequitable worlds. Our dreams are thus largely shaped by a longstand-ing trend towards white visions of suburbia, in which a dark face or an impoverished person or two (but not many more) might be tolerated, but seldom welcomed.[64]

We seek more welcoming forms of storytelling and nation-state building, forms that highlight the lived experience of the disenfranchised and often hid-den from the light of history. Works like Kevin Young's *The Grey Album: On the Blackness of Blackness* (2012) and Michael Rothberg's *Multidirectional Memory: Remembering the Holocaust in the Age of Decolonization* (2009) serve as two examples.[65] Young journeys through many territories of Black history and experience, seen in a wider multicultural frame, discussing the stakes of writing, and its relationship to reality:

I . . . don't think writing . . . is the realm for upholding "reality" as we perceive it, but rather a place to confront reality, and even fictionalize it, in the process remaking it in our image—not necessarily as we live, but as we would like to. Things we *should have been able to read*. For the thing the African American writer might be most interested in, and might ultimately be confronting most often, is the American Dream.

Young's sense of what one *"should have been able to read"* (which is also to say, what one should have been able to write), is very much in keeping with Benjamin's injunction to read (and we would add write) history against the grain.[66] In his "Theses on the Philosophy of History" (1940), written in the aftermath of the Hitler-Stalin Pact, Benjamin sought to critique notions of progress in the context of the emergence and seeming triumph of fascism, in Nazi Germany and beyond.

> As in all previous history, whoever emerges as victor still participates in that triumph in which today's rulers march over the prostrate bodies of their victims. As is customary, the spoils are borne aloft in that triumphal parade. These are generally called the cultural heritage . . . such cultural riches . . . everywhere betray an origin . . . [one] . . . cannot but contemplate with horror. They owe their existence, not merely to the toil of the great creators who have produced them, but equally to the anonymous forced labor of their contemporaries. There has never been a document of culture which was not at one and the same time a document of barbarism. And just as such a document is never free of barbarism, so barbarism taints the manner in which it was transmitted from one hand to another. The historical materialist therefore dissociates himself from this process of transmission as far as possible. He regards it as his task to brush history against the grain.[67]

Rebecca Brenner's "Walter Benjamin, Walter Johnson, & Reading Early African-American History Against the Grain" (2018) looks at the way in which Benjamin took the debris of mass culture and read it against the implied narratives of capitalist progress, and Johnson, in *River of Dark Dreams: Slavery and Empire in the Cotton Kingdom* (2017), used the texts of those who enslaved others human beings and read them against their own racist assumptions. Similarly, Kevin Young re-reads texts against ingrained assumptions, going against the grain, to illuminate the struggle for freedom. Young notes:

> Black authors, and others of course, for years have described the downsides of the dream, its contradictions and far worse its presence as promise unfulfilled—not to mention the nightmare it can become. *Native Son, Autobiography of an Ex-Colored Man, Montage of a Dream Deferred*, Gwendolyn Brooks's *In the Mecca*, Coltrane's "Alabama," Nicolas Guillen's *Grand Zoo*, James Brown's "Payback": all show us the ways in which the dream may be deferred. . . . It would seem that the very denial of dreaming that society seems to impose on black folks, while it hasn't made us dream less, does seem to punish us for what dreams we do have.[68]

Young's work offers a montage element that we find insightful in conveying the kind of multivalent sense of reality we seek, and echoes the methods of

Langston Hughes, Walter Benjamin, Romare Bearden, W. E. B. Du Bois, and others. There is also within our work a desire to confront reality, or more aptly what is presented as reality, and the question of dreams in general, and the American Dream in particular, for those who live with its perpetual deferment.

Michael Rothberg argues for the importance of multidirectional memory, contrasting it against unidirectional memory, to amend and broaden the range of memories and attendant histories brought into view, and to question how they are viewed. We aim at something with elective affinities to Rothberg's work in our own efforts here. Rothberg writes: "Against the framework that understands collective memory as *competitive* memory—as a zero-sum struggle over scarce resources—I suggest that we consider memory as *multidirectional*: as subject to ongoing negotiating, cross-referencing, and borrowing; as productive and not privative."[69] Rothberg's work resonates with that of Michael-Rolph Trouillot's *Silencing the Past: Power and the Production of History* (1995), which critiques Plato's famous theory of memory as recollection, in which memories are set, effectively stored, and then retrieved, without alteration:

> If memories as individual history are constructed . . . how can the past they retrieve be fixed? The storage model has no answer to that problem. Both its popular and scholarly versions assume the independent existence of a fixed past and posit memory as the retrieval of that content. But the past does not exist independently from the present. Indeed, the past is only past because there is a present, just as I can point to something *over there* only because I am *here*. But nothing is inherently there or here. In that sense, the past has no content. The past—or more accurately, pastness—is a position.[70]

The shift in perspective we cultivate considers how concepts such as memory and history are shaped and recognizes that these shapes also then shape what can be seen as memory and history. In other words, what we *imagine* as memory or history, much like what we imagine as a nation-state, to cite Benedict Anderson's important work, *Imagined Communities* (1983), again, becomes seen at some point as fixed, rather than as something actively evolving and continuously imagined.[71] In *Race, Nation, Class: Ambiguous Identities* (1991), co-authored with Immanuel Wallerstein, Etienne Balibar affirms, in "The Nation Form," that memory and history are forms that are constantly being rearticulated, that is to say, remade, in an ongoing, never-ending process:

> Every "people," which is the product of a national process of ethnicization, is forced today to find its own means of going beyond exclusivism or identarian ideology in the world of transnational communications and global relations of force. Or rather: every individual is compelled to find in the transformation of

the imaginary of "his" or "her" people the means to leave it, in order to communicate with the individuals of other peoples which he or she shares the same
interests and, to some extent, the same future.[72]

Balibar seeks to challenge to contemporary versions nationalist exclusivism,
gesturing toward a world beyond hermetically sealed identities of nations
and groups. Revealed here is Immanuel Wallerstein's "construction of
peoplehood," denoting the clay-like ever-changing relational features of all
human groups.[73]

In this work, we insert considerations of the question of the American
Dream, and its ever-changing forms, by often marginalized writers, into
conversation with their Others. We seek nothing less than to explore the dialectical and contested meanings of the American Dream and dreams deferred,
excavating the past to understand the possibilities for creating better multicultural futures.[74] What we will see in the works of literature we take up is
how crucial the making of collective memory and a sense of peoplehood is
for imagined communities, and simultaneously, how these very memories can
divide communities into fratricidal rivalries.

We come at this investigation from different formal disciplinary vantage
points, yet with a multi or interdisciplinary approach, though one which we
prefer to call, following Immanuel Wallerstein, a unidisciplinary approach.[75]
One of us teaches about fairy tales, metaphors, African American and
Interracial literature in a Department of English, the other about the United
States and the global system in a Department of Sociology. Between us, we
have presently, or in the past, affiliations in Ethnic Studies, Women's and
Gender Studies, Asian Studies, and Latin American Studies. In this work,
we continually cross these and other terrains in search of the meanings of
the American Dream and dreams deferred in and in the aftermath of the
American Century, now in ruins.[76] For as Hughes imagined, and as Walter
Benjamin intimated, it is in the ruins of mass culture that we may glimpse
the American Dream and its deferment as a dialectical image, seeing it in
what Benjamin called the now of recognizability.[77] Indeed, the best place to
awake from the American Dream in the new millennium is from the ruins of
its alternative future(s).[78] For the American Dream lives on exactly because
the moment to realize it was missed.[79] And indeed, it *is* missed, consistently,
as James Truslow Adams formulated it in terms that basically express the
idea of a land where there are no arbitrary limits on the development of one's
abilities, where all classes can develop their capabilities to the fullest, rather
to benefit a particular social class that reaps the primary benefits of the efforts
of others.[80]

It should be noted that Adams put up a fight to title his book *The American
Dream*, but this was rejected by his publisher who said no one would ever be

willing to pay $3.00 "for a 'dream.'"[81] Adams sought "to trace . . . the beginnings . . . of many characteristics which are generally considered as being 'typically American,' and, in especial, of that American dream of a better, richer, and happier life for all our citizens of every rank which is the greatest contribution we have as yet made to the thought and welfare of the world."[82] Adams wrote during the days of the Great Depression, and, as noted earlier, can perhaps be lauded for his interest in bolstering the American spirit. Yet in suggesting that the American Dream is America's greatest contribution to the world, he may have been grasping at straws, especially considering current realities. In the context of Adams' own argument, and its contradictions, his assertions are perplexing, suggesting a rather oddly shaped largesse, and a paucity of alternative offerings. The American Dream suggests a better, richer, happier life for Americans, not for the world, unless Adams is imagining the range and sweep of globalization then, now evident some ninety years later. While, arguably, the extent to which the American Dream has bettered the "welfare" of the world over its storied history is worth discussing, few would dispute that it has done much to shape global thought. Also, and importantly, while the American Dream may well express some form of the hopes and dreams of many Americans, this belies the conflict embedded within radically differing notions concerning it, from the visions of America that led to a bloody war over slavery in the 1860s to those that animate social movements and politics today. We trace this tale in an unusual way, that has few disciplinary examples, except perhaps in American Studies or Cultural Studies. We are very informed by the possibilities mentioned above for vignettes and montage, and so, we draw on history, sociology, anthropology, literature, and more to tell a story.

Chapter 1, "The American Dream and Dreams of the Americas," brings the history of America and the Americas, including ideas and realities often ignored, into discussion. We examine the vast gap between America's stated ideals and underlying realities, from the Age of Revolutions to the US Civil War. Myths are productive in establishing a foundation for the construction of any imagined community. Our effort here is to resituate or reformulate what might be a more reasoned basis for discussing the American Dream, and by extension, the dreams of the Americas, including the United States.

Chapter 2, "Embattled Dreams, Memory, and the American Iliad," illustrates the multiple odysseys to and from America and the radically differing American dreams and dreams deferred, most especially between visions of the expansion of slavery and freedom, culminating in the US Civil War and the rise and fall of what W.E.B. Du Bois called *Black Reconstruction*. In this great contestation, we explore the entwining of American dreams of various ethnic groups kaleidoscopically refracted through the poetry of Paul Laurence Dunbar and Langston Hughes.

In chapter 3, "What Happens to a Dream Deferred?," our work centers on Langston Hughes, whose poems and short stories provide us with a poignant portrait of the Dream during a period largely associated with the Harlem Renaissance, after the exodus of Blacks fleeing enslavement and bondage in the South for presumably better opportunities elsewhere. Here, we place the work of Hughes in conversation with another writer chronicling the era, John Steinbeck, in his novel *The Grapes of Wrath* (1939). Yes, these seem odd bedfellows, but a fuller understanding of the American Dream and its recentering on California, compels such interactions, given the centrality of exodus, exit, and migration in American history, from the Okies to the Great Black Migration. Thus, we look too at Chester Himes, whose brutal depictions of life also pose a challenge to the Dream for African Americans and others, illuminating its nightmarish dimensions. We chronicle Himes' novels on Los Angeles, such as *If He Hollers Let Him Go* (1945) and *Lonely Crusade* (1947), and his searing critique of the Dream in the city that is its supposed embodiment, during World War II, as well as in Walter Mosley's *Devil in a Blue Dress* (1990), set in 1948 in Los Angeles.

In chapter 4, "Another California, Another Country, Another World?," we return to California and the possibilities offered there with forays into Washington, D.C. (the District of Columbia), and New York City. We explore what the Eagles dubbed in their haunting song, "Hotel California"—which functions not only or simply as an end goal, but also as a state of mind—in its revisions and extensions of the American Dream. For while the tale of white migrants and farm labor allowed national sympathy for the plight of the Okies, it foreclosed the possibility of imagining the real future of California, with the greatest diversity of any state in the continental US today (and second overall, after Hawaii). In the context of New York City and Los Angeles, we draw upon the work of Luis Rodriguez, James Baldwin, and others who question the cost of the American Dream, even if its possibilities were to be realized, and whether it can ever be worth the price of the ticket.

In chapter 5, "The Dreams and Nightmares that America Bears," we recognize the poignant ways in which Dinaw Mengestu's novel *The Beautiful Things that Heaven Bears* (2007), inspired by a passage from Dante's *Inferno*, as well as select works of August Wilson and Toni Morrison address, yet again, Hughes' question. Answers to his question are repeatedly evident in the myriad depictions of African American life in *The Cycle Plays* of August Wilson. *The Cycle Plays* are a sweeping work, ten plays, chronicling the lives of Black people in Pittsburgh, Pennsylvania, and elsewhere, from roughly 1900 to 2000. Wilson's opus is also a chronicle of American Dreams and dreams deferred, as none of these ten plays result in anything more than hope for an ever-fading better future, in the face of a crippling, living past. Few efforts better articulate the dialectic we seek to encapsulate in our work than these plays, and the other work of significance in this context, Toni Morrison's sweeping genealogy, *Paradise* (1997), the third and final novel in her Dantesque trilogy of African American history, starting with *Beloved* (1987) and continuing with *Jazz* (1992). This chapter closes with a consideration of Imbolo Mbue's, *Behold the Dreamers* (2016), a look at the lives of African immigrants from Cameroon, coming to New York City, and working for the family of a Wall Street powerbroker. The lives of both families are subjected to hardships in the boom-and-bust moments of the Great Recession, which still informs our troubled present and the possible futures we can imagine.[83]

In the epilogue, "Black to the Future," we approach visions of America, of American Dreams and dreams deferred to come, through the works of Black science fiction writers in the literary tradition often referred to today as Afrofuturism. Specifically, we explore the work of Octavia Butler. Butler's novels *Parable of the Sower* (1993), *Parable of the Talents* (1998), and *Fledgling* (2005) are set against current realities. Lauren Olamina, the lead character in *Parable of the Sower* and *Parable of the Talents*, is on the run, migrating, only to find that the future seems to have arrived sooner than expected. In exploring Butler's visions of an increasingly heterogeneous yet disintegrating social fabric, we look to the future of the American Dream and dreams deferred as the gap between myth and reality grows ever sharper. *Fledgling*, Butler's last novel, tells the tale of a Black pansexual interracial and interspecies person. Deprived of all her memory through trauma, Shori, the lead character of *Fledgling,* awakens to find herself caught in a racist world, in which she must struggle against others who would eliminate her and her kind. A profound contrast with Toni Morrison's *Paradise*, oversaturated with memory, *Fledgling* approaches the current world from a vantage point of all memories made anew, providing a counterpoint to questions of shared history but no shared memory, and insight into the dialectical history of the American Dream and dreams deferred.

Today, in the wake of the Great Recession (2007–2008), and the end hopefully of the Trump era, Americans can increasingly relate to the cultural, emotional, social, and economic frustrations of trying to achieve a dream that seems increasingly out of reach, whether it be a college education, a home, or just housing, a steady job, food on the table, accessible and affordable healthcare, and so on. This hollowing out of the American Dream, or its requiem, as a new documentary on Noam Chomsky, *Requiem for the American Dream* (2016), calls it, has been registered in popular culture in many ways.[84] The larger consumer visions, advertised in arcades and malls in the United States and abroad, seem increasingly distant for those whose struggle to stay afloat or ahead of rising costs, and crippling debt. Increasing numbers of young Americans today rightly believe that the prospects that they will be better off than their parents are slim, with many often turning to drugs to escape from the nightmares their American Dreams have become.[85]

In what follows, we trace the American Dream through often ignored narratives, placing them in a dialectical relationship with those narratives with which most of us are familiar. In so doing, we aim to compel a more complex sense of the American Dream, and its possible alternative futures. This is for us the beginning of the next chapter, both in the sense of shifting to a new narrative focus, to a reimagined American history, and hopefully to reimagining new dreams, rising, phoenix-like, alternately, from the ashes of its deferment and realization in space and time.

NOTES

1. See Giovanni Arrighi, "World Income Inequalities & the Future of Socialism," *New Left Review* I/189 (September/October 1991): 39–68. See also, Immanuel Wallerstein, "Introduction: The American Dream Between Yesterday and Tomorrow," *The Decline of American Power* (New York: New Press, 2003).

2. For a discussion of the invention of the term, America, see James Dunkerley, *Dreaming of Freedom in the Americas: Four Minds & a Name* (2004), especially 12–14. Here, Dunkerley quotes the eminent historian John H. Elliot, *Do the Americas Have a Common History?* (Providence, Rhode Island, 1998), 9–10, in which the latter notes: "By default, the inhabitants of the new republic arrogated to themselves the name of 'Americans' for what else could they be called? In the process they deprived all the other peoples of the hemisphere of their collective name, and compelled the pluralisation of 'America' into the Americas."

3. James Truslow Adams, *The Epic of America* (Boston: Little, Brown, & Company, 1931), 405–406.

4. The production of willful blindness and ignorance is a subject to which we shall return.

5. Thomas Piketty, *Capital in the Twenty-first Century* (Cambridge, MA: Belknap Press of Harvard University Press, 2014), 13. Of course, there are occasional, if startling exceptions. Most notably, to use a telling recent example, Jeremy Rudd, on the Board of Governors of the Federal Reserve, in a discussion of neoclassical economics, says he must "leave aside the deeper concern that the primary role of mainstream economics in our society is to provide an apologetics for a criminally oppressive, unsustainable, and unjust social order." Jeremy B. Rudd, "Why Do We Think That Inflation Expectations Matter for Inflation? (And Should We?)," Finance and Economics Discussion Series 2021–062. Washington: Board of Governors of the Federal Reserve System (2021), 1. https://doi.org/10.17016/FEDS.2021.062. Thanks to Noam Chomsky for this reference.

6. For two contrasting uses of the term, humanity, see Martha Nussbaum's *Cultivating Humanity* (Cambridge, MA: Harvard University Press, 1998), and Jonathan

Glover, *Humanity: A Moral History of the Twentieth Century* (New Haven: Yale University Press, 2012).

7. For some recent reflections on this current moment of danger and opportunity, see Azar Nafisi, *Read Dangerously: The Subversive Power of Literature in Troubled Times* (New York: William Morrow, 2022). See also Barbara Abercrombie, *A Year of Writing Dangerously* (Novato, California: New World Library, 2012). See also Anne Lamott, *Bird by Bird: Some Instructions on Writing and Life* (New York: Anchor Books, 1994).

8. Thomas Piketty, *Capital in the Twenty-first Century* (Cambridge, MA: Belknap Press of Harvard University Press, 2014), 368–369. And see more recently, Thomas Piketty, *Capital and Ideology* (Cambridge, MA; Belknap Press of Harvard University Press, 2020), and Amory Gethin, Clara Martinez-Tolanado, and Thomas Piketty, eds., *Political Cleavages & Social Inequalities: A Study of Fifty Democracies, 1948–2020* (Cambridge, MA: Harvard University Press, 2021).

9. For a view analyzing such polarizations within the *longue duree* of historical capitalism, see Giovanni Arrighi's magisterial *The Long Twentieth Century: Money, Power, & the Origins of Our Times* (New York: Verso, 2010).

10. Thomas Piketty, *Capital in the Twenty-first Century* (Cambridge, MA: Belknap Press of Harvard University Press, 2014), 441–442. In a related passage, Piketty notes that "the growth of a true 'patrimonial (or propertied) middle class' was the principal structural transformation of the distribution of wealth in the developed countries in the twentieth century." Thomas Piketty, *Capital in the Twenty-First Century* (Cambridge, MA: Belknap Press of Harvard University Press, 2014), 326. See also the ensuing discussion, 326–329.

11. In the final book of poems released before his death in 1967, *The Panther and the Lash*, New York: Vintage Classics, 1992, 14, Hughes retitled this "Harlem" fragment, arguably the most famous of his poem, taken from his larger *Montage of a Dream Deferred*, simply: "Dreams Deferred."

12. Walter Benjamin, *The Arcades Project* (Cambridge, MA: The Belknap Press of Harvard University Press, 1999). For one of the most profound interpretations of this work, see Susan Buck-Morss, *The Dialectics of Seeing: Walter Benjamin and the Arcades Project* (Cambridge, MA: The MIT Press, 1989). Christopher Tomlins' Benjaminian work, *In the Matter of Nat Turner: A Speculative History* (Princeton, New Jersey: Princeton University Press, 2020), xiv, is also suggestive here regarding Benjamin's notion of "dialectical images," as in writing of the Turner Rebellion as "overdetermined," wherein he cites Ben Brewster, who argued that Freud sought through this concept: "the representation of . . . dream-thoughts in images privileged by their condensation in a number of thoughts in a single image . . . or by the transference of psychic energy from a particularly potent thought to apparently trivial images."

13. Stanley Corngold, "Introduction," Franz Kafka, *The Metamorphosis*, translated and edited by Stanley Corngold, (New York: Modern Library, 2013), xxxii.

14. Max Weber, *Charisma and Disenchantment: The Vocation Lectures*, edited by Paul Reitter and Chad Wellmon (New York: New York Review of Books, 2020).

15. See also Walter Benjamin, *One-Way Street & Other Writings* (London: New Left Books, 1979), 35.

16. Edward Said, *Culture and Imperialism* (New York: Vintage, 1994), x.

17. The debt to the work of Antonio Gramsci and his theory of hegemony explored by Giovanni Arrighi, especially in his "The Three Hegemonies of Historical Capitalism," the first chapter of his *The Long Twentieth Century*, ought to be evident here. See also Charles S. Maier, *Among Empires: American Ascendancy and Its Predecessors* (Cambridge, MA: Harvard University Press, 2006). On hegemony, see especially Antonio Gramsci, *Prison Notebooks, Volume I-III,* edited and translated by Joseph A. Buttigieg (New York: Columbia University Press, 2011). Buttigieg was the father of US Presidential contender and now President Biden's Secretary of Transportation Pete Buttigieg, who is thanked by his father in the introduction to his now standard translation of the *Prison Notebooks.* See also Antonio Gramsci, *Subaltern Social Groups: A Critical Edition of Prison Notebook 25*, edited and translated by Joseph A. Buttigieg and Marcus E. Green (New York: Columbia University Press, 2021).

18. Langston Hughes, "Harlem," in Langston Hughes, *Poems*, Selected and edited by David Roessel (New York: Alfred A. Knopf, Everyman's Library Pocket Poets, 1999), 238.

19. Greta Thunberg, "Everywhere I Go I Seem Surrounded by Fairy Tales," Speech to United States Congress, Washington, D.C., September 18, 2019, Greta Thunberg, *No One is Too Small to Make a Difference* (Updated with New Speeches), (New York: Penguin, 2012), 85–87.

20. Raj Chetty, "Achieving the American Dream Shouldn't Be a Coin Flip," Walton Family Foundation, April 27, 2021.

21. On childism, see Elisabeth Young-Bruehl, *Childism: Confronting Prejudice Against Children* (New Haven: Yale University Press, 2012). See also, Amnesty International, Angelina Jolie, and Geradine Van Bueren, *Know Your Rights and Claim Them: A Guide for Youth* (Minneapolis: Zest Books, 2021).

22. Goran Therborn, "Inequality and World-Political Landscapes," *New Left Review* 129, May/June 2021, p. 7, citing Thomas Piketty, *Capital and Ideology* (Cambridge, MA: Belknap Press, an imprint of Harvard University Press, 2020): 352–354.

23. Isabel Wilkerson, *Caste: The Origins of Our Discontents* (New York: Random House, 2020), 352–354.

24. Ursula K. Le Guin, *The Wind's Twelve Quarters: Stories* (New York: Harper Perennial, 2004), 254–262. N.K. Jemison, *How Long 'Til Black Future Month: Stories* (London: Orbit Books, 2018).

25. Mike Davis, "Who Will Build the Ark?," *New Left Review* (January/February 2010): 29–46.

26. See also Ivan Berend, *A Century of Populist Demagogues* (Central European University Press, 2020).

27. Rousseau's statement and the Declaration can be fruitfully compared with that of James Otis: "Are not women born as free as men?" Quoted in Linda K. Kerber, *Women of the Republic* (Chapel Hill: University of North Carolina Press), 13, 3–31, 80, a powerful work on the patriarchal foundations of Anglo-American law and politics. For an appreciation and critique of the very notion of the Enlightenment and an attempt at an at least partial reframing, see Carlton Floyd and Tom Reifer, "What Happens to a Dream Deferred? W.E.B. Du Bois & the Radical Black Enlightenment/

Endarkenment," *Socialism & Democracy*, Edward Carson, Gerald Horne, & Phillip Luke Sinitiere, eds., Volume 32, No. 3 (November 2018): 52–80.

28. See the discussion in the interview between Noam Chomsky and Tom Reifer, "Language, the Liberal Arts and the Challenges of the Twenty-First Century," University of San Diego, 2021.

29. See Eric Foner, *The Fiery Trial: Abraham Lincoln & American Slavery* (New York: W.W. Norton & Company, 2010), and his earlier fundamental study, *Free Soil, Free Labor, Free Men: The Ideology of the Republican Party Before the Civil War,* with a new introduction by the author (New York: Oxford University Press, 1995). See also Matthew Karp, "The People's Revolution of 1856: Antislavery Populism, National Politics, and the Emergence of the Republican Party," *Journal of the Civil War Era*, Volume 9, Number 4, (December 2019): 524–545. See also Matthew Karp, "The Mass Politics of Antislavery," *Catalyst*, Volume 3, Number 2, Summer 2019. See also LeAnna Keith, *When it Was Grand: The Radical Republican History of the Civil War* (New York: Hill and Wang, 2020). For the Republican Party's subsequent transformation, see especially the following studies: Boris Heersink and Jeffrey A. Jenkins, *Republican Party Politics and the American South, 1865–1968* (New York: Cambridge University Press, 2020), and Angie Maxwell and Todd Shields, *The Long Southern Strategy: How Chasing White Voters in the South Changed American Politics* (New York: Oxford University Press, 2019), and Heather Cox Richardson, *To Make Men Free: A History of the Republican Party* (New York: Basic Books, 2021, updated with a new epilogue). On the abolitionist movement, see the landmark work by Manisha Sinha, *The Slave's Cause: A History of Abolition* (New Haven: Yale University Press, 2017), as well as Sean Wilentz's recent reviews of a new series of works on the abolitionist, Civil Rights, and Black freedom struggles in *The New York Review of Books*.

30. Roland Marchand, *Advertising the American Dream: Making Way for Modernity, 1920–1940* (Berkeley: University of California Press, 1985).

31. Tracy Chapman, *Tracy Chapman*. Elektra Records, 1988.

32. Eric Foner, *Free Labor, Free Men: The Ideology of the Republican Party Before the Civil War* (New York: Oxford University Press, 1995), xxxviii–xxxix.

33. Walter Benjamin, *The Writer of Modern Life: Essays on Charles Baudelaire*, edited by Michael W. Jennings (Cambridge, MA: The Belknap Press of Harvard University Press, 2016). Walter Benjamin, *Charles Baudelaire: A Lyric Poet in the Era of High Capitalism* (London, New York: Verso, 1989).

34. Walter Benjamin, *The Work of Art in the Age of Its Technological Reproducibility & Other Writings on Media*, edited by Michael W. Jennings, Brigid Doherty, & Thomas Y. Levin. (Cambridge, MA: The Belknap Press of Harvard University Press, 2008).

35. Walter Benjamin, *The Arcades Project* (Cambridge, MA: The Belknap Press of Harvard University Press, 1999), 460–461.

36. Nathan Irvin Huggins, *Harlem Renaissance*, updated edition, with a foreword by Arnold Rampersad (New York: Oxford University Press, 2007). See Walter Benjamin's essay, alternately called "A Short History of Photography," or "A Small History of Photography," included in various collections, and Sara Blair, *Harlem Crossroads:*

Black Writers & the Photograph in the Twentieth Century (New Jersey: Princeton University Press, 2007).

37. See August Wilson, "Bearden: Black Life on Its Own Terms," and Toni Morrison, "Abrupt Stops and Unexpected Liquidity: The Aesthetics of Romare Bearden," in Robert G. O'Meally, ed., *The Romare Bearden Reader* (Durham: Duke University Press, 2019): 174–177, 178–184.

38. Neda Ulaby, "The Art of Romare Bearden: Collages Fused Essence of Old Harlem, American South," September 14, 2003. See Branford Marsalis Quartet, *Romare Bearden Revealed* (2003). See Mary Schmidt Campbell, *An American Odyssey: The Life and Work of Romare Bearden* (New York: Oxford University Press, 2018). See Robert G. O'Meally, ed., *The Romare Bearden Reader* (Durham: Duke University Press, 2019). See Glenda Elizabeth Gilmore, *Romare Bearden in the Homeland of His Imagination: An Artists Reckoning With the South* (Chapel Hill: University of North Carolina, 2022).

39. See John Stauffer, Zoe Trodd, and Celeste-Marie Bernier, *Picturing Frederick Douglass: An Illustrated Biography of the Nineteenth Century's Most Photographed American*, and with an afterword by Henry Louis Gates Jr. (London: Liveright, 2015). See also Frederick Douglass, "The Color Line" (1881) in Frederick Douglass, *The Portable Frederick Douglass*, edited by John Stauffer and Henry Louis Gates Jr. (New York: Penguin Classics, 2016), 501–512. See also Henry Louis Gates Jr., *Stony the Road: Reconstruction, White Supremacy, and the Rise of Jim Crow* (New York: Penguin, 2019). See also Raymond Williams, "Means of Communication as Means of Production," in *Problems of Materialism and Culture* (New York: Verso, 1980) and more recently Manuel Castells, *Communication Power* (New York: Oxford University Press, 2013) and his *Networks of Outrage and Hope: Social Movements in the Internet Age* (New York: Polity, 2015. See also Alissa V. Richardson, *Bearing Witness While Black: African Americans, Smartphones, and the New Protest #Journalism* (New York: Oxford University Press, 2020). See also the important work of Jack Goody on these questions of the means of communication, especially *The Logic of Writing and the Organization of Society* (New York: Cambridge University Press, 1986), and *The Interface Between the Written and the Oral* (New York: Cambridge University Press, 1987).

40. For the background on the Jewish world, through the lens of one critical artist, see Benjamin Harshav, *Marc Chagall and His Times: A Documentary Narrative* (Stanford, CA: Stanford University Press, 2004) and his *Marc Chagall: The Lost Jewish World* (New York: Rizzoli, 2006). See also Alain Brossat and Sylvie Klingberg, *Revolutionary Yiddishland: A History of Jewish Radicalism* (New York: Verso, 2017). See also Ilan Halvei, *A History of the Jews* (London: Zed Books, 1987), and the extraordinary online edition of the YIVO Encyclopedia of the Jews of Eastern Europe: https://yivoencyclopedia.org/. For Africa and the diaspora, see the landmark life-long dream of W.E.B. DuBois, *Africana: The Encyclopedia of the African and African-American Experience*, available as a *Concise Desk Reference* (Philadelphia: Running Press, 2003), and in a five-volume edition (2005), excerpts of which are now published in two accessible volumes edited by Kwame Anthony Appiah and Henry Louis Gates Jr., *Africana: Arts and Letters: An A-to-Z Reference of Writers,*

Musicians, and Artists of the African American Experience (Philadelphia: Running Press, 2004), and *Civil Rights: An A-Z Refence of the Movement that Changed America* (Philadelphia: Running Press, 2004). See also David Eltis and David Richardson, *Atlas of the Transatlantic Slave Trade* (New Haven: Yale University Press, 2000), and Jan Pieterse, "The Triangle of Emancipation," *Race & Class: A Journal for Black and Third World Liberation*, Volume 30, Number 2 (October-December 1988): 1–22. See also Ira Berlin, *The Making of African America: The Four Great Migrations* (New York: Penguin, 2010). See also Eddie Glaude Jr., *Exodus: Religion, Race, and Nation in Early Nineteenth Century Black America* (Chicago: University of Chicago Press, 2000).

41. One thinks here of Milan Kundera's *The Book of Laughter and Forgetting* (1978), the work of Primo Levi, Eduardo Galeano's trilogy, *Memories of Fire* (1985), Toni Morrison's "The Site of Memory" (1987), and Laurence E. Prescott, "'Yo tambien soy America': Latin American Receptions of Langston Hughes's American Dream," R. Baxter Miller, ed., *Critical Insights: Langston Hughes* (Ipswich, MA: Salem Press, 2013): 255–274.

42. Marianne Cooper, "The Downsizing of the American Dream" (October 2, 2015). For this excerpt from the longer Hughes poem see Langston Hughes, *Langston Hughes Poems*, Selected & edited by David Roessel (New York: Alfred A. Knopf, 1999), 238. The entire poem is reprinted in this selection by David Roessel, as well as in Langston Hughes, *Selected Poems* (New York: Vintage 1990).

43. In *The Cuban Drumbeat*, Piero Gleijeses quotes the scholar Nancy Mitchell, who notes regarding the United States and Cuba, "we share a past, but have no shared memories." (Seagull Books, 2009), 7. For the sordid background, see Lars Schoultz, *That Infernal Little Republic: The United States & the Cuban Revolution* (Chapel Hill: University of North Carolina Press, 2009).

44. In contrast, compare such normative assumptions to works such as Matthew Frye Jacobson, *Whiteness of a Different Color: European Immigrants and the Alchemy of Race* (Cambridge, MA: Harvard University Press, 1999), and Michel-Rolph Trouillot, "The North Atlantic Universals," Immanuel Wallerstein, ed., *The Modern World-System in the Longue Duree* (Boulder: Paradigm Publishers, 2004), 229–237.

45. For different views on the discussion of the complexity of these processes, see William H. Frey, *Diversity Explosion: How New Racial Demographics are Remaking America* (Washington, D.C.: Brookings, 2018), as well as Richard Alba, *The Great Demographic Illusion: Majority, Minority, and the Expanding American Mainstream* (New Jersey: Princeton University Press, 2022).

46. Michal P. Ginsburg (2022), in her exploration of Victor Hugo's *Les Miserables* (1862), provides a stunning visualization of the novel's characters, and character networks, highlighting, or making visible, those who might otherwise be lost or forgotten: "The discovery that the novel has many, many more characters than readers (myself included) remember or even notice while reading is well worth reflecting upon. . . . Most of these forgotten, unrecognized characters are nameless, playing a marginal role in the novel's plot, appearing only briefly before disappearing without leaving a trace. . . . I would argue, however, that their presence is of the utmost importance since they stand precisely for [the] 'les misérables' of the novel's title.

Thus our habitual reading practices demonstrate the problem Hugo sought to bring to our attention: the invisibility of the miserable ones to the social world we, the readers, represent. Or, put in other words: Realism, which constructs literary characters as 'persons' and 'individuals,' is complicit with the social order that renders the miserable ones invisible. Recognizing these forgotten, marginal characters means countering our tendency (to which filmic adaptations of the novel contribute) to think of the novel as the story of a small number of unforgettable individuals, rather than as the story of 'les misérables.'" Michal P. Ginsburg, "Characters and Characters' Networks in Les Misérables," Visualizing Les Misérables, https://lesmiserables.mla.hcommons .org/. See also Franco Moretti, "Two Theories," *Daedalus: Journal of the American Academy of Arts and Sciences*, Volume 150, Issue 1 (Winter 2021): 18. For some work reflecting on related issues in the digital humanities, see P. Gabriel Foreman and Labanya Mookerjee, "Computing in the Dark: Spreadsheets, Data Collection and DH's Racist Inheritance," *Always Already Computational: Library Collections as Data National Forum Position Statements* (March 2017). https://collectionsasdata .github.io/aac_positionstatements.pdf. For a particularly important work that seeks to deconstruct such master narratives regarding immigrants, see Mai M. Ngai, *Impossible Subjects: Illegal Aliens & the Making of Modern America* (New Jersey: Princeton University Press, 2014).

47. W.E.B. Du Bois, *Black Reconstruction* (New York: Library of America, 2021), 22.

48. James Truslow Adams, *The Epic of America* (Boston: Little, Brown, and Company, 1931).

49. For an important recent contrasting perspective, see Caroline Elkins *Legacy of Violence: A History of the British Empire* (New York: Alfred Knopf, 2022).

50. James Truslow Adams, *The Epic of America* (Boston: Little, Brown, and Company, 1931), 148. See Matthew Frye Jacobson, *Whiteness of a Different Color: European Immigrants and the Alchemy of Race* (Cambridge, MA: Harvard University Press, 1999).

51. James Truslow Adams, *The Epic of America* (Boston: Little, Brown, and Company, 1931), 400.

52. See for example, Kurt Anderson, *Fantasyland: How America Went Haywire: A 500-Year History* (New York: Random House, 2018).

53. J.A. Leo Lemay, "Franklin's Autobiography & the American Dream," in J.A. Leo Lemay & P.M. Zall, ed., *Benjamin Franklin's Autobiography: A Norton Critical Edition* (New York: W.W. Norton & Co., 1986), 350. See also David Waldstreicher, *Runaway America: Benjamin Franklin, Slavery, & the American Revolution* (New York: Hill & Wang, 2005). See also Nian-Sheng Huang & Carla Mulford, "Benjamin Franklin & the American Dream," in Carla Mulford, ed., *The Cambridge Companion to Benjamin Franklin* (New York: Cambridge University Press, 2009): 146–158. See also Carla Mulford, *Benjamin Franklin & the Ends of Empire* (New York: Oxford University Press, 2019).

54. See also Luigi Zingales, "Who Killed Horatio Alger?" *City Journal* (Autumn 2011).

55. Stefan Kanter, "Horatio Alger: The Moral of the Story," *City Journal* (Autumn 2000).

56. See Eric Liu, *A Chinaman's Chance: One Family's Journey & the Chinese American Dream* (New York: Public Affairs, 2016). See also Jeffrey Wasserstrom, "Here's Why Xi Jinping's 'Chinese Dream' Differs Radically from the American Dream," *Time Magazine* (October 29, 2015).

57. On the origins of the word *xenophobia*, or fear of strangers, see Emily Wilson's Introduction to her translation of Homer's *The Odyssey* (New York: W.W. Norton & Co., 2018), 23.

58. Ibram X. Kendi, *Stamped from the Beginning* (New York: Bold Type Books, 2017).

59. John Kenneth White, *The American Dream in the 21st Century* (Philadelphia: Temple University Press, 2011).

60. Michael Kimmage, "The Politics of the American Dream, 1980 to 2008," in Sandra L. Hanson & John Kenneth White, eds., *The American Dream in the 21st Century* (Philadelphia: Temple University Press, 2011), 38.

61. Michael Kimmage, "The Politics of the American Dream, 1980 to 2008," in Sandra L. Hanson & John Kenneth White, eds., *The American Dream in the 21st Century* (Philadelphia: Temple University Press, 2011), 37.

62. Jim Cullen, "Twilight's Gleaming: The American Dream & the Ends of Republics," in Sandra L. Hanson & John Kenneth White, ed., *The American Dream in the 21st Century* (Philadelphia: Temple University Press, 2011), 21.

63. James W. Loewen, "Dreaming in Black & White," in Sandra L. Hanson & John Kenneth White, *The American Dream in the 21st Century* (Philadelphia: Temple University Press, 2011), 59.

64. For a powerful discussion of these themes, see Nancy Fraser, "On Justice: Lessons from Plato, Rawls and Ishiguro," *New Left Review* 74 (March/April 2012), 41–51.

65. And see also Toni Morrison, *Playing in the Dark: Whiteness and the Literary Imagination* (New York: Vintage, 1993).

66. See Rebecca Brenner, "Walter Benjamin, Walter Johnson, & Reading Early African-American History Against the Grain," Society for US Intellectual History, 2018.

67. Walter Benjamin, "Theses on the Philosophy of History, VII": the quote here has been put together from the version quoted in Fredric Jameson, *The Political Unconscious: Narrative as a Socially Symbolic Act* (Ithaca: Cornell University Press, 1981), 281, and in Walter Benjamin, *Illuminations: Essays and Reflections* (New York: Schocken Books, 2007), 256.

68. Kevin Young, *The Grey Album: On the Blackness of Blackness* (Minneapolis: Grey Wolf Press, 2012). See also *Unsung: Unheralded Narratives of Slavery and Abolition*, edited by the Schomburg Center for Research in Black Culture, and with a foreword by Kevin Young (New York: Penguin, 2021).

69. Michael Rothberg, *Multidirectional Memory: The Holocaust in the Age of Decolonization*, (Stanford: Stanford University Press, 2009), 3.

70. Michel-Rolph Trouillot, *Silencing the Past: Power and the Production of History* (Boston: Beacon Press, 1995), 15. See also Michel-Rolph Trouillot, *The Michel-Rolph Trouillot Reader*, edited by Yarimar Bonilla, Greg Beckett, and Mayanthi L. Fernando (Durham: Duke University Press, 2021).

71. Benedict Anderson, *Imagined Communities: Reflections on the Origins and Spread of Nationalism* (New York: Verso, 2016).

72. Etienne Balibar, "The Nation Form," Etienne Balibar and Immanuel Wallerstein, *Race, Nation, Class: Ambiguous Identities* (New York: Verso, 1991), 105.

73. Thus, as Wallerstein forcefully argues: "Would it not make more sense to understand peoplehood for what it is-in no sense a primordial stable social reality, but a complex, clay-like historical product of the capitalist world-economy through which the antagonistic forces struggle with each other. We can never do away with peoplehood in this system not relegate it to a minor role. On the other hand, we must not be bemused by the virtues ascribed to it, or we shall be betrayed by the ways in which it legitimates the existing system. We need to analyze more closely the possible directions in which, as peoplehood becomes ever more central to this historical system, it will push us, at the system's bifurcation point, towards various possible alternative outcomes in the uncertain process of the transition from our present historical system to the one or ones that will replace it." Immanuel Wallerstein, "The Construction of Peoplehood: Racism, Nationalism, Ethnicity," Etienne Balibar and Immanuel Wallerstein, *Race, Nation, Class: Ambiguous Identities* (New York: Verso, 1991), 71–85, especially 84–85. See also the important reflections on these questions in Mike Davis, "Marx's Lost Theory: The Politics of Nationalism in 1848," *New Left Review* 93 (May/June 2015): 45–66. And see also Mike Davis, Unpublished Draft Precis, "Star-Spangled Leviathan: A History of American Nationalism: Volume One: 1763–1900," nd, in the author's possession.

74. While some frame multiculturalism as adding persons of color to the existing structure of unequal power and wealth, and essentialist unchanging identities, we use multiculturalism to describe the changing experiences of different groups experiencing racism who seek to value their own experiences in an ever-changing global system.

75. Immanuel Wallerstein invented the term in his *The Modern World System* (San Diego: Academic Press, 1974), 11, to designate the interconnected nature of knowledge, stating in the "Introduction: On the Study of Social Change": "When one studies a social system, the classical lines of division within social science are meaningless. Anthropology, economics, political science, sociology—and history—are divisions of the discipline anchored in a certain liberal conception of the state and its relation to functional and geographic sectors of the social order. They make a certain limited sense if the focus of one's studies is organizations. They make none at all if the focus is the social system. I am not calling for a multidisciplinary approach to the study of social systems, but for a unidisciplinary approach."

76. See Alan Brinkley, *The Publisher: Henry Luce and His American Century* (New York, Vintage, 2011).

77. See Eduardo Cadava, *Words of Light: Theses on the Photography of History* (New Jersey: Princeton University Press, 1997), 64.

78. Paraphrasing from the first line of Mike Davis's *City of Quartz: Excavating the Future of Los Angeles* (London: Verso, 2018), 1: "Prologue: The View From Futures Past," "The best place to view the Los Angeles of the next millennium is from the ruins of its alternative future." The 2016 Republican National Convention, held in Cleveland, Ohio, featured a four-thousand-pound ice sculpture spelling the words "The American Dream." See the article in *The New Yorker*, "In Cleveland, The American Dream Melts Away" (July 22, 2016), and "The American Dream Melts at the Republican National Convention," *Vice News* (July 20, 2016). In an early draft of the Arcades Project, Benjamin (1999: 13) writes: "Balzac was the first to speak of the ruins of the bourgeoisie. But it was Surrealism that first opened our eyes to them. The development of the forces of production shattered the wish symbols of the previous century, even before the monuments representing them had collapsed. . . . All these products are on the point of entering the market as commodities. But they linger on the threshold. From this epoch derive the arcades and *interieurs*, the exhibition halls and panoramas. They are residues of a dream world. The realization of dream elements, in the course of waking up, is the paradigm of dialectical thinking. Thus, dialectical thinking is the organ of historical awakening. Every epoch, in fact, not only dreams the one to follow but, in dreaming, precipitates its awakening. It bears its end within itself and unfolds it—as Hegel already noticed—by cunning. With the destabilizing of the market economy, we begin to recognize the monuments of the bourgeoisie as ruins even before they have crumbled." Walter Benjamin, *The Arcades Project* (Cambridge, MA: The Belknap Press of Harvard University Press, 1999).

79. Paraphrasing, from the first line of the introduction of Theodor Adorno's *Negative Dialectics* (New York: Continuum, 1981), 3: "Philosophy lives on . . . because the moment to realize it was missed."

80. James Truslow Adams, *The Epic of America* (Boston: Little, Brown, & Company, 1931), 404–405.

81. James Truslow Adams, *Select Correspondence*, edited with a Bibliographic Essay by Allan Nevins (New Brunswick: Transaction Publishers, 2012), 68. Three dollars in 1931 is about $50 today.

82. James Truslow Adams, *The Epic of America* (Boston: Little, Brown, & Company, 1931), vii–viii.

83. See also Janis Sarra & Sara L. Wade, *Predatory Lending & the Destruction of the African-American Dream* (New York: Cambridge University Press, 2020).

84. Noam Chomsky, *Requiem for the American Dream* (New York: Seven Story Books, 2017).

85. See Raj Chetty, et al., "The Fading American Dream: Trends in Absolute Income Mobility Since 1940," *Science* Volume 356, Issue 6336 (April 28, 2017): 398–406. See also reports from the Organization for Economic Cooperation and Development (OECD), including Thorsten Hellmann, Pia Schmidt, and Sascha Matthias Heller, *Social Justice in the EU & OECD, Index Report 2019* (OECD, 2019), *A Broken Social Elevator?* (OECD, 2018); *Social Justice in the OECD—How Do the Member States Compare?* (OECD, 2011). See Ann Case and Agnes Deaton, *Deaths of Despair and the Future of Capitalism* (New Jersey: Princeton University Press, 2021).

Chapter 1

The American Dream and Dreams of the Americas

Here we bring a history of the United States of America (USA) and the Americas that includes ideas and realities often ignored. We examine the vast gap between the USA's stated ideals and underlying realities. The history on which many generally rely, and one very evident in James Truslow Adams' *Epic of America,* is largely myth. Myths are central in producing imagined communities, as Benedict Anderson established in *Imagined Communities: Reflections on the Origin and Spread of Nationalism* (1983). But when a myth is so utterly empty of the lived experiences of so many of the nation's inhabitants, and when it leaves even the realm of myth to constitute what might best be described as a fairy tale, it has traveled too far to relevantly inform our understanding. Our effort here is to reform this myth on what might be a more reasoned basis.

When we look at the architecture of the American Dream, we find in James Truslow Adams' own retelling, a kind of enchanted fairy tale, in which dreams of avarice facilitated the development of the American Dream, although this basis of the Dream seems later to dismay him. Adams begins *The Epic of America* with a prologue entitled "From Time Immemorial," depicting the North American continent as "sparsely inhabited," a typical but ultimately mistaken trope of settler colonialism.[1] Adams goes on to discuss the voyages of exploration of Columbus. Concerning gold, Adams quotes Columbus, who classifies it as: "the most precious of all commodities; [it] constitutes treasure, and he who possesses it has all he needs in this world, as also the means of securing souls from purgatory, and restoring them to the enjoyment of Paradise."[2] Adams indicated that the gold they sought long eluded them, and yet they carried on. Much like Adams' subsequent invocation of the quest for the American Dream, if it's not where you sought it, not to worry! If you keep striving for it, keep searching for it, it will come. You will find it. Around the corner, in another place, or perhaps in another, or with a little more, time. In short, in the words of the song sung by Judy Garland in the movie so apropos of American Life, it is always "Somewhere Over the Rainbow," from *The Wizard of Oz* (1939).[3] Adams phrases this mythical quest, this *Iliad* and *Odyssey*, in just this way.[4]

In Adams' retelling, Columbus, an agent of the Catholic Spanish empire, conjures the Garden of Eden (Paradise), the Fall, and the restoration of paradise. Instead of articulating the Golden Rule as provided by Jesus in the Sermon on the Mount, "Do unto others as you would have them do unto you," Columbus conjures the alternate Golden Rule of the powerful, those who have the gold make the rules. The mythic recurrence and return to paradise here, is not that of the abundance of the Garden, and not a disenchanted world, but for Adams a dream world of commodities, the God of all of them being gold, and in which the forced labor of Columbus's indigenous contemporaries is buried, as with any hint of the brutality that befell them.[5] Later, however, Adams provides an additional register to contemplate:

> The Spaniards had come seeking gold. They had not only found it, but they had also found a highly organized society of barbaric splendor. If the white men robbed the Indians of their independence and wealth, they also felt that they had a gift of priceless value to bestow in return—the gift of the Christian religion, as they understood it, and of eternal salvation. With all their cruelty, it never occurred to the Spaniards but that the Indian was a human soul to be saved, as well as exploited.[6]

Though Adams supposes that Christianity is a gift of priceless value that the Spaniards bestow on the conquered, by Adams' own telling, for the Conquistadores, the values of Christianity are totally inverted. The Conquistadores seek not salvation through Jesus's Golden Rule, but instead seek the gold so they can rule and furthermore purchase their passageway from purgatory to Paradise. There is no hint of the words of Matthew 16:26 in the New Testament here: "What will it profit a man if he gains the whole world, yet forfeits his soul?"

Moreover, the assertion that the Spanish all saw the Indians as having souls is just wrong. For this very question set off a fierce and controversial debate, starting with Dominican Fray Antonio Montesinos and his sermon on Advent Sunday in 1511. Here, Montesinos asked, "Are these [Indians] not men? Have they not rational souls?"[7] This sermon is thought to mark the first open protest by European Christians against the treatment of the indigenous inhabitants of the Americas. This protest culminated in the epic debate between Juan Gines de Sepulveda, author of a book *Democratis Segundo* subtitled *About the Just Causes of the War Against the Indians,* and the first priest to be ordained in the Americas, Bartolome de Las Casas, who wrote in their defense, about just these very issues, and their moral and ethical implications.[8]

Patricia Seed argues that the question of whether the indigenous inhabitants of the Americas had rational souls has a particular meaning in Christian thought, going back to Saint Augustine and Thomas Aquinas, specifically the distinction between humans capable of reason, and thus of receiving the word of Christ and assimilation into Christianity, and those incapable of such. The varied positions at the time of this sixteenth-century debate were that: a) Indians were human, and thus capable of receiving the word of Christ; b) that they were generally incapable of this (not able to receive the word); or c) that they were incapable of such (and thus beasts).[9]

The stakes were high for Spain's Catholic empire abroad, as their very presence in the New World was thought to be based upon the famous Alexandrine or Papal Bulls of 1493–1494, ostensibly giving Spain dominion if it undertook evangelization of the Native inhabitants.[10] For Bartolome de Las Casas all human beings were endowed with souls, and thus bearers of rights that allowed for their moral autonomy. de Las Casas articulated such notions of all humankind being one, centuries before it became fashionable to do so, even in what was considered Radical Enlightenment thought.[11] And here, it is important to note that Bartolome de Las Casas, in his defense of the rights of the Native inhabitants, used centuries of canon law to argue that dominion only allowed for voluntary attempts at conversion, and could not lawfully or justly supplant their rights to their own lands and persons without their express consent. For de Las Casas, this made Imperial Spain's war on the Native inhabitants and related actions in the New World unjust and illegal.[12]

The significance of Bartolome de Las Casas can be gleaned from the fact that he was charged with high treason before the Spanish Royal Council or Council of Castille, in 1547, for advising priests to deny confession and absolution to Spanish colonists unless they returned lands they had unjustly taken and made related restitution as penance for their crimes and wrongdoing.[13] For de Las Casas, there was no amount of gold that could purchase the passageway for the Conquistadores into Paradise; what rules in the realm of Christian ethics is Jesus's Golden Rule expressed in the Sermon on the Mount, of doing unto others as you would have them do unto you.

Even in other areas where Bartolome de Las Casas initially faltered, he reversed course. de Las Casas, like others of his time, initially accepted slavery and supported petitions calling for Black and white slaves from Spain to be transported to augment the labor of the Indians, to ease their hardship.[14] Yet later, probably around 1547, after visiting Lisbon, upon finding out the truth about these matters, de Las Casas, added some eleven chapters to his *Historia de las Indias*, denouncing slavery for both Blacks and Indians.

Gustavo Gutierrez quotes de Las Casas as saying that had he known the truth, "he would not have proposed it for all the world, because blacks were enslaved unjustly, tyrannically, right from the start, *exactly as the Indians had* been," thus lamenting his own earlier advice.[15] In this dramatic reversal, de Las Casas became an early critic of the transatlantic enslavement of Black humanity.

Bartolome de Las Casas argued that there was only one humanity, all endowed with souls, but his opponents vociferously disagreed. So much then for Adams' supposition that it never occurred to the Spaniards that the Indians had no soul capable of being saved. For had it not occurred to them, there would not have been such a fierce debate. Adams never hints about de Las Casas's condemnation of the conquest, forced evangelization, slavery, and exploitation. Adams rationalizes these very destructive aspects of the conquest by proposing that they were just the way things were done. He asserts, and presents such an assertion as a kind of *fait accompli*, that the rich people of all civilizations have always exploited others, may always need to do so, and that notwithstanding the American Dream, the necessity of such exploitation remains

> an unsettled question. . . . The Southerner exploited labor in the shape of legal slavery, the Northerner in the shape of wage slavery. Neither was conscious of any moral guilt in adapting himself to the social structure that had been shaped by the economic situation of his own section. . . . The South had a distinct type of civilization, and its cultural values were dear to it. Those of a highly competitive, complex industrial civilization are bound to be very different, and as the North became definitely committed to such a civilization, the South began instinctively to feel its own threatened. In the same way, what many of the sanest critics of America to-day object to is not its system of life *per se*, but the distorted and debated cultural values which have resulted.[16]

Adams authenticates asymmetric relations of power as not only the way things are, but as most likely, the way things ought to be. Yet if no one in the North or the South experienced or were conscious of the experience of any "moral guilt" concerning "legal slavery" or "wage slavery," then there would have been little reason to protest them. Adams is wrong here too. There was consciousness about the moral problems of both systems, sparking numerous outcries that were critical of both "Negro Slavery" and "wage slavery." In *Walden* (1854), Henry David Thoreau wrote of the "keen and subtle masters that enslave both North and South," going on to note, in contrast to Adams' American Dream, how in the US "the mass of men lead lives of quiet desperation."[17] In fact, the long attempt to deal with the morally problematic issue of chattel slavery, and the critique of wage slavery, including by the emerging Republican Party, was arguably what eventually gave way to efforts to defend them as a positive good, and thereby escape the admission, by its participants, and those protesting against it, at its essentially evil nature. Yet Adams somehow maintains that neither section was conscious of their morally questionable nature, while in effect denying the substantive issues involved in the protestations against them. When Adams does speak of radical abolitionists from William Lloyd Garrison to Henry David Thoreau to John Brown, he can't help but to designate them as fanatics or extremists, terms never applied to those who own other human beings as in the slavery, or who rent them, as in wage slavery.

It is fruitful to compare the perspective of James Truslow Adams, *The Epic of America*, with a book published only four years later, and recently republished by the Library of America in 2021, W.E.B. Du Bois's *Black Reconstruction: An Essay Toward a History of the Part Which Black Folk Played in the Attempt to Reconstruct Democracy in America, 1860–1880* (1935). In his note to the reader, Du Bois writes that he understands that a key determinant for many readers is simply whether they recognize the Negro as ordinary human beings, noting that for those who assume Negro inferiority, they cannot be convinced by facts, and recognizing as well that such views will radically curtail his readership.[18] Perhaps Adams has taken the opposite stance to that proffered by Du Bois, by assuming that people of African descent (and any other non-white persons) are "distinctly inferior," and thus not fit for full enfranchisement or embrace as wholly human, but also thus fully fit for domination and enslavement. Perhaps, Adams has as well considered his audience to be precisely the people that Du Bois is not trying to convince. But that of course is mere speculation.

In contrast to Adams, Du Bois reminds us of the conscience that slavery stirred in colonial America: "At first, black slavery jarred upon them, and as early as the seventeenth century German immigrants to Pennsylvania asked the Quakers if slavery was in accord with the Golden Rule."[19] Du Bois goes on to discuss, in contrast, the ideology of the white slaveholding oligarchy, in "The Planter," and their political representatives, notably that prophet of the Confederacy, John C. Calhoun (1781–1850).[20] For as Du Bois notes, Calhoun "once said with perfect truth: There has never yet existed 'a wealthy and civilized society in which one portion of the community did not, in point of fact, live on the labor of the other.'"[21] Yet, Du Bois goes on to say, "What the planter and his Northern apologist," of whom James Truslow Adams is a supremely representative example, was unwilling to admit, was the degradation of humanity such an attitude implied, especially in the social death that was slavery.[22] Of course, here, Du Bois raises the possibility that the Southern planter oligarchy could hide from its conscience the suffering it imposed through its harsh system of ownership of other human beings. Yet, in "The

Black Worker," Du Bois registers, unlike Adams, the profound differences between chattel and wage slavery: "The whole legal status of slavery was enunciated in the extraordinary statement of a Chief Justice of the United States that Negroes had always been regarded in America 'as having no rights which a white man was bound to respect.'"[23] The person to whom Du Bois refers is none other than Chief Justice Taney, who, in the *Dred Scott v. Sandford Decision* (1857) noted more specifically that Black people "had for more than a century before been regarded as beings of an inferior order, and altogether unfit to associate with the white race, either in social or political relations; and so far inferior, that they had no rights which the white man was bound to respect; and that the negro might justly and lawfully be reduced to slavery for his benefit."[24] Moreover, Taney repeatedly stipulates that Black people, whether enslaved or free, or anyone with any Blackness in them, as in the interracial offspring of Black and White couplings, had no place in the United States as anything other than slaves, contending that such was the reasoning of the Founding Fathers, and every other "free white citizen."[25] Of course, he is wrong in the assumption that all "free white citizens" agreed with him, as the life of John Brown, Henry David Thoreau, and many others attest. But much like Adams, Taney speaks to and for a particular subset of white and white-assimilated society.

It is of note that that the words of Chief Justice Taney, John C. Calhoun and James Truslow Adams are echoed more recently in Jim Cullen's "Twilight's Gleaming: The American Dream and the Ends of Republics," in *The American Dream in the 21st Century* (2011). Cullen too maintains that inequity, or the exploitation of some for the benefit of others is simply, and inevitably, what civilizations do. And the notion that such a social structure calls into question the American Dream in ways that had not then or now been settled is itself questionable. On the one hand, you have an inevitable exploitation "as every civilization has always done . . . may, perhaps, have to do." On the other hand, you have a Dream of a civilization that promises the opportunity for everyone to rise above exploitation, even though it has always exploited labor, and "may, perhaps, have to do" so. Specifically, Adams says, at the end of his famous *Epic of America*, that the American Dream of throwing off fetters which impede human development "has been realized more fully in actual life here than anywhere else, though very imperfectly even among ourselves. It has been a great epic and a great dream. What, now, of the future?"[26] Well, what now of the future indeed! Given that Adams recognized, even then, the prevailing push towards the Dream's materialization, by which is meant its tendency to be focused on "motor cars and high wages," or "material plenty," and that such tendencies "doubtless counted heavy," it is a wonder that he also assumes some grand or significant place within it for "social orders" devoted to a shared communal uplift within it. Where material matters of self-acquisition count heavy, it is likely wise to assume that social or communal uplift count a bit less, and particularly so among populations with deeply egregious social situations, still clearly subjugated under the yoke of social, political, economic, and cultural structures designed to not recognize their humanity.

Adams is also wrong that the white slaveholding South was conscious of no moral guilt for slavery. For as David Brion Davis has shown in *The Problem of Slavery in the Age of Revolution, 1770–1823* (1999), the American Revolution and the Age of Revolutions more generally made the reality of slavery increasingly complicated for Americans arguing for liberty and freedom as the natural state of humankind, as it represented a radical departure from this ostensible universalism articulated in the Declaration of Independence. Moreover, there was also bitter condemnation of both racist chattel slavery and wage slavery during this period, including by the Republican Party, which held up instead the alternative concept of free labor and free men, being one's own master, as a necessary antidote to otherwise servile dependence on the will of another.

In later passages, Adams reconfigures his epic tale, heretofore limited to Catholic Spain, in a Protestant vein. Now, Adams emphasizes the providentialism in the making of the Americas and the American Dream, in ways congruent with the religious beliefs of Protestant Europeans in the continued "discovery" and conquest of America. For Protestant Europeans (largely Anglo-Saxon English in Adams' estimation) finding gold, like Catholic Spain before it, also becomes a means of finding Heaven. The first chapter of Adams' *Epic*, "The Men of Destiny," is an ode to Calvinist Protestant notions of predestination, the subject of Max Weber's famous *The Protestant Ethic and the Spirit of Capitalism* (1905), downplaying the fundamental roles of white settler colonialism, plantation slavery and various forms of labor, free and unfree, in the making of British North America, and subsequent revolt against the British Empire.[27] Though of course many crossed the seas to inhabit what would become known as the Americas, those lands that became the United States with the American Revolution of 1776 were settled primarily by an advanced transplant of the center of capitalist or bourgeois society that was emerging in and around England. These men of wealth and power, most of them slaveowners, shaped the Constitution to their liking in 1787, in what Michael J. Klarman, who has written the standard work on the question, calls *The Framers' Coup* (2016).[28]

Especially given the preference Adams expresses for those he considered real Americans, namely those of good Anglo-Saxon stock, it is useful to examine the dreams of empire that inspired this element, from Europe, even before it turned its sights overseas towards the Americas. Many historians have shown just how central England's conquest of Ireland in the

Elizabethan period was in developing related projects to expand and conquer in the Americas.[29] As Bernard Magubane argues, the conquest of Ireland also played a central role in developing British ideologies about the superiority of the white Anglo-Saxon Protestant race.[30] Such beliefs, in the late nineteenth and early twentieth centuries, inspired the powerful British Round Table movement which sought to make legendary British imperialist Cecil Rhodes visions of empire and white supremacy into a reality. Members and supporters of the British Round Table movement included influential persons with whom James Truslow Adams was quite close.[31]

The combination of voluntary migration from Europe, forced migration from Africa in the era of the transatlantic slave trade, the exploitation of Native American labor, and the ecological appropriation of the riches of the Americas, would be crucial in the growing dominance of Western Europe and its settler colonies. These migrations, in turn, remade New World identities. The forced migration of Africans thus involved what Ira Berlin calls *The Making of African America* (2010).[32] As white settlers continued to arrive, multiply, and move, they brought with them and reinvented racist ideologies of white supremacy, solidifying inequalities that continue to the present. The rise of England was part of the emerging "Anglo-World" outdistancing the Spanish and Portuguese empires, and it, along with the ascent of the United States, became a new factor in world history.[33]

An integral aspect of the emergence of the United States in world history were the efforts of white settlers to conquer the continent. Here, the famous journeys of Lewis and Clark are often thought of as the beginnings of Western history, but of course, they were not, for these early American pioneers entered an already existing history, those of the Native Americans inhabitants, who had been there for thousands of years. When Henry David Thoreau journeyed with "Penobscot guides through the forests of Maine," he began to realize that the lives of Native American Indians in this place went back "three thousand years deep into time," and indeed they went back well before that, from over 15,000 to 23,000 years earlier, in recent estimates by leading experts.[34]

Over a long stretch of time, the incubation of a new empire striving to become a nation, led to the American Revolution. The Declaration of Independence, written primarily by Thomas Jefferson, famously argued that "All men are created equal," endowed with "unalienable rights," which it further stated could not be taken away by governments. Despite its limitations, or perhaps even because of them—ignoring women, the "merciless Indian savages" mentioned later in the Declaration, Black Africans, or other non-whites—the Declaration played a prominent role for successive generations in efforts to expand the realm of human freedom, not only in the United States, but in the Americas and throughout the world.[35]

In his *Epic of America*, Adams counterposes Federalist dreams of empire, wealth, and power with the agrarian democratic vision of Jefferson: "Hamilton stood for strength, wealth, and power; Jefferson stood for the American dream."[36] Of course, Jefferson's radical egalitarianism applied only to free-born whites, not to African slaves, including his own, which were to be brutally exploited, including through the liberty of sexual gratification without consent for the master, a form of sexual assault, or Native Americans, who were to be exterminated. And yet, despite these monstrous horrors, the radical albeit limited egalitarianism expressed in the Declaration of Independence became the basis for successive generations of Americans to continue their fight to make good on the implications of Jefferson's declarations, notwithstanding its grievous omissions and exceptions.[37] John Truslow Adams, after contrasting these visions, further argues that Jefferson's Dream had geohistorical roots.

> The heart of the new Americanism began to find its home in the heart of the continent, in the new empire of the Mississippi Valley. America would not have become what it did in mind and spirit had we clung to the shores of the Atlantic. For better and worse both, the new America was the child of "Ol' Man River," nurtured in the vast domain which had been his through all the ages. It was on frontier after frontier of his vast domain that the American dream could be prolonged until it became part of the American mind.[38]

And this revelation by Adams of what he considers to be the geographical heart of the American Dream is instructive, as it reveals the realities upon which the Dream rested, including the forced enslavement of Blacks, as well as Adams' enduring sympathies with the Confederacy which sought to expand slavery in space and time. In *River of Dark Dreams: Slavery and Empire in the Cotton Kingdom* (2013) Walter Johnson offers an illuminating history of the Mississippi River:

> Downriver was the great city of New Orleans: the commercial emporium of the Midwest, the principal channel through which Southern cotton flowed to the global economy and foreign capital came to the United States, the largest slave market in North America, and the central artery of the continent's white overseers' flirtation with the perverse attractions of global racial domination. Upriver lay hundreds of millions of acres of land. Land that had been forcibly incorporated into the United States . . . for which, in a few short years, young men would fight and die . . . [an] image of the catastrophe—at once imperial, ecological, economic, moral—that haunted the visions of progress and plenty by which the Valley's masters had charted the course of its history.
>   That history—the history of slavery, capitalism, and imperialism in the nineteenth century Mississippi Valley—began with a dream. Specifically, a dream

in the mind of Thomas Jefferson—the philosopher, visionary, slaveholder president of the United States in 1803. Jefferson's hope for the Mississippi Valley was . . . an "empire for liberty."[39]

Adams argues for the identification of Thomas Jefferson with the American Dream. Yet in Jefferson's vision, and thus in Adams' argument for it, the American Dream was bound up simultaneously with dreams deferred and denied, or more forcefully, the American Dreams of some were the hellish nightmare of Dante's inferno for others. Also, the distinctions drawn between Jefferson and Hamilton are not always distinct. Perhaps we might borrow the title for Robert O'Meally's new book, *Antagonistic Cooperation* (2022), to clarify the relationship between these presumably opposing views. For on matters of empire, imperialism, the acquisition of wealth, and the enslavement and degradation of Black and other non-white forms of humanity, they were not so distinctly apart.[40]

It is often pointed out how slavery was the great contradiction between stated ideals in the United States, as articulated in the Declaration of Independence, and American realities, but such comments downplay the extent to which slavery was expanding exponentially at the very time of the founding. Here, the only successful slave revolution in world history, the Haitian Revolution played a critical role in this, in leading to the Louisiana purchase, nearly doubling the size of the United States, facilitating Jefferson's vision of an "empire of liberty" in what was actually becoming the heart of American slavery, the Mississippi River Valley, the "heart" of Adams' "new Americanism."[41] What was really happening here was the creation of an empire of white liberty, erected atop the foundations of an empire of Black slavery.[42] Yet many of the Founding Fathers, such as Thomas Jefferson, but also James Monroe, hesitated to openly reveal their real views, about white liberty being predicated upon a continuous expansion of Black slavery. For the growing prominence of the abolitionist movement, as W.E.B. Du Bois notes, demanded

> that slavery in the United States be immediately abolished. . . . This movement . . . simply said that under any condition of life, the reduction of a human being to real estate was a crime against humanity of such enormity that its existence must be immediately ended. After emancipation there would come questions of labor, wage and political power. But now, first, must be demanded that ordinary human freedom and recognition of their essential manhood which slavery blasphemously denied. This philosophy of freedom was a logical continuation of the freedom philosophy of the eighteenth century which insisted that Freedom was not an End but an indispensable means to the beginning of human progress.[43]

It must be said here, in a point that we will return to later, that this view included the inauguration in 1827 of the first all-Black newspaper in America, *Freedom's Journal*, co-founded by the legendary John Brown Russwurm, and the first meeting of the Convention of People of Color in 1830, inaugurating hundreds that would follow from 1830 to the 1890s. The famous abolitionist William Garrison founded his famous paper, *The Liberator*, the following year in 1831, and the long history of slave revolts that went back to colonial times continued that year with the Nat Turner rebellion. Regarding the Colored Conventions, as St. Clair Drake argues:

> Most of the educated leaders among the freedman had decided that the time had come to make very clear to the nation that they had no intention of supporting any movement for colonizing them in Africa, the West Indies, or anywhere else. They recalled the fact that they had fought, and some of their fellows had died, for The American Dream. They insisted that the Dream must include them.[44]

The opposite views of some of the leading Founders, namely the reality of their continued support for slavery forever in many instances, have often been obscured or totally hidden from view. Yet recent scholarship has demonstrated how deeply felt they were for figures such as Jefferson and Monroe, despite scholarly arguments to the contrary, and many others of the Virginia gentry especially, which played such a decisive role in the making of Black slavery and the American Republic.[45] Here, then, was a critical moment in the remaking of America, namely the construction of the most powerful slaveholding Republic the world had ever seen. And as Karl Marx wrote in 1861, "In . . . foreign, as in the domestic policy of the United States, the slaveholders served as the guiding star."[46]

Though America and the Americas, with the American Revolution and the Hispanic American Wars of Liberation, were to be seen as realms of freedom, they were also the central destination of the transatlantic slave trade that brought some twelve million enslaved Africans to the New World. In the historical retelling, these entwined histories are usually separated, and we seek to correct that sundering herein.[47] There were, to be sure, some attempts, to write a more complete history of the Americas. In the very year after the publication of *The Epic of America*, the President of the American Historical Association, Herbert Eugene Bolton, delivered a famous address in 1932, published in the *American Historical Review* in 1933, inspired by Adams, called "The Epic of Greater America." Lamenting the appropriation of the term only for the United States, Bolton noted that "the study of the thirteen English colonies and the United States in isolation has obscured many of the larger factors in their development and helped to raise up a nation of chauvinists."[48] Bolton knew of what he spoke, for he noted that:

My early environment and outlook were typically Yankee "American," that is to say, provincial, nationalistic. My unquestioned historical beliefs included the following: Democrats were born damned; Catholics, Mormons, and Jews were to be looked upon askance. The Americans licked England; they licked the Indians; all good Indians were dead; the English came to America to build homes, the Spaniards merely explored and hunted gold; Spain failed in the New World; the English always succeeded; their successors, the Americans, were God's elect; American history all happened between the Rio Grande; the Americans virtuously drove the Mexicans out of New Mexico, Colorado, Texas, Arizona, and the rest, and thereby built a great empire. Every one of these concepts is false in whole or in part, but it took me half a lifetime to discover it.[49]

This is not to say that Bolton himself had overthrown such chauvinism. For example, Bolton also wrote: "On the mainland Spaniards first settled among the advanced peoples—Mayas, Aztecs, Pueblos, Chibchas, and Incas. These natives were easier to conquer, were most worth exploiting, and their women made the best cooks."[50] As J. H. Elliot notes, "The culinary skills of the conquered are not usually included among the justifications for conquest."[51] Yet Bolton had a more serious side to his essay, and ends it with the inspiration Adams had stimulated to propose a new retelling of the story on a grander scale:

> A noted historian has written for us the *Epic of America*. In his title, "America" means the United States. We need a [James Truslow] Adams to sketch the high lights and the significant developments of the Western Hemisphere as a whole. Perhaps the person who undertakes the task, as a guarantee of objectivity ought to be an inhabitant of the moon. But such a synthesis, done with similar brilliancy, would give us the "Epic of *Greater America*."[52]

Greater America, in Bolton's terms, or the Americas, in ours, have long exercised a powerful hold, at once a place of discovery, invasion, and captivity–contingent on one's vantage point, a contact zone of cultures, and part of the global imaginary. Here was seen a New World, in stark contrast with the Old.[53] Moreover, the creation of the "Americas" was constitutive of a larger process, that of the emergence of the modern world, and the dawning of global capitalism, with all its attendant inequalities. And then of course there was the global impact of the American and French Revolutions, and the revolutions in the then French colony, Haiti, and across the Americas in turn.

This Age of American Revolutions, including the abolition of colonial slavery in the Americas in the nineteenth century, reflected the contradictions of the dreams of the Americas.[54] The American Revolution in the US led to not the overthrow, but instead of expansion of slavery. Haiti represented instead the only successful slave revolution in world history, and the birth of the first state in the world to outlaw racial discrimination in its Constitution. The independence of Latin America was to be more complicated, and even America's supposed support for the newly independent states was severely limited, never supporting for example the independence of Haiti, the newly independent state that provided critical support for Bolivar's effort to liberate the Americas, or Cuba, because of fears the latter would become another Haiti.[55] Slavery was abolished in some of the newly independent states, but not in others, and even then, the abolition of slavery in some parts, inspired increases in slavery in other nations, most notably Cuba and Brazil. In addition, the Americans brought together persons from across the world to this vast land, joining the indigenous inhabitants who had resided there long before. There are more than two hundred million people of varying ancestries who developed this continent and marked it with their histories.[56]

And so, the American revolution left unresolved questions regarding freedom and modernity, with critical aspects of the Declaration of Independence and its intimations of what later historians would call the American Dream and dreams of the Americas unfulfilled. Soon thereafter, both the massive Tupac Amaru rebellion of 1780–1783—the largest popular uprising in the history of the Spanish empire, and in which the continent's indigenous Indian inhabitants, most especially the descendants of the Incas, played a critical role, and the subsequent wars of Hispanic American liberation led by Simon Bolivar, sought to provide, at least in part, for the egalitarian reconstruction of the Americas.[57] Yet as Perry Anderson poignantly reflected:

> A tragic consciousness of the discrepancies which . . . arose between the avowed objectives and real effects of independence haunts the writings of Bolivar, more lucidly aware than any of his contemporaries of the failure of the Spanish American revolutions as a broader human enterprise of liberation. "I am ashamed to admit it," he wrote, "but independence is the only benefit we have gained, at the cost of all else. They will say of me that he liberated the New World, but not that he improved the felicity or stability of a single nation in America." The lacerated epitaph of the generation that fought for emancipation can be read in his final words: "Those who serve the revolution plough the sea."[58]

This recognition, of the limitations of even Hemispheric-wide continental rebellions, in the context of subsequent revolutionary waves, periodic defeats and contemporary processes of regional integration, saw the reimagining of the Americas. Yet possibilities for solidarity across the Americas have increasingly been reframed in terms of the American Dream, to the exclusion of other spaces and traces of the Americas.[59] This is perhaps especially true for those dreams carried across borders in a search for refuge, jobs, opportunities, escape from violence and civil wars, in which the US has been deeply implicated, as during its century or more support of murderous oligarchical rule throughout the Americas.[60]

The reshaping here, of course, also had to do with the continued US continental expansion in the era of Manifest Destiny, including the invasion of and conquest of a third of Mexico, in the US-Mexican War of 1846–1848, and the subsequent discovery of gold in California in 1848. The subsequent Gold Rush, played a central role in the making of the American and California Dream, as the state, today the most populous in the nation, increasingly came to represent what Kevin Starr, in his Americans and the California Dream Series, called the "cutting edge of the American Dream."

Tragically, the discovery of gold in California coincided with the genocidal extermination of the state's Native American peoples, and the narrowing or extinguishing of their dreams. Yet Native American Californians, who had lived on the land for thousands of years, would continue to do so. In an important work, *We Are the Land: A History of Native California* (2021), Damon B. Akins and William Bauer Jr. note that:

> One cannot separate Indigenous Peoples from the land that makes up California. But as an idea, or as it was often described, a dream-that colonial entities brought with them, "California" represented a natural abundance of resources to be exploited. . . . People misunderstand the settler invasion of Indigenous California *as* California history rather than as an unsustainable and disruptive episode in it.[61]

California today, Los Angeles County specifically, still has the largest populations of indigenous descent in the US. And today, even with the loss of luster, globally, the California Dream resonates still. In recent years Lady Gaga sang the lines "It's buried in my soul like California Gold."[62] California historian Kevin Starr and historian Malcolm J. Rohrbough both underscored the relationship between the discoveries and American and California Dreams, with the latter noting: "the gold rush was the beginning of the nation's and the world's fascination with California and things Californian as the embodiment of the American Dream."[63] Yet long ago, it was no less a figure than Karl Marx that heralded the epoch-making nature of the discovery of gold in California. In 1849, the year after the failed world revolutions of 1848 and the publication of Marx and Engel's *Communist Manifesto*, Marx would write that "the dreams of gold had replaced the dreams of socialism among the proletariat of Paris."[64] Recently, Mae Ngai, in *The Chinese Question: Gold Rushes and Global Politics* (2021), has underscored the fundamental significance of the discovery and subsequent gold rushes, in not only California but globally. Across much of the Anglo-Saxon world, in white settler colonies from California, in the United States, to Australia and later South Africa, the Chinese question provided for a reformulation of white supremacist dreams, in ways that sought to exclude the Chinese, and persons of color from participation. And though largely lost to historical memory, this Chinese question intersected in important ways with the Black freedom struggle.

In 1869, for example, Frederick Douglass, in a speech to the National Colored Persons Union, spoke out strongly against the anti-Chinese movement, arguing

> for the elevation of those deemed worthless. . . . I have said that the Chinese will come, and have given some reasons why we may expect them in very large numbers in no very distant future. Do you ask, if I favor such immigration, I answer I would. Would you have them naturalized, and have them invested with all the rights of American citizenship? I would. Would you allow them to vote? I would. Would you allow them to hold office? I would. . . . I submit that this question of Chinese immigration should be settled upon higher principles than those of a cold and selfish expediency. There are such things in the world as human rights . . . eternal, universal, and indestructible. Among these, is the right of locomotion; the right of migration . . . which . . . belongs . . . to all. . . . It is the right you assert by staying here, and your fathers by coming here. It is this great right that I assert for the Chinese and Japanese, and for all other varieties of men equally with yourselves, now and forever. I know of no rights or race superior to the rights of humanity, and when there is a supposed conflict between human rights and national rights, it is safe to go to the side of humanity. . . . I reject the arrogant and scornful theory by which they would limit migratory rights, or any other essential human rights to themselves, and which would make them the owners of this great continent to the exclusion of other races of men. I want a home here not only for the negro, the mulatto and the Latin races; but I want the Asiatic to find a home here in the United States, and feel at home here, both for his sake and ours.[65]

Douglass's eloquent plea was indicative of the larger questions of racism and antiracist struggles for equality soon to become bound up with the US Civil War with Black Reconstruction, and central to the attempt to remake the United States on new and enlarged, anti-racist social foundations. Just a few years before this speech by Frederick Douglass, Karl Marx noted in *Capital* (1867) that "in the United States of America, every independent workers' movement was paralyzed as long as slavery disfigured a part of the republic. Labor in a white skin cannot emancipate itself where it is branded in a black skin."[66] Du Bois extends Marx's important insight here, in *Black Reconstruction*, noting that "the emancipation of labor is the freeing of that basic majority of workers who are yellow, brown and black."[67] Yet here too there were terrible divisions in the Abolitionist and emerging women's and feminist movements, not only in terms of the color of one's skin, but also in terms of gender. At the first women's rights convention, in Seneca Falls, New York, of 1848, despite the proclamation of the ideal that all women and men were created equal, thus announcing a fuller vision of human equality, subsequent divisions were tearing this movement apart.[68] In the aftermath of the US Civil War, as the debate over the Fifteenth Amendment got underway, enfranchising African American men, but not women, some of the most prominent leaders of the women's or feminist movement, notably Elizabeth Cady Stanton, revealed invectives that were seeped in racism, classism, and ethnic and religious stereotypes against immigrants, both voluntary and forced. Stanton offered up traditional racist tropes about the vulnerabilities of white womanhood to Black masculinity, for example.[69] Though almost wholly unknown still, the stark realities went even beyond this. As Gary Y. Okihiro relates: "advances in U.S. democracy illustrated the complexity of the intersections and articulations of race, gender, and class. The National Woman Suffrage Association, led by Elizabeth Cady Stanton and Susan B. Anthony, opposed the Fifteenth Amendment because it gave political power to 'the lower orders of Chinese, Africans, Germans, and Irish, along with their low ideals of womanhood.'"[70] Despite the limitations of the Abolitionist movement, it played a heroic role in the overthrow of American slavery. One might suppose that the very person who coined the term, the American Dream, would be an eloquent support of a movement arguably indispensable for its realization. Revealingly, however, Adams himself is torn on the subject. At one moment, Adams talks of the American Dream as based on "the belief in the value of the common man," stating that "like every great thought that has stirred and advanced humanity, it was a religious emotion, a great act of faith a courageous leap into the dark unknown." And then, just a few pages later, in discussing the Abolitionist movement, Adams says, "Opinion will perhaps always remain divided as to whether in the long run the movement served the genuine good of the negro or not."[71] Aside from racist opinion, there is no divide about whether the movement advanced the cause of Black freedom.[72] There is this different debate, however, on the limits of freedom after the abolition of slavery, and the question of how to make freedom a blessing, instead of a burden or curse, to the newly free.

Of course, the prerequisite for any debate concerning the meaning of freedom was the titanic battle for the abolition of racist slavery in America, by the enslaved themselves and their allies. Blacks led this freedom struggle, part and parcel of one of the great multiracial coalitions in American history, and one in which abolitionism and an emerging women's rights movement played especially critical roles. Adams' stance on these matters is fraught with angst, as on the one hand, he considered the southern white slaveholding states as real America. According to Adams, "until past the mid-century the Mississippi Valley was racially, as well as in its enforced economic democracy, the real home of Americanism."[73] Since Adams lauds America as the land of opportunity for everyone, he thus poses a contradiction here, of immense proportions. How is it possible to construct a dream around, by, and for white slaveholding people, that is also a dream for non-white or partially white non-slaveholding people, to whom Adams refers to, incidentally, as the ignorant immigrant hordes?[74] It is also disturbing to consider Adams' phrasing in describing the South as a place of "enforced economic democracy." How is it even remotely possible that democracy can exist, a notion predicated on the freedom to participate in self-governance, if this participation is predicated upon the forced compulsion of racist slavery?

Instead of recognizing these realities, which one might expect to be necessary for the realization of the Dream, Adams continues to uphold the myth of the benevolent slavery of the South versus the malevolent wage slavery of the North, noting: "The negro slave had at least one great advantage over the Northern factory worker. He was property, and had to be taken care of. What the Northern manufacturer considered *his* property was the mill with its machinery, and he came to care no more for the worker than for the bale of cotton."[75] The point Adams appears to make is for some absurdly ridiculous notion of compassionate enslavement. Because the slaveholder values their property, which are their slaves, they are compelled to take care of that property. Because the Northern manufacturer values their property, which are mills and machinery, they have no need to, and are not inclined to, care for the mill worker. The logic here is astounding and horrifying. It is also, sadly, the logic of capitalism, in the sense that Adams is presciently speaking to the direction that capitalism takes in the future before him. Such is evident in recent revelations that the field of economics, to cite one instance, conventionally uses terms like "human capital stock" to refer to workers, placing these people as both a kind of property, much like how Adams understood the white southern system of slavery, and simultaneously identifying such people as non-human. In short, the system of enforced economic democracy to which Adams refers becomes the frame for our presumably democratic capitalism. The South rises again, so to speak, embedded in a system that reaches far beyond it. In today's distaste of any notion of economic redistribution, one can hear the reality of the Southern racist oligarchy, whose "property" rose up against their enslavement, and with the support of the Union armies, including some 200,000 Black soldiers, effected the largest expropriation of property, in this instance enslaved humanity, in American history.

Nevertheless, Adams continues on upholding Southern honor in his mind anyway, noting that for the white slaveholding oligarchy (antiseptically referred to as gentlemen): "To have these Yankees, who drove their wage slaves twelve and fourteen hours a day in badly ventilated mills for a few cents' pay, and who never assumed the slightest responsibility for them when sick, old, or out of work, tell the Southerner that *his* form of slavery only was immoral, and thus assume airs of superiority, was galling."[76] Certainly, there is some hypocrisy here on the part of the North, as Adams rightly points out. But beyond such, what Adams never seems to consider is the possibility that in a place where most people are without property, and where the ownership of property, or being owned as property, determines one's voting rights, democracy, or rule of the people without property, is but a chimera. To do so, Adams would be forced to deepen his critique of both chattel and wage slavery, holding up the notions of liberty that animated the early Republican Party in its critique of both systems of slavery, but this he cannot seem to bring himself to do. Yet where Adams fails, Du Bois succeeds. For Du Bois understood, and articulated better than ever before, that it was the rise of the Black freedom struggle, most especially the abolitionist movement, and with it the emergence of a Republican Party dedicated to stopping the expansion of slavery, that would bring the contradictions to a bursting point, and give the moment for enslaved humanity, as Du Bois notes, to rise from the dead and enter history, an astonishing achievement unrecognized by their brethren, with tragic consequences.[77]

There is no recognition of this tragedy in any part of Adams' epic. And this is not surprising as among Adams' admiring correspondents was none other than Claude Bowers, author of arguably the most influential history of Reconstruction, *The Tragic Era: The Revolution After Lincoln* (1929), and an integral part of the infamous Dunning School of racist historiography, which dominated the history of the period.[78] Bowers' letter to Adams discusses an admiring review of his book in the *Baltimore Sun*, among other things.[79] Of course, Adams wrote four years before Du Bois's magnum opus was published, in which the latter dubbed Bowers' book pure and simple propaganda, but the admiration for Bowers can be seen in the similar enough title and arguments Adams narrates in *The Epic of America* and *The American Tragedy* (1934). Adams evidently sided with those who deemed that Blacks were not ordinary human beings. Later historiography, for some time, was not much better. As David Roediger wrote in the introduction to his edited collection, *Black on White: Black Writes on What it Means to Be White* (1998):

> In my own field, that of history, the leading U.S. professional organization recently published a poll which asked members to list the most important historian and books treating the American South. Not a single respondent named W.E.B. Du Bois's *Black Reconstruction*. This omission, the rough equivalent of a group of theologians neglecting the Bible in listing important books bearing on the Christian tradition, came as part of a pattern.[80]

The war on historical memory, the erasure of history, and the substitution of racist fairy tales for historical truth led Du Bois to title his last chapter in *Black Reconstruction*, "The Propaganda of History," arguing that: "No serious and unbiased student can be deceived by the fairy tale of a beautiful Southern slave civilization."[81] In explaining the longevity of this fairy tale, Du Bois focuses on what he sees as the key element in its persistence, namely that: "The chief witness in Reconstruction, the emancipated slave . . . has been almost barred from court"; *Black Reconstruction* sought to correct this.[82] In the face of this "epistemology of white ignorance," as Charles Mills calls it, W. E. B. Du Bois's *Black Reconstruction* (1935), and also his earlier biography, *John Brown* (1909), provides a literary window through which we can see the humanity of the resistance and rebellion of the enslaved at the heart of radical abolitionism, as does the work of scholars such as Cedric Robinson, in *Black Marxism: The Making of the Black Radical Tradition* (1983) and other works.[83]

In the story of John Brown, the Civil War, and beyond, in radical abolitionism or what Du Bois called abolition-democracy, we get a rare glimpse of one of those moments where the American Dream seems possible, simultaneous with Langston Hughes's dialectical image of the dream deferred. This connection to Langston Hughes, and the drama of John Brown, and his allies that inspired him, most especially former enslaved persons turn freedom fighters, such as Harriet Tubman and Frederick Douglass, was personal. For Lewis Sheridan Leary, the first husband of Langston Hughes' maternal grandmother, Mary Langston, joined John Brown's raid at Harper's Ferry. So, Hughes himself, who like Douglass, was of mixed-race origins, had an experience in his close familial history of this most-loved white American among Blacks. Mary Langston used to say about John Brown, "His soul is marching on," and use the blood-stained shawl rescued from her martyred husband's body to cover young Langston at night.

In 1859, John Brown attempted to overthrow slavery in the US through his raid on Harpers Ferry, the federal armory, and along with Du Bois's biography of Brown, the story has now been immortalized in fiction. As Robert Blauner notes, arguably "no single work gets to the heart of race in America as well or as profoundly as Russell Banks' *Cloudsplitter*" (1998), a work that David Roediger, in his new introduction to Du Bois's biography comes closest to grasping Du Bois's understanding of how militancy and racial egalitarianism were inseparable for John Brown.[84] The book is told through the lens of John Brown's third son, Owen Brown. Here, Owen Brown voices the lens through which the radical abolitionists of the Brown family saw the world:

> The three-hundred-year-long War between the Races, from before the Revolution up to and including Harpers Ferry, was being found mainly as the War Against

Slavery. . . . The truth is, for us, the so-called Civil War was . . . part of a continuum. Just another protracted battle. Ours was very much a minority view,
however. It still is. But from the day it began, to Northerner and Southerner
alike, the Civil War was a concussive trauma that erased all memory of what
life had been like before it. On both sides, white Americans woke to war and
forgot altogether the preceding nightmare, which had awakened them in the
first place."[85]

North American settler colonial history and that of the US thereafter
had long been a delicate balance between the rights of slaveholders and
non-slaveholders, protecting the former from potential threats by the latter.[86] With a revolutionary generation riding the tide of popular rebellion, the
Founding Fathers nevertheless, as the secret proceedings of the Constitutional
Convention articulated, moved to protect the opulent minority against the
propertyless majority, as James Madison alluded to in *The Federalist Papers*,
Number 10, while simultaneously excluding African Americans, Native
Americans, all others designated non-whites, and women.[87]

Eventually, the conflict increasingly expressed itself in terms of the battle
between the slaveholding oligarchy controlling the slave states, and free
states. Each entrance of a state or territory into the union became the basis
for a power struggle. Over time, this battle became more and more fierce. The
coming of the Civil War reflected embattled versions of the American Dream,
as each side believed in its vision of America, each reading the vision articulated in the Declaration of Independence as supportive of their perspective.
Some may scoff at such an idea, seeing in the Declaration of Independence
a promissory note of liberty, to be claimed by future generations, yet the
long-time domination of the US federal government by the slave states cau-
tions against such optimistic readings. So too does a host of new evidence,
troubling, but plausible, that a key aspect of the motivation for the American
Revolution, at least in the eyes of the Southern states and the Southern oligarchy, was the fear that the *Somerset* decision in England, providing for the
freedom of England's slaves, given the place of the American colonies, could
be extended to them, depriving them of their most important property.[88]

Still other evidence, alluded to before, attempts to reconcile the seeming
contradiction between the language of enslavement and that of freedom that
animated the new revolutionary Americans. This would not be the first time
in world history that notions of freedom were animated by the realities of
slavery, as Orlando Patterson argued in *Freedom* (1991).[89] Here, we focus
on the intersecting histories of some of the leading actors in the abolitionist movement, part of the larger "antislavery enterprise," in which Lincoln
played a key role, though interestingly, he was not an abolitionist, despite his

fervent belief that slavery was morally wrong, and his personal desire to see it abolished.

In *Cloudsplitter*, Banks explores the historical person of revolutionary John Brown, and his most unusual quality as a "white" man, of empathetic identification with Blacks in their struggle and treatment of them on the basis of full equality, even while realizing the centrality of the fiction or witchcraft of "race," which is to say historical racism, in every interaction not only between Blacks and whites, but also between whites themselves. Many African Americans who Brown met with, including Harriet Tubman and Frederick Douglass, knew of Brown's plans, and attested to his qualities. And while declining to follow Brown in his path, they were supportive of his general efforts. Brown realized too, as Banks expresses it, that whites are as burdened with color and race as Blacks, not of course as the oppressed, but instead in terms of the centrality of oppressive race relations in the United States. Part of the political importance of Brown, in addition to this relatively unique form of antiracist consciousness, is the extent to which he demonstrated the possibility of those of European American descent being willing to give their lives to create a new American dream, to wrest it, that is, from the long-simmering American nightmare of slavery, dispossession, racism and genocide.

Banks draws here on John Brown's autobiographical account of his transformative experience of seeing an enslaved Black child, when he himself was only a child, in describing the man who Du Bois argued came nearest to touching the souls of Black folk.[90] In *Cloudsplitter,* John Brown's son Owen reflects on his father's love for African Americans, noting:

> Negroes . . . did not need white people to love them. They merely needed us to deal justly with them. . . . To Negroes, white was as much a color as black, red, or yellow—if not more so. . . . Father . . . loved *American* blacks, and he loved them, I believe, because of their relation to the dominant race of American whites. He saw our nation as divided unfairly between light-colored people and dark, and he chose early and passionately to side with the dark. Something deep within his soul . . . went out to the souls of American Negroes, so that he was able to ally himself with them in their struggle against slavery and American racialism, not merely because he believed they were in the right, but because he believed that somehow he was one of them. Of course, he was *not* one of them. He was a white man, with all the inescapable powers, privileges, and prerogatives of his race and sex . . . he was a white man, and he knew it.[91]

Through Brown, Banks acknowledges the ways in which adults remain in, carry within them, their childhood, and in so doing, are enabled to see the world from their perspectives as adults, but also as children, if time or trauma does not block their ability to continue to do so.[92]

Frederick Douglass, in a "Lecture on Pictures," on December 3, 1861, on roughly the second anniversary of John Brown's execution, noted: "Tonight . . . the brave spirit of John Brown serenely looks from his eternal rest, beholding his guilty murderers in torments of their own kindling—and the faith for which he nobly died, rapidly becoming the saving faith of the nation. Two years ago, young John Brown was hunted in Ohio like a felon. Today he is a captain under the broad seal of the U.S. Government."[93] Subsequently in an April 1881 letter to the *New York Times*, just after his *Life and Times of Frederick Douglass* (1881) appeared, with a number of chapters on John Brown, Douglass wrote the following: "I never had under my roof at any time such an incarnation of justice and the true martyr spirit as when John Brown lived with me. He was a constant thorn in my side. I could not help feeling that this man's zeal in my enslaved people was holier and higher than mine. I could speak for my race—he could fight for my race. I could live for my race—John Brown could die for my race."[94] The next month, in May 1881, Douglas eloquently spoke his truth in a speech at Harper's Ferry:

> If John Brown did not end the war that ended slavery, he did, at least, begin the war that ended slavery. If we look over the dates, places, and men for which this honor is claimed, we shall find that not Carolina, but Virginia, not Fort Sumter, but Harper's Ferry and the arsenal, not Major Anderson, but John Brown began the war that ended American slavery, and made this a free republic. Until the blow was stuck, the prospect for freedom was dim, shadowy, and uncertain. The irrepressible conflict was one of words, votes, and compromises. When John Brown stretched forth his arm the sky was cleared, the armed hosts of freedom stood face to face over the chasm of a broken Union, and the clash of arms was at hand.[95]

Rather than receding, slavery was still expanding, however. In 1850, the Fugitive Slave Act was passed, providing for the return of runaway enslaved persons. Just four years later, in 1854, the Missouri Compromise, which had at least some limits on slavery's further expansion, was repealed. Simultaneously, John Brown and his sons threw themselves into battle against slavery's expansion into Kansas, founding the Radical Abolition Party. And Brown was not alone, finding support from the likes of Henry David Thoreau, Ralph Waldo Emerson, Senator Charles Sumner, Frederick Douglass, Martin Delany, and Harriet Tubman, who Brown called "General Tubman," and who helped in its planning. These actions were followed by the most infamous decision in Supreme Court history, the *Dred Scott* decision, handed down just two days after President James Buchanan's inauguration, on March 5, 1857. The judgement of the highest court in the land declared that Negroes were not part of the American people, never were and never could be, having no rights that white men needed respect. The clear implication was that Black slavery could not thereby be legally constrained in the new territories, or anywhere else for that matter, in the United States.

In June of that year, Democratic Senator Stephen Douglas, Lincoln's archrival, in a speech in Springfield, Illinois announced his vociferous support for the decision. Just two weeks later, on June 26, 1857, Lincoln gave his rejoinder in that same city, declaring that all the forces seemed now bent on

> making the bondage of the negro universal and eternal. . . . All the powers of earth seem rapidly combining against him. Mammon is after him; ambition follows, and philosophy follows, and the Theology of the day is fast joining the cry. They have him in his prison house; they have searched his person, and left no prying instrument with him. One after another they have closed the heavy iron doors upon him, and now they have him, as it were, bolted in with a lock of a hundred keys, which can never be unlocked without the concurrence of every key; the keys in the hands of a hundred different men, and they scattered to a hundred different and distant places; and they stand musing as to what invention, in all the dominions of mind and matter, can be produced to make the impossibility of his escape more complete than it is.[96]

Just eight months later, in February of 1858, as Lincoln was preparing for his Senate run against Douglas, one that proved unsuccessful, "a political earthquake dramatically altered the landscape of party politics. In the wake of the *Dred Scott* decision, President Buchanan announced that slavery now existed in all the territories, 'by virtue of the Constitution.' In the spring of 1858 . . . Buchanan attempted to bring Kansas into the Union as a slave state under the Lecompton Constitution."[97] As Lincoln famously said earlier in his Peoria, Illinois speech of October 16, 1854: "The doctrine of self-government is right—absolutely and eternally right—but it has no just application, as here attempted . . . if the negro *is* a man," then slavery "is despotism."[98] This in turn led to Lincoln's famous House Divided speech of June 16, 1858, where he declared, conjuring Matthew 12:25:

> "A house divided cannot stand." I believe that this government cannot endure, permanently half *slave* and half *free*. . . . It will become all one thing or the other. Either the *opponents* of slavery, will arrest the further spread of it, and place it where the public mind shall rest in the belief that it is in the course of ultimate extinction; or its *advocates* will push it forward, till it shall become alike lawful in *all* the States, *old* as well as *new*—*North* as well as *South*. Have we no *tendency* to the latter condition?[99]

A little over a year later, on October 16, 1859, John Brown, with some 21 other men, 5 Black and 16 white, launched a daring raid to capture the federal arsenal at Harper's Ferry in West Virginia, some 60 miles from Washington, D.C., and just a few days later they were killed or captured. Brown was tried for attempting to incite a slave insurrection, murder, and treason, and executed. Among those who captured Brown and his men on that day were future Confederate General, Robert E. Lee, and the head of the Virginia Military Institute, Thomas F. Jackson, who also aided in overseeing Brown's execution, and was later nicknamed Stonewall Jackson and fought with Lee. One of those who witnessed Brown's hanging with Jackson was Edmund Ruffin, who was later granted "the honor of firing the first shot on Fort Sumter, a kind of christening of the Confederacy," while another who witnessed the event was none other than John Wilkes Booth, who later assassinated President Lincoln shortly after attending his historic second and final inaugural address.[100] No more than six months after attending John Brown's execution, Ruffin revealed the American Dream he sought in a novel, *Anticipations of the Future* (1860), which imagined secession, civil war, and a Southern triumph.[101]

On the day of Brown's execution, Harriet Tubman, reflecting on Brown's unflinching dedication to the Black freedom struggle, is supposed to have said: "I've been studying and studying upon it . . . and its clar to me, it wasn't John Brown that died on that gallows . . . its clar to me it wasn't a mortal man, it was God in him."[102] And according to one of her leading biographers, Lois E. Horton, in *Harriet Tubman and the Fight for Freedom* (2013), "After Brown's death Tubman redoubled her efforts and was even more convinced that a war against slavery was imminent."[103] Tubman, of course, became famously identified with the war effort, serving as a spy and military scout gathering intelligence for the Union Army and leading a military raid on the Combahee River in enemy territory in South Carolina, one of the few in American history to do so, risking her own life and freedom. Tubman later assisted the famous Black Fifty-Fourth Massachusetts Regiment, in which two of Frederick Douglass's sons, Charles and Lewis, and the white abolitionist Robert Gould Shaw served, before their famed attack on Fort Wagner in Charleston, South Carolina. Over 100 of the 600 men were killed, including Sergeant William H. Carney, the first African American in history to be awarded the Congressional Medal of Honor; Tubman helped to bury the dead.[104]

It must be stressed here, though, that at that time, Lincoln, as he himself stated, had no intention of interfering with Southern slavery, beyond being unwilling to allow for its further expansion. Yet, even this limitation was totally unacceptable to the Southern slaveholding oligarchy. Such points were acknowledged by Lincoln at the time, in a letter to the soon to be Vice-President of the Confederacy, Alexander Stephens, dated December 22, 1860:

I fully appreciate the present peril the country is in, and the weight of responsibility on me.

Do the people of the South really entertain fears that a Republican administration would, *directly*, or *indirectly*, interfere with their slaves, or with them, about their slaves? If they do, I wish to assure you, as once a friend, and still, I hope, not an enemy, that there is no cause for such fears.

The South would be in no more danger in this respect, than it was in the days of Washington. I suppose, however, that this does not meet the case. You think slavery is right and ought to be extended; while we think it is wrong and ought to be restricted. That I suppose is the rub. It certainly is the only substantial difference between us.[105]

The full reply, we are told by leading Civil War scholars, is currently lost to history but in his infamous "cornerstone" speech of March 21, 1861, a month after his appointment as the Vice-President of the Confederacy, Stephens spoke of what he called the false idea upon with the United States was founded, that all men are created equal, to highlight, by way of contrast, that the Confederacy

is founded upon exactly the opposite idea; its foundations are laid, its cornerstone rests, upon the great truth that the negro is not equal to the white man; that slavery, subordination to the superior race, is his natural condition. This, our new government, is the first, in the history of the world, based on this great physical, philosophical and moral truth.[106]

As to what unfolded after Lincoln's letter to Stephens, and less than a month after the latter's cornerstone speech of March 1861, ironies abound. As Du Bois wrote in *Black Reconstruction*, "When Edwin Ruffin, white-haired and mad, fired the first gun at Fort Sumter [on April 12, 1861], he freed the slaves. It was the last thing he meant to do." Initially, the response of Lincoln and the North was simply to restore the Union, for reasons that Du Bois expertly underscored.[107] But as Emerson once said, "Things are in the saddle, And ride mankind." With the continuation of the war and the advancement of the Union armies, enslaved humans increasingly escaped to join the Union armies in an assertion of their humanity and freedom, and rebelled in a thousand different ways, in what Du Bois called "the general strike." As the war dragged on, the logic of harnessing enslaved African American humanity's struggle for freedom, increasingly tied with American freedom, became more and more evident to some, and it was from here too that the ideas of the post–Civil War Bureau of Refugees, Freedman, and Abandoned Lands, or the Freedmen's Bureau, was born.[108]

In his *The Long Road to Antietam: How the Civil War Became a Revolution* (2012), Richard Slotkin underscored the great challenges that Lincoln, the

Union, and all those who sought the overthrow of slavery and a new birth of freedom faced. Here the Battle of Antietam was important, for the victory allowed Lincoln to issue the news of his preliminary Emancipation Proclamation five days later, on September 22, 1862. This landmark document stated: "That on the first day of January in the year of our Lord one thousand eight hundred and sixty-three, all persons held as slaves in any state, or designated part of a state, the people whereof shall be in rebellion against the United States shall be then, thenceforth, and forever free."[109] The issuing of the Emancipation Proclamation of January 1, 1863 in turn paved the way for the incorporation of some 200,000 African-Americans into the U.S. armed forces, with the formation of Black Regiments and the heroic exploits of Harriet Tubman. Paul Dunbar, whose father served in the 55th Massachusetts Infantry Regiment during the Civil War and who Henry Louis Gates Jr. has called "the greatest African American poet before the Harlem Renaissance," first chronicled their exploits in poems such as "The Colored Soldiers" (1913). The heroism of these men finally made its way to Hollywood screens in the film *Glory* (1989), after a half-century of Hollywood's glorifications of Confederate dreams.

Like Hollywood largely before and after him, Adams somehow cannot bring himself to evoke the very moment when the American Dream seemed at once closest to possible realization, for the first time, or utter destruction, in the US Civil War, as very different conceptions of the American Dream erupted into apocalyptic conflict, as they are arguably again today, nor can he acknowledge the centrality of an enslaved Black humanity struggling for freedom in American and world history. In the fatal moment of the US Civil War, for the briefest of moments at least, the struggle for African American freedom and American freedom became one. Here was revealed the entwining of the destiny of which Martin Luther King Jr. later wrote in his famous "Letter from Birmingham Jail" just a little over 100 years after Lincoln's Emancipation Proclamation, in 1963:

> I am cognizant of the interrelatedness of all communities and states. . . . Injustice anywhere is a threat to justice everywhere. We are all caught in an inescapable network of mutuality, tied in a single garment of destiny. Whatever affects one directly, affects all indirectly. . . . Just as Socrates felt that it was necessary to create a tension in the mind so that individuals could rise from the bondage of myths and half-trusts to the unfettered realm of creative analysis and objective appraisal, so much we see the need for nonviolent gadflies to create the kind of tension in society that will help men rise from the dark depths of prejudice and racism to the majestic heights of human brotherhood. . . . We must use time creatively, in the knowledge that the time is always ripe to do right.[110]

Adams too sees an interrelationship, but a vastly different one than Du Bois or King, in the sense that Adams insists on not seeing what they insist on seeing, which is Black humanity's importance in the Americas, for the question of the American Dream, and thus for the world and humanity. In fact, and to his credit if any credit can be given, Adams readily admits his limited and limiting vision when he states:

> We had always had to shut one eye when we looked at the negro, and after 1865 we had had to shut it also when we looked at the South and those in it who objected to being "reconstructed." We had had slaves and we had had "rebels," and now over 10 percent of our population were "subjects." It was getting a bit hard to maintain the fiction of the free man giving his free consent to a free government; and if that were no longer to be held by us as the one infallible political philosophy for freedom, might not the inroads on the old conception extend yet further?[111]

Perhaps not surprisingly, Du Bois, in *Black Reconstruction*, in attempting to understand the failure of European Americans to seize the moment and transform themselves, writes:

> Efforts were made to show that Negro labor could only achieve its end by political organization. Frederick Douglass wrote an editorial to this effect, and concluded with the words: "The Republican Party is the true workingmen's party of the country." This sounded strange for the North but it was at the time true of the South. . . . As the Negroes moved from unionism toward political action, white labor in the North not only moved from political action to union organization, but also evolved the American Blindspot for the Negro and his problems. It lost interest and vital touch with Southern labor and acted as though the millions of laborers in the South did not exist . . . it was the American Blindspot that made the experiment all the more difficult, and to the South incomprehensible. For several generations the South had been taught to look upon the Negro as a think apart. He was different from other human beings . . . the color problem became the Blindspot of American political and social development and made logical argument almost impossible. The only power to curtail the rising empire of finance in the United States was industrial democracy—votes and intelligence in the hands of the laboring class, black and white, North and South.[112]

Stephen O'Connor's *Thomas Jefferson Dreams of Sally Hemmings: A Novel* (2016) conjures this notion of eyes wide shut and blind spots with his epigraph from Thomas Jefferson, in a letter from 1786:

> What a stupendous, what an incomprehensible machine is man!

> Who can endure toil, famine, stripes, imprisonment or death

Itself in vindication of his own liberty, and the next moment be

deaf to all those motives whose power supported him thro' his

trial, and inflict upon his fellow men a bondage, one hour of which

is fraught with more misery than ages of that which he rose in

rebellion to oppose.[113]

Jefferson augments Adams' notion of limited sight with an additional diminishment of the senses, one of limited or selective hearing. Adams' one eye shut arguably underplays dramatically the war against, and erasure of historical memory of American racism and the Black freedom struggle, the interrelatedness of this to humanity and sentient beings more generally, and the unwillingness of many Americans to use their eyes and their minds to see, understand, and act on such understanding. Indeed, Adams himself seems unable to simply recognize the presence of Black humanity in the lands that became the United States of America and the entwining of this into a larger history. It is the blindness that registers legible in Adams' *Epic of America* a series of aporia regarding the whole notion of the American Dream and dreams deferred, which he and many others, are simply unwilling to see. To quote once again from Reverend Dr. Martin Luther King Jr.:

> Abused and scorned though we may be, our destiny is tied up with America's destiny. Before the pilgrims landed at Plymouth, we were here. Before the pen of Jefferson etched the majestic words of the Declaration of Independence across the pages of history, we were here. For more than two centuries our forebears labored in this country without wages; they made cotton king; they built the homes of their masters while suffering gross injustice and shameful humiliation—and yet out of a bottomless vitality they continued to thrive and develop.[114]

Remarking upon these passages, Jonathan Reider, in *Gospel of Freedom: Martin Luther King, Jr.'s Letter from Birmingham Jail and the Struggle that Changed a Nation* (2013), cites the work of King in a way that provides a powerful dialectical counterpart to Adams' notion of the American Dream, invoking instead, at least implicitly, Hughes' *Montage of a Dream Deferred.*

> This veneration of the slaves reminds us why it is a mistake to place King into the civil religious tradition evoked by his use of the imagery of the American dream. When he reviewed American history, King read it in the light of the Black experience in America, in which coerced work was central. The labor of a slave was not the labor of a lonely individual who came to the pristine state of

American nature, worked the land and acquired a right to property. Nor was it an errand in the wilderness, the story of Providence watching out and over the unfolding of American glory. The slave's story was always of a people in exile, who "were here" but not allowed to be part of the nation, whose skin color and forced labor made for a different kind of "exceptionalism": They were other people's property, the instruments of somebody else's dream.[115]

This inability to see, and the need for corrective vision, was perhaps why Susan Buck-Morss titled her book *The Dialectics of Seeing: Walter Benjamin and the Arcades Project* (1989). The brilliant montage artist of the Harlem Renaissance, Romare Bearden, in "The Negro Artist's Dilemma" (1946), reacting to the success of the romanticization of white supremacy in *Birth of a Nation* and *Gone With the Wind,* "made pointed reference to . . . the debilitating influence of cinematic as well as fine arts images of a people and their culture," arguing "that cinematic caricatures were making seeing impossible."[116] For as the Frankfurt School theorists Max Horkheimer and Theodor Adorno pointed out in *The Dialectic of Enlightenment* (1946) this very same year, in a chapter subtitled "Enlightenment as Mass Deception," what they called "the Culture Industry" was harnessed for mythmaking and sleep, rather than awakening.[117] And this is true as well, of many tropes of the American Dream, for as Stephen Daedalus, widely considered the "literary alterego" of the author James Joyce, who first makes his appearance in *A Portrait of the Artist as a Young Man* (1916), later puts it in a book published 100 years ago, *Ulysses* (1922), "History . . . is a nightmare from which I'm trying to awake."[118]

NOTES

1. On the actual historiography regarding the population of the Americas, including North America, see the important recent study by Alexander Kock, Chris Brierly, Mark M. Maslin, and Simon L. Lewis, "Earth System Impacts of the European Arrival and Great Dying in the Americas after 1492," *Quaternary Science Reviews* 207, 2019: 13–36.

2. James Truslow Adams, *The Epic of America* (Boston: Little, Brown, and Company, 1931), 12.

3. A wonderful version of the song is sung by Hawaiian artist Israel Kamakawiwo'ole.

4. James Truslow Adams, *The Epic of America* (Boston: Little, Brown, and Company, 1931), 12, 14–15.

5. For a profound exploration of the background of Columbus's voyage and the subsequent encounter with the "Other," see Nicolas Wey Gomez, *The Tropics of Empire: Why Columbus Sailed South to the Indies* (Cambridge, MA: MIT Press, 2006).

6. James Truslow Adams, *The Epic of America* (Boston: Little, Brown, and Company, 1931), 19.

7. Quoted in Lewis Hanke, *The Spanish Struggle for Justice in the Conquest of America* (Dallas: Southern Methodist University Press, 2002), 17.

8. For the debate, see Lewis Hanke, *All Mankind is One: A Study of the Disputation Between Bartolome de Las Casas and Juan Gines de Sepulveda in 1550 on the Intellectual and Religious Capacity of the American Indians* (De Kalb: Northern Illinois University Press, 1974), and Immanuel Wallerstein, *European Universalism: The Rhetoric of Power*, especially Chapter 1, "Whose Right to Intervene? Universal Values Against Barbarism" (New York: New Press, 2006), 1–31, and Patricia Seed, "Are These Not Also Men? The Indians' Humanity and Capacity for Spanish Civilization," *Journal of Latin American Studies* 24, No. 3 (October 1993): 629–652.

9. Patricia Seed, "'Are These Not Also Men?' The Indians' Humanity and Capacity for Spanish Civilization," *Journal of Latin American Studies* 24, No. 3 (October 1993): 629–652, especially 629, 634–640. See also David M. Lantigua, *Infidels and Empires in a New World Order: Early Modern Spanish Contributions to International Legal Thought* (New York: Cambridge University Press, 2020).

10. J.H. Elliot, *Empires of the Atlantic World: Britain and Spain in America 1492–1830* (New Haven: Yale University Press, 2006), 11.

11. Lewis Hanke, *All Mankind is One: A Study of the Disputation Between Bartolome de Las Casas and Juan Gines de Sepulveda in 1550 on the Intellectual and Religious Capacity of the American Indians* (De Kalb: Northern Illinois University Press, 1974). See also Carlton D. Floyd and Thomas E. Reifer, "What Happens to a Dream Deferred? W.E.B. Du Bois and the Radical Black Enlightenment/Endarkenment," *Socialism and Democracy in W.E.B. Du Bois's Life, Thought and Legacy*, eds., Edward Carson, Gerald Horne, and Philip Luke Sintiere (New York: Routledge, 2022), 52–80.

12. Kenneth J. Pennington Jr., "Bartolome de Las Casas and the Tradition of Medieval Law," *Church History* 39, No. 2 (June 1970): 149–161. See also Lawrence A. Clayton, *Bartolome de Las Casas and the Conquest of the Americas* (New York: Wiley-Blackwell, 2011), and his *Bartolome de Las Casas: A Biography* (New York: Cambridge University Press, 2012).

13. See David Orique, OP, *To Heaven or to Hell: Bartolome de Las Casas's Confesionario* (University Park, PA: Pennsylvania State University Press, 2018). On the charges of high treason, see Nicolas Wey Gomez, *The Tropics of Empire: Why Columbus Sailed South to the Indies* (Cambridge, MA: MIT Press, 2006), 449–450, footnote 31.

14. In *Abolition: A History of Slavery and Antislavery* (New York: Cambridge University Press, 2007), 40–87, Seymour Drescher, building upon earlier historiography, discussed the racialization of slavery over time, and its settlement on Black slavery which brought Africans to the New World, where a combination of factors, including the invention of racism as a justification for enslavement itself, eventually led to the end of the enslavement of Native Americans, European Americans, and Asians, and the turning to Africa in the transatlantic slavery trade.

15. Gustavo Gutierrez, *Las Casas: In Search of the Poor of Jesus Christ* (Maryknoll, New York: Orbis Books, 1993), 327.

16. James Truslow Adams, *The Epic of America* (Boston: Little, Brown and Company, 1931), 200–202.

17. Henry David Thoreau, *Walden*, edited with an introduction and notes by Stephen Fender (New York: Oxford World Classics, 2008), 9.

18. W.E.B. Du Bois, *Black Reconstruction in America* (New York: The Library of America, 2021), 3–4.

19. W.E.B. Du Bois, *Black Reconstruction* (New York: The Library of America, 2021), 25. See also Brycchan Carey, *From Peace to Freedom: Quaker Rhetoric & the Birth of American Antislavery, 1657–1761* (New Haven: Yale University Press, 2012). See also Charles Grier Sellers Jr.'s edited collection, *The Southerner as American*, and related chapter, "The Travail of Slavery" (New York: E.P. Dutton & Co., 1966), 40–71. For more recent evidence regarding the question of whether slaveholders or Southerners felt any guilt about slavery, see Gaines M. Foster, "Guilt Over Slavery: A Historiographical Analysis," *Journal of Southern History* 56 (November 1990): 665–694, and Patricia Roberts-Miller, *Fanatical Schemes: Proslavery Rhetoric and the Tragedy of Consensus* (Tuscaloosa: University of Alabama Press, 2009). See the short discussion of this article and book in William L. Barney, "Rush to Disaster: Secession and the Slaves' Revenge," in *Secession Winter: When the Union Fell Apart*, eds., Robert J. Cook, William L. Barney, and Elizabeth R. Varon (Baltimore: The Johns Hopkins University Press, 2013), 10–33, and page 92, footnote 3.

20. For the most recent biography, see Robert Elder, *Calhoun: American Heretic* (New York: Basic Books, 2021).

21. W.E.B. Du Bois, *Black Reconstruction* (New York: The Library of America, 2021), 59.

22. W.E.B. Du Bois, *Black Reconstruction* (New York: The Library of America, 2021), 65–66.

23. W.E.B. Du Bois, *Black Reconstruction* (New York: The Library of America, 2021), 15–16.

24. https://caselaw.findlaw.com/us-supreme-court/60/393.html. For two important reviews of questions of slavery, and of racism and "race" more generally in the Supreme Court, see Paul Finkelman, *Supreme Injustice: Slavery in the Nation's Highest Court* (Cambridge, MA: Harvard University Press, 2018), and Orville Vernon Burton and Armand Derfner, *Justice Deferred: Race and the Supreme Court* (Cambridge, MA: The Belknap Press of Harvard University Press, 2021).

25. https://caselaw.findlaw.com/us-supreme-court/60/393.html.

26. James Truslow Adams, *The Epic of America* (Little, Brown, and Company, 1931), 405.

27. For two fascinating analyses of some of these questions, ranging from Europe's violent colonization of the America's and the globe to Protestantism (including in the first essay a profound appreciation and critique of Weber's famous book), slavery in the Americas, including British North America, and more, see Carlo Ginzburg, "Latitude, Slaves and the Bible: An Experiment in Microhistory," *Critical Inquiry* 31 (Spring 2005): 665–683, and Peter Ghosh, *Max Weber and "The Protestant Ethic":*

Twin Histories (New York: Oxford University Press, 2017). The phrase, Manifest Destiny, is thought to have been coined by expansionist John O'Sullivan in 1845 to promote the annexation of Texas, which was secured, along with the conquest of a third of Mexico, including the state that would become California, during the war which began in 1846 and ended in 1848. Manifest Destiny was thus fundamentally the belief that the expansion of Protestantism, and hence America, across the continent through conquest and the bringing of capitalism and democracy, was providential. See also Bruce Gordon, *Calvin* (New Haven: Yale University Press, 2009). See also Nicholas Guyatt, *Providence and the Invention of the United States, 1607–1876* (New York: Cambridge University Press, 2007). Here, the burst of overseas expansion was part and parcel of what Alfred Crosby called *Ecological Imperialism: The Biological Expansion of Europe: 900–1900* (New York: Cambridge University Press, 2015). On the central role of English colonization and labor, free and unfree, see Christopher Tomlins, *Freedom Bound: Law, Labor, and Civic Identity in Colonizing America, 1580–1865* (New York: Cambridge University Press, 2010). See also Aziz Rana, *The Two Faces of American Freedom* (Cambridge, MA: Harvard University Press, 2010).

28. Louis Hartz, *The Founding of the New Societies: Studies in the Histories of the United States, Latin America, South Africa, Canada, and Australia* (New York: Harcourt, Brace and World, 1964). See Michael J. Klarman, *The Framers' Coup: The Making of the United States Constitution* (New York: Oxford University Press, 2016). See also Jennifer Nedelsky, *Private Property and the Limits of American Constitutionalism: The Madisonian Framework and its Legacy* (Chicago: University of Chicago Press, 1994).

29. Eric Hinderaker and Peter C. Mancall, *At the Edge of Empire: The Backcountry in British North America* (Baltimore: Johns Hopkins University Press, 2003). J.H. Elliot, *Empires of the Atlantic World: Britain and Spain in America 1492–1830* (New Haven: Yale University Press, 2006), 23–24, 418, footnote 96.

30. Bernard Magubane, *The Making of a Racist State: British Imperialism and the Union of South Africa, 1875–1910* (New Jersey: Africa World Press, 1996), Chapter 6, "The Irish Precedent," 139–162.

31. See Allan Nevins, *James Truslow Adams: Historian of the American Dream* (Champaign: University of Illinois Press, 1970).

32. Ira Berlin, *The Making of African America: The Four Great Migrations* (New York: Viking, 2010).

33. James Belich, *Replenishing the Earth: The Settler Revolution and the Rise of the Anglo-World, 1783–1939* (New York: Oxford University Press, 2009). James Belich, "Exploding Wests: Boom and Bust in Nineteenth Century Settler Societies," *Natural Experiments of History*, eds., Jared Diamond and James A. Robinson, (Cambridge, MA: Harvard University Press, 2010), 53–87. See also E. Digby Baltzell, *The Protestant Establishment: Aristocracy and Caste in America* (New Haven: Yale University Press, 1964).

34. The quote is from Colin G. Calloway, *One Vast Winter Count: The Native American West before Lewis & Clark* (Lincoln: University of Nebraska Press, 2009), especially his "Prologue: Land & History in the American West," 18, 1–21, from

which this paragraph draws heavily. See also Andrew C. Isenberg, *The Destruction of the Bison: An Environmental History, 1750–1920* (New York: Cambridge University Press, 2000). David J. Meltzer, *First Peoples in a New World: Populating Ice Age America* (New York: Cambridge University Press, 2021). Matthew R. Bennett, et al., "Evidence of Humans in North America During the Last Glacial Maximum," *Science* 373, September 24, 2021, 1528–1531. Ellen Callaway, "Ancient Footprints Could Be Oldest Traces of Humans in the Americas," *Nature* 597 (September 30, 2021), 601–602. *New York Times*, "Ancient Footprints Push Back Date of Human Arrival in the Americas: Human Footprints Found in the Americas are about 23,000 Years Old, a Study Reported, Suggesting That People May Have Arrived Long Before the Ice Age's Glaciers Melted," Carl Zimmer, September 23, 2021.

35. See for example Kate Masur, *Until Justice Be Done: America's First Civil Rights Movement, From the Revolution to Reconstruction* (New York: W.W. Norton and Company, 2021). See also David Armitage, *The Declaration of Independence: A Global History* (Cambridge, MA: Harvard University Press, 2007).

36. James Truslow Adams, *The Epic of America* (Boston: Little, Brown & Co., 1931), 112.

37. In addition to Kate Masur, *Until Justice Be Done: America's First Civil Rights Movement, From the Revolution to Reconstruction* (New York: W.W. Norton and Company, 2021), see Van Gosse, *The First Reconstruction: Black Politics in America from the Revolution to the Civil War* (Chapel Hill: University of North Carolina Press, 2021).

38. James Truslow Adams, *The Epic of America* (Boston: Little, Brown, and Company, 1931), 119.

39. Walter Johnson, *River of Dark Dreams: Slavery and Empire in the Cotton Kingdom* (Cambridge, MA: The Belknap Press of Harvard University Press, 2013). See also Sven Beckert, *Empire of Cotton: A Global History* (New York: Vintage Books, 2014).

40. Robert O'Meally, *Antagonistic Cooperation: Jazz, Collage, Fiction, & the Shaping of African American Culture* (New York: Columbia University Press, 2022), 10. See also Ralph Ellison, *The Collected Essays of Ralph Ellison*, edited and with an introduction by John F. Callahan (New York: Modern Library, 2003), and Ralph Ellison, *Living with Music: Ralph Ellison's Jazz Writings*, edited and with an introduction by Robert G. O'Meally (New York: The Modern Library, 2002). For an exploration of this in action, see Charles Sellers, *The Market Revolution* (New York: Oxford University Press, 1991).

41. For the background, see David Geggus, "The Louisiana Purchase & the Haitian Revolution," in Elizabeth Maddock Dillon & Michael Drexler, eds., *The Haitian Revolution & the Early United States* (Philadelphia: University of Pennsylvania Press, 2016): 117–129. The best current account in our estimation is now Piero Gleijeses, "Napoleon, Jefferson, & the Louisiana Purchase," *The International History Review* (2017), Volume 39, Number 2: 237–255.

42. This point is forcefully argued in Peter S. Onuf, "The Empire of Liberty: Land of the Free and Home of the Slave," *The World of the Revolutionary American*

Republic: Land, Labor, and the Conflict for a Continent, ed. Andrew Shankman (New York: Routledge, 2014), 195–217.

43. W.E.B. Du Bois, *Black Reconstruction* (New York: The Library of America, 2021), 27–28.

44. St. Clair Drake, *The American Dream and the Negro: 100 Years of Freedom?* The Emancipation Proclamation Centennial Lectures, January-February, 1963 (Chicago, Illinois: Roosevelt University), 23. See P. Gabrielle Foreman, Jim Casey and Sarah Lynn Patterson, eds., *The Colored Conventions Movement: Black Organizing in the Nineteenth Century* (Chapel Hill: University of North Carolina Press, 2021). See also the Colored Conventions Project, https://coloredconventions.org/about-conventions/. See also Winston James, *The Struggles of John Brown Russwurm: The Life and Writings of a Pan-Africanist Pioneer, 1799–1851* (New York: New York University Press, 2010). See also Henry Mayer, *All on Fire: William Lloyd Garrison and American Slavery* (New York: St. Martins, 1998).

45. On the hidden history, only recently established decisively in historical scholarship, see especially John Craig Hammond, "Mastery over Slaves, Sovereignty over Slavery: James Monroe, Virginia, and the Missouri Crisis," in *Revolutionary Prophecies: The Founders and America's Future*, eds., Robert M.S. McDonald and Peter S. Onuf (Charlottesville: University of Virginia Press, 2021), 194–222, and John Craig Hammond, "President, Planter, Politician: James Monroe, the Missouri Crisis, and the Politics of Slavery," *Journal of American History* 105, Issue Number 4, (March 2019): 843–867. See also Christa Dierksheide, *Amelioration and Empire: Progress and Slavery in the Plantation Americas* (Charlottesville: University of Virginia Press, 2014).

46. Quoted as the epigraph of Matthew Karp's important study, *This Vast Southern Empire: Slaveholders at the Helm of American Foreign Policy* (Cambridge, MA: Harvard University Press, 2016).

47. For a critically important study about the racist exclusions during the Revolutionary War that were central in forming the United States as what Benedict Anderson calls "an imagined community," see Robert G. Parkinson, *The Common Cause: Creating Race & Nation in the American Revolution* (Chapel Hill: University of North Carolina Press, 2016).

48. Herbert Eugene Bolton, "The Epic of Greater America," in *Do the Americas Have a Common History? A Critique of the Bolton Theory*, ed. Lewis Hanke (New York: Alfred A. Knopf, 1964), 68.

49. Jose de Onis, "The Americas of Herbert E. Bolton," *The Americas* XII, Washington (1955), 157–168, quoted in Lewis Hanke, "Introduction," in *Do the Americas Have a Common History? A Critique of the Bolton Theory*, ed., Louis Hanke (New York: Alfred A. Knopf, 1964), 11.

50. Herbert Eugene Bolton, "The Epic of Greater America," in *Do the Americas Have a Common History? A Critique of the Bolton Theory*, ed., Lewis Hanke (New York: Alfred A. Knopf, 1964), 70. See also Albert L. Hurtado, *Herbert Eugene Bolton: Historian of the American Borderlands*, (Berkeley, CA: University of California Press, 2012).

51. J.H. Elliot, *Do the Americas Have a Common History?* (Providence, Rhode Island: John Carter Brown Library, 1998).

52. Herbert Eugene Bolton, "The Epic of Greater America," in *Do the Americas Have a Common History? A Critique of the Bolton Theory*, ed., Louis Hanke (New York: Alfred A. Knopf, 1964), 100.

53. Tzvetan Todorov, *The Conquest of America* (New York: Harper Perennial, 1982), 5. Also see Richard Drinnon, *Facing West: The Metaphysics of Indian Hating & Empire Building* (New York: Schocken, 1990).

54. The term is taken from the important book by Caitlin Fitz, *Our Sister Republics: The United States in an Age of American Revolutions* (New York: Liveright, 2016). See also Alan Taylor, *American Revolutions: A Continental History, 1750–1804* (New York: W.W. Norton & Co., 2016). There are few works that attempt an integrated approach towards the Americas. For two iconoclastic attempts, though, see James Dunkerley, *Americana: The Americas in the World, around 1850* (New York: Verso, 2000), and Felipe Fernández-Armesto, *The Americas: A Hemispheric History* (New York: The Modern Library, 2003).

55. See Piero Gleijeses, "Haiti's Contribution to the Independence of Spanish America: A Forgotten Chapter," *Revista/Review Interamericana* (Winter 1979): 511–528; Piero Gleijeses, "The Limits of Sympathy: The United States & the Independence of Spanish America," *Journal of Latin American Studies* 24, Number 3 (October 1992): 481–505; Piero Gleijeses, *America's Road to Empire: Foreign Policy from Independence to World War I* (New York: Bloomsbury Academic, 2021).

56. Enrique Dussel, *The Invention of the Americas: Eclipse of "The Other" and the Myth of Modernity*, (Continuum International Publishing Group, 1995), 124–125.

57. For a world-systems analysis of the Age of Revolutions and this entire period and the rebellions, see Immanuel Wallerstein, *The Modern World-System: The Second Era of Great Expansion of the Capitalist World-Economy, 1730s–1840s* (San Diego: Academic Press, 1989), Chapter 4, "The Settler Decolonization of the Americas: 1763–1833," 191–256. See also Charles F. Walker, *The Tupac Amaru Rebellion* (Cambridge, MA: The Belknap Press of Harvard University Press, 2014), and Charles F. Walker and Liz Clarke, *Witness to the Age of Revolution: The Odyssey of Juan Bautista Tupac Amaru* (New York: Oxford University Press, 2020). See also, J.H. Elliot, *Empires of the Atlantic World* (New Haven: Yale University Press, 2006), 353–402. See also Piero Gleijeses, *America's Road to Empire: Foreign Policy from Independence to World War I* (New York: Bloomsbury, 2022), Chapter 6, "The Limits of Sympathy: The United States and the Independence of Latin America," 101–111.

58. Perry Anderson, "The Nature & Meaning of the Wars of Hispanic American Liberation," in *World Society Studies*, eds., Volker Bornschier and Peter Lengyel (Frankfurt: Campus Verlag, 1990), 108.

59. We note here that the poetry of Langston Hughes has long thrived throughout the Americas, with over 164 of his poems translated in much of the Spanish-speaking world, with over three hundred versions of them in circulation. See W. Jason Miller, *Langston Hughes* (London: Reaktion Books, 2020), 49. See also Vera M. Kutzinski, *The Worlds of Langston Hughes: Modernism and Translation in the Americas* (Ithaca: Cornell University Press, 2012).

60. See James Dunkerley, *Power in the Isthmus: A Political History of Modern Central America* (New York: Verso, 1988). See Jeffrey M. Paige, *Coffee and Power: Revolution and the Rise of Democracy in Central America* (Cambridge, MA: Harvard University Press, 1998). See also Douglas V. Porpora, *How Holocausts Happen: The United States in Central America* (Philadelphia: Temple University Press, 1992).

61. Damon B. Akins and William J. Bauer Jr., *We Are the Land: A History of Native California* (Oakland: University of California Press, 2021), 4.

62. Lady Gaga, "Always Remember Us This Way," Bradley Cooper and Lady Gaga, *A Star is Born*, Soundtrack, 2018.

63. Malcolm J. Rohrbough, "'We Will Make Our Fortunes—No Doubt of It': The Worldwide Rush to California," in *Riches for All: The California Gold Rush and the World*, ed., Kenneth N. Owens (Lincoln: University of Nebraska Press, 2002), 54.

64. Quoted in Malcolm J. Rohrbough, "'We Will Make Our Fortunes—No Doubt of It': The Worldwide Rush to California," in *Riches for All: The California Gold Rush and the World*, ed., Kenneth N. Owens (Lincoln: University of Nebraska Press, 2002), 66. See also Andrew C. Isenberg, *The California Gold Rush: A Brief History with Documents* (Boston: Bedford/St. Martin's, 2018).

65. Frederick Douglass, "Composite Nation." Speech to the Colored National Labor Union Founding Convention, 1869. https://www.blackpast.org/african-american -history/1869-frederick-douglass-describes-composite-nation/.

66. Karl Marx, *Capital, Volume 1* (New York: Penguin, 1992), 414.

67. W.E.B. Du Bois, *Black Reconstruction* (New York: The Library of America, 2021), 22.

68. See Faye E. Dudden, *Fighting Chance: The Struggle Over Woman Suffrage and Black Suffrage in Reconstruction America* (New York: Oxford University Press, 2011). See also Lisa Tetrault, *The Myth of Seneca Falls: Memory and the Women's Suffrage Movement, 1848–1898* (Chapel Hill: University of North Carolina Press, 2014).

69. See the preceding references, along with Brett Staples, "The Racism Behind Women's Suffrage," *New York Times*, July 29, 2018, A8.

70. Quoted in Gary Y. Okihiro, *American History Unbound: Asians and Pacific Islanders* (Oakland: University of California Press, 2015), 88.

71. John Truslow Adams, *The Epic of America* (Boston: Little, Brown, and Company, 1931), 198, 200.

72. Recently, Manisha Sinha, in *The Slave's Cause: A History of Abolition* (2016), has underscored the radicalism of this movement, its multiracial and transnational character, and the centrality of Black leadership, notably from those humans who resisted their enslavement, whose voices provided the most stirring calls for freedom, with women playing a central role.

73. James Truslow Adams, The *Epic of America* (Boston: Little, Brown, and Company, 1931), 148.

74. "Hordes of underpaid ignorant immigrants, with little training in government of any sort, replaced the old American stock with its long experience of town meetings and politics." James Truslow Adams, *The Epic of America* (Boston: Little, Brown, and Company, 1931), 183.

75. James Truslow Adams, *The Epic of America* (Boston: Little, Brown, and Company, 1931), 180.

76. James Truslow Adams, *The Epic of America* (Little, Brown, and Company, 1931), 201.

77. W.E.B. Du Bois, *Black Reconstruction in America* (New York: Library of America, 2021), 873–874.

78. John David Smith and J. Vincent Lowery, eds., *The Dunning School: Historians, Race, and the Meaning of Reconstruction*, with a foreword by Eric Foner (University Press of Kentucky, 2013).

79. Claude G. Bowers to James Truslow Adams, in *James Truslow Adams, Select Correspondence*, edited with a Bibliographical Essay by Allan Nevins, (New Brunswick: Transaction Publishers, 2012), 192–194.

80. David R. Roediger, "Introduction," *Black on White: Black Writers on What it Means to Be White*, ed., David R. Roediger (New York: Schocken Books, 1998), 8.

81. W.E.B. Du Bois, *Black Reconstruction* (New York: The Library of America, 2021), 858–859. See also the important work by David W. Blight, *Beyond the Battlefield: Race, Memory, & the American Civil War* (Amherst: University of Massachusetts, 2002.

82. W.E.B. Du Bois, *Black Reconstruction*, New York: The Library of America, 2021, 866.

83. Charles Mills, "White Ignorance," in *Race & the Epistemology of Ignorance*, ed., Shannon Sullivan & Nancy Ruana (Albany: State University of New York Press, 2007), 13. Mills writes: "White ignorance . . . It's a big subject. How much time do you have? It's not enough. Ignorance is usually thought of as the passive obverse to knowledge, the darkness retreating before the speak of the Enlightenment. But . . . Imagine an ignorance that fights back. Imagine an ignorance militant, aggressive, not to be intimidated, an ignorance that is active, dynamic, that refuses to go quietly—not at all confined to the illiterate and uneducated but propagated at the highest levels of the land, indeed presenting itself as knowledge." See also Charles Mills, "White Ignorance," in *Agnotology: The Making & Unmaking of Ignorance*, ed., Robert N. Proctor & Londa Schiebinger (Stanford, CA: Stanford University Press, 2008), 230–249. W.E.B. DuBois, *Black Reconstruction: An Essays Towards the Part Which Black Folks Played in the Attempt to Reconstruct Democracy in America, 1860–1880, & Other Essays*, edited by Eric Foner & Henry Louis Gates Jr. (New York: Library of America, 2021). First published in 1935. W.E.B. Du Bois, *John Brown*, edited and with an Introduction by David Roediger (New York: The Modern Library Classics, 2001). See also Ralph Hertwig & Christoph Engel, eds., *Deliberate Ignorance: Choosing Not to Know* (Cambridge, MA and London, England: Massachusetts Institute of Technology & the Frankfurt Institute of Advanced Studies, 2020). See Cedric J. Robinson, *Black Marxism: The Making of the Black Radical Tradition*, revised and updated 3rd edition (Chapel Hill: University of North Carolina Press, 2021). See also Walter Johnson, with Robin D.G. Kelley, *Boston Review: Forum 1: Race, Capitalism, Justice* (Cambridge, MA, 2017). See also Michael Omi and Howard Winant, *Racial Formation in the United States*. 3rd edition (New York: Routledge, 2014).

84. Bob Blauner, *Still the Big News: Racial Oppression in America* (Philadelphia: Temple University Press, 2001), ix. David Roediger, "Introduction," to W.E.B. Du Bois, *John Brown* (New York: Random House, Modern Library, 2001), xvi–xvii.

85. Russell Banks, *Cloudsplitter: A Novel* (New York: Harper Perennial, 1998), 7–8. James M. McPherson, Russell Banks, *Cloudsplitter* (1998); "Russell Banks's Fictional Portrait of John Brown," Mark C. Carnes, ed., *Novel History: Historians & Novelists Confront America's Past (and Each Other)* (New York: Simon & Schuster, 2001), 61. See also Bob Blauner, *Still the Big News: Racial Oppression in America* (Philadelphia: Temple University Press, 2001).

86. For a fundamental work chronicling these complex processes, see Barbara J. Fields, "Slavery, Race, & Ideology in the United States of America," *New Left Review* 181 (May/June 1990): 95–118, also incorporated into Karen E. Fields & Barbara J. Fields, *Racecraft: The Soul of Inequality in American Life* (New York: Verso, 2012).

87. See Jennifer Nedelsky, *Private Property and the Limits of American Constitutionalism: The Madison Framework and its Legacy* (Chicago: University of Chicago Press, 1994).

88. The *Somerset v Stewart* decision of 1772 found that Charles Stewart, the nominal owner of an enslaved African, James Somerset, could not return him to slavery in England's colony, Jamaica, having now set his feet upon British soil. Here, the Judge in the case, Lord Mansfield, stated that "the state of slavery is of such nature that it is incapable of being introduced on any reasons, moral or political . . . it is so odious that nothing can be suffered to support it but positive law." Quoted in Trevor Burnard, *Jamaica in an Age of Revolution* (Pittsburgh: University of Pennsylvania Press, 2020), 151. Yet the decision had implications far beyond its actual ruling, soon thereafter taking on a life of its own, and inspired the development of antislavery sentiment long thereafter, becoming became part of the basis for legal thinking thereafter in the American Republic, as James Oakes argues in *Freedom National* (New York: W.W. Norton & Co., 2014). See especially William M. Wiecek, "*Somerset:* Lord Manfield and the Legitimacy of Slavery in the Anglo-American World," *University of Chicago Law Review* 42, (1975): 84–146, and his *The Sources of Antislavery Constitutionalism in America, 1760–1848* (Ithaca: Cornell University Press, 1977). See also Steven M. Wise, *Though the Heavens May Fall: The Landmark Trial That Led to the End of Human Slavery* (Lebanon, IN: De Capo Press, 2006).

89. Orlando Patterson, *Freedom: Freedom in the Making of Western Culture* (New York: Basic Books, 1991).

90. Paraphrased from W.E.B. Du Bois's preface to his *John Brown* (New York: Modern Library, 2001). See also, W.E.B. Du Bois, *The Souls of Black Folk*, W.E.B. Du Bois, *Writings* (New York: Library of America, 1986), 357–547. See also, W.E.B. Du Bois, *The Souls of Black Folk*, with "The Talented Tenth," and "The Souls of White Folk" New York: Penguin Classics 150th Anniversary Edition, 1868–2018, with an introduction by Ibram X. Kendi (New York: Penguin Books, 2018).

91. Russell Banks, *Cloudsplitter* (New York: Harper Perennial, 1998), 415–425, with quotes here and above taken from 415–417.

92. Russell Banks, *Cloudsplitter* (New York: Harper Perennial, 1998), 415–418, with the quote from 418.

93. Frederick Douglass, "Lecture on Pictures," Boston's Tremont Temple, December 3, 1861, in *Picturing Frederick Douglass: An Illustrated History of the Nineteenth Century's Most Photographed American*, with an epilogue by Henry Louis Gates Jr., and an afterword by Kenneth B. Morris Jr., edited by John Stauffer, Zoe Trod, & Celeste-Marie Bernier (New York: W.W. Norton & Co., 2015), 126–141. Douglass is referring here to John Brown's oldest son, who did not accompany him in the raid on Harper's Ferry but was then serving in the Civil War captaining a company of soldiers from Kansas.

94. Frederick Douglass, quoted in Robert S. Levine, *The Lives of Frederick Douglass* (Cambridge, MA: Harvard University Press, 2016), 185.

95. Quoted in W.E.B. Du Bois, *John Brown* (New York: The Modern Library, 2001), 211.

96. Abraham Lincoln, "Speech on the *Dred Scott* Decision at Springfield, Illinois," June 26, 1857, in *The Annotated Lincoln*, ed., Harold Holzer and Thomas A. Horrocks (Cambridge, MA: The Belknap Press of Harvard University Press, 2016), 194.

97. Eric Foner, *The Fiery Trial: Abraham Lincoln & American Slavery* (New York: W.W. Norton & Co., 2010), 98.

98. The quotes are drawn from Eric Foner's *The Fiery Trial* (New York: W.W. Norton & Co., 2010), 98, and Allen C. Guelzo, ed., *Lincoln Speeches* (New York: Penguin Books, 2012), 47–48, 167, footnote 38, the latter noting that the actual quote from Matthew 12:25 is: "Every kingdom divided against itself is brought into desolation; and every city or house divided against itself shall not stand."

99. Allen C. Guelzo, ed., *Lincoln Speeches* (New York: Penguin Books, 2012), 56.

100. See Ronald C. White Jr., "Abraham Lincoln's Sermon on the Mount: The Second Inaugural," in *1865: America Makes War and Peace in Lincoln's Final Year*, eds., Harold Holzer and Sara Vaughn Gabbard (Carbondale: Southern Illinois University Press, 2015), 52–65.

101. John Stauffer and Zoe Trod, "Introduction: The Meaning & Significance of John Brown, eds., *The Tribunal: Responses to John Brown & the Harper's Ferry Raid* (Cambridge, MA: The Belknap Press of Harvard University Press, 2012), xlvi, xliii, 262–269.

102. Harriet Tubman, quoted in Lois E. Horton, *Harriet Tubman and the Fight for Freedom: A Brief History with Documents* (The Bedford Series in History and Culture. Boston: Bedford/St. Martin's, 2013), 134–139, 48.

103. Lois E. Horton, *Harriet Tubman & the Fight for Freedom: A Brief History with Documents* (The Bedford Series in History & Culture, Boston: Bedford/St. Martin's, 2013), 49.

104. This paragraph is drawn from the account given in Lois E. Horton, *Harriet Tubman & the Fight for Freedom: A Brief History with Documents* (Boston: Bedford/St. Martin's, 2013).

105. Harold Holzer and Thomas A. Horrocks, ed., *The Annotated Lincoln* (Cambridge, MA: The Belknap Press of Harvard University Press, 2016), 361. And though it is widely believed that the January 6, 2021, attack by a pro-Trump mob was the first time since the War of 1812 that the Capitol was stormed, in fact there was an organized plan to stop the electors when they met to certify the electoral votes for then

President-elect Lincoln on February 13, 1861. Fortuitously, however, the celebrated war hero General Winfred Scott was ready and organized, and threatened to blow to smithereens anyone who tried to interfere with the certification of the votes. Ted Widmer, Opinion: "The Capitol Takeover That Wasn't: In 1861, a pro-Southern mob wanted to block the tallying of electoral votes for Lincoln. So did some congressmen," *New York Times* (January 8, 2021). Ted Widmer, *Lincoln on the Verge: Thirteen Days to Washington* (New York: Simon & Schuster, 2020).

106. Quoted in James M. McPherson, *What They Fought For, 1861–1865* (New York: Anchor Books, 1995), 47–48. See also James M. McPherson, *For Cause and Comrades: Why Men Fought in the Civil War* (New York: Oxford University Press, 1997), and his *The Negro's Civil War: How American Blacks Felt and Acted During the War for the Union* (New York: Vintage, 2003). The earlier part of the speech, underscoring the profound differences between the US Constitution and that of the Confederacy, right before the excerpt quoted here, is as follows: "But not to be tedious in enumerating the numerous changes for the better, allow me to allude to one other though last, not least. The new constitution has put at rest, forever, all the agitating questions relating to our peculiar institution African slavery as it exists amongst us the proper status of the negro in our form of civilization. This was the immediate cause of the late rupture and present revolution. Jefferson in his forecast, had anticipated this, as the 'rock upon which the old Union would split.' He was right. What was conjecture with him, is now a realized fact. But whether he fully comprehended the great truth upon which that rock stood and stands, may be doubted. The prevailing ideas entertained by him and most of the leading statesmen at the time of the formation of the old constitution, were that the enslavement of the African was in violation of the laws of nature; that it was wrong in principle, socially, morally, and politically. It was an evil they knew not well how to deal with, but the general opinion of the men of that day was that, somehow or other in the order of Providence, the institution would be evanescent and pass away. This idea, though not incorporated in the constitution, was the prevailing idea at that time. The constitution, it is true, secured every essential guarantee to the institution while it should last, and hence no argument can be justly urged against the constitutional guarantees thus secured, because of the common sentiment of the day. Those ideas, however, were fundamentally wrong. They rested upon the assumption of the equality of races. This was an error. It was a sandy foundation, and the government built upon it fell when the 'storm came and the wind blew.'" https://www.battlefields.org/learn/primary-sources/cornerstone-speech See also Keith Herbert, *Cornerstone of the Confederacy: Alexander Stephens and the Speech that Defined the Lost Cause* (Knoxville, Tennessee: University of Tennessee Press, 2021). See also Sean Wilentz, "Forging an Early Black Politics," *New York Review of* Books, July 1, 2021, 42–44.

107. Both the quote and an analysis of the quest to restore the Union can be found in W.E.B. Du Bois, *Black Reconstruction* (New York: The Library of America, 2021), 70–71.

108. See Du Bois's *Black Reconstruction* (New York: The Library of America, 2021), Steven Hahn, *A Nation Under Our Feet: Black Political Struggles in the Rural South from Slavery to the Great Migration* (Cambridge, MA: The Belknap Press of

Harvard University Press, 2004), and his subsequent *The Political Worlds of Slavery and Freedom* (Cambridge, MA: Harvard University Press, 2009), and more recently Chandra Manning, *Troubled Refuge: Struggling for Freedom in the Civil War* (New York: Alfred A. Knopf, 2016), as well as Thavolia Glymph, *The Women's Fight: The Civil War's Battles for Home, Freedom, & Nation* (Chapel Hill: University of North Carolina Press, 2020). For an original reconsideration of the background, see Kate Masur, *Until Justice Be Done* (New York: W.W. Norton & Co., 2021).

109. See Abraham Lincoln, "Preliminary Emancipation Proclamation," September 22, 1862, in Michael Vorenberg, *The Emancipation Proclamation: A Brief History in Documents* (New York: Bedford/St. Martin's, 2010), 59–61.

110. Martin Luther King Jr., *Letter from Birmingham Jail* (UK: Penguin, 2018), 2–3, 6, 16. For an exploration of King's meditations, in the context of questions about time, influenced by Walter Benjamin's "Theses on the Philosophy of History," see David Luban, *Legal Modernism* (Ann Arbor: University of Michigan Press, 1994), especially 209–283.

111. James Truslow Adams, *The Epic of America* (Boston: Little, Brown, and Company, 1931), 340.

112. W.E.B. Du Bois, *Black Reconstruction*, (New York: Library of America, 2021), 443, 446, 455.

113. Thomas Jefferson to John Nicolas Demeunier, 26 June 1786, https://founders.archives.gov/documents/Jefferson/01-10-02-0001-0006. This quote serves as one of the epigraphs for Stephen O'Connor, *Thomas Jefferson Dreams of Sally Hemmings: A Novel* (New York: Penguin, 2016).

114. Martin Luther King Jr., *Letter from Birmingham Jail* (UK: Penguin, 2018), 26.

115. Jonathan Reider, *Gospel of Freedom: Martin Luther King, Jr.'s Letter from Birmingham Jail and the Struggle that Changed a Nation* (New York: Bloomsbury, 2013), 95–96.

116. Mary Schmidt Campbell, *An American Odyssey: The Life and Work of Romare Bearden* (New York: Oxford University Press, 2018), 129. Romare Bearden, "The Negro Artist's Dilemma," in The *Romare Bearden Reader,* Robert G. O'Meally, ed., (Durham: Duke University Press, 2019), 91–98. And see most recently the powerful work with resonates with many of the arguments put forward here, Glenda Elizabeth Gilmore, *Romare Bearden in the Homeland of His Imagination: An Artist's Reckoning With the South* (Durham: Duke University Press, 2022).

117. Max Horkheimer and Theodor W. Adorno, *Dialectic of Enlightenment: Philosophical Fragment*, edited by Gunzelin Schmid Noerr and translated by Edmund Jephcott (Stanford, California: Stanford University Press, 2002). As David Frisby notes, "The world of modernity, for Benjamin, was a world of fantasy and illusion generated, ultimately, by the domination of commodity production and exchange. . . . With increasing urgency, Benjamin sought to break through this reified world by means of his dialectical images in order to awaken the 'dreaming collectivity' from its dream. This could only be achieved by the remembrance of what had been forgotten about this reified world. Adorno hopes that Benjamin's theory of the experience of modernity would include 'the whole opposition between individual lived experience [*Erlebnis*] and concrete experience [*Erfahrung*] in a dialectical theory of

forgetfulness.'" David Frisby, *Fragments of Modernity* (Cambridge, MA: The MIT Press, 1986), 272. See also Paul Ricoeur, *Memory, History, Forgetting* (Chicago: University of Chicago Press, 2004).

118. James Joyce, *Ulysses: The 1922 Text* (New York: Oxford World Classics, 1998), 34. See also the Introduction by Seamus Deane to James Joyce, *The Portrait of the Artist as a Young Man* (New York: Penguin Classics Centennial Deluxe edition, 2016), xliii, who notes the similarity here with Karl Marx's famous comment in *The Eighteenth Brumaire of Louis Bonaparte* (1852) that "the tradition of the dead generations weighs like a nightmare on the minds of the living." Note: the translation here comes from Karl Marx, *The Political Writings* (New York: Verso 2019), 481. See also, Fredric Jameson, *The Political Unconscious: Narrative as a Socially Symbolic Act* (Ithaca, New York: Cornell University Press, 1981), Hayden White, "Getting Out Of History: Jameson's Redemption of Narrative," *The Content of the Form: Narrative Discourse and Historical Representation* (Baltimore: The Johns Hopkins University Press, 1987), 142–168, and Perry Anderson, "Fredric Jameson: The Fruits of Time," Hoberg Prize Symposium, 2008. See also Franco Moretti, "The Long Goodbye: *Ulysses* and the End of Liberal Capitalism," *Signs Taken for Wonders: Essays in the Sociology of Literary Forms* (New York: Verso, 1993), 182–208.

Chapter 2

Embattled Dreams, Memory,
and the American Iliad

The shattering of the hopes and dreams of Black Reconstruction in the aftermath of the US Civil War gave birth to the blues and jazz, or what Amiri Baraka and others call *Blues People* and the invention of "American classical music."[1] Of course, we have witnessed the creation and global expansion of rap or hip-hop, most recently at the 2022 Superbowl in Los Angeles. And hip-hop, as William Jelali Cobb has so eloquently written, "is blues filtered through a century of experience and a thousand miles of asphalt."[2] Central in the emergence of the blues was the presence of African American soldiers during the Civil War, called alternately the Blues, the Black and Blues, or what Vincent Harding referred to as "the black men in blue in the year of Jubilee," 1865.[3] As so, with unending irony, the "death of the blues" or the Black men in blue gave "birth to the blues" and with it "the blues epistemology," or what Robert G. O'Meally, riffing off of Ralph Ellison and others, referred to as the "jazz cadence of American culture."[4]

As Clyde Woods argued in *Development Arrested: The Blues and Plantation Power in the Mississippi Delta* (2017), "After the Civil War, African American soldiers in Mississippi served as the backbone of the Union Leagues movement . . . that emerged to defend the land, labor, social and political reform agenda. As the Reconstruction governments were overthrown, the Union Leagues and similar organizations were assassinated throughout the South."[5] "The blues perspective emerged among the two generations that witnessed the overthrow of slavery, ten years of freedom, the overthrow of Reconstruction and the beginning of ninety-five years of what has been called the "Second Slavery," replete with the widespread criminalization of Black life in the South and the beginning of the convict lease system.[6] In contrast, the origins and evolution of the jazz cadence of U.S. culture came especially from New Orleans, Louisiana, specifically Congo Square, or what is now known as Louis Armstrong Park. Both musical forms, and the places where they formed, influenced Langston Hughes's *Montage of a Dream Deferred.* There is a real sense in which the bard of Harlem was continuing the struggles of what we might call the long 1860s, whose spark went back at least to the 1859 raid on Harper's Ferry, if not earlier. Returning to Langston Hughes's grandmother's evocative words on John Brown, "His soul goes marching on," we can see here that John Brown was taking up, like his friends and comrades Harriet Tubman and Frederick Douglass, those souls cast into the detritus of history, and it is here that we find another affinity to both Hughes and Walter Benjamin. Benjamin, like Hughes before him, sought "the 'refuse' and 'detritus' of history, the half-concealed, variegated traces of the daily life of 'the collective,' as the object worthy of study, and with the aid of methods generally distinct from those of the modern historian. something like dream interpretation was the model, not conceptual analysis. The nineteenth century was the collective dream which we, its heirs, were obliged to reenter, as patiently and minutely as possible."[7]

Among the most important artists attempting to usher in this historical awakening from the nation's romanticized myth of slavery was the poet Paul Laurence Dunbar, and the US Civil War, the American Iliad, was the crucible of this awakening. Paul Laurence Dunbar's eyes wide open stunning visualization, "The Colored Soldiers," depicts Black soldiers fighting simultaneously for American and Black freedom in the Civil War. Like the film *Glory* (1989), Dunbar's poem evokes very different American Dreams and dreams deferred than the one-eyed vision of Adams, yet the ability of this poem's inspired words to penetrate the wall of white supremacy in the US and around the world was limited indeed, though the words are no less powerful:

> If the muse were mine to tempt it
> And my feeble voice were strong,
> If my tongue were trained to measures,

Here Dunbar expresses humility in the face of seeking to tell such a powerful storage of courage, bravery, resilience, and fortitude.

> I would sing a stirring song.
> I would sing a song heroic
> Of those noble sons of Ham,

Dunbar strives through his poetic voice to give wings to the soaring story of freemen and enslaved persons called upon to save the nation and fight for their own freedom, in the country's time of need. Dunbar writes of selfless sacrifice, immortalizing the hundreds of thousands who answered the call to arms, to fight for freedom.

> Of the gallant colored soldiers
> Who fought for Uncle Sam!

The bravery, and gallantry, are underscored here, the destiny of two nations, come together as one.

> In the early days you scorned them,
> And with many a flip and flout

Yet, like Langston Hughes later, Dunbar underscores the memory of times past, when the possibilities for freedom and progress were not given a thought, where the majority was unable to consider the precious lives and suffering of their brothers and sisters of color.

> Said "These battles are the white man's,
> And the whites will fight them out."
> Up the hills you fought and faltered,

Dunbar here underscores the vanity and conceit, the arrogance of racism, of exclusion, of homogenous conceptions of the nation, that belie its true and poignant reality of heterogeneity, the diversity of voices making up the true embroidered tapestry of the land, despite the horrific treatment of many, at the hands of those blinded to its beauty.

> In the vales you strove and bled,
> While your ears still heard the thunder
> Of the foes' advancing tread.

Dunbar depicts the movement into battle, the blind leading the blind, hearing only the thunder, yet unable to see the need for solidarity in the face of the impending storm.

> Then distress fell on the nation,
> And the flag was drooping low;
> Should the dust pollute your banner?

Chronicled here is the ostensible progress of the war, actually regress, defeat, humiliation, all because of an inability to call upon those most dedicated to the august principles, belied in reality, but ready to be taken up by the countrys forgotten ones, of "life, liberty and the pursuit of happiness for all," in a land claiming its dedication to the principles of equality for all.

> No! the nation shouted, No!

> So when War, in savage triumph,
> Spread abroad his funeral pall—

Here Dunbar gestures again to the suffering, the needless loss of life, because of racism, on the sides of both the Confederacy, dedicated to the principle that all men are not created equal, and the Union, the latter claiming to fight for the principles of the Declaration of Independence.

> Then you called the colored soldiers,
> And they answered to your call.

And yet, strange fruit. The nation calls, and those long scorned, rejected, set aside, pick up arms and the flag ready to fight for all in the hour of need.

> And like hounds unleashed and eager
> For the life blood of the prey,
> Sprung they forth and bore them bravely

The spring in the step of those promised freedom, many for the first time, underscores the willingness of those enslaved to fight for freedom, justice and equality like none else, no matter the cost.

> In the thickest of the fray.
> And where'er the fight was hottest,
> Where the bullets fastest fell,

Here, Dunbar underscores the heroism of those, who faced willingly, death, dismemberment, and destruction, now that they were given a chance, regardless of the degree of danger encountered.

> There they pressed unblanched and fearless
> At the very mouth of hell.

And once again, we come to now, the willingness of African Americans to walk into the gates of hell, if so doing, will purchase a new birth of freedom, upon new and enlarged foundations for all.

> Ah, they rallied to the standard
> To uphold it by their might;
> None were stronger in the labors,

The irony is not lost on our poet bard, of those rallying to the cries, of the strength of the oppressed, now called upon to fight a common adversary, and thus uphold the truth expounded in the nation's founding documents, yet long denied.

> None were braver in the fight.
> From the blazing breach of Wagner
> To the plains of Olustee,

And here Dunbar makes his testament to men facing certain death, who accepted their fate for the sake of future generations to come.

> They were foremost in the fight
> Of the battles of the free.

And here our poet expresses the formation of those steeled in battles for freedom, free in what they offer for others, resurrected from the death of enslavement to the heroic self-making of free men choosing death to advance the cause of liberty for all.

> And at Pillow! God have mercy
> On the deeds committed there,
> And the souls of those poor victims

In these lines, Dunbar harkens to the terrible massacres of Black men, after capture, in violation of all the laws of war, underscoring the depths of racisms inhumanity, that would rather kill a man, than call him brother, and realize that thy brethren indeed have souls.

> Sent to Thee without a prayer.
> Let the fulness of Thy pity
> O'er the hot wrought spirits sway

Dunbar's poem here becomes a sort of lamentation, an elegy for the fallen.

> Of the gallant colored soldiers
> Who fell fighting on that day!

Here, the dead are immortalized in memory, their fallen bodies consecrating the ground on which they fought.

> Yes, the Blacks enjoy their freedom,
> And they won it dearly, too;

We come here to the simple ability to enjoy freedom, to partake in the blessings of liberty, unencumbered, as in Adams' famous dream, long denied, long deferred.

> For the life blood of their thousands
> Did the southern fields bedew.

Articulated here, the notion of Black freedom fighters as the life blood of the Republic, the life blood of Democracy, only worth the name when it fights for the freedom not of some, but of all.

> In the darkness of their bondage,
> In the depths of slavery's night,
> Their muskets flashed the dawning,

Once again, nodded to hear, the long night of bondage and oppression in the home of the brave and the land of the free, for those men of color, who sought so long for this to be. The long night of slavery is here highlighted, with the flashing of the muskets heralding the new dawn, a new day, out of the land of Canaan, from bondage in Egypt, to freedom land.

> And they fought their way to light.
> They were comrades then and brothers,
> Are they more or less to–day?

Articulated here is the light of freedom, solidarity, brotherhood, and a query for the nation, a plea, a Socratic question hauntingly articulated, bringing forth the ghosts of slavery, and the possibilities for repeating the mistakes of the past, unless due recognition is given to the fallen soldiers.

> They were good to stop a bullet
> And to front the fearful fray.
> They were citizens and soldiers,

Here, Dunbar, heralding the citizen-soldiers of color, whose patriotism was deemed true, to take the fearful fire of bullets, to lay their bodies down, overcoming fear, for a higher cause.

> When rebellion raised its head;
> And the traits that made them worthy,—
> Ah! those virtues are not dead.

Dunbar reminds us here that the colored soldiers stayed true, that even when these men who fought for freedom died, the virtues for which they fought and died live on, among the dead, and among the living, if only this can be recognized but once, and for all time. It is for the nation to choose he seems to be saying.

> They have shared your nightly vigils,
> They have shared your daily toil;
> And their blood with yours commingling

Blood brothers, from different fathers and mothers, who have shared vigils, laboring for the same cause, willing to die for each other.

> Has enriched the Southern soil.

The blood of martyrs, the true heroes of Southern soil, the true men, for which monuments ought to have been erected around the nation, instead of those for the Confederacy and the evil for which it fought, arrayed against the formal principles on which the USA declared its independence.

> They have slept and marched and suffered
> 'Neath the same dark skies as you,
> They have met as fierce a foeman,

The daily marches, suffering, training, under night skies, the fierce determination, the willingness to die for some as yet unseen freedom, that those who gave the fullest measure of devotion sought to will into existence through their noble sacrifice.

> And have been as brave and true.
> And their deeds shall find a record
> In the registry of Fame;

Here is revealed those who were willing to live and die in bravery and truth, for all time, their sacrifice recorded in the annals of freedom forever.

> For their blood has cleansed completely
> Every blot of Slavery's shame.
> So all honor and all glory

Can the nobility of such selfless sacrifice redeem principles long trampled underfoot, in the shame and blood, and unique sufferings of hundreds of years of enslavement, of every inequity, of millions of horrors that sullied eloquent sermons for freedom? Can what one might think of as everlasting shame, somehow be taken into the memory of the nation, and all humanity, to ensure that never again will the treatment of its citizens of color be forgotten, so that a new tapestry can be embroidered, to sing a new song?

> To those noble sons of Ham—
> The gallant colored soldiers
> Who fought for Uncle Sam![8]

Their truth, Dunbar tells us, is marching on, their battle cry of freedom will forever sing and soar, no matter what the future brings, though what it brings matters deeply, in light of such a tragic and astonishing tale of betrayal, and heroism, the likes of which humankind has not often seen.

And in a poem written and published in 1900, in response to the erection of the Augustus Saint-Gaudens Shaw Memorial in 1897, entitled "Robert Gould Shaw," Dunbar strikes a more mournful tone.

> Why was it that the thunder voice of Fate
> Should call thee, studious, from the classic groves,
>   . . .
> To lead th' unlettered and despised droves . . .

The bitter ironies, Dunbar seems to be saying, that those driven and despised, are now called upon by fate, to step out of one inferno, and into another, for themselves and their compatriots.

>   . . .
> Far better the slow blaze of Learning's Light,
> The cool and quiet of her dearer fane,
> Than this hot terror of a hopeless fight,

Here, Dunbar seems to be saying that though the road to redemption and learning may sometimes be slow, and seem hopeless, that it is not so, for slow learning is better than none at all, and the ebbing away of ignorance and hatred gives hope where once all seemed forlorn.

> This cold endurance of the final pain,
> Since thou and those who with thee died for right
> Have died, the Present teaches, but in vain![9]

And yet, Dubar mournfully articulates that it is our actions in the present that shall determine the meaning of these actions, and whether they were or are truly in vain.

In commenting on this poem, James Smethurst, notes:

Dunbar sees Shaw buried with his nameless and forgotten black troops once again. Of course, these soldiers had names, as Dunbar knows well from his family history. He implicitly suggests here, as he would state in "Unsung Heroes," that these black "droves" are rendered nameless through a national forgetfulness. The ending, then, is one of defeat—or at best, a deferred dream of citizenship.[10]

Subsequently, Dunbar, in a poem entitled "To the South, on Its New Slavery," (1913) would pen these tragic words:

> What, was it all for naught, those awful years,
> That drenched a groaning land with blood and tears?

Again, hauntingly, Dunbar questions the nation, asking all to search their heart and soul to answer the mournful cries and wailing of suffering souls, akin to those Dante encountered in hell, but these men, in hell, not because they were not true, but because the nation was not true to them, to their dedication, their suffering, and their ultimate sacrifice.

> Was it to leave this sly inconvenient hell,
> That brother fell fighting his own brother fell?[11]

In a tongue eminently adequate to the task, Dunbar laid out this still oft ignored history, ignored by Adams in his day, and largely since then. Of special interest here is that Dunbar wrote the second to last paragraph of this poem for the 1893 World Columbian Exposition, or World's Fair in Chicago, timed to commemorate the 400th anniversary of Columbus's arrival in the Americas. Benjamin took a keen interest in such exhibitions in his *Arcades Project*, for they represented the utopian dreams of capitalist progress in the late nineteenth and early twentieth centuries. At the time of the Columbia Exposition, Chicago was regarded as "The White City." At the Fair, Dunbar befriended Frederick Douglass, and they worked together on August 25, for what was alternately called Colored People's Day, Colored American Day, or Jubilee Day, to present an alternative positive image of the Black freedom struggle that contrasted with the racist depictions of Africa and the Black diaspora.[12] W.E.B. Du Bois would continue this tradition at later world fairs, such as the Paris Exposition of 1900.[13]

Subsequently, General Colin Powell fittingly addressed this history and its absence from our history books at the 1997 centennial commemoration of Augustus Saint-Gauden's monument to the 54th Massachusetts Regiment noting:

What a powerful image—the proud, young, fatalistic Colonel Robert Gould Shaw and his black soldiers, heads high, rifles on their shoulders, resolution in their every step, marching southward with fortitude, looking just as they did when they marched past the site of this statue on May 28, 1863, on their way to hope, on their way to glory, and for many of them, on their way to death. . . . Soldiers returned from the doomed assault [on Fort Wagner] bearing the flag they believed in, and Sergeant William H. Carney, though severely wounded, carried that flag back. Sergeant Carney became the first black soldier to earn the new Congressional Medal of Honor.

Battery Wagner was not the first battle for black troops, and it certainly would not be the last. But it served as a gleaming example of their courage and fortitude. . . . They have earned in blood the blessings of liberty. Two more deadly years would pass before the war and slavery came to an end. The Reconstruction period that followed the Civil War brought hope to black Americans. Now that they had earned in blood the blessings of life, liberty, and the pursuit of happiness, that was what they would receive. . . . Certainly, we had proved that skin color was not the measure of a man or a woman. But it was not to be.

Reconstruction came to an end as the political consensus for it collapsed. After the Civil War, we entered a new dark period of American history: the period of Jim Crow and segregation, poll taxes, repression, and the denial of justice. All of this was codified in the terrible doctrine known as "separate but equal," enshrined by the U.S. Supreme Court in *Plessy vs. Ferguson* in 1896 just as the Saint-Gaudens memorial was being completed.

. . . One hundred summers after Battery Wagner, Martin Luther King, Jr. would stand in front of the Lincoln Memorial and give his famous "I Have a Dream" speech, praying for the day once again when the content of a person's character would be the sole measure of a person's worth. It was the same prayer that had inspired the soldiers of the Fifty-fourth Massachusetts. It is a prayer that still must inspire us today.

Despite the obstacles that are before us, remarkable progress had been made of course, since 1864 and since 1963. . . . I was privileged to become the first black person to be appointed chairman of the Joint Chiefs of Staff of the Armed Forces of the United States, but I was not the first one qualified. . . . To my dying day, I will also never forget that I became chairman because there were men of the Fifty-fourth, Buffalo Soldiers, Tuskegee Airmen, and others who were willing to serve and shed their blood for this country. They served this country knowing full well that their country would not serve them . . . we dare not believe that our work is done.[14]

The Shaw Memorial has been called, by noted Yale Art Historian Vincent Scully, "the greatest public sculpture of America's greatest period of public sculpture . . . that begins with the World's Columbian Exposition in 1893."[15] And as Kirk Savage notes: "There had never been an American monument more elite than this."[16] Yet the supreme irony of the legacy, highlighted here, was that these soldiers of color bravely served a country that never served them; they fought for a country that never fought for them. The biblical reference to the sons of Ham in Dunbar's poem, Noah's darker than white second son and his progeny, renews the life of an age-old mythology in a presumably newly emerging world. Here, Dunbar, flips the script accorded to Ham, thought of as populating Africa, the so-called dark continent, and as a defilement on the earth, produces noble rather than ignoble sons, "gallant colored soldiers" rather than pitiful and weak ones. In running the words *gallant* and *colored* together without additional adornment or qualification, Dunbar leaves room for at least two interpretations, that of soldiers whose Blackness is itself a gallant color, and that of soldiers who are both gallant and colored. We learn, as Dunbar continues, that these Black soldiers, once rejected and vilified, take on a distinctly elevated stance in the eyes of white soldiers and citizens who found themselves on the losing end of this war, at least until no longer needed.

The invisibility of the sacrifice of Blacks in the American Civil War to win their own freedom and preserve American freedom, was mirrored in the invisibility of the nation's first preeminent Black modern poet. But of course, it was more than simply invisibility, for the South and the nation have untold numbers of monuments glorifying the Confederacy, and those who fought to keep Black slavery.[17] As Kevin Young writes, "As the first widely popular black poet, Paul Laurence Dunbar occupies the unenviable position of being at once extremely influential and strangely invisible. . . . The son of slaves himself, Dunbar's influence is still felt, invisibly."[18] Young goes on to chronicle the influence of the man Henry Louis Gates Jr. called "the greatest African American poet before the Harlem Renaissance," across a range of mediums, moments, and cultural awakenings, from the work of Zora Neal Hurston and the Harlem Renaissance, to Maya Angelou's *I Know Why the Caged Bird Sings* (one of Dunbar's stirring lines of poetry, from his poem "Sympathy"), to Dunbar's inclusion in Young's edited *African American Poetry: 250 Years of Struggle and Song* (2020), prefaced with his beautiful introduction, "The Difficult Miracle," with its epigraph from June Jordan, "This is the difficult miracle of Black poetry in America: that we persist, published or not, and loved or unloved: we persist."[19] Young goes on to note:

> For more than 250 years, African Americans have written and recited and published poetry about beauty and injustice, music and muses, Africa and America, freedom and foodways, Harlem and history, funk and opera, boredom and longing, jazz and joy. They wrote about what they saw around them and also what they dreamt up—even if was a dream deferred, derailed, or outright denied.[20]

In fact, the whole history of the Black freedom struggle, and popular movements to abolish slavery, has been deleted from the historical record.

For example, in the film *Lincoln* (2012), the Black activism evident in Washington, D.C., is all but erased, as is the fact that this activism was part of a massive popular movement—sponsored by the Women's National Loyal League, led by abolitionist-feminists and African American activists—for a popular constitutional amendment abolishing slavery, initiatives resulting in some 400,000 petitions to the Senate by mid-1864 that drove the process forward.[21] Of course, an assassin's bullet ended Lincoln's life before Black Reconstruction, the period as Henry Louis Gates Jr. rightly recalled, of maximum Black freedom, followed by an alt-right rollback, reminiscent of our present day.[22] Still today Black Reconstruction remains one of the least known, most misunderstood, and yet one of the most important periods of US history, as Du Bois argued.

Typically, Reconstruction is divided by historians into specific periods, the ill-fated Presidential Reconstruction of 1865–1866, soon done in by President Andrew Johnson's racism, and then Congressional or Radical Reconstruction, beginning in the Spring of 1866, where the struggle for racial progress was taken over and led by the Radical Republicans, continuing their overriding of President Johnson's recurrent vetoes of progressive legislation for progressive multiracial democracy, such as the 1866 Civil Rights Bill.[23] Brooks D. Simpson, editor of the Library of America's recent collection, *Reconstruction: Voices from America's First Great Struggle for Racial Equality* (2018), makes the important point that despite the oft-used term Radical Reconstruction during this period, its use "overlooks the extent to which several measures associated with Radical Republicans—a prolonged military occupation of the former Confederacy, the confiscation and redistribution of land to the freed people, and the continuing exclusion of former Confederates from voting and holding office—faded from the realm of the politically possible."[24] At the same time, as Simpson goes on to recognize, "guarantees of equality before the law, the enfranchisement of the black adult males in the South, and in increased federal role in the establishing new state governments with the participation of southern freedmen seemed radical enough to those seeking to maintain a white supremacist America."[25]

In this effort, the self-agency of African Americans combined with new initiatives such as the Freedmen's Bureau, to facilitate the move to labor free from the bounds of legal enslavement. Du Bois called this new agency "the most extraordinary and far-reaching institution for social uplift that America has ever attempted," albeit one that faced the "Twelve labors of Hercules."[26] And yet, the Freedmen's Bureau was vetoed by President Andrew Johnson twice, only to be revived by an override of the second veto led by the Radical Republicans. Eventually the Freedmen's Bureau became, in the words of Clyde Woods, "the first, the largest, and the most powerful federal regional planning entity ever created in the United States."[27] The road forward was clear and arguably never better expressed than by "Major Martin R. Delany, the most distinguished Northern Negro in South Carolina . . . 'What becomes necessary to secure and perpetuate the Union is simply the *enfranchisement* and recognition of *political equality* of the power that saved the nation from destruction—a recognition of the political equality of the blacks with the whites in all their relations as American citizens'" (emphasis in the original).[28]

Along with the veto of the bill that would have continued the Freedmen's Bureau and expanded its powers, Johnson also vetoed the 1866 Civil Rights Act, allying himself with the white supremacists of the South at a time when many states of the former Confederacy had already passed the Black Codes depriving African Americans yet again of their rights. The Senate over-rode Johnson's veto of the Civil Rights Act and eventually of the revised Freedmen's Bureau Bill. The 1866 Civil Rights Act and Second Freedmen's Bureau Bill was an attempt to effectuate Delaney's demands for civil equal-ity, as was the Fourteenth Amendment to the Constitution, guaranteeing equal protection and providing for birthright citizenship.[29] And yet, this move was not enough, as the Radical Republican Thaddeus Stevens argued: "The black man . . . must have the ballot or he would continue to be a slave. . . . 'I know it is easy,' he said, to protect the interests of the rich and powerful; but it is a great labor to guard the rights of the poor and downtrodden—it is the eternal labor of Sisyphus, forever to be renewed."[30]

The triumph of the election of 1866 which gave Republicans resounding majorities allowed for such a renewal, especially given the open discussion of the need for the uplift of the formerly enslaved. In 1870, the Fifteenth Amendment to the US Constitution was ratified, enfranchising African American men. These changes helped lead to the election of thousands of African Americans to local, state, and federal offices across the United States. None of this happened without a titanic struggle, however. Du Bois records the incredulity of African Americans who were called on to save American democracy, only to see others attempting to take back their victories, quoting the African American, William Murphy, who noted:

When the late war resulted in the issuing of the Emancipation Proclamation by Abraham Lincoln, four million of our enslaved brethren were called to aid in the establishment of this union of loyalty. For the colored troops have proved their loyalty; they protected the Union flag. . . . I would have never spoken, but to say this to the men that have been our masters, men who we have brought to the very condition they are now in, and have not only fed them, but have clothed them, have tied their shoes, and finally have fought until they are obliged to surrender. . . . Has not the man who has conquered upon the battlefield gained any rights? Have we gained none by the sacrifice of our brethren?[31]

And yet, despite the possibilities for making a new world on the ashes of the old, in the face of persistent violence, and the panic that set off the Great Depression of 1873–1896, the Democrats emerged victorious in the mid-term elections of 1874, thereby returning them to control of Congress in 1875. At the time, the Democratic Party was the party of white supremacy. As Eric Foner noted in *Reconstruction: America's Unfinished Revolution, 1863–1877* (2014):

> only the depression can explain the electoral tide . . . in 1874. . . . In the greatest reversal of partisan alignments in the entire nineteenth century, they erased the massive Congressional majority Republicans had enjoyed since the South's secession, transforming the party's 110-vote margin in the House into a Democratic majority of sixty seats. . . . Not until 1896 would Republicans reestablish their electoral dominance; until then, the same party would control both Houses only three times, and only twice the White House and the Congress. . . . Although the depression far outweighed Reconstruction as a cause of the Republican defeat, the implications for the party's Southern wing were indeed ominous. When Democrats assumed control of the House in 1875, the South would receive half of the committee chairmanships. Southern Republicans feared the results portended the abandonment of national efforts to bolster their party and protect their rights.[32]

And they were not proved wrong. The moment signaled the beginning of the end of Reconstruction. The victories won for African American and American freedom at Gettysburg and other battlefields were now in ignominious peril. America's unfinished revolution paused, and the counterrevolution gained speed. With the subsequent infamous bargain of 1877, the Democrats allowed the Republican Party to ascend to the White House in the contested Presidential elections of 1876 in exchange for the Republican Party's return of federal troops to their barracks. The South then destroyed most of the historic achievements of Black Reconstruction, erecting upon on its ruins the structures of Jim Crow white supremacy, with world historical implications for the US and the global system.[33] In *Black Reconstruction*, Du Bois eloquently sums up the broken promise of possibility in words as tragic as they are unforgettable:

> America thus stepped forward in the first blossoming of the modern age and added to the Art of Beauty, gift of Renaissance, and to Freedom of Belief, gift of Martin Luther and Leo X, a vision of democratic self-government. . . . What an idea and what an area for its realization—endless land of richest fertility, natural resources such as earth seldom exhibited before, a population infinite in variety. . . . It was the Supreme Adventure, in the last Great Battle of the West,

for that human freedom which would release the human spirit from lower lust for mere meat, and set it free to dream and sing.

And then some unjust God leaned, laughing, over the ramparts of heaven and dropped a black man in the midst.

It transformed the world. It turned democracy back to Roman Imperialism and Fascism; it restored caste and oligarchy; it replaced freedom with slavery and withdrew the name of humanity from the vast majority of human beings.

But not without struggle. Not without writhing and rendering of spirit and pitiable wail of lost souls. . . .

Then came this battle called Civil War, beginning in Kansas in 1854, and ending in the presidential election of 1876—twenty awful years. The slave went free, stood for a brief moment in the sun; then moved back again towards slavery. The whole weight of America was thrown to color caste. . . . A new slavery arose. The upwards moving of white labor was betrayed into wars for profit based on color caste. Democracy died save in the hearts of black folk.

Indeed, the plight of the white working class throughout the world is directly traceable to Negro slavery in America. . . . The resulting color caste founded and approved by capitalism was adopted, forwarded and approved by white labor, and resulted in subordination of colored labor to white profits the world over.[34]

In later years, most notably with the election of America's first African and European American President, Barack Obama, most of the United States, bereft of the knowledge or memory of *Black Reconstruction,* seemed unable to understand that progress towards racial and gender equality and greater respect for immigrants and others was not inexorable. In this, they succumbed to notions of progress prominent on both the left and right. Learning from Du Bois and our earlier history might have instructed us better. For in the early twenty-first century, Du Bois might have said, as in the late nineteenth, "some unjust God leaned, laughing, over the ramparts of heaven and dropped a black man in the midst." And today, once again, democracy seems in danger of dying, save in the hearts of those who have long sought an alternative vision counter to the dreams of white supremacy to which so many are still wedded. During the Civil War and Reconstruction millions of ordinary persons went to extraordinary lengths to keep the dream of freedom and justice alive. Today, millions are doing the same.[35] For James Truslow Adams, Black Reconstruction, Black people, and people of color more generally, barely register or warrant registering. Hence, the history Adams creates on which the Dream rests is without much acknowledged or visible bodies of any color or shade really, other than white. Adams could have drawn on several texts and contexts in his reading of this nation-state, and the numerous populations beyond it, that might have inspired a differently framed American Dream than that depicted in *The Epic of America.* (We admit to many more populations ourselves that we are not currently knowledgeable of, or currently capable of more fully acknowledging, which must be included. We hope by others who take up this work. Our lapse is one of limited time and limited ability. His lapse is one of studied indifference and willful blindness or ignorance.) There are many writers who published rejoinders to Adams' sense of America prior to *The Epic of America* of which Adams could have been aware, or could have shown some interest in including in his work and thought. We point particularly to the works of Paul Laurence Dunbar (1872–1906), James Weldon Johnson (1871–1938), W. E. B. Du Bois (1868–1963), Claude McKay (1889–1948), and Emma Lazarus (1849–1887), whose poem, "The New Colossus," is appended to the Statute of Liberty. Dunbar published his first book of poems *Oak and Ivy* in 1893. The work of his we cite on Black soldiers in the Civil War, is published in 1902. We also noted his presence at the 1893 World's Columbian Exhibition in Chicago, and Frederick Douglass's note of such. We did not mention that "a review of Paul's dialect poems for *Harper's Weekly* by prominent literary critic William Dean Howells in 1896 brought Dunbar national acclaim and sales, after which he began touring the United States and Great Britain to deliver public readings."[36] James Weldon Johnson wrote what is now known as the Black National Anthem, "Lift Every Voice and Sing" (1900), with his brother, J. Rosamond Johnson. James Weldon Johnson also published *The Autobiography of an Ex-Colored Man* (1912) detailing life as someone who lived on both sides of the color line. We have spoken extensively of W. E. B. Du Bois, whose book *The Souls of Black Folk* (1903) is likely the most well-known of his numerous texts. His co-founding of the National Association for the Advancement of Colored People (NAACP), and his editing of their magazine *The Crisis,* both established in 1910, should also be noted. Adams might have known about Alain Locke (1885–1954) who proposed that a new kind of Blackness had arisen out of the preceding turbulent times that came to be known as the Harlem Renaissance, although it extended much beyond Harlem, in his essay "Enter the New Negro" in *Survey Graphic: Harlem: Mecca of the New Negro* (1925). Perhaps Adams heard or at least heard of the poem "If we must Die" (1919), by Claude McKay, in response to the spate of lynching around and during what is now called the Red Summer of 1919. All these writers published prior to Adams' *Epic of America* (1939) and offered a rejoinder to his sense of America; they could have shown him a different world than he imagined, if he had opened both eyes, instead of insisting that one remain closed.

It would be a mistake not to mention texts such as Harriet Beecher Stowe's *Uncle Tom's Cabin* (1852), which, despite its significant problems, still provides a different and better sense of the world than the one Adams proposes we come from. Stowe's book, which sold exceptionally well, had some positive impact on Abolitionism, for which it can be revered, and a markedly negative impact on Black male representation, for which it can be reviled; it was adapted to film far too many times to recount. And then there is the spectacularly controversial work of Mark Twain (1835–1910) whose depictions of Huck and Jim as they traverse the Mississippi River, a site for which Adams shows some love, and texts we find it hard to believe he did not hear of, read, or see. A recent opinion piece about Mark Twain sheds some instructive light here. Laura Skandera Trombley and Ann Ryan write in "Mark Twain was American Lit's first critical race theorist" (2021):

> Mark Twain was American literature's first critical race theorist as well as America's greatest writer. His most famous work, *Adventures of Huckleberry Finn*, is a nihilistic satire about systematic racial and gender oppression, a rejection of sanctioned education and religion, and a searing metaphor for the failure of Reconstruction. But for over 130 years, no one got the joke, so to speak, or, if they did, their voices went unheard. Instead, *Adventures of Huckleberry Finn* was turned into a comic book, a Disney riverboat ride, a movie vehicle for Mickey Rooney's overacting and Ken Burns' slow pan. The joke that Twain so artfully and ironically crafted was that America was a nation of freedom and equality where everyone had "unalienable rights." And since *Adventures of Huckleberry Finn*'s publication in 1886, in addition to being one of the most frequently banned novels, it has been consistently and carefully misread by generations of scholars who, consciously or not, were collaborators in the whitewashing of American literature and history. Twain's covert and disruptive meanings were as submerged as the wrecked steamboat *Walter Scott*, and his audience both then and now was inclined not to look beneath the surface of the muddy Mississippi.[37]

These covert and disruptive meanings were also apparently submerged for Adams. One might say that if Jim and Huck were floating on the Mississippi, so too was Adams, except that he thought he was floating to a brighter future based on a glorious, mythic past, and they thought they were floating toward freedom, but were floating instead, sadly, back towards Dixie.

In the decades immediately before Adams' *Epic of America*, and in the one in which he was writing, a host of books and Hollywood films came out that further developed the fairy tale out of which the American Dream is formed. Walter Benjamin's "The Work of Art in the Age of Its Technological Reproducibility" is important here, for in it, he noted: "*Just as the entire mode of existence of human collectives changes over long historical periods, so too does their mode of perception.*"[38] Crucial here was the emergence of photography and the new visual culture of mass reproduction, and most especially the new medium of film. Henry Louis Gates Jr. had recently brought out the fundamental role of these new technologies, drawing on Walter Benjamin and others, in his *Stony the Road: Reconstruction, White Supremacy, and the*

Rise of Jim Crow (2019), emphasizing the technological reproducibility of the mass-produced racist images of Blacks.[39] Hollywood, California, would soon capitalize on the new technologies to hammer the nail into the coffin of Reconstruction and more.

The film *The Birth of a Nation* (1915), made by David Wark Griffith, based on the novel *The Clansman: A Historical Romance of the Ku Klux Klan* (1905) by Thomas Dixon Jr., and *Gone with the Wind* (1936), by Margaret Mitchell, published just a year after Du Bois's *Black Reconstruction*, deserve mention. *Birth of a Nation* and *The Clansman* were best sellers in the US, with *Birth of a Nation* being the first film to be screened at the White House on February 18, 1915, with President Wilson supposedly saying, "It is like writing history with lightning, and my only regret is that it is all so terribly true."[40] Mark E. Benbow argues that though one can't be absolutely certain, Wilson likely did tell the filmmaker that the movie could be useful in teaching, and that it could "teach history by lightning." There is less evidence for the latter remark by Wilson, regarding his only regret, and he notes that this may have been the filmmakers' own invention.[41]

The subtitle to *The Clansman* tellingly provides a clue as to concerns already raised in our examination of Adams' work and ultimately on the formative inspirations that shape his Dream. The *Epic of America* might have been fittingly subtitled, like *The Clansman*, a historical romance. Both treat history as a kind of fictionalized fact. What arises from them, wherein the interpretation of events is presented as and understood as facts, creates an edifice built not on solid ground, but rather on shifting sand. Add to the notion of the historical the concept of romance, and we get something like a love or passion for a particular historical interpretation, which is a problem when such a conceptualization is taken as an accurate rendition of history, and serves as foundational to a nation-state, and its mythology.

The Clansman was part of what was sometimes called the "Reconstruction Trilogy" written by Thomas Dixon (1864–1946). This trilogy included: *The Leopard's Spots: A Romance of the White Man's Burden 1865–1900* (1902); *The Clansman: A Historical Romance of the Ku Klux Klan* (1905); and *The Traitor: A Story of the Fall of the Invisible Empire* (1907). Both *The Leopard's Spots* and *The Clansman* were significantly popular. Andrew Leiter notes concerning Dixon and his work:

> His version of Reconstruction and "redemption" (the restoration of white supremacy) in North Carolina was overt propaganda that sought both to remind the white South of its racial duties and to justify segregation and racial violence to critics outside the South. Reaching a vast national audience, Dixon was wildly successful in this endeavor. According to Joel Williamson, Doubleday, Page & Company printed approximately one copy of *The Leopard's Spots* "for

every eight Americans," and when D. W. Griffith combined portions of *The Leopard's Spots* with Dixon's companion novel *The Clansman* to create the landmark film *The Birth of a Nation* (1915), Dixon's vitriolic racism, vaguely disguised as chivalry, reached an even broader audience through the compelling new medium of film.[42]

In *Mixed Race Hollywood* (2008), the editors, Mary Beltran and Camilla Fojas, validate a point made earlier here, when they remark: "*Birth of a Nation*, based on Thomas Dixon's novels *The Clansman* and *The Leopard's Spots*, is a historical fiction of social relations after the Civil War and, as the title suggests, a major foundational fiction of the United States"[43] Among the many other things this film depicts, at its heart it is a story of the horrors of racial integration. The story begins with white and Black people living in some sense of relative, and certainly short-lived harmony until Reconstruction. The film presents racial groups existing just beyond the bounds of legal, or chattel, slavery. This relationship, one of relative social equality, is evident at the personal or individual level, as it plays out in its interracial intimacies. As Heidi Ardizzone articulates:

> The link between marriage and racial politics had always been present in the public debate over intermarriage and segregation. Segregationists, after all, used intermarriage as the final argument against racial equality. It was perhaps the issue that encapsulated most concisely white Americans' fears about the gender and race implications of an egalitarian society: What if a black person married *your* child?
> . . . D. W. Griffith's blockbuster narrative of post-Reconstruction racial politics infamously depicted two narratives of black or mulatto men threatening white women with "forced marriage" as an extension of their newly won political rights.[44]

The gist of the story, or plot, a distinction we will approach again shortly, is quite simple, although it takes a long time to visually depict, with an original runtime of three hours and fifteen minutes.[45] To cite Ardizzone again, the story centers on the following:

> Senator Stoneham, a northern white, is in the South supporting African American politicians and voting rights for former slaves. Although the widowed Senator Stoneham is seen keeping house with a mixed-race woman, when his mixed race protégé kidnaps and tries to forcibly marry his daughter Elsie, the senator finally sees the error of racial equality.[46]

Of course, order is restored, the error of racial equality corrected, by the Ku Klux Klan. A white supremacist order is restored, and Reconstruction is rescinded. Interracial relations of any kind, and Black lives of virtually every shade, yet again, take a massive hit. What is revealed is a social and cultural reliance on racial disintegration, a way of maintaining a one-eye-shut perspective on the social order that Adams' perhaps unwittingly reveals. Maintaining this order also then includes any number of ways to not see a fuller historical picture. One such way is captured in the notion of historical romance, a notion too often skewed towards a closely related but non-synonymous other, that of historical fiction. Historical romance, admittedly a subset of historical fiction, but an important subset, nonetheless, seems often overlooked.

While the following definitions are simplistic, they are generally how people understand and experience the terms history and fiction. History points us to something factual, or actual. Fiction points us to something neither factual, nor actual. Romance, however, points us to a particular understanding, a way of reading, that may apply or be applied to both fact and fiction. As Janice A. Radway suggests in *Reading the Romance: Women, Patriarchy, and Popular Literature* (1991), romance functions as a form of escape, that is as access to a particularized fictional world, and as a form of knowledge acquisition, a window to a real world. In terms of the first notion, Radway comments that the women she studied treated escape in the context of reading romance in two ways, primarily:

> On the one hand, they used the term literally to describe the act of denying the present, which they believe they accomplish each time they begin to read a book and are drawn into its story. On the other hand, they used the word in a more figurative fashion to give substance to the somewhat vague but nonetheless intense sense of relief they experience by identifying with a heroine whose life does not resemble their own in certain crucial aspects.[47]

And in terms of the second notion, Radway asserts that for the women observed, reading romance offered some sense of historical accuracy, or factuality:

> If it seems curious that the very same readers who willingly admit that romances are fairy tales or fantasies also insist that they contain accurate information about the real world, it should be noted that the contradictory assertions seem to result from a separation of plot and setting. When the Smithton women declare that romantic fiction is escapist because it isn't like real life, they are usually referring to their belief that reality is neither as just nor as happy as the romances would have it. . . . A romance is a fantasy, they believe, because it portrays people who are happier and better than real individuals and because events occur as the women wish they would in day-to-day existence.
>
> The fact that the story is fantastic, however, *does not compromise the accuracy of the portrayal of the physical environment within which the idealized*

characters move. Even though the Smithton women know the stories are improb-
able, they also assume that the world that serves as the backdrop for those
stories is exactly congruent with their own [Italics added].[48]

Effectively, then one ends up with escapism: the first a "denial of the present," the second an identification with a simultaneously distinct but linked
heroine, and the third an access to "accurate information about the real world"
particularly concerning the "physical environment within which the idealized
characters move."[49] These contradictions are significant in understanding the
reach, range, and sweep of tales like *Birth of a Nation* and *Gone with the
Wind,* as the notion of romance functions to bridge the typical distinctions
drawn between history, historical interpretation, fact, and fiction (fairy tales,
romance). The historical romance presents, or is often perceived, as fact, in
its presumably accurate depiction of some historical setting, and fiction, in its
ode to fairy tale or romance.

While Radway is interpreting the world of women readers of this genre, the
reading she submits seems a reasonable approximation of readers of historical
romance more generally, with some readers identifying with the hero, rather
than the heroine, some with the heroine rather than the hero, and some with
both or neither. Let us look at the least commonly entertained position here,
that of the people who identify with neither. This positionality is not hard to
fathom in the two stories under examination. In *Birth of a Nation,* consider
the Black and mixed-race characters for whom this fairy tale or fantasy, this
historical romance, is a nightmare. Effectively, a set of characters central to
the historical romance must not be privy to its history or romance. Moreover,
a blind eye must be turned towards those characters of mixed-race who are as
white as they are Black, or who are involved in relationships that carry across
these racial lines.

The plot of the story is an attempt to eradicate the very human forms of
existence it denies access to the fantasy or fairy tale of history it makes. Or, as
James Baldwin so expressly states, "*The Birth of a Nation* is really an elabo-
rate justification of mass murder."[50] What else might be said to issue from
a plot wholly dependent upon the subjugation of Black and Mixed people,
where, in fact does the happily ever after exist in this subjugation? No wonder
James Baldwin says concerning *The Birth of a Nation* that:

It is impossible to do justice to the story, such story as attempts to make an
appearance being immediately submerged by the tidal wave of the plot; and, in
Griffith's handling of this fable, anyway, the key is to be found in the images.
The film cannot be called dishonest: it has the Niagara force of an obsession.
   A story is impelled by the necessity to reveal: the aim of the story is revela-
tion, which means that a story can have nothing—at least not deliberately—to

hide. This also means that a story resolves nothing. The resolution of a story must occur in us, with what we make of the questions with which the story leaves us. A plot, on the other hand, must come to a resolution, prove a point: a plot must answer all the questions which it pretends to pose.[51]

And indeed, the plot of this historical romance does "answer all the questions it pretends to pose." As Ardizzone would have it, and it bears repeating, all questions here can be subsumed into one: "that encapsulated most concisely white Americans' fears about the gender and race implications of an egalitarian society: What if a black person married *your* child?" More aptly, the question is, what if a black man married your white daughter, with marriage functioning as a euphemism for any kind of sexual mingling between these two particular social positionalities? The senator is already in some form of a relationship with his mixed-race companion, so that kind of a relationship doesn't seem to pose a problem. The problem appears to be Black people who don't know their place across as opposed to crossing the color line. They can't enter the happily ever after realm that whiteness is presumed to bring; they must therefore be happy, or more accurately, depicted as happy, where they are. Here white supremacist American Dreams rise above reality, always and forever forward and upward, with one eye closed, of course, to other racial dreams or realities; non-white American Dreams are submerged, much like non-white life, never reaching much less rising above sea-level.

Such a project or strategy is also evident in what might also be classified as a historical romance, *Gone with the Wind* by Margaret Mitchell (1936), and adapted to film in 1939. Certainly, it would seem so in aspects of Blanche H. Gelfant's "'Gone with the Wind' and the Impossibilities of Fiction."[52] Despite the essay's many charms, Gelfant sadly insists on the universality of some significantly non-universal themes:

> Secrets are *Gone With The Wind's* explicit concern—hinted at, withheld, hunted, and exposed. The story begins with the Tarleton twins telling Scarlett their secret, and ends with Rhett telling her his—that he has always loved her. Love is a mystery that Scarlett has always skirted but never solved, one of many mysteries in the novel, all of them sexual, and all hidden behind the novel's closed doors, a detail of setting which appears so recurrently that it becomes an obsessive symbol, autonomous and dreamlike rather than incidental. Reality in the novel is frequently transmuted into dream or so confused with it that finally Scarlett asks, "Was she dreaming again or was this her dream come true?" Her sleeping dream—the nightmare of a child who is lost in the fog—seems impossible to reconcile with her heroic accomplishments. But the reconciling of irreconcilable desires is, I believe, the ultimate secret of *Gone With The Wind*, a secret it shares with great fiction, which accomplishes this same end in muted and much more difficult ways. *Gone With The Wind* fulfills the reader's

irreconcilable desires openly, again and again, in a manner that makes gratification immediately accessible.[53]

The reading posed here in which secrets and mysteries suffuse the story seems a relevant and significant reading, or viewing, and intimacies in some implicit form or another can also be said to resonate. One wonders whether some of those secrets, mysteries, and intimacies, offer deeper meaning. Put another way, mysteries that recur so often reveal a problem. While Georg Lukacs sought to illuminate this with the concept of "false consciousness," Fredric Jameson has reframed these issues in *The Political Unconscious: Narrative as a Socially Symbolic Act* (1991).[54] What these narratives reveal is the ways in which they conceal in plain view, life on and of the plantation writ large, that of the house slave, and then house maid, Mammy, whose role both on and off the screen reveals so much to us about the US, and the American Dream in the interstices of the historical romance. Off the screen, Hattie McDaniel, who played Mammy, won an Academy Award for Best Supporting Actress in this role, but had to get special permission to even attend the dinner at which the award was given, because of the realities of segregation in Hollywood. It is not clear how one can fathom the resolution of irreconcilabilities within this scenario. It seems no clearer, in the following reading of the novel's closure by Gelfant:

> As Scarlett imagines Tara and its red earth, her final vision in the novel, the figure of Mammy emerges, and once again earth and mother become one: "Suddenly she wanted Mammy desperately, as she had wanted her when she was a little girl, wanted the broad bosom on which to lay her head." Return to the earth's broad bosom satisfies conflicting desires that *Gone With The Wind* evokes—a desire for renewal and continuation (promised by its *tomorrow*) and a desire for rest, for ending (promised, indeed, by narrative form).[55]

There is much here that is difficult to wrap one's head around. If Mammy is representative of earth and mother, if she is so desperately desired as a source of comfort, if she is the sight and site of return, rejuvenation, and "continuation," if then, Mammy is the past, the present, and the future, one should be deeply concerned about her! Alas, the concern expressed is self-absorbed. Rhett's line, "Frankly, my dear, I don't give a damn," would work delightfully well coming from just about anyone in the film concerning any interest in Mammy's life. No one frankly seems to give a damn about a character so apparently central to the story.

Some value can be drawn from a look at the concept of historical fiction in this context. In "History Lessons from *Gone with the Wind*," Kathryne

Bevilacqua points out the general focus on history at the expense of its twinned term, fiction, noting:

> Critics of the novel have argued that *Gone with the Wind* "propagandizes history" in order to advance a Lost Cause mythology. Others have attempted to apologize for the novel's inaccuracies by historicizing its flaws: Mildred Seydell argues that the novel provides not a "true picture of the South of those days," but "a true picture of the picture of those days." Still others attempt to absolve the novel of its historiographical offenses by universalist appeals to "truths . . . of a mythic, epic and indeed tragic nature"—in short, by de-historicizing the novel altogether. All these readings of *Gone with the Wind*, however, still emphasize the historical in historical fiction at the expense of the fictional.
>
> Distilling history from memory in *Gone with the Wind* is a fruitless pursuit, and such efforts ignore the real work that fictionalizing history—making history something that can be read and interpreted—performs within the novel.[56]

Distilling history from fantasy may be more to the point if such distillation is even possible. For the strategy such work imposes in this context, and in those other historical fictions mentioned here, is to not simply make history readable and open to interpretation, but to remake history into something palatable for a particular audience, and to do so in ways that hide from view significant aspects thereof. In short, where history presumably recounts what has happened, its fictionalization reframes it, isolating, supposedly, what matters about what has happened. Interpretation is already present in both instances of history and its fictionalization, but in the latter case it is explicitly, rather than implicitly evident. The problem is this latter reading then as history, represented under the guise of readability, as if history itself is somehow unreadable. What would make it so? Bevilacqua goes on to point out that Scarlett's position toward history is untenable:

> As the narrator of the novel presents history in a deluge of metaphorically significant material details, Scarlett refuses to "read" these details properly—or even at all. Time and again she goes against the grain of the narrator's historical hermeneutics, and the reader is caught in a crossfire of memory and forgetting, metaphor and material, nostalgia and futurity. Ultimately, as Scarlett stares stridently into tomorrow, *Gone with the Wind* shows how history need not be measured in units of accuracy or pathos; rather, history becomes a strategy not for remembering, but for forgetting.[57]

Instead of Proust's *Remembrances of Things Past*, we are back to Fredric Jameson's "political unconscious," that which is forgotten, repressed, only to return in some unknown form. So, then the history presented in this historical romance is effectively rejected by Scarlett, who "refused to 'read' these details properly—or even at all," but then the question becomes, what is histories proper reading, and what is accomplished by its rejection? An answer may well indeed be tied up in history, or more relevantly, in its use as "a strategy not for remembering, but for forgetting." Perhaps Scarlett refuses to "read" the historical romance in which she exists and from which she issues because the task of both is to re-present history, to remake it in the shape of one's fantasies, and thus to grow a future that cannot exist, cannot arise out of an unreconstructed past. So, yes, the strategy does seem to be about forgetting, and about revisiting and revising, reimagining the past so that a particular vision and version of the future may arise. There is an old saying, if you don't like the answers you are getting, change the questions; in similar fashion, one might say for Scarlett and *Gone with the Wind*, that if you don't like the answers you are getting, which is, in these cases, the future you see coming, then the task becomes to change the questions, or the past upon which that untenable future is based. This form of reading and revision is also evident in *Birth of a Nation*, and *Epic of America*. One does well to heed James Baldwin's words concerning the film version of *Gone with the Wind*, and of the image the camera produces. Baldwin asserts, "It is said that the camera cannot lie, but rarely do we allow it to do anything else, since the camera sees what you point it at: the camera sees what you want it to see. The language of the camera is the language of our dreams."[58] Here, the camera can stand in metaphorically for the lens through and by which we see, or more accurately perceive that which we see. What is seen or perceived is shaped significantly by what we focus on or, in Scarlett's case, refuse to focus on. Notice here the distinction Baldwin draws between what we say, the camera cannot lie, and what we do, use the camera to lie. The use of a truth, cameras cannot lie, hides from view the camera's user, who can. Scarlett is filmed to not see history, to reject it in favor of a fantasy, a romance, that her history, unvarnished, untouched, unedited, cannot bear.

In fact, rarely are the authors of these very disparate tales of America contrasted with each other. Yet consider this. W.E.B. Du Bois and Alain Locke are Adams' contemporaries, as is also Marcus Garvey (1887–1940). Louis Adamic (1898–1951) is publishing regularly around the time that Adams publishes *Epic of America* (1931). Langston Hughes' (1901–1967) first book of poems, *The Weary Blues*, comes out around 1926, and offers that alternative perspective that Adams hints at but does his best to reject. *Black No More* by George Schuyler (1895–1977) is published in 1931. We mention these various select writers to offer a history that superimposes texts and contexts generally constructed in separate or distinct, and sadly still unequal canonical streams, rarely contextualized in relationship with each other. Yet consider reading Margaret Mitchell's *Gone with the Wind* (1936) in relationship to authors such as Zora Neale Hurston and *Their Eyes Were Watching*

God (1937). The setting for these tales is the south, Georgia for *Gone with the Wind*, during the Civil War and Reconstruction, and Florida for *Their Eyes Were Watching God* in the days following Reconstruction. The former is set primarily on southern plantations, and the latter is set primarily in an all-Black town, one of several that settled during and following Reconstruction. Both texts are deeply embedded in southern culture, both are centered on two presumably strong female characters, and both celebrate southern cultures, albeit distinct versions of such, positing two versions of this nation-state, as Sarah Churchwell points out:

> But even as *Gone with the Wind* was in its ascendancy, another national narrative was slowly gaining traction. Black writers including W E B DuBois, Zora Neale Hurston, Langston Hughes and Richard Wright were vigorously challenging the dominant racist narrative, while white southern writers such as Ellen Glasgow and, especially, William Faulkner, also began debunking and complicating this facile tradition. Faulkner took from the Lost Cause legends that he, too, had heard as a child in Mississippi, some much darker truths about memory, history, distortion, perspective. Faulkner's *Absalom, Absalom!* is probably his greatest meditation on the processes of myth-making and how they intersect with national history, writing a Homeric epic of America. *Absalom* came out in 1936, the same year as *Gone with the Wind*, and in many ways can be read as a corrective to it, shaking off the dreams of moonlight and magnolia to show the Gothic nightmare underneath.[59]

In short, we have on the one hand "dreams of moonlight and magnolia" and a "Gothic nightmare underneath" in *Gone with the Wind* and nightmares of moonlight and magnolia in *Their Eyes Were Watching God* and a waking memory underneath evident in the closing passage of the latter text. A summary of Hurston's text is that its central character, Janie, is born out of generational trauma. Janie's grandmother is raped by her slave master during slavery, and her mother is raped by her white teacher after slavery. Janie is raised by her grandmother and married off to a man who wants a helper on his farm, not a lover, which Janie cannot abide. She leaves him and ultimately finds the love she seeks in a man named Tea Cake, also known as Vergible Woods. Ultimately, he ends up getting rabies, attacks her, and she kills him. So, no happy ending here in one sense, but in the joy, experience, and maturity life brings her, there is a level of contentment. The novel ends with Janie, having shuttered the house for the night, heading up the stairs to her room:

> She closed in and sat down. Combing road-dust out of her hair. Thinking.
>   The day of the gun, and the bloody body, and the courthouse came and commenced to sing a sobbing sigh out of every corner in the room; out of each and every chair and thing. Commenced to sing, commenced to sob and sigh, singing

and sobbing. Then Tea Cake come prancing around her where she was and the song of the sigh flew out the window and lit in the top of the pine trees. Tea Cake, with the sun for a shawl. Of course he wasn't dead. He could never be dead until she herself had finished feeling and thinking. The kiss of his memory made pictures of love and light against the wall. Here was peace. She pulled in her horizons like a great fish-net. Pulled it from around the waist of the world and draped it over her shoulder. So much of life in its meshes! She called in her soul to see.[60]

In the closing passage of *Gone with the Wind*, Scarlett shuts down the world inside her, in direct contrast to the actions of Janie. Rhett has left her, much as Tea Cake left Janie, although Rhett is still alive, and Tea Cake is dead. Scarlett refuses to accept Rhett's departure. "'I won't think of it now,' she said again, aloud, trying to push her misery to the back of her mind, trying to find some bulwark against the rising tide of pain."[61] Janie fully accepts Tea Cake's death, but not his departure. She knows what Scarlett will not acknowledge, which is that the dearly departed aren't gone, just not physically, materially present. Scarlett wants to go home, wants to return to the plantation, Tara, and more specifically, to the arms of her former slave, now servant, Mammy, and, most importantly, she wants to return to a place that no longer exists:

Suddenly she wanted Mammy desperately, as she had wanted her when she was a little girl, wanted the broad bosom on which to lay her head, the gnarled black hand on her hair. Mammy, the last link with the old days.

With the spirit of her people who would not know defeat, even when it stared them in the face, she raised her chin. She could get Rhett back. She knew she could. There had never been a man she couldn't get, once she set her mind upon him.

I'll think of it all tomorrow, at Tara. I can stand it then. Tomorrow, I'll think of some way to get him back. After all, tomorrow is another day.[62]

Scarlett, thus, rejects memory, and embraces instead mythology, a past home in the arms of Mammy and a childhood that can longer exist beyond her insistence of it mythologized presence. Janie embraces memory and rejects mythology. For Janie, history sits just outside the window in the trees, and for Scarlett, history exists in make believe. Her last link with the old days is no longer there, in large part because Scarlett is no longer a child.

Gone with the Wind advances a south and a national landscape that never was, in the vein that Adams depicts, and on which his dominant and desired version of the American Dream depends. *Their Eyes Were Watching God* advances a south and a national landscape that was, in the vein that Adams depicts and downplays by keeping one eye closed to it. *Gone with the Wind* captures and ignites public interest, to this day, whereas *Their Eyes Were*

Watching God languished in relative obscurity until wrested from the dust-bins of history largely by Alice Walker in the 1960s.[63]

And yet it is this alternative vision of the national landscape, and the American Dream that invigorates not only Hurston, but also Hughes, Du Bois, Louis Adamic, and many others we mention, and many more we don't. This alternative vision animated the literary magazine *Common Ground*, published by the *Common Council for American Unity*, and Adamic functioned as one of its editors. As Matthew M. Briones notes:

> The Carnegie Corporation eagerly funded the quarterly: the foundation hoped to unify morale on the home front and promote the relatively unsuccessful philosophy of intercultural education during the early to mid 1940s. Thus, the magazine enjoyed reasonably high circulation and subscription rates for its first six years, when the Adamic-inflected theme of immigrant diversity reigned over the majority of volumes, while attracting the finest writers and thinkers of the day: the folklorist Zora Neale Hurston, equally iconoclastic George Schuyler, the immigrant activist and author Mary Antin, University of Chicago president Robert M. Hutchins, literary giant Van Wyck Brooks, the novelist Mary Ellen Chase, the Chinese author Lin Yutang, and Hurston's erstwhile writing companion, the polymath Langston Hughes, the last four of whom were editorial board members for the magazine.[64]

This vision insisted on a multiracial and multiethnic understanding of the United States, as John P. Enyeart notes, and articulates in the following passage:

> During the Progressive Era, advocates of cultural pluralism rejected the idea that an "American race," largely defined by its Anglo-Saxon blood and culture, existed. Instead, they claimed that a nation composed of various ethnic and racial groups speaking a multitude of languages and keeping old- world traditions alive made the country stronger. To them, a commitment to the nation's founding principles—a civic nationalism—best defined the US identity. Nativists succeeded in muting the pluralist arguments in 1919 by capitalizing on the fears of "alien" radicalism caused by the Russian Revolution and gained widespread support for the quota laws of 1921 and 1924. Asian exclusion statutes and Jim Crow policies allowed the racial nationalists who equated Anglo to white and white to American to officially define the nation's identity.[65]

The list above can be extended to include what is called the red summer of 1919, which Erik Ortiz describes as follows:

> Racial strife flaring across the United States. Black Americans standing up to societal structures in unpredictable ways. People enduring months of a deadly pandemic infecting millions worldwide, shuttering businesses and heightening

fears of a lengthy economic downturn. That was 1919, during what would later be coined the "Red Summer," when communities across America were reeling from white mobs inciting brutality against Black people and cities were still wrestling with a third wave of the so-called Spanish flu pandemic that emerged the previous year.[66]

Ortiz rightly sees some likeness between this moment and our current one. Of course, the violence of the red summer of 1919 did not abate then. Our point is that one is not just seeing warring racial factions; one is also seeing opposing versions of the United States, the Americas, and the American Dream. Of these opposing versions, it seems pertinent to quote the words of Diane Roberts: "The problem was that, while the North won on the battlefield, the South won in the political and cultural sphere."[67]

As World War II approached, two versions of the American Dream, arguably diametrically opposed, and yet dialectically entwined, contended for their place locally, and globally. One version of the Dream reflected Du Bois's critique of the American Blindspot, and our critique of Adams' one-eye-closed notion, a telling admission of the limited vision of both the author and many Americans. The other version of the Dream sought to encompass a fuller vision of the U.S. and the Americas. This vision, recurrently glimpsed as a possible alternative future, has yet to come to fruition. Despite heroic efforts to find common ground and create a truly multicultural democracy, this vision did not have the powers of Hollywood harnessed to promote it and did not achieve the cultural resonance of the Southern romance. Not until 2016 would Hollywood make another film, also entitled *Birth of a Nation*, but this one devoted to the famous uprising of the enslaved in Virginia in 1831 led by Nat Turner, which had largely vanished from historical consciousness, despite it being "the deadliest slave rebellion in American history and a momentous warning shot in our march towards Civil War."[68] And so it was that sadly, these malevolent visions set to film played an integral role in solidifying the fairy tale of American racism, the benevolent genteel South of Adams' myth, desecrating the memory of those who gave their lives for an inclusive American freedom for all. It is not surprising then, that some of the most racist literary works and films made in the U.S. inspired so many across the world, including in Nazi Germany. Yes, the artists associated with the efforts to link and fight racism at home and racism and fascism abroad were not wrong in their understanding of these entwined threats. As Timothy Snyder writes: "For generations of German imperialists, and for Hitler himself, the exemplary land of empire was the United States of America."[69] Moreover, as Hitler wrote, "Europeans often without realizing it—take the circumstances of American life as the benchmark for their own lives."[70] In quoting this passage, Timothy Snyder points out that "Globalization led Hitler to the American dream."[71] As John Haag relates:

> The sensational success of Margaret Mitchell's *Gone with the Wind* was a universal phenomenon of the late 1930s, eventually resulting in the novel appearing in translation in virtually all the world's languages. . . . One of the most successful . . . books to appear in Nazi Germany before the war was . . . *Gone with the Wind* . . . it became an immediate bestseller in the Third Reich. . . . It may well have been read by as many as a million Germans by 1945."[72]

Hitler himself was saddened at the defeat of the Confederacy, lamenting that "the beginnings of a great new social order based on the principle of slavery and inequality were destroyed by that war . . . and with them the embryo of a future truly great America."[73] And so it was that among the "Lost Cause enthusiasts of these years was the Nazi leader Adolph Hitler," who saw the Confederacy as having "anticipated his goal of creating a society that rested on racial hierarchy and slave labor," and thus not surprisingly, was reportedly "fascinated" with *Gone with the Wind.*[74] After all, the South's racial laws had provided inspiration for the Nazi's own Nuremberg Laws against the Jews, though even Nazi officials thought that some of the South's laws went too far.[75] As Hitler stated, "Our Mississippi must be the Volga." In their plan for continental conquest, the Nazi's famous hunger plan envisioned killing up to thirty million Slavs to pave the way for what they imagined as a Garden of Eden, as they believed North America had been remade before through colonization, extermination, slavery, and conquest.[76] How fitting, then, that Hitler's propaganda minister, Joseph Goebbels, sleepless after the hour struck midnight on the morning of their invasion of Russia against the supposed threat of Judeo-Bolshevism, Operation Barbarossa, on June 22, 1941, spent his time watching a pre-release of *Gone with the Wind*, with invited guests.[77]

In this chapter, we have connected James Truslow Adams' *The Epic of America* to a particular vision of the US, that of the historical southern romance, and to a particular version of the American Dream, which arises from it. This version of the American Dream, a one-eye-shut version, intentionally hides from itself the historical understanding that comes from a both eyes open view of the world. This alternative view, which we attempt to expose, is itself insufficient without recognition that the body in which any two eyes are open, is just one body among many that deserves recognition in the imagined community we call a nation-state, be these bodies individual or collective, and in the vision of the American Dream they shape. In other words, this view must both historically and currently inclusive. This vision cannot be reserved for white and white-like people and associated institutions, it cannot be only for the rich or otherwise advantaged, it must also be for people of early color, race, ethnicity, and creed, and from every social and economic dimension. In what follows, we continue to place stress on this alternative vision of the US, its alternative vision of the American Dream, and the voices unheard, and the faces unseen, in the first version, the southern historical romance, or the fairy tale, which redirects us away from any collectively empowering and empowered location.

NOTES

1. LeRoi Jones (Amiri Baraka), *Blues People* (New York: Harper Perennial, 2002). Amiri Baraka, *Digging: The Afro-American Soul of Classical Music* (Berkeley: University of California Press, 2009).

2. William Jelali Cobb, *To the Break of Dawn: A Freestyle on the Hip Hop Aesthetic* (New York: New York University Press, 2008), 26.

3. Clyde Woods, *Development Arrested: The Blues and Plantation Power in the Mississippi Delta* (New York: Verso, 2017), 81. See also Bennett Parten, "'Blow Ye Trumpet, Blow': The Idea of Jubilee in Slavery and Freedom," *The Journal of the Civil War Era*, Volume 10, Number 3 (September 2020): 298–318, and David W. Blight, *Frederick Douglass's Civil War: Keeping Faith in Jubilee* (Baton Rouge: Louisiana State University Press, 1989).

4. Robert G. O'Meally, ed., *The Jazz Cadence of American Culture* (New York: Columbia University Press, 1998).

5. Clyde Woods, *Development Arrested: The Blues and Plantation Power in the Mississippi Delta* (New York: Verso, 2017), 7.

6. Clyde Woods, *Development Arrested: The Blues and Plantation Power in the Mississippi Delta* (New York: Verso, 2017), 16. On the imposition of the new slavery with the criminalization of Black life and the convict lease system, see Douglas A. Blackmon, *Slavery By Another Name: The Re-enslavement of Black Americans from the Civil War to World War II* (New York: Anchor Books, 2008). See also the PBS film *Slavery By Another Name* (2001). See also Risa Goluboff, *The Lost Promise of Civil Rights* (Cambridge, MA: Harvard University Press, 2010).

7. Howard Eiland and Kevin McLaughlin, Translators' Foreword, in Walter Benjamin, *The Arcades Project* (Cambridge, MA: The Belknap Press of Harvard University Press, 1999), x.

8. Paul Dunbar "The Colored Soldiers," originally published 1913. Reprinted in *Lyrics of Lowly Life* (Lit2Go Edition). Retrieved February 26, 2021, from https://etc.usf.edu/lit2go/187/lyrics-of-lowly-life/3691/the-colored-soldiers/. See also Paul Laurence Dunbar, *The Sport of the Gods & Other Essential Writings*, edited & introduced by Shelley Fisher Fishkin and David Bradley (New York: The Modern Library Classics, 2005), "The Colored Soldiers," 44–46.

9. Quoted in David W. Blight, *Beyond the Battlefield: Race, Memory, & the American Civil War* (University of Massachusetts Press, 2002), 153. See also Paul Laurence Dunbar, *The Sport of the Gods & Other Essential Writings*, edited and introduced by

Shelley Fisher Fishkin and David Bradley (New York: The Modern Library Classics, 2005), "To the South: On Its New Slavery," 86–88.

10. James Smethurst, "'Those Noble Sons of Ham': Poetry, Soldiers, and Citizens at the End of Reconstruction," in *Hope and Glory: Essays on the Legacy of the 54th Massachusetts Regiment*, eds. Martin H. Blatt, Thomas J. Brown, and Donald Yacovone, (Amherst and Boston: University of Massachusetts Press, in association with the Massachusetts Historical Society, 2001), 184.

11. Quoted in David W. Blight, *Beyond the Battlefield: Race, Memory, & the American Civil War* (University of Massachusetts Press, 2002), 153. See also Paul Laurence Dunbar, *The Sport of the Gods and Other Essential Writings*, edited and introduced by Shelley Fisher Fishkin & David Bradley, "To the South: On Its New Slavery," (New York: The Modern Library Classics, 2005), 86–88.

12. This section is largely drawn from Gene Andrew Jarrett, *Paul Laurence Dunbar: The Life and Times of a Caged Bird*, (New Jersey: Princeton University Press, 2022), 152–170.

13. W.E.B. Du Bois, *Black Lives 1900: W.E.B. Du Bois at the Paris Exposition* (London: Redstone Press, 2019).

14. General Colin L. Powell, "Foreword: Hope and Glory: The Monument to Colonel Robert Gould Shaw and the Fifty-fourth Massachusetts Regiment," in *Hope and Glory: Essays on the Legacy of the 54th Massachusetts Regiment*, eds., Martin H. Blatt, Thomas J. Brown, and Donald Yacovone (Amherst and Boston: University of Massachusetts Press, in Association with the Massachusetts Historical Society, 2001), xv–xx. See also Sarah Greenough, *Tell it With Pride: The 54th Massachusetts Regiment and Augustus Saint-Gaudens's Shaw Memorial* (New Haven: Yale University Press, 2013). See also David W. Blight, *Beyond the Battlefield: Race, Memory, & the American Civil War*, "The Shaw Memorial & the Landscape of Historical Memory" (Amherst: University of Massachusetts Press, 2002), 153–169. See also Douglas R. Egerton, *Thunder at the Gates: The Black Civil War Regiments that Redeemed America* (New York: Basic Books, 2016).

15. PBS Documentary, "Augustus Saint-Gaudens, Master of American Sculpture—The Shaw Memorial," 2009, https://www.youtube.com/watch?v=8t8K7Aisx8U.

16. Kirk Savage, *Standing Soldiers, Kneeling Slaves: Race, War, and Monument in Nineteenth Century America* (Princeton: Princeton University Press, 2019), 193.

17. See James W. Loewen, *Lies Across America: What Our Historic Sites Get Wrong* (New York: New Press, 2019). See also Karen L. Cox, *Dixie's Daughters: The United Daughters of the Confederacy and the Preservation of Confederate Culture* (Tallahassee, Florida: University Press of Florida, 2019). See also Thomas J. Brown, *Civil War Monuments and the Militarization of America* (Chapel Hill: University of North Carolina Press, 2019), and his earlier *The Public Art of Civil War Commemoration: A Brief History with Documents* (Boston: Bedford/St. Martin's, 2004).

18. Kevin Young, "Broken Tongue: Paul Laurence Dunbar, His Descendants, and the Dance of Dialect," *The Grey Album: On the Blackness of Blackness* (Minneapolis, Minnesota: Grey Wolf Press, 2012), 89.

19. Kevin Young, "Introduction: The Difficult Miracle," *African American Poetry: 250 Years of Struggle and Song, A Library of America* Anthology, ed., Kevin Young (New York: Library of America, 2020), xxxix. See also Paul Laurence Dunbar, *The Sport of the Gods and Other Essential Writings*, edited and introduced by Shelley Fisher Fishkin and David Bradley, (New York: Random House, Modern Library Classics, 2005), especially "Sympathy," 69. The quote from Henry Louis Gates Jr. appears on the cover of this book.

20. Kevin Young, "Introduction: The Difficult Miracle," *African American Poetry: 250 Years of Struggle and Song, A Library of America Anthology*, ed., Kevin Young (New York: Library of America, 2020), xxxix–lx.

21. See Eric Foner, *The Fiery Trial: Abraham Lincoln and American Slavery* (New York: W.W. Norton & Company, 2010), 291, though one ought to read the whole illuminating Chapter 9, "'A Fitting & Necessary Conclusion': Abolition, Reelection, & the Challenge of Reconstruction," 290–322. Such popular movements, and the central role of African American activists here, are totally missing from the Hollywood film, Lincoln, which presents an inside the beltway story of slavery's abolition, in contrast to the realities historians continue to document. See also Kate Masur, *An Example for All the Land: Emancipation and the Struggle for Equality in Washington, D.C.* (Chapel Hill: University of North Carolina Press, 2010).

22. "Henry Louis Gates Jr. Points to Reconstruction as the Genesis of White Supremacy," National Public Radio (April 3, 2019). See also Edward Steers Jr., "Why Was Lincoln Murdered?" in *1865: America Makes War and Peace in Lincoln's Final Year*, edited by Harold Holzer and Sara Vaughn Gabbard (Carbondale: Southern Illinois University Press, 2015), 81–100. See also Edward Steers Jr., *Lincoln's Assassination* (Carbondale: Southern Illinois University Press, 2014).

23. See the timeline in Brooks D. Simpson, *Reconstruction: Voices from America's First Great Struggle for Racial Equality* (New York: Library of America, 2018). See also Hans L. Trefousse, *The Radical Republicans: Lincoln's Vanguard for Racial Justice* (Baton Rouge: Louisiana State University Press, 1968). See also K. Stephen Prince, *Radical Reconstruction: A Brief History With Documents* (Boston: Bedford/ St. Martin's, 2016).

24. Brooks D. Simpson, ed., *Reconstruction: Voices from America's First Great Struggle for Racial Equality* (New York: Library of America, 2018), 225.

25. Brooks D. Simpson, ed., *Reconstruction: Voices from America's First Great Struggle for Racial Equality* (New York: Library of America, 2018), 225.

26. W.E.B. Du Bois, *Black Reconstruction* (New York: Library of America, 2021), 266, 273.

27. Clyde Woods, *Development Arrested: The Blues & Plantation Power in the Mississippi Delta* (New York: Verso, 2017), 306, footnote 25.

28. W.E.B. Du Bois, *Black Reconstruction* (New York: Library of America, 2021), 282.

29. See Laura F. Edwards, *A Legal History of the Civil War & Reconstruction: A Nation of Rights* (New York: Cambridge University Press, 2015), and Martha S. Jones, *Birthright Citizens: A History of Race & Rights in Antebellum America* (New York: Cambridge University Press, 2018). See also Eric Foner, *The Second Founding:*

How the Civil War and Reconstruction Remade the Constitution (New York: W.W. Norton & Co., 2019). See also Randy E. Barnett and Evan D. Bernick, *The Original Meaning of the 14th Amendment: Its Letter & Spirit*, with a foreword by James Oakes (Cambridge, MA: The Belknap Press of Harvard University Press, 2021).

30. W.E.B. Du Bois, *Black Reconstruction* (New York: Library of America, 2021), 379.

31. W.E.B. Du Bois, *Black Reconstruction* (New York: Library of America, 2021), 661.

32. Eric Foner, *Reconstruction: America's Unfinished Revolution, 1863–1877* (New York: Harper Perennial, 2014), 523–524.

33. Eric Foner, *Reconstruction: America's Unfinished Revolution, 1863–1877* (New York: Harper Perennial, 2014), 524–612. See also Douglas R. Egerton, *The Wars of Reconstruction: The Brief, Violent History of America's Most Progressive Era* (New York: Bloomsbury, 2014). See also Richard M. Valelly, *The Two Reconstructions: The Struggle for Black Enfranchisement* (Chicago: University of Chicago Press, 2004).

34. W.E.B. Du Bois, *Black Reconstruction* (New York: Library of America, 2021), 39–40. Du Bois ends this part by noting, "And this book seeks to tell that story."

35. On the racist backlash against President Obama and its centrality in reshaping the Democratic and Republican parties, including its crucial role in the remaking of Republican primaries, and now the party, see John Sides, Michael Tesler, and Lynn Vavreck, *Identity Crisis: The 2016 Presidential Campaign and the Battle for the Meaning of America* (2nd edition, New Jersey: Princeton University Press, 2019). For reflections from Eric Foner after Trump's attempted coup and related storming of the Capitol, see Isaac Chotiner, "Learning from the Failure of Reconstruction," *New Yorker*, January 13, 2021, https://www.newyorker.com/news/q-and-a/learning-from -the-failure-of-reconstruction. See also Sidney Blumenthal, "The Insurrection is Only the Tip of the Iceberg," *The Guardian*, January 6, 2022. On the passage of the US from being considered a democracy according to largely agreed upon international criteria, and the coming danger of a new US Civil War (albeit radically different from the late nineteenth-century US Civil War), see Barbara F. Walter, *How Civil Wars Start: And How to Stop Them* (New York: Crown Books, 2022).

36. "Paul Laurence Dunbar's Life Story," Dayton Aviation Heritage, National Park Service, updated February 5, 2018, https://www.nps.gov/daav/learn/historyculture/ paullaurencedunbarslifestory.htm.

37. Laura Skandera Trombley and Ann Ryan, "Mark Twain and Critical Race Theory," *Inside Higher Ed*, October 7, 2021, https://www.insidehighered.com/views /2021/10/07/mark-twain-was-american-lits-first-critical-race-theorist-opinion.

38. Walter Benjamin, "The Work of Art in the Age of Its Technological Repro- ducibility," in Walter Benjamin, *The Work of Art in the Age of Its Technological Reproducibility and Other Writings on Media*, edited by Michael W. Jennings, Brigid Doherty, and Thomas Y. Levin (Cambridge, MA: The Belknap Press of Harvard Uni- versity Press, 2008), 23.

39. Henry Louis Gates Jr., *Stony the Road: Reconstruction, White Supremacy, and the Rise of Jim Crow* (New York: Penguin Press, 2019), especially 129–130. See also his PBS Series, *Reconstruction: America After the Civil War* (2019). See also Romare

Bearden, "The Negro Artist's Dilemma," in Robert G. O'Meally, ed., *The Romare Bearden Reader* (Durham: Duke University Press, 2019), 91–98.

40. *Gone With the Wind* achieved the status of the number one bestseller in the United States for two years in a row, won the Pulitzer Prize in 1937, and ultimately went on to see 25 million copies in some 37 countries, and was on the bestseller list again in the late 1980s for its 50th anniversary republication. See *New York Times*, Edwin McDowell, "Gone with the Wind Best Seller Again at 50," June 24, 1986.

41. Mark E. Benbow, "Birth of a Quotation: Woodrow Wilson and 'Like Writing History with Lightning,'" *The Journal of the Gilded Age and Progressive Era*, October 2010, Vol. 9, No. 4, 528.

42. Andrew Leiter, "Thomas Dixon Jr.: Conflicts in History and Literature." *Documenting the American South.* The University of North Carolina at Chapel Hill. https://docsouth.unc.edu/southlit/dixon_intro.html#titles_by_author

43. Mary Beltran and Camilla Fojas, "Introduction," *Mixed Race Hollywood*, ed., Mary Beltrán and Camilla Fojas (New York University Press, 2008), 99.

44. Heidi Ardizzone, "Catching Up with History: Night of the Quarter Moon, the Rhinelander Case, and Interracial Marriage in 1959," in *Mixed Race Hollywood*, ed., Mary Beltrán and Camilla Fojas (New York University Press, 2008), 99.

45. https://www.imdb.com/title/tt0004972/

46. Heidi Ardizzone, "Catching Up with History: Night of the Quarter Moon, the Rhinelander Case, and Interracial Marriage in 1959," in *Mixed Race Hollywood*, ed., Mary Beltrán and Camilla Fojas (New York University Press, 2008), 99.

47. Janice A. Radway, *Reading the Romance: Women, Patriarchy, and Popular Literature*, (Chapel Hill, University of North Carolina Press, 1991), 90.

48. Janice A. Radway, *Reading the Romance: Women, Patriarchy, and Popular Literature* (Chapel Hill, University of North Carolina Press, 1991), 109.

49. Janice Radway, *Reading the Romance* (Chapel Hill: The University of North Carolina Press, 1991), 109.

50. James Baldwin, "The Devil Finds Work," *The Price of the Ticket* (New York: St. Martin's Press, 1985), 585.

51. James Baldwin, "The Devil Finds Work," *The Price of the Ticket* (New York: St. Martin's Press, 1985), 585.

52. Blanche H. Gelfort, "'Gone with the Wind' and the Impossibilities of Fiction," *The Southern Literary Journal*, Vol. 13, No. 1 (Fall, 1980): 3–31.

53. Blanche H. Gelfant, "'Gone with the Wind' and the Impossibilities of Fiction," *The Southern Literary Journal* 13, No. 1 (Fall, 1980): 3–31.

54. Georg Lukacs, *History and Class Consciousness* (Cambridge, MA: MIT, 1972). See also Fredric Jameson, *"History and Class Consciousness* as an Unfinished Project," *Valences of the Dialectic* (New York: Verso, 2010), 201–222.

55. Blanche H. Gelfant, "'Gone with the Wind' and the Impossibilities of Fiction," *The Southern Literary Journal* 13, No. 1 (Fall, 1980): 13.

56. Kathryne Bevilacqua, "History Lessons from *Gone with the Wind," The Mississippi Quarterly* 67, No. 1 (Winter 2014), 100–101. On the history of the Lost Cause ideology and myth, see especially Karen L. Cox, *Dixie's Daughters: The United Daughters of the Confederacy and the Preservation of Confederate Culture*

(Gainesville, Florida: University Press of Florida, 2019), especially the new preface, xv–xxviii.

57. Kathryne Bevilacqua, "History Lessons from *Gone with the* Wind," *The Mississippi Quarterly* 67, No. 1 (Winter 2014): 101.

58. James Baldwin, "The Devil Finds Work," *The Price of the* Ticket (New York: St. Martin's Press, 1985), 579.

59. Sarah Churchwell, "Moonlight and magnolias: The fictions that sustained the American South." *New Statesman* (August 21–27, 2015): 37.

60. Zora Neale Hurston. *Their Eyes Were Watching God* (New York: Harper Perennial, 1937), 193.

61. Margaret Mitchell, *Gone with the Wind* (New York: The Macmillan Company, Anniversary Edition, 1961), 953.

62. Margaret Mitchell, *Gone with the Wind* (New York: The Macmillan Company, Anniversary Edition 1961), 953–954.

63. Walker's article, "In search of Zora Neale Hurston" (1975), published in *Ms. Magazine* is credited with sparking renewed interest in Hurston's work.

64. Matthew M. Briones, "'A Multitude of Complexes': Finding Common Ground with Louis Adamic." *Jim and Jap Crow: A Cultural History of 1940s Interracial America* (New Jersey: Princeton University Press, 2012), 68.
Stable URL: https://www.jstor.org/stable/j.ctt7t4kq.7

65. John P. Enyeart, *Death to Fascism: Louis Adamic's Fight for Democracy* (Champaign: University of Illinois Press, 2019), 41–42.
Stable URL: https://www.jstor.org/stable/10.5406/j.ctvkjb3bg.6.

66. Erik Ortiz, "Racial violence and a pandemic: How the Red Summer of 1919 relates to 2020." June 21, 2020. https://www.nbcnews.com/news/us-news/racial-violence-pandemic-how-red-summer-1919-relates-2020-n1231499.

67. Diane Roberts, "The Great Granddaddy of White Nationalism," *Southern Cultures* 25, Number 3 (Fall, 2019): 137. See also Karen L. Cox, *Dreaming of Dixie: How the South Was Created in American Popular Culture* (Chapel Hill: University of North Carolina Press, 2011).

68. Quoting the powerful National Geographic film "Rise Up: The Legacy of Nat Turner," 2016, where at the end it is said: "America's future depends on how we remember our past." For a discussion, including of the original 1916 version of *Birth of a Nation*, see "*The Birth of a Nation*: A Roundtable," with Vernon Burton, Kenneth S. Greenberg, John Craig Hammond, Catherine Stewart, and Ryan Keating, in *Civil War History*, Volume 64, Number 1 (March 2018): 56–91. See also Stephen B. Oakes, *The Fires of Jubilee: Nat Turner's Fierce Rebellion* (New York: Harper Perennial, 2016). See also Vanessa M. Holden, *Surviving Southampton: African American Women and Resistance in Nat Turner's Community* (Champaign, Illinois: University of Illinois Press), 2021. See also Christopher Tomlins, *In the Matter of Nat Turner: A Speculative History* (Princeton, New Jersey: Princeton University Press, 2022).

69. Timothy Snyder, *Black Earth: The Holocaust as History and Warning* (New York: Tim Duggan Books, 2015), 12.

70. Hitler, quoted in Timothy Snyder, *Black Earth: The Holocaust as History and Warning* (New York: Tim Duggan Books, 2015), 13.

71. Timothy Snyder, *Black Earth: The Holocaust as History and Warning* (New York: Tim Duggan Books, 2015), 13.

72. John Haag, "Gone with the Wind in Nazi Germany," *The Georgia Historical Quarterly*, Volume 73, Number 2, (Summer 1989): 278–279.

73. Quoted in Robert E. Bonner, "Confederate Racialism and the Anticipation of Nazi Evil," in *The Problem of Evil: Slavery, Freedom, and the Ambiguities of American Reform*, edited by Steven Mintz & John Stauffer (Amherst: University of Massachusetts Press, 2007), 115.

74. Robert E. Bonner, "Confederate Racialism and the Anticipation of Nazi Evil," in *The Problem of Evil: Slavery, Freedom, and the Ambiguities of American Reform*, edited by Steven Mintz and John Stauffer (Amherst: University of Massachusetts Press, 2007), 115. See also Susan Neiman, *Learning from the Germans: Race and the Memory of Evil* (New York: Picador, 2020, with a new afterword).

75. See James Q. Whitman, *Hitler's American Model: The United States and the Making of Nazi Race Law* (Princeton, New Jersey: Princeton University Press, 2018).

76. Timothy Snyder, *Black Earth: The Holocaust as History and Warning* (New York: Tim Duggan, 2015), 20–21. See also Alex J. Kay, "'The Purpose of the Russian Campaign Is the Decimation of the Slavic Population by Thirty Million': The Radicalization of German Food Policy in Early 1941," in *Nazi Policy on the Eastern Front, 1941: Total War, Genocide, and Radicalization* (Rochester, New York: University of Rochester Press, 2012), 101–129. See also Alex J. Kay, *Empire of Destruction: A History of Nazi Mass Killing* (New Haven: Yale University Press, 2021).

77. Ira Katznelson, *Fear Itself* (New York: Liveright, 2013), 283, 587. See also Christopher R. Browning, *The Origins of the Final Solution* (Lincoln and Jerusalem: University of Nebraska Press and Yad Vashem, 2004). See also Paul Hanebrink, *A Specter Haunting Europe: The Myth of Judeo-Bolshevism* (Cambridge, MA: The Belknap Press of Harvard University Press, 2018).

Chapter 3

What Happens to a Dream Deferred?

We begin within a frame that invites the proverbial refuse, the detritus of American life, the outliers of the United States, and their American Dream into conversation. We refer to the African American, and those similarly situated, no matter for how brief or long a period, which James Truslow Adams depicted as a problematic people for two specific, interconnected reasons, although we suspect more reasons may come, vividly evident in Adams' assessment of the costs he associates with the development of America's capitalist-driven labor system. To wit, Adams notes concerning such that: "The earlier demand for slave labor had left us with the free-negro problem. This later demand for cheap white labor left us with another racial problem, although one somewhat less serious, since, after a generation or two, these people can be absorbed, whereas the negro cannot."[1]

Assuredly, the question W.E.B. DuBois posited in his book *The Souls of Black Folk* (1903), "How Does it Feel to be a Problem?" resonates in multivalent ways here. If indeed we now inhabit or have been inhabiting a cultural space in which the Negro sees him or herself as a problem (and thus in need of a solution), we are, and the American Dream is, always already in serious trouble. The free-Negro problem—which can and should be read as a problem, not only because they are Negro, but also because they are free—is a serious problem for capitalism. As Adams notes, demand for slave labor left a problem in the political and economic system; left, ironically, the "refuse" of its own teeming shores, on its shores, with no knowledge or sense of what to do with them. So much for the "Give me your tired, your poor, your huddled masses yearning to be free." At least Adams suggests an origin and impetus for the Negro problem in his comments concerning the "demand for slave labor," which, then, shifts to a demand for "cheap white labor," the latter of which is less of a problem than the formerly enslaved labor, for white labor was absorbable in a generation or two, while the free Negro was not.[2]

Adams never raises the possibility that our brethren are brothers and sisters to be loved, rather than problems to be solved.[3] The problem might be understood then, as the incapacity of the America Adams imagined, and its dreams, to absorb the free Negro: "Again, although various factors combined in Europe to foster the emigration thence, perhaps the chief one in starting this different migration to the New World was the demand by the new great industrial corporations here for cheap and ignorant labor which might prove more docile than the restive American laboring man, and more helpless."[4] The notion that cuts across both quotes from James Truslow Adams is the continuing demand for labor.[5] This notion must be set in its dialectical relationship to the story often told about migrants and migration, and immigrants and immigration, also evident in Adams' work, which is the demand for better opportunities, if not better lives.[6] Adams also speaks to this part of the dialectic when he asserts much earlier in his book, "It must be noted, for one thing, that however badly off a large multitude of the new immigrants might be at the lowest rung of the American economic ladder, they were used to a low standard of living, and in almost every respect, not least in the independent political atmosphere, they found themselves far better off than they had been in the countries from which they came."[7] The forgotten or ignored "Constitutional questions which had perforce been the chief study of the earlier generations for so many decades were considered settled, except perhaps slavery, which everyone thought of as little as possible when allowed to forget it."[8] The constitutional questions Adams seems to reference concern "self-governance and manhood suffrage . . . the quality of the electorate . . . [and] statesmanship and the future."[9] Critical to his thoughts on the United States and its American Dream then is that the formerly enslaved pose a nagging and perhaps insurmountable problem, one from which dreamers would rather run than confront. In fact, elsewhere Adams suggests that American dreamers tend to avoid troublesome considerations; we speculate that this might have to do with not wanting to wake up.

Yet as many have argued, the American Dream is not a static concept, but one that has evolved over time. And in the late nineteenth and first half or more of the twentieth centuries, the American Dream was reimagined. Arguably, no three states and cities were more central in this reimagining than New York, with its teeming immigrant masses, Ellis Island, and the Statue of Liberty; California, with its Angel Island, the so-called Ellis Island of the West; and Chicago, Illinois, to which we turn in the next chapter. And in the state of California, no city was more important in this than the City of Angels (the fallen angels in Joni Mitchell's nomenclature), Los Angeles, and the city within the city, Hollywood, manufacturer of dreams, though perhaps we might emphasize, the manufacturer of Confederate dreams. For not only did the filmmaker D.W. Griffith, the son of an officer in the Confederate Army, move to California to work in the film industry, he did so with a purpose, "to tell American what he regarded as the true story of the Civil War and Reconstruction. Convinced that Americans in the new age of mass culture would learn about the past through visual media rather than reading history books, he set about creating a convincing narrative that would educate as well as thrill audiences."[10] Not only was the film a spectacular hit, bringing about "a revolution in American moviegoing," in addition to being the first film shown at the White House, it was also "the first to be projected for the judges of the Supreme Court and members of Congress" and "the first to be viewed by countless millions of ordinary Americans," and perhaps some 200 million globally, the most profitable film, perhaps of all time, and this despite protests by Black Americans of the film across the country.[11] Tellingly, the film was shot in California, including Los Angeles, and Orange County, the latter long the promised land of the New Right.

Thus, if the rise of California, Los Angeles, and Hollywood signaled the growing centrality of the visual medium of film and television, chronicled by Benjamin and his friends and colleagues in the Frankfurt School and the larger European diaspora, fleeing European fascism, including Theodor Adorno, Max Horkheimer, and Bertolt Brecht, Hollywood filmmakers and related publishers were in important senses, as Mike Davis argues, "our own cultural I.G., Farbens." Only in 1989, "three-quarters of a century after Griffith's celebration of the Ku Klux Klan, and after an estimated 800 previous Civil War-based films, TriStar released *Glory*—Hollywood's first's honorable and unequivocally pro-Union film. There has been no sequel."[12] Here, during the ravages of World War II and accompanying destruction of European Jewry, and countless others, from the Roma to the Russians during the Nazi's aggressive war, the high priests of European critical theory reimagined the making of US, European, and world capitalism, and the triumph not of the will, to allude to the famous Nazi film which signaled the triumph of fascist aesthetics and politics in the 1930s, but of the image, of which the American Dream was and is arguably the penultimate expression.[13] Yet critically, the American Dream reflected and encapsulated not only its historical contradictions, but those of what became for a time two nations, one of these the Confederacy, defeated on the battlefield, but victorious culturally in the public sphere, and the other an American Dream upholding ideals of equality and opportunity, with its own internal contradictions in turn. Upon these contradictions, antinomies and aporia, really, the American Century was to unfold.

For Benjamin, Paris was the Capital of the Nineteenth Century. For many others, New York was the Capital of the Twentieth. And within New York of course, there was Harlem, which spawned the Harlem Renaissance and became known throughout Africa, the diaspora, and beyond. And along this itinerary of cities, Chicago and Los Angeles also emerged as particularly important sites historically and in the imagination of the American Dream and related tales of dreams deferred. Developments in these cities and beyond, including in the South and Midwest, were part and parcel of the making of what Michael Denning calls the Cultural Front, "a radical social-democratic movement forged around anti-fascism, anti-lynching and the industrial unionism of the CIO." Here, the fusion of race, ethnic and class struggles at home, and campaigns of international solidarity against imperialism and fascism abroad were central. This was in the 1930s and 1940s, when a substantial number of Americans, as today, were supportive of or open to socialist ideas more broadly, though the internationalist emphasis seemed much greater in the past than in the present.[14] Here was a dialectical counterpart to Confederate versions of the American Dream, one animated by visions of global human solidarity, equality, and equity.

These contradictions can be seen in Adams' own visions of the American Dream, one in which each is afforded equal opportunity, unhindered by social, cultural, and economic conditions that impinged on the full development of their abilities, and their humanity, yet which simultaneously could not imagine African Americans as part of the American people. For Adams, and many others then and now who struggled with the question of who should be considered people; we assert that such a question has a ready answer, but not, for some, a desirable one. In our paraphrase of the Declaration of Independence, Lincoln's touchstone, we assert that all people are created equal, and that as such those in the United States, and the American Dream, ought to be available to everyone here, and moreover, that human flourishing ought to be possible for all more generally.[15] Yet the regional dreams of the South's Confederate nationalism, based on the principle that all are not created equal—and hence some are entitled not even to dream of a better life—achieved just at this moment, arguably unparalleled influence on national and global dreams, through novels and films. So once again, here, we have two dialectically entwined dreams, the latter racist dream revealed in the aporia of American ideals, blinded to the reality of racism, and of Adams' American Dream, unable to open both eyes to confront the contradictions in his own quest for that to be achieved over the rainbow.

Another critical site registering these disparate visions was New York City, sometimes called the Capital of the Twentieth or American Century, or perhaps the dialectical fairyland of the American Dream, to paraphrase Benjamin. New York, or the Big Apple, is often thought of as the main portal of immigration into the US. Yet, of course, New York's Black population, and that of Colonial North America as well, has a history and legacy going back over 400 years or more.[16] Here, at just about the same time that Adams was writing his *Epic of America* and laying out his vision of the American

Dream, African Americans were laying claim to their own cultural heritage and promissory note embodied in the Declaration of Independence, to which they ostensibly fell heir, as Martin Luther King Jr. was to later argue in his famous speech, yet which was simultaneously denied to them at every level.

Though enslaved African Americans had helped to build Harlem and New York going back to the seventeenth century and beyond, by the late nineteenth and early twentieth centuries, African Americans drawn to New York, along with a significant migration from the Caribbean, had already made that city "A Black Metropolis," as James Weldon Johnson chronicled in *Black Manhattan* (1930). Prominent figures here included: W.E.B. Du Bois; the legendary A. Philip Randolph, head of the Brotherhood of Sleeping Car Porters and Maids; the equally legendary Madam C.J. Walker, a close friend of Randolph's wife, the socialist Lucille Campbell, and also an owner of a beauty shop; the Caribbean-born Hubert Harrison, the so-called "Father of Harlem Radicalism," who later became known as the "Black Socrates."[17] Also notable were the now famous novelist Zora Neale Hurston, whose work would inspire the likes of Alice Walker and who first published her now famous *Their Eyes Were Watching God* (1937); the Bard of the legendary Harlem Hellfighters of World War I, who brought ragtime and jazz to Europe, James Reese Europe; the incomparable visual artist Aaron Douglas; Claude McKay and Marcus Garvey, the latter head of the Universal Negro Improvement Association (UNIA), both of whom were from Jamaica); and Arturo Alfonso Schomburg, the Afro–Puerto Rican, whose essential contributions to the works of this period, and creation of what is today the Schomburg Center for Research in Black Culture, with some 11 million items, are only now becoming more adequately recognized. Rounding out this list are of course Paul Robeson, Langston Hughes, and many others, making Harlem the place to be.[18] And as the largest center of urban Blacks at the time in the United States, "Harlem would be at the forefront of black America's resistance to white America's racism."[19]

This renaissance and resistance were, in fact, international. The Caribbean surrealist poets from Martinique, including Suzanne Césaire and Aimé Césaire, were of decisive importance here, as was their larger milieu. The concept of Negritude was developed and promoted by Léopold Sédar Senghor, poet and politician, one-time French government minister who became the first President of Senegal, general secretary of the Society of African Culture, a member of the *Académie Française*. Senghor, who helped found the famous journal *Présence Africaine*, gave pride of place in the development of this concept to leading poet, novelist, and scholar-activist of the Harlem Renaissance, Claude McKay, who was bisexual, as "the true inventor of [the values] of Negritude. . . . Far from seeing in one's blackness an inferiority, one accepts it, one lays claim to it with pride one cultivates it lovingly."[20] Such developments of course were seen around the world: from Black Pride in the United States to the Black Consciousness Movement led by Stephen Biko in South Africa. And of course, this was a time when blues and jazz travelled to New York City, with such maestros as Duke Ellington, Louis Armstrong, and virtuoso pianists Fats Waller, Willie "The Lion" Smith, and Art Tatum.

An indispensable, highly original voice inspiring the Harlem Renaissance was Alain Locke, who was gay, and while though he himself never lived in Harlem, promoted the likes of Langston Hughes, Claude McKay, and others. Locke's 1925 collection, *The New Negro*, originally published as part of the magazine *Survey Graphic*, was illustrated by visual artist Aaron Douglas, who also provided illustrations for James Weldon Johnson's *God's Trombones: Seven Negro Sermons in Verse* (1927), and the National Association for the Advancement of Colored Peoples (NAACP) magazine founded and edited by Du Bois, *The Crisis*, as well as famous murals such as his 1934 *Aspects of Negro Life* for the New York Public Library (what is today the Countee Cullen Branch).[21] Locke believed in the simultaneous pursuit of the good, the true, and the beautiful, as they were all entwined. In the words of Jeffrey C. Stewart, this visionary sought to "re-create politics by teaching a new genera-tion of Black artists that they had a lofty mission—to march the Negro race out of the Plato's cave of American racism and allow them to see themselves through art as a great people."[22]

Though the Harlem Renaissance is the most well-known site of the flow-ering of a self-conscious African American cultural reawakening, there are lesser-known, interconnected, and important sites, such as New Orleans, Louisiana, but here we provide a very brief and incomplete glimpse into what historians today refer to as the Chicago Renaissance or Black Chicago Renaissance.[23] Like New York, Chicago was a critical portal for immigration into the US. Chicago was a magnet for Black migrants from the United States South. As Davarian L. Baldwin notes in *Chicago's New Negroes: Modernity, the Great Migration and Black Urban Life* (2007), "While Harlem has been heralded as the center of early-twentieth-century black culture, when most migrants connected freedom with the urban North, 'the mecca was Chicago.'"[24] As Baldwin shows too, many Southern migrants had first had their experiences of the city not in the North but in the rapidly industrializing South, noting that Chicago's Stroll, its African American commercial district, "was not a unique phenomenon but part of a larger circuit of city strips, strolls, and jukes."[25]

The new world of commodity-centered capitalism in America's urban-industrial cities represented contradictory spaces for articulations of the self. In advertising, consumption, and commodified leisure, subjects could seek to fulfill desires individually, and sometimes even register their dissent collectively, at the structures of white supremacy and "dreams deferred in urban industrial life."[26] Lacking autonomy and fulfillment, they could seek out through conspicuous consumption the fulfillment denied to them in their lives. As opposed to Max Weber's notion of the disenchantment of the world, Benjamin realized that the new world of consumer capitalism provided for a re-enchantment of the world, simulating the idea of a new world of commodities and abundance. Expressions of an alternate world, however, could only be realized by going beyond actually existing capitalism and the dreams it manufactured. As Marx and Benjamin pointed out earlier in different albeit complementary ways, the new consumer capitalism often went hand in hand with the increasing mystification of the natural and social world.[27]

Once again, here, the great city of Chicago has exceptional importance. The famous novelist Richard Wright, in his little-known and seldom remembered introduction to the Black Chicago School's famous *Black Metropolis* (1945), writes:

> Chicago is the city from which the most incisive and radical Negro thought has come. . . . Chicago is the *known* city; perhaps more is known about it, how it is run, how it kills, how it loves, steals, helps, gives, cheats, and crushes than any other city in the world. Chicago is a new city; it grew to be bigger in one hundred years than did Paris in two thousand. . . . Because Chicago is so young, it is possible to know it in a way that many other cities cannot be known. The stages of its complex growth are living memories.[28]

Sadly, some of the most important literary expressions of urban industrial life, including new forms of commercialized information with the rise of newspapers, took decades to come to the public eye. So, for example, among the first and finest of Black novelists to reach a broad audience, Richard Wright, who along with Langston Hughes and others nurtured such talent as Ralph Ellison, Margaret Walker, and so many others, composed his first novel *Lawd Today!* (1935) set in Chicago's famous South Side. Originally titled *Cesspool*, the book "levelled a trenchant critique of the American Dream."[29] Yet because of its successive rejection by publishers, the book was not actually published until 1963, three years after Wright's death, long after Wright's novel *Native Son* and autobiographical novel, *Black Boy*.[30] *Black Boy*, set in Chicago, featured Bigger Thomas, born in Mississippi, like Wright himself, and captured important elements of the tragicomic existential situations confronting African Americans in America, a theme emphasized to varying degrees by writers and scholars from Ralph Ellison to Cornel West.[31]

Du Bois was critical of Wright's *Black Boy*, and his critique inspired Ralph Ellison's defense of Wright's literary autobiography in a famous 1945 essay in the *Antioch Review*, entitled "Richard Wright's Blues." Here, arguably,

the background of Wright and Ellison came into play, contrasting as it did
with Du Bois's more affluent background. Most especially, Ellison argues
that Wright's autobiography was that of the Negro blues, which, he continued, requires

> a word of explanation. The blues is an impulse to keep the painful details and
> episodes of a brutal experience alive in one's aching consciousness, to finger its
> jagged grain, and to transcend it, not by the consolation of philosophy but by
> squeezing from it a near-tragic, near-comic lyricism. As a form, the blues is an
> autobiographical chronicle of personal catastrophe expressed lyrically.[32]

These themes are present from Wright's first novel, chronicling the day in
the life of a Black postal worker (as Wright himself had been), and not a very
sympathetic character at that. In *Lawd Today!* Wright provides a scene in
which the character, Jake, regales his wife, Lil, about a headline in the paper,
which proclaims, "Hitler Calls on the World to Smash Jews." Jake exclaims:

> Now, that's something for everybody to think about. It shows that people's wak-
> ing up. That's what's wrong with this country, too many Jews, Dagos, Hunkies,
> and Mexicans. We colored people would be much better off if they had kept
> them rascals out. Naw, the American white man went to sleep; he didn't have
> enough sense to let us black people have a break. He had to let them Jews and all
> in. Now they got the country sewed up; every story you see is run by a Jew, and
> the foreigners. And they don't think about nobody but themselves. They ought
> to send 'em all back where they came from. That's what I say.

Jake then turns to other stories in the newspaper, including one on Einstein,
who he claims is just fooling everyone with his theories, and another on
Communists rioting in New York, where Jake asserts that such people should
have stayed in Russia, where they are in power, and where their people are
"starving to death." To this comment, Lil counters:

> "But, Jake!"
>
> "Hunh?"
>
> "Folks is starving over here, too."
>
> "Aw, you talk like a fool!"
>
> "The papers said so."
>
> "Nobody but lazy folks can starve in this country!"
>
> "But they can't get no work."
>
> "They don't want no work!"

"And they burned a colored man alive the other day."

"Who?"

"The white people in this country."

"Shut up! You don't know what you talking about!"

"Well, they *did*!"

"How you know?"

"It was in the papers."

"Aw, that was down South, anyhow."

"But the South's a part of this country."

Jake stopped chewing and stared at her.

"Woman, is you a *red*?"[33]

In his introductory essay to *Black Metropolis*, Wright expanded on his critique, first begun in *Cesspool/Lawd Today!*

> Capitalists today hate Hitler for his wholesale, gratuitous murders; but they hate him for another and subtler reason. They hate him for revealing the shaky, class foundations of their society; for reminding them of their sundered consciousness, for flaunting their hypocrisy, for sneering at their hesitations, for manipulating their racial hatreds to a degree that they had never dared. . . .
>
> In *Black Metropolis*, the authors . . . have shown how *any* human beings can become mangled, how *any* personalities can become distorted when men are caught in the psychological trap of being emotionally committed to the living of a life of freedom . . . denied him. . . .
>
> It is distinctly possible to know, *before it happens*, that certain forms of violence will occur. It can be known that a native-born white man, the end-product of all our strivings, educated, healthy, apparently mentally normal, having the stability of a wife and family, possessing the security of a good job with high wages, enjoying more freedom than any other country on earth accords its citizens, *but devoid of the most elementary satisfactions*, will seize upon an adolescent, zoot-suited Mexican and derive deep feelings of pleasure from stomping his hopeless guts out upon the pavements of Los Angeles.[34]

Given recent political, social, and economic developments in today's world, Wright's work is surprisingly contemporary. For despite rampant racism and sexism, as depicted above, some clear evidence of interracial solidarity among the working class at least, did occur. Given the trajectory of fascism in Europe during this period, and the seeming resurgence of what might be called neofascism in the US today, the achievements of the multiracial left during the New Deal, with all their limitations, stand out in sharp relief.[35] Among the most important of these accounts, in addition to those already noted earlier, are Lizabeth Cohen's *Making a New Deal* (2014), and Mike Davis's broader analysis in *Prisoners of the American Dream* (1986), as well as related works, with a different emphasis, such as David Roediger's *Working Towards Whiteness: How America's Immigrants Became White, the Strange Journey from Ellis Islands to the Suburbs* (2018).

Lizabeth Cohen stresses the importance of the new more inclusive industrial unionism of the Congress of Industrial Organizations (CIO), which sought to challenge the racist American Federation of Labor. Central in the efforts of the CIO was the building of a "culture of unity," expressing a class-based ethos against the bosses, cutting across the ethnic and racial divisions of the workforce. These could be seen in the various organizing vanguards, the Packinghouse Workers Organizing Committee (PWOC), the Steel Workers Organizing Committee (SWOC), in places like Gary, Indiana, against US Steel, America's first billion-dollar corporation. A key emphasis of the CIO was to organize Black workers as part of multiracial alliances necessary to fight the bosses. Cohen describes some of the important achievements here:

> In organizing campaigns within Chicago, organizers lost no time responding to black concerns. . . . The CIO's determined efforts to woo black workers succeeded. Blacks responded with tremendous enthusiasm to the CIO's drive. . . . Racial unity became a watchword of the CIO's campaign in the 1930s, and to an astonishing degree in the early years - given both the long history of prejudice and many of the racial conflicts that would later erupt - it became a reality in locals everywhere. . . . The CIO hardly created a racially integrated society, but it went further in promoting racial harmony than any other institution in existence at the time.[36]

CIO unions also sought to make sure that employers would never again take advantage of another potential division within the industrial workforce—nationality. So that all ethnic groups as well as natives would participate, organizers worked closely with the ethnic and religious communities feeding workers into Chicago plants. Whereas by now many younger workers did not have strong ethnic identities, other Chicago workers still spoke Croatian or Polish or Spanish as their first language. Signs and other material were prepared in all the appropriate languages and special events such as Polish dances and Mexican fiestas aimed to attract people of different ethnicities to union events.[37] The CIO's progressive achievements extended, albeit fleetingly, to the inclusion of women, with women's auxiliaries, and Mexican workers, the latter especially being a tremendous boon to its organizing drives and successes.[38]

Here, the culture of unity found solidarity in diversity, inclusion in ways that added to the complex constellation of cultures harnessed for the growth of working-class power for the common good. One steel worker recalled the class and cultural achievements here: "I, who had been confined to the four walls of a steel mill, now found out . . . about Hungarian goulash, minestrone soup, lox and blintzes of creamed cheese, corned beef on hard rolls or rye bread, gefilte fish, and other exotic dishes."[39] Stephen Schienberg, in turn, recalls: "a powerful memory of sitting on his father's shoulders in a racially mixed crowd at Packinghouse Workers' Hall in Chicago around 1943–44, listening to the great Black singer and activist Paul Robeson . . . bring his audience together with renditions of spirituals, Yiddish lullabies, and Russian songs."[40] Chicago, along with other urban-industrial areas, in the context of industrialization and proletarianization, created the basis for the rise of the second-generation immigrants who came to be considered on the white side of the color line. Along with their parents, they were forty million strong, and in historic alliances with Blacks, Mexicans, and others, they created the industrial unionism of the CIO as shop-floor citizens and were the electoral base for Roosevelt's New Deal, electing him first in 1932, with FDR entering office in March of 1933, with the Great Depression still raging. Many of course would go on to serve as citizen-soldiers in World War II, with women entering the factories during the era of Rosie the Riveter.

Involved here was a profound attempt to remake American culture. Despite the impressive achievements, the limitations of the CIO's efforts must be emphasized here too. As David Roediger stresses, roughly two-thirds of the twelve million persons that made up the organized trade union movement were outside the CIO. Additionally, practices among CIO locals varied greatly, including in their commitment to challenging racism, and much was dependent of course, on the self-organizing capabilities of communities of color, in the face of massive repression and structural racism and discrimination.[41] Moreover, barriers to new immigrant homeownership also hampered efforts towards equity and inclusion across the color line, though originally, as David Roediger notes, drawing on Oliver Zunz: "As Zunz boldly puts it, 'Owning a home . . . was not a middle class phenomenon, nor was it a sign of any movement into the middle class.' Instead, it stood as 'more an emblem of immigrant working-class culture than of established middle-class native white American culture.' The new immigrant did not so much 'buy into' the American Dream of home ownership as help to create it."[42]

Of course, structural racism and discrimination in housing, along with post–World War II trends, would make home ownership increasingly indicative of middle-income status and "whiteness," representing the major source of wealth accumulation from which initially Jews and Asian Americans, but especially Mexican Americans and Blacks, were excluded. Passage of the Fair Housing Act after King's assassination in 1968 did nothing to reverse the massive differential opportunities for wealth accumulation, especially for Blacks, permanently pricing many out of home ownership. And then there was the great crime against the human rights of Japanese Americans, with FDR's forcible incarceration of them into concentration camps during World War II.[43] There were some notable figures who protested.

A consistent ally since the beginning of evacuation, Du Bois courageously and frequently spoke out against the internment. For example, in February 1942, he was the sole African American leader to sign Norman Thomas's open letter to FDR protesting the order, while intellectuals, editorial boards, and national organizations initially remained silent, fearful of the potential charges of un-American activity for supporting enemy aliens. Two years later, in 1944, Du Bois would remind readers in his "As the Crow Flies" column that economic competition and deeply ingrained racism colluded to scapegoat their Japanese American brethren:

> The driving out of people of Japanese descent on the West Coast was not only the attempt to confiscate their savings without return, but to foment and prolong racial antagonism. The persons back of this wanted to keep serf Japanese labor in the Hawaiian Islands and prevent the Japanese from working anywhere in the United States outside the West Coast.

The federal government hardly needed to exert itself, since nativist, militia-like citizen groups hungered for a racialized witch hunt. Du Bois continues, "Among the organizations back of this movement is the Americanism Educational League, and the Homefront Commandos, Inc., whose slogan is 'Slap the Rat Jap' and 'No Jap is Fit to Associate With Human Beings.'"[44]

Nevertheless, despite the efforts a courageous few, expressed here were some of the profound limits of the attempts to remake the United States and the global system on more egalitarian anti-racist and equitable social foundations, with hatred directed against the Japanese and in the vicious war on all sides in the Pacific theatre, as Ikira Ayiye, John Dower, and others have chronicled, not to mention the infamous hate strikes against workers of color in the burgeoning war industries.[45]

Indeed, what David Roediger calls the CIO's nonracial syndicalism failed to address larger questions of equity outside the factory floor: "Chicago labor organizer Stella Nowicki recalled her time as a packinghouse union militant in the early CIO: 'We worked in the stockyards with blacks but when we came home, we went to lily-white neighborhoods and blacks went to their ghetto. How were we going to bridge that?'"[46] Despite all its limitations, however, the tentative alliances across the color line did involve profound mutations and changes in American culture and in the meaning of the American Dream. Critical to this reimagining was not only the ferment of organizing across the United States during the high-water mark of class struggle and related strike waves during the Great Depression, but also a series of great migrations, from that of African Americans leaving the South, to Okies leaving the Dust Bowl. California was particularly crucial for this reimagining.

As Kevin Starr argues in his Americans and the California Dream series, the so-called Golden or Sunshine state became increasingly seen as on the cutting edge of the American Dream. California was imagined, for its incoming migrants, as a new land of milk and honey. This was poignantly expressed in John Steinbeck's *The Grapes of Wrath* (1939). Yet by whitening the characters, and not chronicling the struggles of those workers of color who struggled against capitalist exploitation in agriculture, the realities of America's racial capitalism gained little to no resonance in the larger popular culture. These realities were unable to break through the cultural wall of white supremacy that such depictions would have necessitated.[47] Left out here too was the massive deportation of over one million persons of Mexican descent, 60 percent or more being US citizens of Mexican descent, along with whatever dreams they might have had.[48] And so instead, it was John Steinbeck's *The Grapes of Wrath* that was of fundamental importance in remaking the American Dream and its recentering out West, in California.[49]

The *Grapes of Wrath* is structured like the biblical story of Exodus. Cast out of Eden, a new Eden, a promised land, a new land of milk and honey, beckons. Here, God's poor seek new possibilities. Yet as Denning notes, "The roots of *The Grapes of Wrath* lie in the great 1933 strikes of Mexican, Filipino, and Japanese farmworkers . . . [they] began with the spring pea harvest and continued throughout the summer, culminating in the cotton fields of the San Joaquin Valley; they were the largest strikes in the history of American agriculture and the great majority succeeded in winning wage increases."[50] Yet Denning also noted that these realities had already been displaced in earlier fictional accounts, notably in Steinbeck's earlier book, *In Dubious Battle* (1936).[51] Denning here raises the question of what was it about *The Grapes of Wrath* that gave it such cultural resonance that the imaginary became the reality through which so many narrated the Great Depression. The novel has undeniable power. Yet there were other striking works with powerful representations as well, as Denning chronicles. Denning's answer in part is the centrality of migration to the narrative:

Perhaps the central difference lay in . . . the exodus . . . the story and struggles in California's agricultural valleys was built around a mass migration. The ideological crisis of the depression was a crisis of narrative, an inability to imagine what had happened and what would happen next. . . . The way out was migration, and the representation of mass migration became one of the fundamental forms of the popular front. Many of the most powerful works of art of the cultural front are migration stories: the portrayals of the Alabama terror become the first act in the grand narratives of African American migration in Jacob Lawrence's *Migration of the Negro*, Langston Hughes's *One-Way Ticket*, Duke Ellington's *Black, Brown and Beige*, the Chicago novels of Richard Wright, the Chicago blues of Muddy Waters, and Ralph Ellison's *Invisible Man*, which begins with a sharecropping narrative and ends in Harlem. . . . However, California had long seemed a promised land to the nation, and the betrayal of that promise gave the "grapes of wrath" story much of its dramatic power; "California's a Garden of Eden," Woody Guthrie sang in the enduring "Do Re Mi," "a paradise to live in or see / But believe it or not, you won't find it so hot / if you ain't got the do re mi."[52]

These words also presciently anticipate the crisis of the California Dream today, what with astronomical housing prices, amidst a crisis of affordable housing and a burgeoning homeless population, especially among communities of color. The influence and limits of the novels of John Steinbeck are important here. For even though it was in "the fields of California," that "the multi-ethnic, poly-cultural destiny of California first asserted itself," in popular representation, in a still white supremacist nation, this reality could not be seen, anticipating a similar enough situation, albeit with an even more radical ethno-racial and religious composition in the twenty-first century.[53] Starr gives us a vivid picture of the stark contrast:

Set squarely in the center of the Great Valley, Fresno County—with its large Armenian population, its five thousand Albanian Italians from Potenza Province, its ten thousand Volga Germans from Russia, its seventy-five thousand residents of Portuguese descent, its twenty-five hundred Swedes in and around Kingsbury, together with assorted pockets of Danes, Greeks, Norwegians, and Yugoslavs—was perhaps the most multi-cultural county in the State.

As colorful as all this might be, it obscured another reality. . . . As of 1930 the state remained overwhelmingly white (88 percent), and that percentage was even higher among those who controlled the land. White people owned the land, and people of color—368,000 Mexicans most notably—did the work.[54]

And in addition to Mexican and Mexican American labor, there was also that of Native Americans, in conditions that approximated slavery. In other words, at the time, and still today, the white racism at the heart of successive iterations of the American Dream mitigated against the possibilities of imagining Asian Americans, Mexican Americans, or African Americans, not to mention multiracial coalitions of farmworkers, as lighting the way for a new rebirth of American freedom. And yet is was only the dreaming of different dreams that broke out of the prismatic experience of structural racism. Think of how many times in the last five to ten years one has heard discussion of the "white working class" versus the actual reality that most working-class people in the United States are increasingly multiracial, persons of color, and women. This has deep roots, however. Steinbeck reframed the story through the eyes of the Okies, whitening them, and thereby gaining cultural resonance. Tom Joad, his family, and company, set off from Oklahoma, in search of a better life, and the haunting and brilliant narrative has retained a resonance in American history, so much so that Bruce Springsteen, long the chronicler of the experience of America's forgotten, entitled one of his most powerful songs, and related albums, *The Ghost of Tom Joad.*[55]

The arrival of over 300,000 migrants into the state in the late 1930s, notably from the Dust Bowl, in search of work, adding to roughly that same number already there, along with Steinbeck's recasting of the struggle in the California fields as the plight of primarily white rather than multiracial migrants played a major role in catapulting the Joads into the national imaginary. And while this tale of "white" migrants and "white" farm labor allowed national sympathy for the plight of the Okies, it foreclosed the possibility of imagining the real future of California, as a state with the greatest demographic diversity of any state in the continental United States today.[56]

Steinbeck's novel begins with Tom's release from prison, where he had been sent for killing a man in a barroom brawl, and his coming home to the double catastrophe of the Great Depression and the Dust Bowl. Significantly, this image of the Dust Bowl has increasingly captured the American imagination in the twenty-first century. In the film *Interstellar* (2014), set in the future, and replete with actual scenes from the *Dust Bowl* (2012) series by documentary filmmaker Ken Burns, unacknowledged references to one of the apocalypses of the American Century, but framed as relating to some mysterious catastrophe that was then in the process of destroying much of American civilization. More ironic is this eclipse of historical memory, as the current drought in California threatens to turn much of the state into a sort of permanent dust bowl.

The imaginary tale of the Joads, and the more complex realities underlying the Okie migration, and well as that of other workers, is highlighted by looking at the complex realities of multicultural Los Angeles. For example, the powerful imagery of the African American story, with its theological and even messianic notions of exodus, provide an ongoing and compelling critique of the American Dream and its often grim and haunting lived realities. Among the most evocative takes of this journey are some of the poems in Langston Hughes' 1949 collection, *One-Way Ticket.*[57] Hughes' poem "Flight," from this collection, starts off with the imagery of the fugitive slave, and the related flight from the South's new slavery after the defeat of Black

Reconstruction, noting that one must leave no tracks, lest the hounds that are nipping at your heels, and back, catch the track, seizing one's brief moment of precious freedom. And the poem finishes with the old racist stereotypes against Black men, the dangers they supposedly pose to white women, and the resultant ever-present danger for Black men of white lynch mobs.

The book's title poem draws out the line of flight. Like so many tales of the Great Black Migration, and that of other despised humans, whose labor is sought, but whose humanity goes unrecognized, this is a tale of being constantly on the move. The destination? Anywhere other than the South, or in Hughes' words, "Dixie." Here, we see the ever-present desire to escape from the particular cruelties of Southern racism, and yet with the knowledge that the color line knows no geographic boundaries in the United States, in terms of the omnipresence of racism, and this, despite efforts for its overthrow. A repeated refrain here is that one doesn't just jump on a train or get in a car or even just walk away, unencumbered, but rather that one takes one's "life" with them, in whatever tattered state it exists in, and in this poem the protagonist takes his life on the road away from Dixie land, and ends up in, or adjacent to, Disneyland. Once again, we see the beckoning of California, the idea of coming out West, or going North, anywhere that is not South. Anywhere that is not governed by Jim Crow. Anywhere that one might find people who are not mean and spiteful, which is effectively the heart of Jim Crow statutes. Registered here are the daily cruelties, large, small, the indignities, the primacy of history as pain, hurt, suffering, lynching, and other unspeakable atrocities. The ironies abound here, of racists afraid of their projected fears and fantasies, of the Other, and in so doing, become the Other, themselves. Fear is reciprocal, it's a relationship, emanating from this structure of domination, residues of the social death of slavery, and the failure to truly do what real abolition requires, for freedom, justice, and quality, so that emancipation is a blessing and not a burden.

What the poem references repeatedly is the movement of a life, in its entirety, at least that which can be carried, away from the land of Dixie, and the journey taken, is one way, away. Once again, we see the tale of Black suffering, yet today and earlier it could also be that of the refugee, the immigrant, the deportee, in whose faces the doors are increasingly jarred shut; unless of course, they are part of lucrative pieces of geopolitical real estate and ongoing wars without end, and seen as white, and Christian. Gone. Vanished. Some never to return. Some who come back because it was too much, the promissory note unfulfilled, except with the stamp of rejection, hurt, closed hearts and closed doors. Yet this poem is immediately followed by one entitled "Restrictive Covenants," which details what happens to the life that has moved North, or West, or anywhere not Dixie. When that life the protagonist has picked up is put down, the place where it is laid to rest becomes restless, as no sooner than one moves in, those residing there fly away. Underscored here is the omnipresence of white flight, the racial sorting out process of a land not unlike apartheid South Africa, where walls are erected to segregate the Other, caging them in ghettos.

We see the recurrent question here, are we human? Then why, can our humanity not simply be recognized, even accepted? What is this difference between us? More importantly, arguably, is the question, why is this difference between us? The sun rises and sets on us equally, the moon lights our ways in nights darkness. We are under the same moon, and the same sun, and yet it seems at times we are on different planets, or perhaps in different circles of hell, in Dante's inferno. Hughes takes us from the atrocities of the South to the atrocities of the North, East, and West, from Jim Crow to restrictive covenants. We move from the dark side of the southern towns often split between white and dark by railroad tracks, to the dark side of cities, the south side of Chicago, specifically, where people of color are separated, segregated, where, in Hughes terms they are unable to breathe freely. Hughes gestures here towards the legal process of restrictive covenants, where Blacks, and oftentimes Asians and Mexican Americans and sometimes Jews, were told not to apply. So instead of the mythical belief, that the city air makes you free, for Black Americans, the struggle is to breathe, and this even before the global pandemic of recent years, and before George Floyd, and so many others, who can't breathe, what with a knee of a white police officer on their neck, while other police sit by and watch the life flow out of a fellow human being, calling out for mercy, calling out for his mother. Finally, Hughes returns to his other refrain. Nature doesn't seem to care for the differences we see between us. The sun and the moon make no such distinction. Neither it would seem does the wind, for the wind blows on everyone, everywhere. Hughes reckons that wind has to care, even if other humans, tragically divided by racial animus, do not.[58] Hughes finds beauty, even in the face of ever-present suffering, with the wind at his back, feeling the air, as its blows with the mass movement of the millions of masses, each one precious, an individual, a human being, with inherent dignity, even if not accorded such respect by others.

Among the places Hughes invokes in *One-Way Ticket* (1949) is Los Angeles, and he knew of what he wrote. Already in his autobiographical *The Big Sea* (1940), Hughes remained sanguine about the Harlem Renaissance, noting that most Blacks hadn't heard about the period of cultural efflorescence, and famously stated that if they had "it hadn't raised their wages any."[59] Hughes was to become, in his words, "a literary sharecropper," expressing feelings informed by the Black experience, noting that he "had chosen a career at writing simply because he did not know how to do anything else."[60] Hughes finally saw California for the first time in 1931, later securing a Hollywood contract as a screenwriter. This was a disillusioning experience to say the least. In a June 1939 speech, just some three months after the Nazi invasion of Czechoslovakia, Hughes noted:

All the problems known to the Jews today in Hitler's Germany, we who are Negroes know here in America—with one difference. Here, we may speak openly about our problems, write about them, protest, and seek to better our conditions. In Germany the Jews may do none of these things. Democracy permits us the freedom of a hope, and some action towards the realization of that hope. . . .

Here are our problems. . . . It is very hard for a negro to become a professional writer. Magazine offices, daily newspapers, publishers' offices are as tightly closed to us in American as if we were pure non-Aryans in Berlin. . . .

Hollywood insofar as Negroes are concerned, might just as well be controlled by Hitler.

. . . These are some of our problems. What can you . . . do to help us solve them? What can you, our public, do to help us solve them? My problem, your problem. No, I'm wrong! It is not a matter of *mine* and *yours.* It is a matter of *ours.* We are all Americans. We want to create the American dream, a finer and more democratic America. I cannot do it without you. You cannot do it omitting me. . . .

. . . Can we not put our heads together and think and plan—not merely dream—the future America? And then create it with our hands?

. . . We do not want a weak and imperfect democracy. We do not want poverty and hunger and prejudice and fear on the part of any portion of our population. We want America to really be America for everybody. Let us make it so![61]

If Langston revealed some of the underside of Hollywood and the Studio system, it was the extraordinary Black writer Chester Himes' experiences in Los Angeles that grippingly portrayed some of its realities. Himes was born in 1909 in Jefferson, Missouri, but his family moved often, to Mississippi, St. Louis, Arkansas, Georgia, eventually graduating from High School in Cleveland, Ohio, or what migrants called Alabama North. After working as a busboy, Himes accidentally fell forty feet down an elevator shaft, was badly injured, and used a disability stipend to enroll at Ohio State University. He ended up spending some time in the slums of Cleveland, got into trouble there, and was sent to the penitentiary for armed robbery in Chicago and served hard time, where he began his writing. After his parole, he worked odd jobs, including writing for the Works Progress Administration (WPA), and for the newly formed CIO, feeling validation in work with an organization taking an active anti-racist stance in the union movement. Subsequently, Himes and his wife, Jean Johnson, moved to Los Angeles, at a time in which Los Angeles was becoming increasingly home to Southern Blacks and whites. And we must remember here that those two very different great migrations brought with them radically different versions of the American Dream, one rooted in dreams of emancipation and Black Reconstruction, and efforts to build a multiracial society before the imposition of Jim Crow upon the ruins of its destruction, and the other buoyed by visions of Southern gentility and white supremacy and Black inferiority, as articulated in *Birth of a Nation*, *The Epic of America,* and *Gone with the Wind.*[62]

Himes, of course, brought with him dreams from Jefferson City, Missouri, and then Cleveland, Ohio, his place of birth and sojourn before his trip out to the new land of dreams out West. The stunning articulation of these dreams and dreams deferred that Himes arrestingly portrayed was in none other than Los Angeles. Here, dreams were in short supply, but dreams deferred were the order of the day. Thus, Himes' first two books, *If He Hollers, Let Him Go* (1945) and the subsequent *The Lonely Crusade* (1947), portray Los Angeles as a Dostoyevskian hellhole where all the psychological brutalities of American racism scrape at the consciousness of the characters akin to what it must have felt like to fall into that elevator shaft, except here it was the unrelenting racism of America, pummeling the human soul. As Himes noted in the first volume of his biography, *The Quality of Hurt,*

> Los Angeles hurt me racially as much as any city I have ever known—much more than any city I remember from the South. It was the lying hypocrisy that hurt me. Black people were treated much the same as they were in an industrial city of the South. They were Jim-Crowed in housing, in employment, in public accommodations, such as hotels and restaurants. . . . The difference was that the white people of Los Angeles seemed to be saying, "Nigger, ain't we good to you?"
>
> The only thing that surprised me about the race riots in Watts in 1965 is that they waited so long to happen. We are a very patient people . . .
>
> It was from the accumulation of my racial hurts that I wrote my bitter novel of protest, *If He Hollers, Let Him Go.* . . .
>
> Up to the age of thirty-one I had been hurt emotionally, spiritually, and physically as much as thirty-one years can bear; I had lived in the South, I had fallen down an elevator shaft, I had been kicked out of college, I had served seven and one half years in prison, I had survived the humiliating last five years of the Depression in Cleveland; and still I was entire, complete, functional; my mind was sharp, my reflexes were good, and I was not bitter. But under the mental corrosion of race prejudice in Los Angeles I had become bitter and saturated with hate. . . . I was thirty-one and whole when I went to Los Angeles and thirty-five and shattered when I left to go to New York.[63]

Just a few years later Himes followed his powerful first novel with an even more powerful one, *The Lonely Crusade*. The novel depicts the rabid racism and antisemitism and fusion of race and class of Los Angeles during the war.

Himes chronicles a scene straight from modern times but set during World War II. When the young Negro labor organizer, jaded about the realities of unionism, and his wife are invited to the millionaire boss's mansion, a discussion is related where the inner mind of important parts of European America, or the social construction of white power, is revealed:

"Were your parents in business here, Lee?" Foster asked.
"No sir, they were domestic servants." Just the recollection of his background had compelled him to give the title of respect.
"And you completed college?"
"Yes sir—U.C.L.A. My mother helped and I worked also."
"There is no place like America," Foster said, and the emotion in his voice was genuine because the opportunity for betterment afforded by America was his special love. He was convinced that any American (except women, whom he did not consider men's equal; Negroes, whom he did not consider as men; Jews, whom he did not consider as Americans; and the foreign born, whom he did not consider at all), possessed of ingenuity, aggressiveness, and blessed with good fortune, could pull himself up by his bootstraps to become one of the most wealthy and influential men in the nation—even President. The fact that neither he nor any of his associates had been faced with this necessity had no bearing on his conviction. Like other fables of the American legend, the truth made little difference—as long as he believed, just as he now believed that there was no other place on earth where a Negro son of servant parents could achieve a college education. "No place like America," he repeated.[64]

The one eye closed of which Adams spoke, and Du Bois's American Blindspot, reveals itself here, blissfully ignorant of its arrogance and ignorance. Himes' work, though neglected today, nevertheless carried its influence among the artists of the Black freedom struggle. The famous poet of the Black Arts Movement Nikki Giovanni captured the special qualities of the author's prose here by noting of her friend: "When he opened the special door . . . we all could peep inside to a special genius. . . . Chester Himes is to writing what Miles Davis is to the trumpet, what John Coltrane is to the saxophone, what lips are to love. . . . Chester deserves this sun to cast his shadow over the library that is the hope of black Americans."[65]

Making the sojourn to Los Angeles as well during this period were exiles from Nazi Europe associated with the Frankfurt School, including Theodor Adorno and Max Horkheimer, as well as poet and playwright Bertolt Brecht. As Mike Davis notes in *City of Quartz: Excavating the Future in Los Angeles* (1990), it was an important moment in the European reconceptualization of the New World, which they saw in many ways as a nightmarish inversion of the critical hopes of the Enlightenment. In LA, they saw an absence of critical intellectuals and the submersion of the hopes of the urban working class and cafe life into the monastic suburbs of Los Angeles. LA was the place that Horkheimer and Adorno composed arguably their most famous work, *Dialectic of Enlightenment* (1944). At the same time, Adorno penned his beautiful book of short entries, *Minima Moralia: Reflections from Damaged Life* (1951), the same year as Hughes' *Montage of a Dream Deferred*. Sadly, though, Horkheimer's and Adorno's antipathies at the time failed to register Chester Himes' powerful depiction of Los Angeles as a racist hell.

As for Brecht, his reactions to the climate were just as pessimistic, if not more so. As his biographer notes, "For Brecht, everything in California had been commodified, any sense of history and culture lost only in the market," apocalyptic observations that were registered for posterity in his famous poems where hell, like in the poems of Hughes cited here, takes center stage. Here Brecht notes that while his brother Shelley thought hell much like London, he thought that people who lived in Los Angeles might think it much like hell, as well.[66] Here the ironies abound. For not too long after Horkheimer and Adorno wrote their magnum opus about the transformation of the dialectic of enlightenment and its descent to cruel myth, Langston Hughes penned the work that ironically was arguably closest to that member of the Frankfurt School who stayed in Europe too long, writing that he thought there were still things there to defend, Walter Benjamin. Two books by three exiles, albeit one exiled into the land into which they were born. Hughes' work, in contrast to Benjamin, and Horkheimer and Adorno, was framed not in the context of Nazi fascism, but instead in the relentless onslaught of American racism, refracted through the myth of the American Dream, and his poetic refrain, that of the dreams deferred. And yet, today, as the demons of that Dream seem to have increasingly escaped Pandora's Box all at once, as the dream turns into cruel myth, it is perhaps the time when Hughes's *Montage of a Dream Deferred* can finally be seen in what Benjamin called "the now of a specific recognizability."

Here, in excavating the kinds of relationships to the past of which we think Benjamin and Hughes speak, it is important to remember that the past is always present, the nightmare from which we are trying to awake. Benjamin and Hughes see the past as not static but suffused with current and future dangers and possibilities. We see the work of Black feminist science fiction writer Octavia Butler, who we approach in our final chapter, as also following this line of thinking. Indeed, we see ourselves situated within these entwined ways of looking at the imbrication of past, present, and possible alternative futures.

Returning to our analysis then with these thoughts in mind, we continue to note that the new culture being born in Los Angeles was impressive. There is one additional person of importance we wish to mention, whose journey also took him to Los Angeles, and that is none other than a Slovenian peasant immigrant to America, Louis Adamic, discussed earlier. Adamic was one of Los Angeles' famous "debunkers," as Mike Davis put it, puncturing the excesses associated with the boosters that sold the Los Angeles and California Dream. From the lands of the Austro-Hungarian empire and its disintegration, from which he and many other immigrants and refugees fled, Adamic had come to America via Pennsylvania, having fought with the American Expeditionary Forces in Europe in World War I, then becoming a long-time resident of Los Angeles. His first two books, *Dynamite: The Story of Class Violence in America* (1931) and his autobiography *Laughing in the Jungle: An Immigrant Story in America* (1932), told the story of the unrelenting class warfare of Los Angeles. Socialists came close to taking over City Hall, only to be brought up on charges of blowing up the *Los Angeles Times*, as the newspaper empire was the leader of the Open Shop movement in the city. After their narrow defeat in the mayoral elections, the socialists founded a utopian colony in the desert, in Llano Del Rio, staying until their credit failed.[67]

But the real importance of Adamic to our story is his recounting of the immigrant experience. In his autobiography, Adamic relates fantastic tales of the great and endless promise of America, all of which he believed. Adamic could not understand a Slovenian who had returned home penniless. When Adamic finally met the man, Peter Molek showed him Upton Sinclair's *The Jungle* (1906), proceeding to tell him that America was one great jungle, and that America had swallowed him whole, but could not digest him and so spit him out! Peter recounts the lure of America, the land of promise, noting that many refer to the immigrants as dung, true enough he says, since they fertilize America. Yet Peter notes the hope persists that those who go will be the lucky ones, getting the better of America instead of the other way around. Ironically, Peter later decides to return to America and Louis Adamic travels with him.[68] When Adamic finally comes to Los Angeles, he describes it vividly: "Los Angeles is America. A jungle . . . From Mount Hollywood, Los Angeles looks very nice, enveloped in a haze of changing colors. . . . Actually, and in spite of all the healthful sunshine and ocean breezes, it is a *bad* place . . . full of curious wild and poisonous growths, decadent religions and cults and fake science, and wildcat business enterprises, which, with their aim for quick profits, are doomed to collapse and drag down multitudes of people."[69]

Even more important than Adamic's tales of his immigrant experience was his tireless efforts to popularize Emma Lazarus's iconic poem, "The New Colossus" (1883), placed inside the lower level of the Statue of Liberty in 1903:

> Not like the brazen giant of Greek fame,
> With conquering limbs astride from land to land;
> Here at our sea-washed, sunset gates shall stand

Here we see the image of America, for some, though today increasingly, and for many, over may years, not open, but closed, for most of those from Africa, except those brought in chains. Yet for Emma, passionate about her brethren overseas, the image was to welcome these persons.

> A mighty woman with a torch, whose flame
> Is the imprisoned lightning, and her name
> Mother of Exiles. From her beacon-hand

Instead of refusing those forced into exile, she hopes for a different and brighter future.

> Glows world-wide welcome; her mild eyes command
> The air-bridged harbor that twin cities frame.

An image, that flitters increasingly from the past, of hope for some, and thus all the more bitterly experienced when it is denied, historically, and in the light of the crisis of the present world.

> "Keep, ancient lands, your storied pomp!" cries she
> With silent lips. "Give me your tired, your poor,
> Your huddled masses yearning to breathe free,
> The wretched refuse of your teeming shore.

An image, of what Frantz Fanon would later call in a different way, harkening to the sons and daughters of colonial rule in Algeria, Africa, and the Third World, of the wretched of the earth. And the seeking of a refuge in the living hearts of men and women.

> Send these, the homeless, tempest-tost to me,
> I lift my lamp beside the golden door!"

As Lazarus' biographer Esther Schor writes: "Despite the prominent placement in her manuscript, 'The New Colossus,' was forgotten for decades. It was only rescued from oblivion by two latter-day champions of the oppressed—[including] . . . a Slovenian immigrant named Louis Adamic—who secured for the poem its enduring fame."[70]

There are many ironies to this story, for the poem only gained recognition after the passage of the nativist and xenophobic Immigration Act of 1924, directed above all at the very Jewish refugees that helped inspire Emma's poem. The plight of these refugees, with the rise of Adolph Hitler and the Nazi Party in Germany, brought the dire circumstances facing the Jews to public attention. Historian of American immigration and nativism John Higham notes:

> Their efforts to escape Nazi barbarism coincided with a growing revulsion of American opinion against racism and Germany. In contrast to the situation of the 1880s, when Americans were turning away from a cosmopolitan, humane outlook, the circumstances of the late 1930s united a particular concern for the Jews with a broader movement to strengthen ethnic democracy. Immigration policy did not change significantly. But a nation striving to overcome its own ethnic hatreds, to dignify influential minority groups, and to gird for war against Hitler needed to define itself anew as a bastion against persecution.
>
> Louis Adamic . . . launched a one-man crusade to elevate the status of the recent immigrant groups and to propagate an eclectic sense of American nationality. His immediate object was not to revise the immigration laws but to get American history rewritten along lines that would recognize the contributions of the newer ethnic groups. After 1938 he adopted the Lazarus sonnet as the keynote of practically everything he said and wrote. He quoted it endlessly in books, pamphlets and public lectures. During the 1940s the words of the poem became a familiar litany in mass circulation magazines, children's stories, and high-school history texts.[71]

Though for many the name is still unfamiliar, in more recent years, historians have increasingly recognized the centrality of the work of Louis Adamic in the making of the Cultural Front during the era of the Great Depression and the making of the New Deal, and the war against fascism, recognizing Adamic's contributions regarding race and ethnicity. Thus, it is not surprising that Adamic was deeply influenced by W.E.B. Du Bois, most especially by his essay "The Souls of White Folk," his counterpart to *The Souls of Black Folk* (1903), and part of his larger autobiographical book, *Darkwater: Voices from the Veil* (1940).

What is critical here is to understand the centrality of the anti-fascist ethos for much of the 1930s Cultural Front in general, and for Du Bois, Adamic, and others. Adamic would express the continuing importance of this after the war. For as Adamic noted, though the Allies had achieved victory against the Axis powers in World War II, the fascist threat was very much alive.[72] For Adamic, defeating fascism meant overturning ethnic chauvinism and nativism in all forms, and corporate dominance as well. Adamic was inspired instead by the hope of compassion, empathy, and solidarity with the racialized other, through the uplifting of what Randolph Bourne before him, and Martin Luther King Jr. after him, called "the beloved community." As a recent biographer of Adamic notes, Bourne had especially great influence on Adamic:

Bourne argued that when people . . . synthesized their values and beliefs, a new federation of cultures emerged that redefined national identity. . . . He emphasized that identities were always in flux and that the interactions . . . held the potential for . . . individuals and groups forging new histories. . . . Adamic helped to revive cultural pluralism during the 1930s and 1940s by contrasting it with expressions of national identity in authoritarian Europe. . . . Adamic viewed . . . Hitler and Mussolini similarly, called Hitler a gangster who terrorized his own people into accepting a version of their national identity based on an imagined history of past national greatness. In response to a supporter asking how to stop the spread of fascism, Adamic proclaimed that Hitler . . . could be defeated by exposing his mendacious rendering of the past with a call for compassion . . . he gave lectures pointing out the limits of tolerance, advocating a revolutionary version of pluralism and attacking whiteness as an impediment to democracy.[73]

In *From Many Lands* (1940), Adamic, after discussing the dominance of Anglo-Saxons in the Eastern United States, notes that: "In connection with these cultural beginnings, there appeared a system of national hopes and aspirations that came to be called the American Dream—a matter mostly of faith in the human individual and the concepts of liberty, fraternity and equality, of general welfare and democracy embodied in the Declaration of Independence and the Constitution."[74] Adamic goes on to discuss the great surge of immigration in the late nineteenth century, noting that it was as if the newcomers were responding to the lines of the 1886 poem of Emma Lazarus put on the Statue of Liberty. Adamic waxed poetic: "This is one of the greatest stories under the sun, the story of the coming and meeting of all these peoples, in so brief a period, on this vast and beautiful continent."[75] Adamic goes on to talk about the spread of prejudice, the feeling among old stock immigrants that the country is no longer theirs. Anticipating the writings of Adorno in *Minima Moralia* at roughly the same time, Adamic criticizes the emphasis on tolerance, noting its potential connotations of superiority, and argues boldly: "Let's make America safe for differences. Let us work for unity within diversity. Let us begin to accept one another as we are." Adamic seeks to enliven the dreams of old immigrants with the dreams and aspirations of the new immigrants, when they cast their eyes upon the Statue of Liberty. Also, he warned us that we should not allow prejudice to turn the American Dream into a Nightmare. In his final reflection, Adamic stated: "The American Dream is a lovely thing, but to keep it alive, to keep it from turning into a Nightmare, every once in a while we've got to wake up."[76] Here Adamic also parallels Benjamin's *Arcades Project*, Hughes' *Montage of a Dream Deferred*, and as we will see later, Octavia Butler's final novel, *Fledgling* (2005).

On the eve of World War II, as Daniel Widener discusses in his *Black Arts West: Culture and Struggle in Postwar Los Angeles*, Duke Ellington, speaking to a Black church in Los Angeles, in February 1941, asked to take as the basis of his remarks Langston Hughes's famous poem, "I Too, Sing America," registered a dissonant chord from Langston's call to honor Black Americans for their contribution to American culture and society. Ellington argues:

> This is all well and good, but I believe it to be only half the story. We play more than a minority role, in singing "America." Although numerically but ten percent of the mammoth chorus that today, with an eye overseas, sings "America" with fervor and thanksgiving, I say our ten percent is the very heart of the chorus: the sopranos, so to speak, carrying the melody, the rhythm section of the band, the violins, pointing the way. . . .
>
> We stirred in our shackles and our unrest awakened Justice in the hearts of a courageous few, and we recreated in America the desire for true democracy, freedom for all, the brotherhood of man [sic], principles on which the country had been founded. . . . We were freed and as before, we fought America's wars, provided her labor, gave her music, kept alive her flickering conscience, prodded her on toward the yet unachieved goal, democracy, until we became more than part of America![77]

Ellington went on to say, "Hear that chord! . . . That's us. Dissonance is our way of life in America. We are something apart, yet an integral part."[78] Increasingly, in the years after World War II, that dissonant chord of which Ellington so eloquently spoke would be expressed, and heard. The rise of fascism in Spain and the Axis powers, the Japanese attack on Pearl Harbor on December 7, 1941, and Hitler's declaration of war against the US immediately thereafter gave rise to the Double V campaign in the US, against racism at home and fascism abroad. The false notion of wartime unity, while paving the way for important reforms, as later during the Cold War, simultaneously concealed the stark realities of racism in the US.[79]

The moment of World War II, with the Double V campaign, and which saw the entrance of mass numbers of Blacks into the US armed forces as citizen-soldiers, and into the factories, most especially women, as shop-floor citizens, along with domestic political protests, seemed to offer up, once again, possible ways forward to make good on America's promissory note of the Declaration of Independence. Yet, as Mike Davis recounts, in contrast to the tentative class solidarity that the unprecedented economic crisis of the Great Depression and the subsequent strike wave in American industry achieved in the 1930s, the equally unprecedented transformation of the US workforce during the 1940s in World War II, resulted not in a new wave of multiracial progress, but instead a wave of hate strikes against the just demands of Black workers or working-class solidarity and racial equality. The earlier achievements of the CIO against racism, including the effort to break the back of racist power in the South through Operation Dixie, fell prey to renewed racism and sexism against Blacks and women in the workplace, and Cold War anti-communism, posing an immense challenge to forward movement on civil, labor, and women's rights in the 1950s and beyond.[80]

Critical here was Du Bois's warning from *Black Reconstruction* about the centrality of racism, and Southern racism, particularly, in the United States:

> The South . . . is for the most part against unions and the labor movement. . . . The whole phantasmagoria has been built on the most miserable of human fictions: that in addition to the manifest differences between men there is a deep, awful and ineradicable cleft which condemns most men to eternal degradation. . . . My rise does not involve your fall. Humanity is one and its vast variety is its glory. . . . If all men make the best of themselves, if all men have the chance to meet and know each other, the result is the love born of knowledge and not the hate based on ignorance. . . . The chief obstacle in this rich realm of the United States . . . to the coming of that kingdom of economic equality which is the only logical end of work is the determination of the white world to keep the black world poor and themselves rich. A clear vision of a world without inordinate individual wealth, of capital without profit and if income based on work alone, is the path out, not only for America and for all men. Across this path stands the South with flaming sword.[81]

Here, Du Bois puts his finger on a central aspect of America's political and social evolution, namely the exclusion of Blacks in the South, though we must add too, the exclusion of Latinos in the Southwest as well, from the New Deal coalition, and the related cleavages of race, class, gender, and nation that became part of its unequal fabric.[82] The betrayal of the Black freedom struggle in the late nineteenth century and beyond had as its critical counterpart, the power of the Southern Democrats in Congress, their control over the Congressional committees, based as they were on seniority.[83] As Dr. Martin Luther King Jr. argued: "Since before the Civil War, the alliance of Southern racism and Northern reaction has been the major obstacle to social advancement. The cohesive political structure of the South working through this alliance enabled a minority of the population to imprint its ideology on the nation's laws. This explains why the United States is still far behind European nations in all forms of social legislation."[84] Such realities, too, were at the heart of the defeat of the ambitious programs of the post–World War II labor movement, to organize the South, in Operation Dixie, moves that faltered in the context of the Red Scare and purges of the 1940s and 1950s.[85] Tragically, as Mike Davis notes, the heart of the industrial trade union movement, the CIO,

> failed to make a sustained attack on the citadel of right-wing political power: the Rotton-borough system of the South. The entire edifice of Democratic conservatism, as well as the interlinked corporate and Cold War political alliances

which it sustained, ultimately rested on linchpins of Black disenfranchisement and the poll tax. At the same time, however, the influx of African Americans into the Democratic Party outside the South made them critical for Truman's Democratic victory in 1948.[86]

Truman's embrace of a Civil Rights program was combined with powerful articulations among Black artists and intellectuals, about the possibilities and need to overcome America's Blindspot, most notably Langston Hughes' *Montage of a Dream Deferred* (1951), dedicated to Ralph and Fanny Ellison, and Ralph Ellison's landmark *Invisible Man* (1952), the first novel by a Black author to win America's National Book Award in 1953.

At this exact time of crisis, however, both opportunity and danger, there appeared a powerful articulation of the present moment by Ward Moore, whose novel, *Bring the Jubilee* (1953), really began the whole genre of alternative history novels, exploring the contingencies of history, and promises, possibilities, and dangers. The book imagined a United States in which the South won the Civil War. In this novel, the North is a union of twenty-six backward and defeated states.[87] Here there was unfree labor, mass xenophobia, scapegoating, expulsion, and deportation (evocative of the period after the defeat of Reconstruction and eerily reminiscent of the Trump era), while aspirants for a better life hoped to make it into the elite Confederate universities. All of this emanates from an imaginary Confederate victory at Gettysburg. Moore invents an anti-hero protagonist, Hodgins Backmaker, whose grandfather was a veteran of the struggle for racial equality. Backmaker, born in 1921, in a backwater town in New York, heads to New York City where he meets the Ambassador of Haiti, Enfandin, representative of the country that saw the only successful slave revolution in history. The two get into a discussion at the bookstore Hodgins is working in, where he tells Enfandin that the book he is holding by Randoph Bourne is a novel. Ralph Bourne was of course the famous radical who denounced World War I, and made famous the saying "War is the health of the state." Renee Enfandin, the US Ambassador from Haiti, asks Hodgins:

> "But you do not approve of fiction, is that so?" . . .
>
> I thought of the adventure tales I had once swallowed so breathlessly. "Well, it does seem to be a sort of waste of time."
>
> He nodded, "Time, yes . . . We waste it or save it or use it. . . . Yet are all novels really a waste of the precious dimension? Perhaps you under-estimate the value of invention."
>
> "No," I said; "but what value has the invention of happenings that never happened, or characters who never existed?"
>
> "Who is to say what never happened? It is a matter of definition."

"All right," I said, "suppose the characters exist in the author's mind, like the events; where does the value of the invention come in?"

"Where the value of any invention comes in," he answered. "In its purpose or use. A wheel spinning aimlessly is worth nothing; the same wheel or a cart or pulley changes destiny."

"You can't learn anything from fairy tales," I persisted stubbornly.

He smiled. "Maybe you haven't read the right fairy tales."[88]

Subsequently, through a series of complicated events, an associate of Hogins opens a wormhole in time. Backmaker uses the wormhole to go back to Gettysburg, July 2, 1861, albeit only to look at the battle as a Civil War historian. As Mike Davis relates the story in "Ward Moore's Freedom Ride" (2011), unintentionally, Backmaker's going back in time, from 1951 to 1863, changes events, and the Union wins the battle. Backmaker hides, not wanting to change the past again, though he takes solace in the abolitionist hopes of his grandfather, now redeemed:

"The Negro is free," he [Backmaker] reflects in 1877, "black legislatures pass advanced laws in South Carolina; black Congressmen comport with dignity in Washington. The Pacific railroad is built, immigrants pour into a welcoming country to make it strong and wealthy; no one suggests they should be shut out or hindered." But he apprehends another imminent bifurcation that will erase much of the gain. "There are rumors of a deal between the northern Republicans and southern Democrats betraying the victory of the Civil War. . . . If this is true, my brave new world is not so brave." This is a brilliant final twist: our Gettysburgs are always at risk.[89]

Backmaker ends up being stranded in another time, and thus he opens his book with the opening arresting sentence: "Although I'm writing this in the year 1877, I wasn't born until 1921."[90] Davis goes on to chronicle the serious reality behind *Bring the Jubilee's* counterfactual history; namely, that in many ways, the South, politically, and culturally, effectively won the Civil War. Obliterating here from much of historical memory were the realities of racist slavery, the heroism of those of bravely overthrew it, albeit temporarily, and the sordid reality of white violence and disenfranchisement that led to the destruction of Black Reconstruction and the imposition of Jim Crow upon its ruins.[91]

The racist backwaters of the defeated North, Moore seems to be saying, are not simply reminiscences of times past, as in Proust's *In Search of Lost Time*, but a kind of return of the repression, an involuntary memory arising from the past, as a warning for the coming of a possible dangerous future, if the present moment is not seized to continue the Black freedom struggle and the effort to build a truly egalitarian multiracial and multicultural society.

After all, in the time of its writing, Senator Joe McCarthy's Red Scare was reaching its height, with universities demanding loyalty oaths, and the House Un-American Activities Committee going at full tilt. And in 1948, of course, in response to President Truman's embracing of Civil Rights, the Dixiecrats had bolted from the Democratic Party to thwart such an embrace and make the region safe for white supremacy for another century. The image, then, of a country in which the South won the Civil War, was not so much a message of the possibilities of the past, but the realities of the present, and the portent of an even more terrifying future, the danger being, in the words of Lincoln, "a house divided cannot stand . . . the country will become all one thing or another." In highlighting the ignominious bargain of 1877, Moore portended an equally insidious possible bargain in the making, between the Dixiecrats and the Republican Party's "long Southern strategy," which dates to this very era, that of Eisenhower. For in the year 1952, "many Dixiecrats supported the Republican candidate, Dwight Eisenhower. The year 1952 saw the beginning of what would eventually become a wholesale transfer of the political allegiance of the segregationist white Southerners to the Republican Party. . . . The history-changing time travel plot is, therefore, used to release certain social dynamics from their coordinates in time and space, allowing us to see the similarities between the readers' present that Hodge learned when mastering the historian's craft."[92]

In "Ward Moore's Freedom Ride," Mike Davis highlight the author's wonderful "eccentricity," namely his commitment to what Eric Foner has referred to as America's unfinished revolution of Reconstruction, noting that Moore "wrote *Jubilee* seven years before Lowell, a year before *Brown vs. Topeka*, in the shadow of the Dixiecrat rebellion and McCarthyism, at a time when every significant mainstream literary voice in America, from Faulkner, Saroyan, and Steinbeck to Shulberg, Mailer, and the Beats, kept a stony silence on civil rights. In contesting Southern legend, but even more in extolling the greatness and justice of abolitionism, Moore was recruiting Freedom Writers. He was struggling to create an alternate world."[93]

The 1950s, for all its supposed conservatism, were an important time in the literature of dreams deferred, from Langston Hughes's *Montage* (1951) to Ralph Ellison's *Invisible Man* (1952). Yet here we also find a crucial innovation in this literature from Toni Morrison. In *"Who Set You Flowin'?" The African-American Migration Narrative* (1995) Farah Jasmine Griffin, quoting Melvin Dixon, highlights the sharp turn in the work of Toni Morrison, noting that she

> manipulates and enlarges the conventions of surrealism and the *bildungsroman*, which Ellison viewed as granting the writer freedom from the sociological predilections and realistic persuasions most readers impose upon black American

fiction. This was Ellison's main criticism of Wright . . . but his injunction stops there. Morrison undercuts the hegemony of Eillison's preferred narrative strategy . . . by enlarging the structure to encompass multiple lives and points of view as her characters aim for motion. . . . The multiplicity of perspectives and situations in Morrison's fiction requires protagonists writ large; her novels are *bildungsromans* of entire communities rather than the voice of a single individual.[94]

Griffin goes on to note that Morrison draws especially here from Baldwin, much more so than Wright or Ellison. Of Baldwin, she says, "[He] gave me a language to dwell in."[95] And so, in the work of Toni Morrison's novel, *The Bluest Eye* (1970), set in the 1940s, were the virulent inner workings of racism, and its deleterious impact on the human soul, in both its systemic and surface forms, and its unpacking, not in Los Angeles, Chicago, or New York, but in what is thought of as the heartland of America, Lorain, Ohio. Its title points to a focus on vision, among other things, a focus that Thomas H. Fick associates with American realism and notes about such that:

As a mode realism has been characterized by its emphasis on sight: as Jeffrey Mehlman remarks, "excellence of vision is the distinguishing mark of realism" and Edwin Cady finds that the principal American realists share a common concern with sight. To "look and look," therefore, is to accept the world's immediate existence, as Pecola does when she accepts the whore's insistent presence, but to look with eyes other than one's own is to falsify both self and world. Pecola's wish for blue eyes is not only a wish to match the ideal of the white child, it is also a rejection of right seeing, of the premises of realism for those of romance.[96]

This insistence on realism over romance is a key point that we have carried through our preceding chapters, as the mode of expression that characterizes the trajectory that has gotten lost, or rather that is generally hidden, whereas the romance trajectory, or the fairy tale, is generally highlighted. These trajectories are on full display in *The Bluest Eye*, except here the romance of the latter provides the ugliness evident in the former. In other words, instead of simply two choices or paths to take, we are shown the cost of the path taken, at least to the Breedloves of this world.

The Bluest Eye is told primarily from the perspective of two young Black girls, Claudia and Frieda MacTeer, neighbors of Pecola, the young daughter of the Breedlove family, a family consisting of Cholly Breedlove, the father, Pauline, the mother, Sammy, their son, and Pecola, their daughter. The story begins with a story from childhood, The Dick and Jane Story that took shape in classroom materials, readers, in the 1930s, and continued in various iterations, until the mid-1960s. The story evokes that state of memory in which childhood stories like Dick and Jane begin to consolidate in our minds, to take up less space and solidify its shape, leaving less in terms of its arc or prurient events, and more in terms of its salient imagery and iterative resonance. "Mother, Father, Dick, and Jane" are, we are told, "very happy."[97] And Jane, the story's primary focus, has one particular concern. Who will play with her? The kitten will not play with her. Mother laughs and father smiles, but neither play with Jane. The Dog runs away, but wait, when the search for all apparent playmates is exhausted—"Here comes a friend. The friend will play with Jane. They will play a good game. Play, Jane, play."

Dick and Jane live in a very pretty green and white house with a red door. The Breedloves live in a rundown storefront. Jane's primary concern is who will play with her. Pecola's primary concern is, well, seeing and being seen as ugly, worthless. This is not a temporary accommodation, we are told. They are not there because of a momentary setback in circumstance. They are poor, Black, and they are convinced that they are ugly: "No one could have convinced them that they were not relentlessly and aggressively ugly. Except for the father, Cholly, whose ugliness (the result of despair, dissipation, and violence directed towards petty things and weak people) was behavior, the rest of the family—Mrs. Breedlove, Sammy Breedlove, and Pecola Breedlove— wore their ugliness, put it on . . . although it did not belong to them."[98] As Thomas H. Fick notes:

> Each segment of this story is used as a section "title" to introduce its counterpart in 1940s racist America: the green and white house of Dick and Jane introduces the Breedloves's "irritating and melancholy" storefront apartment; the strong and smiling father is a bitter drunk; the happy family is poor and miserable. The commitment to realist discourse implied in this ironic juxtaposition is made explicit in the characterization of Pecola's friendly whores [who live upstairs]. Marie, China, and Poland "did not belong to those generations of prostitutes created in novels, with great and generous hearts, dedicated, because of the horror of circumstance, to ameliorating the luckless, barren life of men, taking money incidentally and humbly for their 'understanding.'" Instead, they are "whores in whores' clothing."[99]

This sense of prostitution as "real" rather than as "romanticized" mirrors the sense of ugliness that is attached to the Breedloves, in the sense that their ugliness is also real; there is nothing romanticized about it. This ugliness is, however, unique in the sense of its imperceptibility, its way of being in the world without seemingly being there; its way of being an overshadowing enveloping presence that, like the air we breathe that animates us, leaves us, quite literally and figuratively, either gasping for cleaner air, or drawn under, surviving. We are drawing an analogy here that, while an impoverished one in some respects is meant to suggest that we need a sense of ourselves as beautiful, as having worth or value, balanced against a sense of ourselves as ugly. It is also meant to suggest that we need some sense of ourselves as real. Here the comparison we draw moves in an entirely different direction. Marie, China, and Poland are clear about who and what they are, and there is no shame there within them, even as they live in a world that would shame them. The Breedloves, however, are creations of a world that shames them. Their ugliness, or more aptly, the label of ugliness given them, is not theirs, does not belong to them, even though they accept it, given so little evidence to the contrary, as their own.

For a moment in her life Mrs. Breedlove, Pauline, saw herself as beautiful, and then that moment transformed, ugliness reasserted, reinstated. Much like the endless battles between good and evil that play across novels, television, and movies, there are also battles between ugliness and beauty. Pauline saw some sense of herself as beautiful when she first met Cholly. Pauline, with a damaged foot that caused her to walk with a slight limp, yearning for a life and a love she had never had, wanting to be noticed in a life-affirming way, leaning on the fence in her front yard, listening to a young man whistling, as he walks down the street near her, feeling the young man tickle her foot, her infirmity, as if it was a mark of beauty, rather than some deformity: "She laughed aloud and turned to see. The whistler was bending down tickling her broken foot and kissing her leg. She could not stop her laughter—not until he looked up at her and she saw the Kentucky sun drenching the yellow, heavy lidded eyes of Cholly Breedlove."[100] In this moment, for Pauline, the world she experiences bursts into technicolor, sun-washed, happy moment memories: she remembers the deep purple of the berries she used to pick with other children in her youth, the coolness of the lemonade her mother would make, the green flash of the fireflies back down in her hometown, as if they have freshly arrived, again, all at once.[101]

Cholly shows her affection and care, instead of seeing her broken foot as a deformity, he caused her to see it as "something special and endearing. For the first time Pauline felt that her bad foot was an asset" and not a liability.[102] Pauline and Cholly marry, move further north, to Lorain, Ohio, the place, incidentally, of Morrison's birth. Pauline finds herself up north in Ohio in a strange and inhospitable place, a place with mean folks, white and Black surrounding her, having started in what appears to be the deep south of Alabama to Kentucky, and from Kentucky, with Cholly, to Ohio; she is lonesome, Cholly begins to behave in ugly ways, and then Pauline loses a tooth, and while the moment itself is not singularly momentous, it yields for her a point of focus for her despair.[103] And the movies, Cholly's one source of pleasure, became where she learned "all there was to love and all there was to hate," in the world, in the movies, and in herself. The problem was not really her damaged foot, or even her lost tooth; the problem was the lenses she was given, via the movies, life, and her love, Cholly, through which to see herself. Pauline would go to the movies, the one place where she felt the weight of her world lift off her, the room would fade to Black, the movie would start: *"and I'd move right on in them pictures. . . . I don't know. I 'member one time I went to see Clark Gable and Jean Harlow. I fixed my hair up like I'd seen hers on a magazine. . . . It looked just like her. Well, almost just like."* And then she lost a tooth, which set her world back on the track of the reality from which she had at least temporarily escaped. This event, which by itself, would, without other mitigating factors, have little impact, brings her close to tears, and, in retrospect, she thinks that she never recovered from that moment.[104]

And in fact, she does not get over this moment, or the culmination of events preceding and following it. Pauline settles into accepting herself as just downright ugly. This ugliness is not of her own making. It is embedded in the relationship between what is presented to her as beauty, and as ugliness. It is in her desire to be beautiful, the attempt to look even a little like Jean Harlow, an attempt to dream dreams in which she is or is like Jean Harlow, to, in Pauline's words, when the silver screen would light up, to then "move right on in them pictures," to fix her hair like Harlow, to have at least her hair, some small malleable part of her, look "just like her," while even then recognizing the difficulty of realizing this desire, well, she says, "almost just like." And for a few more wonderful minutes Pauline is just fine, until her tooth falls out. Now, truthfully, the loss of the tooth is only the moment of realization that her efforts at beauty, and the kind and thoughtful treatment by others that beauty presumably brings, are for naught. Things change, and not always for the better, and in this moment of recognizability, she sees herself as her world sees her. The problem is not with her foot, although the text indicates that placing blame on it might be her easiest, most obvious, perhaps, option. Nor is her problem with the lost tooth. The problem is her relationship with and to the world surrounding her, the one on the silver screen, her one last place of hope, dreams, companionship, and solace, and the material matters of her existence, her mean and getting meaner husband, her unempathetic employer, her fake friends, the few that could even be said to exist, her lonely life and still then vulnerable heart. For these reasons if not more, the narrator tells the reader that if one really wants to know the truth about "how dreams die, one should never take the word of the dreamer."[105] The dreamer has as much difficulty determining how their dreams die as they do understanding how their dreams live; this is particularly so if the dreamer sees their dream as their life; neither can assess or access the moment when their lives or dreams begin and end. Both the dreaming and the living can, however, trace their path between arrival and departure, beginning and ending. And for the Breedloves, tracing this path brought to their senses, their experiences, their relationships, their interactions a singular point of clarity concerning their existence, which is that they were ugly. Fick rightfully asserts that:

> Thus while Pauline's experience in the movies can usefully be read as a general warning to dreamers it is also something more. As Marcia Westkott argues in "Dialectics of Fantasy," "Fantasy not only opposes real conditions, but also reflects them. The opposition that fantasy expresses is not abstract, but is rooted in the real conditions themselves, in concrete social relations." In *The Bluest Eye* the real conditions are those of American consumer culture, the continuing "gilded age" that began after the Civil War and replaced physical slavery with other forms of mastery.[106]

By mastery, Fick references the numerous forms that asymmetric power relations take, and, particularly, the forms of enslavement embedded in them. More importantly, Fick asserts, "As Pecola's experience suggests, *The Bluest Eye* is as critical of economic and political systems, of the underlying 'concrete social relations' that generate fantasy, as it is of fantasy itself."[107] Sikivu Hutchinson makes these "concrete social relations" plain, using the words of Senator Strom Thurmond, the longstanding senator from South Carolina, serving as senator for nearly fifty years, to ground the following assessment:

> True to the brutal myth of the noble Southern patriarch, Thurmond hewed to a particularly noxious brand of rationalization: "Just as there are in this country two main and quite distinct cultures, a northern culture and a southern culture, so there are in this country two different species of genus segregation. . . . Segregation in the South is open, honest, and aboveboard. Northern segregation is founded on hypocrisy and deceit." The open, honest, and aboveboard segregation that Thurmond speaks of is the blood price of slavery, a code bred on the ships that etched the Middle Passage, as black men and women lay shackled together belly deep in each other's waste, plowing into the unknown, time meted out into beatings, mutilations, rape, and suicide. Open, honest, and aboveboard, lynchings, public humiliations, and the squalor of "separate but equal" gave the children's stories captured in the first generation of Dick and Jane grade-school primers their ethereal sheen of innocence. . . . Dick and Jane taught America how to read the American dream. Picture book primers with these two characters snaked through every schoolhouse from the Deep South to the rugged West Coast of African American "Promised Land" reveries. . . . In their sun-kissed freckle faced averageness, they schooled America in the cultural literacy of suburbia and the holy trinity of nuclear family, heterosexual marriage, and white supremacy. . . . Father was breadwinning and boozing. Mother was homemaking and Easy-Off sniffing. Spot, the family dog, brooded faithfully at brother Dick's side, primed to rip off the balls of any intruder. Government-subsidized Federal Housing Administration (FHA) loans and GI Bill-funded college educations

smoothed the pathway for Dick and Jane's nuclear bootstrapping. Black vets and black families need not apply.[108]

Morrison then taught America how to reread or resee the American Dream. It is not simply the future vision arising from a historical romance. It is not the happily ever after of the national fairy tale or myth. Or rather it is only in a world gone insane, one so intent in keeping one eye closed that it can consistently, continuously, not see a sizable part of its population, as well as not see what it does with them.

The Breedloves' ugliness is not who they are, at least not in terms of how they were born; it was not something intrinsic to them. Rather, their ugliness, except for the ugliness of Cholly, which is something else altogether, had been given them:

> It was as though some mysterious all-knowing master had given each one a cloak of ugliness to wear, and they had each accepted it without question. The master had said, "You are ugly people." They had looked about themselves and saw nothing to contradict the statement; saw in fact, support for it leaning at them from every billboard, every movie, every glance. "Yes," they had said. "You are right."[109]

This passage can fill one with despair and an unanswerable anger and anguish. To convince so deeply and completely someone of their ugliness suggests a sinister, premeditated, institutionalized power structure intent on a particularly virulent form of dehumanization. It is not that one is simply understood as not human, but that they are too ugly to be accorded the dignity one might accord a human. It is not that even in one's dehumanization some sense of worth still exists, it is to be understood and experienced as something even less than those animals that are still found to be worth something; even a stray dog gets some love from a dog lover; the Breedloves do not even get that kind of affection; they are simply beyond being worthy of love in any form, or even pity. They are cloaked in the ugliness we do not wish to see in or as a part of ourselves. They become the anointed undesirable, unwanted; they come to see themselves, to understand themselves as perpetually, unceasingly, irredeemably ugly. Their culture has given them Harry Potter's cloak of invisibility, except in their case, this cloak is permanently attached attire. You register in the eyes of others that reflect what they see of you when they see you, what a young light-skinned black woman, Geraldine, sees in Pecola, when the woman's son, Junior, kills Geraldine's cat and blames it on Pecola. The woman looks at Pecola's disheveled condition, and thinks:

She had seen this little girl all of her life. . . . Eyes that questioned nothing and asked everything. Unblinking and unabashed, they stared up at her. The end of the world lay in their eyes, and the beginning, and all the waste in between.

. . .

"Get out," she said, her voice quiet. "You nasty little black bitch. Get out of my house."

. . .

Pecola backed out of the room, staring at the pretty milk-brown lady in the pretty gold-and-green house who was talking to her. . . . Pecola turned to find the front door and saw Jesus looking down at her with sad and unsurprised eyes.[110]

What we see here is a source of Pecola's ugliness. It is not of her own making, but evident in the assumptions about her, and her supposed kind. Her ugliness is unique, but not uniquely hers. As in she is classified as and with a particular kind of child, the Black and impoverished child, in a particular kind of world, one in which whiteness and money equates to beauty, and Black and impoverished, equals ugly. Even among her own presumed kind, a Black, albeit pretty milk-brown lady, with, one can surmise, enough white in her to temper her blackness, with enough money to see herself as not among the poor, even as her grip on prosperity may itself be tenuous, as is her linkage to whiteness, Pecola is lashed with words that may hurt more than the proverbial sticks and stones that might be thrown her way. Pecola's vision of the Geraldine in this moment too closely parallels the vision of *Dick and Jane* with which this novel, and each chapter within it, begins.

The very pretty green and white house with the red door in the milk-white version of the *Dick and Jane Reader* is juxtaposed to its milk-brown version of Geraldine's, Junior's, and their black cat with blue eyes, pretty green and gold house, this latter one replete with nothing less than a painting, one surmises, as we are not specifically told, of "Jesus looking down at her with sad and unsurprised eyes." And Pecola leaves, head bent as low as it could go, bent low by the cold March air, the cold condemnation of the people like Geraldine around her, under the gaze of an unhappy, broken-hearted, son of God, who Pecola may well see as condemnation, disapproval of her very existence, but which we would like to think of as an unhappiness of being placed on the wall or and associated with the ugliness of Junior and Geraldine. Unlike Pecola, who wears her ugliness like a cloak, wrapped around her, Junior's and Geraldine's ugliness is hidden within and beneath a cloak of presumed beauty.

The people like Pecola and Pauline are condemned to this definition, to their sense of themselves as ugliness personified, by the culture of their country, America, the beautiful; ultimately, they condemn themselves, cloak their ugliness in a self-assigned sense of themselves as beauty personified, and in the culture of their country, by association, America, the beautiful, becomes externally light or white, and yet internally becomes what it always already has become, the ugliness within which it drapes a Pauline or Pecola.

In the afterword to this text, Morrison notes in a critique of her own novel that there is an emptiness in the heart of the novel, a void, representative of the thing that is "Pecola's 'unbeing.'" Morrison did not find herself capable of fleshing out that void, and, in the humbleness felt when confronted by work, and by a writer, of such enormous talent and skill, the void remains in some sense without definition, and yet Morrison's non-definition is a definition. We know that Pecola's "unbeing" takes shape there, and that no other eyes reflect her being in any life-affirming way, save the eyes that her twisted life creates within her.[111] Nevertheless, this silence that Morrison sees in the heart of the novel is in some sense still elusive, difficult to articulate or grasp, all while it is a palpable entity that pervades our inner lives. Those people like Pauline and Pecola internalize the ways in which they are seen by and in the outer world; the Geraldines and the Dicks and Janes of our world, our country, externalize the ways in which they are seen by and in the outer world, almost always blissfully unaware of the ways in which they are seen by and in the outer world. They do not see themselves any more than Pecola and Pauline see themselves, until they hallucinate a self.

The irony here is ocean deep, the see-er and the seen, both forced to see a self that is itself only a dream, an imagined thing, a fiction that squeezes life from any need for fact. To be or not to be, of Shakespearean fame morphs into, to appear to be, or not appear to be. For Pecola, ultimately, appearing to be pretty requires the conjuring of attributes she does not possess, like blue eyes, the bluest of eyes, a synecdoche for the prettiest of features, the nicest of lives, and for its alterity, the most twisted of hearts, the most disturbed of minds, the emptiest of souls. Nothing grows for the girls, Pecola's sole companions, friends even perhaps if she could have seen herself as worthy of any, who had planted some seeds that season. The soil is barren. Something grows in Pecola, however, a child conceived out of Cholly's fraudulent twisted, if not evil, sense of care for her, and Pecola's American dreams turn fully towards hallucinations, nightmares, the wish-fulfillment of something she should have never had reason to wish for, to want, something that should never have had cause to enter her dreams, something that has broken her into two personas: Pecola and Pecola with the bluest eyes. In talking with her second self, Pecola considers the occasion that brought her new friend, her best friend, into her life:

Why didn't I know you before?
You didn't need me before.

. . .

I mean . . . you were so unhappy before. I guess you didn't notice me before.
I guess you're right. And I was so lonely for friends. And you were right here.
Right before my eyes.
No, honey. Right after your eyes.[112]

And so Pecola's delusion must seem complete, and yet it is, and it is not, existing as and consisting of a larger, broader, and deeper delusional abyss. As we have been told, for anyone who cares to look, they might see that for those people like Pecola and Pauline: "The end of the world lay in their eyes, and the beginning, and all the waste in between." And so, in these eyes one sees endings and beginning, and the worlds of waste, of wasted human beings, who long to be what they cannot be outside of the worlds of illusory words and images; cannot be or not be without illusion. And: "So it was," the narrator tells us, "a little black girl yearns for the blue eyes of a little white girl, and the horror at the heart of her yearning is exceeded by the evil of fulfillment."[113] Be careful what you wish or dream for, might be one moral or message of this story, and yet another might be an assessment of our individual and collective relationships with the material world, with that space and place we name reality. Here we ignore the ways in which Pecola encapsulates a larger illusion, one in which misery has its gradations, its asymmetries, much like everything else we classify, and shape in our image. Dreams have consequences, so we must be careful not only what we wish for but what we dream. That is one of the central messages we want to share. And it is to the question of dreams, and the possibilities of creating alternative worlds, and the contradictions therein, that we turn to the land long imagined as the cutting edge of the American Dream, the land sometimes called America's fifty-first nation-state, California (Dreamin).

NOTES

1. James Truslow Adams, *The Epic of America* (Boston: Little, Brown, and Company, 1931), 315.

2. See also Leon Litwack, *North of Slavery: The Free Negro in the Northern States* (Chicago: University of Chicago Press, 1965). See also Ira Berlin, *Slaves Without Masters: The Free Negro in the Antebellum South* (New York: New Press, 2007). For an incisive analysis of these issues, see Etienne Balibar and Immanuel Wallerstein, *Race, Nation, Class: Ambiguous Identities* (New York: Verso, 1991).

3. We thank Father Michael White for this formulation.

4. James Truslow Adams, *The Epic of America* (Boston: Little, Brown, and Company, 1931), 313.

5. See the important discussion of some of these issues of the continuing demand for immigrant labor in Alejandro Portes and Rueben G. Rumbaut, *Immigrant America: A Portrait* (Berkeley: University of California Press, 2014).

6. For a powerful exploration of these questions, see Mai Ngai, *Impossible Subjects: Illegal Aliens and the Making of Modern America* (Princeton, New Jersey: Princeton University Press, 2014, 2nd updated edition).

7. James Truslow Adams, *The Epic of America* (Boston: Little, Brown, and Company, 1931), 184.

8. James Truslow Adams, *The Epic of America* (Boston: Little, Brown, and Company, 1931) 183.

9. James Truslow Adams, *The Epic of America* (Boston: Little, Brown, and Company, 1931), 183.

10. Robert J. Cook, *Civil War Memories: Contesting the Past in the United States Since 1865* (Baltimore: Johns Hopkins University Press, 2017), 131.

11. Quoting and paraphrasing from Melvyn Stokes, *D.W. Griffith's Birth of a Nation: A History of the Most Controversial Picture of All Time* (New York: Oxford University Press, 2008), 3.

12. Mike Davis, "Ward Moore's Freedom Ride," *Science Fiction Studies* 38, Part I (November 2011): 390–3901. I.G., Farben was the chemical combine that prospered under the Nazi regime, for which it worked assiduously. See Peter Hayes, *Industry and Ideology: I.G., Farben in the Nazi Era* (New York: Cambridge University Press, 2000, 2nd edition). For an analysis of the over 800 films made about the Civil War, and their glorification of the myths of the South, see Bruce Chadwick, *The Reel Civil War: Mythmaking in American Film* (New York: Vintage Books, 2001). For a fascinating account of the some of the coordinates of Hollywood's hegemonic hold over visual filmic culture during the age of American hegemony, see Perry Anderson, "Force and Consent," *New Left Review* 17 (September/October 2002): especially 24–25. See also the related discussion in Franco Moretti, *Far Country: Scenes from American Culture* (New York: Picador, 2019), 91–93.

13. See most recently, Alex J. Kay, *Empire of Destruction: A History of Nazi Mass Killing* (New Haven, CT: Yale University Press, 2021). See also Arno J. Mayer, "Memory and History: On the Poverty of Remembering and Forgetting the Judeocide," *Why did the Heavens Not Darken: The "Final Solution" in History* (New York: Verso Books, 2012), 467–482.

14. See Michael Denning, *The Cultural Front: The Laboring of American Culture in the Twentieth Century* (New York: Verso, 2010), including the new afterword where the author responds to comments and criticisms. For one appreciation and critique of this landmark work, see David Roediger, "Radical Culture Without Surrealism," *Socialist Review* 28, No. 1+2 (2001): 74–88.

15. See Harold Holzer and Norton Garfinkle, *A Just and Generous Nation: Abraham Lincoln and the Fight for American Opportunity* (New York: Basic Books, 2015).

16. See for example, the important work of Nell Irvin Painter, *Creating Black Americans: African-American History and Its Meanings, 1619 to the Present* (New York: Oxford University Press, 2006).

17. See Jeffrey B. Perry, *Hubert Harrison: The Voice of Harlem Radicalism, 1883–1918* (New York: Columbia University Press, 2011) and the sequel, *Hubert Harrison: The Struggle for Equality, 1918–1927* (New York: Columbia University Press, 2021).

18. See Mike Wallace, *Greater Gotham: A History of New York from 1898 to 1919* (New York: Oxford University Press, 2017), especially the section on "Harlem" & "New Negroes," 846–862. See also Reid Badger, *A Life in Ragtime: A Biography of James Reese Europe* (New York: Oxford University Press, 1995), as well as Richard Slotkin, *Lost Battalions: The Great War and the Crisis of American Nationality* (New York: Henry Holt and Company, 1995). On the centrality of Caribbean migrants here, see Winston James, *Holding Aloft the Banner of Ethiopia: Caribbean Radicalism in Early Twentieth-Century America* (New York: Verso, 2020). And for a long-lost landmark publication of Claude McKay, see his *Romance in Marseille*, edited and with an Introduction by Gary Edward Holcomb and William J. Maxwell (New York: Penguin Classics, 2020). And see Winston James, *Claude McKay* (New York: Columbia University Press, 2022).

19. Mike Wallace, *Greater Gotham: A History of New York from 1898 to 1919* (New York: Oxford University Press, 2017), 861. On the contributions of Schomburg and others, see work by Winston James: *Holding Aloft the Banner of Ethiopia: Caribbean Radicalism in Early Twentieth-Century America* (New York: Verso, 1998, 2020), and more recently, Kevin Young's foreword to *Unsung: Unheralded Narratives of American Slavery & Abolition*, edited by the Schomburg Center for Research in Black Culture, with an Introduction by Michelle D. Commander (New York: Penguin, 2021), xi–xvi.

20. See the entry, "Negritude," in *Africana: Arts & Letters: An A-to-Z Reference of Writers, Musicians, & Artists of the African American Experience*, eds., Kwame Anthony Appiah & Henry Louis Gates Jr. (Philadelphia: Running Press, 2004): 401–413. On Césaire's extraordinary lifelong accomplishments, including his encounter with Andre Breton and company, deported from Vichy France, see *Aimé Césaire: Une Parole Pour Le XXIeme Siècle/A Voice for the 21st Century*, California Newsreel, 1994/2006. See also Franklin Rosemont and Robin D.G. Kelley, *Black, Brown & Beige: Surrealist Writings from Africa & the Diaspora* (University of Texas Press, 2010).

21. *God's Trombones* is included in James Weldon Johnson, *Writings* (New York: Library of America, 2004).

22. Jeffrey C. Stewart, *The New Negro: The Life of Alain Locke* (New York: Oxford University Press, 2018), 11–12. For a recent analysis, see Henry Louis Gates Jr., *Stony the Road: Reconstruction, White Supremacy, and the Rise of Jim Crow* (New York: Penguin, 2019), Chapter Four, "The New Negro," 185–246.

23. See Craig H. Werner, "Chicago Renaissance," *The Oxford Companion to African American Literature*, William L. Andrews, Frances Smith Foster, and Trudier Harris, eds., with a foreword by Henry Louis Gates Jr. (New York: Oxford University Press, 1997), 132–133.

24. Davarian L. Baldwin, *Chicago's New Negroes: Modernity, the Great Migration and Black Urban Life* (Chapel Hill: University of North Carolina Press, 2007), 14.

25. Davarian L. Baldwin, *Chicago's New Negroes: Modernity, the Great Migration and Black Urban Life* (Chapel Hill: University of North Carolina Press, 2007), 38–44; the quote is from 39.

26. Paraphrasing and quoting here from Davarian L. Baldwin, *Chicago's New Negroes: Modernity, The Great Black Migration, and Black Urban Life* (Chapel Hill: University of North Carolina Press, 2007), 39.

27. See Walter Benjamin, *The Writer of Modern Life: Essays on Charles Baudelaire*, edited by Michael W. Jennings (Cambridge, MA: The Belknap Press of Harvard University Press, 2016). Susan Buck-Morss, *The Dialectics of Seeing: Walter Benjamin and the Arcades Project* (Cambridge, MA: MIT Press, 1989).

28. Richard Wright, "Introduction," to St. Clair Drake & Horace R. Cayton, *Black Metropolis: A Study of Negro Life in a Northern City* (New York: Harcourt, Brace, & Company, 1945), xvii. For a landmark study of Black Chicago's deferred dreams and more, see the enlarged edition of *Black Ghetto* (Chicago: University of Chicago Press, 2015), and Robert J. Sampson, *Great American City: Chicago and the Enduring Neighborhood Effect* (Chicago: University of Chicago Press, 2013). See also Tom Reifer, "The Reassertion of Race, Space and Punishment's Place in Urban Sociology and Critical Criminology," *Environment & Planning D: Society & Space* 31 (April 2013):372–380. See also M. Christine Boyer, *The City of Collective Memory: Its Historical Imagery & Architectural Entertainments* (Cambridge, MA: MIT Press, 1994).

29. Davarian L. Baldwin, *Chicago's New Negroes* (Chapel Hill: University of North Carolina Press, 2007), 43. See also Owen Brady, "Wright's 'Lawd Today': The American Dream Festering in the Sun," *College Language Association Journal* 22, Number 2 (December 1978): 167–172.

30. In 1940, *Native Son* was the first African American novel accepted for the Book-of-the-Month-Club selection.

31. See especially Cornel West, "W.E.B. Du Bois: An Interpretation," in *Africana: Civil Rights: An A-to-Z Reference of the Movement that Changed America*, eds., Kwame Anthony Appiah & Henry Louis Gates Jr. (Philadelphia: Running Press, 2004), 432–458.

32. Ralph Ellison, "Richard Wright's Blues," in *The Collected Essays of Ralph Ellison* (New York: The Modern Library, 1995), 129. See also Ralph Ellison, *Living with Music: Ralph Ellison's Jazz Writings*, edited and with an introduction by Robert G. O'Meally (New York: Modern Library, 2002). The influence of the Russian masters, such as Dostoyevsky, are also apparent here, as Ellison's friend, the famous biographer of Dostoyevsky, Joseph Frank, pointed out.

33. Richard Wright, *Lawd Today!* in Richard Wright, *Early Works*, edited by Arnold Rampersad (New York: The Library of America, 1991), 31–32. The tragicomic realism here was anchored in the complex realities of the city of Chicago. "In the heart of the Black Belt, the Avenue Theater (31st and Indiana) preserved the main floor for white customers while restricting even 'our most representative' blacks to the balcony. In this setting, where Black citizens were the primary consumers, leaders were able to exert full indignation. The *Chicago Defender* took an overtly nativist stance, contrasting the historic role of black soldiers in the U.S. military with the 'foreign' ethnic identity of the theater owner: 'The management should be deported to

his home country—the American citizens of color who fought in all America's wars will not stand the insult.'" Davarian L. Baldwin, *Chicago's New Negroes: Modernity, the Great Black Migration, & Black Urban Life* (Chapel Hill: University of North Carolina Press, 2007), 96.

34. Richard Wright, "Introduction," to St. Clair Drake and Horace R. Cayton, *Black Metropolis: A Study of Negro Life in a Northern City* (New York: Harcourt, Brace, & Company, 1945), xxiv–xxvii.

35. See, for but one example, Anthony DiMaggio, *Rising Fascism in America* (New York: Routledge, 2021).

36. Lizabeth Cohen, *Making a New Deal: Industrial Workers in Chicago, 1919–1939*, 2nd edition (New York: Cambridge University Press, 2014), 333–338. See also Roger Horowitz, *"Negro & White, United & Fight!" A Social History of Industrial Unionism in Meatpacking, 1930–90* (Urbana: University of Illinois Press, 1990).

37. Lizabeth Cohen, *Making a New Deal: Industrial Workers in Chicago, 1919–1939*, 2nd edition (New York: Cambridge University Press, 2014), 333–338.

38. Lizabeth Cohen, *Making a New Deal: Industrial Workers in Chicago, 1919–1939*, (New York: Cambridge University Press, 2014), 337–349.

39. Lizabeth Cohen, *Making a New Deal: Industrial Workers in Chicago, 1919–1939* (New York: Cambridge University Press, 2014), 339.

40. Lizabeth Cohen, *Making a New Deal: Industrial Workers in Chicago, 1919–1939* (New York: Cambridge University Press, 2014), "Preface to the 2nd edition," xxx–xxxi.

41. See David R. Roediger, *Working Toward Whiteness* (New York: Basic Books, 2018), especially the important section, "Regardless of Race: The CIO, the New Immigrants, & Interracial White Unionism," 207–224.

42. David R. Roediger, *Working Toward Whiteness* (New York: Basic Books, 2018), 159.

43. See especially Matthew M. Briones, *Jap and Jim Crow: A Cultural History of 1940s Interracial America* (New York: Oxford University Press, 2012). See also "Jap Crow" in Mark Brilliant, *The Color of America Has Changed: How Racial Diversity Shaped Civil Rights Reform in California, 1941–1978* (New York: Oxford University Press, 2010), 28–57. On the specificity and importance of the terminology used here, see Roger Daniels, "Words Do Matter: A Note on Inappropriate Terminology & the Incarceration of Japanese Americans," in *Nikkei in the Pacific Northwest: Japanese Americans & Japanese Canadians in the Twentieth Century*, eds., Louis Fiset & Gail M. Nomura (Seattle: University of Washington Press, 2005), 190–214, as well as Lane Ryo Hirabayashi, "Incarceration," in *Keywords for Asian American Studies*, Cathy J. Schlund-Vials, Linda Trinh Vo, and K. Scott Wong (New York University Press, 2015), 133–138. See also Gregory D. Squires, ed., *The Fight for Fair Housing* (New York: Routledge, 2017).

44. Matthew M. Briones, "'A Multitude of Complexes': Finding Common Ground with Louis Adamic." *Jim and Jap Crow: A Cultural History of 1940s Interracial America* (Princeton University Press, 2012), 53–54. Stable URL: https://www.jstor.org/stable/j.ctt7t4kq.7

45. Akia Iyire, *Power and Culture: The Japanese-American War, 1941–1945* (Cambridge, MA: Harvard University Press, 1982). John W. Dower, *Race and Power in the Pacific War* (New York: Pantheon, 1987).

46. David R. Roediger, *Working Toward Whiteness* (New York: Basic Books, 2018), 222.

47. Kevin Starr, *Endangered Dreams* (New York: Oxford, 1996), 226, 240. Michael Denning, *The Cultural Front* (New York: Verso, 2011), "Migrant Narratives," 269–282.

48. See Camille Guerin-Gonzalez, *Mexican Workers and the American Dream: Immigration, Repatriation, & California Farm Labor* (New Jersey: Rutgers University Press, 1994). See also Francisco E. Balderrama and Raymond Rodriguez, *Decade of Betrayal: Mexican Americans in the 1930s* (University of New Mexico Press, 2006). See also NPR, "America's Forgotten History of Mexican-American 'Repatriation'" (September 10, 2015).

49. Also important were Steinbeck's *In Dubious Battle* (1936), which like his later work was written after years studying and documenting the conditions of migrant workers in the California fields and which was joined by a host of other reports and images, notably the photography of Dorothea Lange and Paul Taylor, including in their book, *American Exodus* (1940), simultaneous with the Hollywood release of *The Grapes of Wrath* on film. And though, too little known, we now have a record of Lange's photographs of the tragic unjust incarceration of Japanese Americans during World War II. See Linda Gordon & Gary Y. Okihiro, ed., *Impounded: Dorothea Lange & the Censored Images of Japanese American Internment* (New York: W.W. Norton & Co., 2006).

50. Michael Denning, *The Cultural Front* (New York: Verso, 2011), 260.

51. Michael Denning, *The Cultural Front* (New York: Verso, 2011), 266.

52. Michael Denning, *The Cultural Front* (New York: Verso, 2011), 264. See also Roxanne Dunbar-Ortiz, *Growing Up Okie*, with a foreword by Mike Davis (Norman: University of Oklahoma Press, 2006).

53. Kevin Starr, *Endangered Dreams* (New York: Oxford University Press, 1996), 61. See also Sucheng Chan, *The Bittersweet Soil: The Chinese in California Agriculture* (Berkeley: University of California Press, 1987).

54. Kevin Starr, *Endangered Dreams* (New York: Oxford University Press, 1996), 75.

55. Kevin Starr, *Endangered Dreams* (New York: Oxford University Press, 1996), 75.

56. Michael Denning, *The Cultural Front* (New York: Verso, 2011), 267. Carey McWilliams, *Factories in the Field: The Story of Migratory Farm Labor in California*, with a new foreword by Douglas C. Sackman (Berkeley: University of California Press, 2000). A "broad rainbow" of minority groups in California has long been subjected to the brutal realities of California agribusiness. In contrast to Steinbeck, Carey McWilliams' *Factories in the Field* depicts the realities of California agriculture, and the country from its very beginning, chronicling the history of racial dispossession that facilitated such exploitation. Justin Akers Chacon and Mike Davis, *No One is*

Illegal: Fighting Racism & State Violence on the U.S.-Mexico Border (Chicago: Haymarket, 2018).

57. The book is illustrated by one of the twentieth century's most acclaimed African American artists, also coming out of the Harlem Renaissance, whose themes of migration and flight documented the African American experience, Jacob Lawrence, at the same time the latter was exhibiting his series on *The Migration of the Negro* at the Harlem Arts Center, and known for his prolific work on these subjects, which included Harriet Tubman and John Brown, along with artists such as Romare Bearden.

58. These poems are taken from Langston Hughes, *The Collected Works of Langston Hughes: Volume II: The Poems, 1941–1950*, edited with an introduction by Arnold Rampersad (Columbia: University of Missouri Press, 2001), 186, 188–189, 192, referenced also in the original, Langston Hughes, *One-Way Ticket*, illustrated by Jacob Lawrence (New York: Knopf, 1949). For an important articulation of these themes, see Farah Jasmine Griffin, *"Who Set You Flowin?" The African-American Migration Narrative* (New York: Oxford University Press, 1996).

59. Langston Hughes, *The Big Sea* (New York: Hill & Wang, 1940), 228.

60. Arnold Rampersad, *The Life of Langston Hughes: Volume II: 1941–1967, I Dream a World* (New York: Oxford University Press, 1988), 286. Arnold Rampersad, *The Life of Langston Hughes: Volume I: 1902–1941, I Too Sing America* (New York: Oxford University Press, 1988), 221. Here Hughes has again an elective affinity with Benjamin, who once noted he could find a place where he could afford to live, and find a place to make a living, but never both in the same place, struggles he wrote of in his essay "The Author as Producer."

61. Langston Hughes, "Democracy & Me," Speech Made at the Public Session of the Third American Writers' Congress, Carnegie Hall, New York City, June 1939, in Langston Hughes, *Collected Works of Langston Hughes: Essays on Art, Race, Politics & World Affairs, Volume 9* (University of Missouri Press, 2002), 203–206, with the bolded emphasis added. Elements of this story were first recounted, to our knowledge in Arnold Rampersad, *The Life of Langston Hughes: Volume 1: 1902–1941, I, Too, Sing America* (New York: Oxford University Press, 1986), and we were reminded of elements of the story in Mike Davis, *City of Quartz: Excavating the Future in Los Angeles*, London: Verso, 2018, in his section, "The Noirs," 33–43.

62. Details of Himes' life are drawn in part from Edward Margolies and Michel Fabre, *The Several Lives of Chester Himes* (Jackson: University Press of Mississippi, 1997). On the great migration of both Southern Blacks and whites and its impact on popular culture and that of the left, see Michael Denning, *The Cultural Front* (New York: Verso, 2011), 35–38, as well as James N. Gregory, *The Southern Diaspora: How the Great Migrations of Black & White Southerners Transformed America* (Durham: University of North Carolina Press, 2005).

63. Chester Himes, *The Quality of Hurt* (New York: Paragon House, 1971), 73–76.

64. Chester Himes, *The Lonely Crusade* (New York: Thunder's Mouth Press, 1997), 174–175. Note that when we are referring to characters in these novels, we use the language of the time, as our intent is also to grasp an era, and the underlying realities that arguably continue to exist today, in however modified a language or forms.

65. Blurb on the back of Lawrence P. Jackson, *Chester B. Himes: A Biography* (New York: W.W. Norton & Co., 2017).

66. Stephen Parker, *Bertolt Brecht: A Literary Life* (New York: Bloomsbury, 2014), 434. Brecht's poem is quoted in Mike Davis, *City of Quartz* (New York: Verso, 2018), 49. See also Quinn Latimer, "Kalifornientraumen: Bertolt Brecht's Los Angeles Poems & Other Sunstruck German Spectres," *East of Borneo* (October 13, 2010).

67. The Open Shop drive refers to the campaigns to ensure there were no unions, as opposed to a closed shop where all workers are unionized.

68. Louis Adamic, *Laughing in the Jungle* (New York: Harper & Brothers, 1932), 1–20.

69. Louis Adamic, *Laughing in the Jungle* (New York: Harper & Brothers, 1932), 220. Parts of this passage are quoted in Carey McWilliams, *Louis Adamic & Shadow America* (Arthur Whipple, 1935), and Mike Davis, *City of Quartz* (London: Verso, 2018). For a sampling of the Slovenian American's oeuvre, which is no substitute, however, for reading his full works in their entirety, see Louis Adamic, *The Old Alien By the Kitchen Window: Selected Writings* (New York: Modern Times Press, 2022).

70. Esther Schor, *Emma Lazarus* (New York: Schocken, 2017), 231.

71. John Higham, *Send These to Me: Immigrants in Urban America* (Baltimore: Johns Hopkins University Press, 1984), 77–78.

72. This is of course an important theme of Albert Camus's *The Plague* (New York: Knopf Doubleday, 1991.

73. John P. Enyeart, *Death to Fascism: Louis Adamic's Fight for Democracy* (Urbana, Chicago & Springfield: University of Illinois Press, 2019), 4–5.

74. Louis Adamic, *From Many Lands* (New York: Harper & Row, 1940), 291.

75. Louis Adamic, *From Many Lands* (New York: Harper & Row, 1940), 292.

76. Louis Adamic, *From Many Lands* (New York: Harper & Row, 1940), 301. These passages are from Adamic's speech reprinted here, "Plymouth Rock and Ellis Island," which the author notes he delivered hundreds of times. See also Henry A. Christian, "Louis Adamic & the American Dream," *Journal of General Education* 27, Number 23 (Summer 1975): 113–123.

77. Duke Ellington, "'We Too, Sing 'America,'" in *The Duke Ellington Reader* (New York: Oxford University Press, 1993), ed., Mark Tucker 146–148.

78. Duke Ellington, "Interview in Los Angeles: On *Jump for Joy*, Opera, and Dissonance as a 'Way of Life,'" in *The Duke Ellington Reader*, ed., Mark Tucker (New York: Oxford University Press, 1993), 148–151.

79. See Ronald Takaki, *Double Victory: A Multicultural History of America in World War II* (Boston: Little, Brown & Co., 2000). This process was of course contradictory and uneven. See Mary L. Dudziak, *Cold War Civil Rights: Race & the Image of American Democracy* (New Jersey: Princeton University Press, 2000). See Mike Davis, *Prisoners of the American Dream* (New York: Verso, 2018). See also Philip A. Klinker, with Rogers M. Smith, *The Unsteady March: The Rise & Decline of Racial Equality in America* (University of Chicago Press, 1994).

80. See the important discussion of these issues in Mike Davis, *Prisoners of the American Dream* (New York: Verso, 2018), 77–85. See also Bruce Nelson, *Divided We Stand: American Workers and the Struggle for Black Equality* (New Jersey:

Princeton University Press, 2001). See also Michael Goldfield, *The Southern Key: Class, Race, and Radicalism in the 1930s and 1940s* (New York: Oxford University Press, 2020).

81. W.E.B. Du Bois, *Black Reconstruction* (New York: Library of America, 2021), 845, 847–848. See also Richard Iton, *Solidarity Blues: Race, Culture, and the American Left* (Chapel Hill: University of North Carolina Press, 2000). See also Michael Goldfield, *The Color of Politics: Race and the Mainsprings of American Politics* (New York: New Press, 1997).

82. See Linda Gordon, *Pitied but Not Entitled: Single Mothers and the History of Welfare, 1890–1935* (Cambridge, MA: Harvard University Press, 1998), and her "Welfare Reform: A History Lesson," *Dissent* (Summer 1994). See Cybelle Fox, *Three Worlds of Relief: Immigration and the American Welfare State from the Progressive Era to the New Deal* (New Jersey: Princeton University Press, 2012). See Linda Faye Williams, *The Constraint of Race: Legacies of White Skin Privilege in America* (Philadelphia: Pennsylvania State University Press, 2003). See Evelyn Nakano Glenn, *Unequal Freedom: How Race and Gender Shaped American Citizenship and Labor* (Cambridge, MA: Harvard University Press, 2004). See Devra Weber, *Dark Sweat, White Gold: California Farm Workers, Cotton, and the New Deal* (Berkeley: University of California Press, 1994).

83. On these questions, the following works are essential: V.O. Key Jr., *Southern Politics in State and Nation* (Knoxville: University of Tennessee Press, 2006); Angie Maxwell and Todd G. Shields, eds., *Unlocking V.O. Key Jr: Southern Politics for the Twenty-First Century* (University of Arkansas Press, 2011); Robert Caro, *Master of the Senate: The Years of Lyndon Johnson* (New York: Vintage, 2003); Sean Farhang and Ira Katznelson, "The Southern Imposition: Congress and Labor in the New Deal and Fair Deal," *Studies in American Political Development* 19 (Spring 2005): 1–30; G. William Domhoff and Michael J. Webber, *Class Power in the New Deal: Corporate Moderates, Southern Democrats, and the Liberal-Labor Coalition* (Stanford: Stanford University Press, 2011); Ira Katznelson and Quinn Murray, "Was the South Pivotal? Situated Partisanship and Policy Coalitions During the New Deal and Fair Deal," *The Journal of Politics* 74, No. 2 (March 2012): 604–620; Ira Katznelson, *Fear Itself: The New Deal and the Origins of Our Time* (New York: Liveright, 2013); David A. Bateman, Ira Katznelson, and John S. Lapinski, *Southern Nation: Congress and White Supremacy after Reconstruction* (New York and Princeton: Russell Sage Foundation and Princeton University Press, 2018).

84. Martin Luther King Jr., *Where Do We Go from Here: Chaos or Community?* (New York: Bantam, 1967), p. 16.

85. See the landmark work here, of Barbara S. Griffith, *The Crisis of American Labor: Operation Dixie and the Defeat of the CIO* (Philadelphia: Temple University Press, 1988); Judith Stepan-Norris and Maurice Zeitlin, *Left Out: Reds and America's Industrial Unions* (New York: Cambridge University Press, 2003); Elizabeth Fones-Wolf and Ken Fones-Wolf, *Struggle for the Soul of the Postwar South: White Evangelical Protestants and Operation Dixie* (Urbana, Chicago: University of Illinois Press, 2015); Elizabeth Fones-Wolf and Ken Fones-Wolf, "'Termites in the Temple':

Fundamentalism and Anti-Liberal Politics in the Post-World War II South," *Religion and American Culture: A Journal of Interpretation* (2018) 28, Issue 2: 167–205.

86. Mike Davis, *Prisoners of the American Dream* (New York: Verso, 2018), 99–100. See Eric Schickler, *Racial Realignment: The Transformation of American Liberalism* (New Jersey: Princeton University Press, 2016), and Boris Heersink and Jeffery A. Jenkins, *Republican Party Politics and the American South, 1865–1968* (New York: Cambridge University Press, 2020), 169–171.

87. Ward Moore, *Bring the Jubilee* (New York: Farrar, Straus and Young, Inc., with Ballantine Books, 1953).

88. Ward Moore, *Bring the Jubilee* (New York: Farrar, Straus and Young, Inc., with Ballantine Books, 1953), 55–56.

89. Mike Davis, "Ward Moore's Freedom Ride," *Science Fiction Studies* 38, Part 3 (November 2011), 389.

90. Ward Moore, *Bring the Jubilee* (New York: Farrar, Straus and Young, Inc., with Ballantine Books, 1953), 1.

91. Mike Davis, "Ward Moore's Freedom Ride," *Science Fiction Studies*, volume 38, Part 3 (November 2011): 385–392, especially 390–392.

92. Catherine Gallagher, *Telling it Like it Wasn't: The Counterfactual Imagination in History and Fiction* (Chicago: University of Chicago Press, 2018), 159–160. See also Kari Frederickson, *The Dixiecrat Revolt and the End of the Solid South, 1932–1968* (Chapel Hill: University of North Carolina Press, 2001), as well as her recent brilliant analysis of Alabama, the Southern region, and the nation, through the lens of one of its leading families of the white ruling class in Alabama and the related exploitation and oppression of Blacks, from the mid-nineteenth century to the mid-twentieth, *Deep South Dynasty: The Bankheads of Alabama* (Tuscaloosa: University of Alabama Press, 2022).

93. Mike Davis, "Ward Moore's Freedom Ride," *Science Fiction Studies* 38, Part 3 (November 2011): 392.

94. Melvin Dixon, *Ride Out the Wilderness: Geography and Identity in Afro-American Literature* (Urbana: University of Illinois Press, 1987), 164, quoted in Farah Jasmine Griffin, *"Who Set You Flowin'?" The African-American Migration Narrative* (New York: Oxford University Press, 1995), 43. And see also Farah Jasmine Griffin, *Read Until You Understand: The Profound Wisdom of Black Life and Literature* (New York: W.W. Norton & Co., 2022).

95. Quoted in Farah Jasmine Griffin, *"Who Set You Flowin'?" The African-American Migration Narrative* (New York: Oxford University Press, 1995), 43.

96. Thomas H. Fick, "Toni Morrison's 'Allegory of the Cave': Movies, Consumption, and Platonic Realism in *The Bluest Eye*," *Journal of the Midwest Modern Language Association* 22, No. 1 (Spring, 1989): 12, Midwest Modern Language Association. Stable URL: https://www.jstor.org/stable/1315270.

97. Toni Morrison, *The Bluest Eye* (New York: Plume, 1994), 3.

98. Toni Morrison, *The Bluest Eye* (New York: Plume, 1994), 38.

99. Thomas H. Fick, "Toni Morrison's 'Allegory of the Cave': Movies, Consumption, and Platonic Realism in The Bluest Eye," *Journal of the Midwest Modern*

Language Association, 22, No. 1 (Spring, 1989): 10–22. Midwest Modern Language Association. Stable URL: https://www.jstor.org/stable/1315270. P. 12.

100. Toni Morrison, *The Bluest Eye* (New York: Plume, 1994), 125.

101. Toni Morrison, *The Bluest Eye* (New York: Plume, 1994), 115.

102. Toni Morrison, *The Bluest Eye* (New York: Plume, 1994), 116.

103. Toni Morrison, *The Bluest Eye* (New York: Plume, 1994), 117–123.

104. Toni Morrison, *The Bluest Eye* (New York: Plume, 1994), 123 (italics in the original).

105. Toni Morrison, *The Bluest Eye* (New York: Plume, 1994), 110.

106. Thomas H. Fick, "Toni Morrison's 'Allegory of the Cave': Movies, Consumption, and Platonic Realism in *The Bluest Eye*," *Journal of the Midwest Modern Language Association*, 22, No. 1 (Spring, 1989): 15–16. Midwest Modern Language Association. https://www.jstor.org/stable/1315270.

107. Thomas H. Fick, "Toni Morrison's 'Allegory of the Cave': Movies, Consumption, and Platonic Realism in *The Bluest Eye*," *Journal of the Midwest Modern Language Association*, 22, No. 1 (Spring, 1989): 17. Midwest Modern Language Association. https://www.jstor.org/stable/1315270.

108. Sikivu Hutchinson, "White Picket Fences, White Innocence." *The Journal of Religious Ethics* 42, No. 4 (December 2014): 618–619. https://www.jstor.org/stable /24586116.

109. Toni Morrison, *The Bluest Eye* (New York: Plume, 1994), 38–39.

110. Toni Morrison, *The Bluest Eye* (New York: Plume, 1994), 91–93.

111. Toni Morrison, *The Bluest Eye* (New York: Plume, 1994), 214–215

112. Toni Morrison, *The Bluest Eye* (New York: Plume, 1994), 196.

113. Toni Morrison, *The Bluest Eye* (New York: Plume, 1994), 204.

Chapter 4

Another California, Another Country, Another World?[1]

California was the last frontier before California native and science fiction writer extraordinaire Octavia Butler, whose work we take up later, set our sights on the stars. The transformation of the idea of California in popular culture and globally goes back to the discovery of gold soon after it was conquered and annexed with the US aggressive war against Mexico in 1846, and the earlier imaginings of the conquistadors, who told of a land full of Black female Amazons (perhaps an early articulation of the Afro-futurist imagination associated with the work of Octavia Butler).[2] Not surprisingly then, Kevin Starr's Americans and the California Dream series, one of the most accomplished of American regional histories, takes as its theme, the notion of California as the cutting edge of the American Dream, though his last book in the series is fittingly titled *Coast of Dreams: California on the Edge, 1990–2003* (2004). Earlier, we dealt with these themes, in the field of migration, from the Dust Bowl to the Great Depression, to the Ghost of Tom Joad and beyond. Here, we fast forward to California in the Sixties and thereafter, with glimpses back to wartime and post–World War II visions, and of mappings of the possible bad futures, and alternative glimpses of better one's imagined by the ancestors, ahead.

Evocatively enough, and exemplifying the power of the California Dream, later Eagles band member Don Henley tells the story of hearing the famous Mamas and the Papas song, "California Dreamin," in Texas and deciding then and there to head out to California. And no surprise, for after arriving, the band's song "Hotel California," Henley later reflected, was about the dark underside of the American and California Dream. And as Richard Slotkin's epic three-volume history of the myth of the frontier in the American imagination would suggest, there is an elective affinity with the Eagles' last song on the album *Hotel California* (1976), "The Last Resort": "There is no new frontier, we have got to make it here," and the theme of awakening from the

165

Dream that we touch upon in this work.³ And so, drawing on these navigation sights to set and trim our sails for the journey, we turn to what is America's second most diverse state after Hawaii, and the most diverse in the continental United States, California. We do so to explore the possibilities of California dreaming, for the making of another California, another country, and another world.

A crucial aspect of California dreaming, redoubling the effect of the American Dream as a whole, was the enormous gap between the dream as advertised, magnified of course by the global expansion of Hollywood, and the reality. Perry Anderson outlines some of the essential contours of its role in the rise and evolution of US hegemony in the global system:

> Historically, it has been the attractive power of US models of production and culture that has extended the reach of this hegemony. . . . The power of what Gramsci theorized as Fordism—the development of scientific management and the world's first assembly lines—lay in its technological and organizational innovations, which by his time already made the United States the richest society in existence. So long as this economic lead was maintained . . . America could figure in a world-wide imaginary as the vanishing point of modernity: in the eyes of millions of people overseas, the form of life that traced an ideal shape of their own future. . . .
>
> The cultural mirror the US has offered the world . . . owes its success to something else. Here the secret of American hegemony has lain rather in formulaic *abstraction*, the basis for the fortune of Hollywood. In a vast continent of heterogeneous immigrants, coming from all corners of Europe, the products of industrial culture had from the start to be as generic as possible, to maximize their share of the market. . . . In America . . . immigrant publics, with weakened connexions to heteroclite pasts, could only be aggregated by narrative and visual schemas stripped to their most abstract, recursive denominators. The filmic languages that resolved this problem were, quite logically, those that went on to conquer the world, where the premium on dramatic simplification and repetition, across far more heterogeneous markets, was still greater. The universality of Hollywood forms . . . derives from this originating task.⁴

And yet, like the American Dream itself, as Horkheimer and Adorno so poignantly express in the *Dialectic of Enlightenment* (1944), composed in Los Angeles during the wartime period: "The culture industry endlessly cheats its consumers out of what it endlessly promises. The promissory note of pleasure issued by plot and packaging is indefinitely prolonged: the promise, which comprises the entire show, disdainfully intimates that there is nothing more to come, that the diner must be satisfied by reading the menu."⁵ Such entwined realities of Los Angeles as California's utopia-dystopia were especially pronounced for its communities of color, and the poor. Indeed, the cultural contradictions between the endless dreams of California sunshine, open to white youth, and the exclusion of the growing populations of Blacks, Chicanos, and Asians, not to mention restrictions for youth as political beings as a whole, is the basis for both Kirse Granat May's *Golden State, Golden Youth: The California Image in Popular Culture, 1955–1966* (2002) and Mike Davis and Jon Wiener's more recent *Set the Night on Fire: L.A. in the Sixties* (2021).

Mentioned earlier is the African American communities long search for the promised land, which Eddie S. Glaude Jr. has chronicled in his *Exodus!* (2000). And so, it is perhaps no surprise that in the movie *Tupac, Resurrection* (2003), when chronicling the famous prophet of the hood's journey from the East Coast, where he was born in Harlem, and then lived for a time in Baltimore, before moving to California, the accompanying theme music is none other than Bob Marley's *Exodus* (1977), replete with the lines "Movement of the people."

Yet the African American communities' long sojourn and migration to escape Southern Jim Crow and Northern ghettoes by moving West found them confronting confinement in the largest Black ghetto west of the Mississippi. Jim Crow Los Angeles was constructed by white society and its public and private institutions, including the federal government, banks, insurance companies, homeowner associations, restrictive covenants, and the Los Angeles Police Department (LAPD), as the legendary film by Los Angeles resident Cle Bone Sloan, *Bastards of the Party* (2005), powerfully illustrates.[6] Many white residents fought prolonged battles against incoming Black migrants, and attempts to integrate city schools in South Los Angeles, with conspicuous displays of performative racism, such as minstrel shows in high schools in the 1930s. In 1941, a mob of 500 students at Fremont High, built as a haven for white students during the Great Black Migration when neighborhoods and schools were becoming integrated, responded to the presence of six Black students by burning them in effigy. The indefatigable editor of the Black newspaper, the *California Eagle*, the legendary activist Charlotta Bass, referred to the incident as "Alabama on Avalon."[7] As Gaye Theresa Johnson notes in *Spaces of Conflict, Sounds of Solidarity: Music, Race, and Spatial Entitlement in Los Angeles* (2013):

> Bass's writings and activism transformed the political import of Black Los Angeles to both local communities of color and international organizations. Well known for her public campaigns against racially restrictive covenants in housing and persistent efforts on behalf of Black community development and empowerment, Bass also championed the rights and dignity of Mexican Americans. She served as a member of the sponsoring commission for the Sleepy Lagoon Defense Committee, which was organized on behalf of a group

of young Mexican Americans falsely accused of murder, and she campaigned forcefully against the racial brutalities exacted upon Mexican American zoot suiters during the summer of 1943.[8]

Also, and of equally noteworthy mention, Johnson elucidates the relevance of another often unsung activist, Luisa Moreno, collocated historically alongside Bass:

> At nearly the same moment, Luisa Moreno, one of the most visible Latina labor and civil rights activists in the United States from the 1930s to 1950, was facing deportation for her own interethnic activism that she had begun two decades previously. Moreno had organized Latino, Black, and Italian cigar rollers in Florida, cannery workers in California, migrant workers in the Rio Grande Valley, and pecan shellers in San Antonio. In her work from 1935 to 1947 in Los Angeles, she had encouraged cross-plant interethnic alliances and women's leadership inside several area food-processing firms. Rather than emphasize the primacy of the individual, Moreno distinguished herself as an educator, agitator, and mobilizer by focusing on the relationship between individuals and their communities.[9]

The wholesale exclusion and exploitation of communities of color in the supposed paradisical lands of Carey McWilliams' *Southern California: An Island on the Land* (1946) generated a unique resistance. For such racist segregation, including in California public schools, where Native Americans, Mexican Americans, and Blacks were excluded, had long been upheld by the courts. Racist segregation of swimming pools and many other public facilities existed into 1950s, with interracial marriage illegal in the state until 1948. After the landmark US Supreme Court decision on *Brown v. Board of Education* in 1954, segregation in Los Angeles, rather than improving, further worsened, and by 1960 it was more segregated than any Southern city. And yet this shared oppression brought together otherwise disparate groups to confront white supremacist ideologies that rejected an inclusive history, and embraced the illusion of fairy tale, a historical romance, instead. Pushing against this embrace of historical romance was a call for a fleshed-out history that compelled what Gaye Theresa Johnson names:

> The twofold demand for the full spectrum of human rights, as well as white historical accountability, illumines a long-shared philosophy among Blacks and Browns in the United States about the nature of their rights as human beings. For example, in the struggle for emancipation, slaves in the mid-nineteenth century created what W.E.B. Du Bois named "abolition democracy." In the years leading up to the victory of the passage of the Fourteenth Amendment, Blacks articulated a radical political perspective that demanded freedom in its entirety—nothing less than the material realization of all of the rights supplied

to elite whites. In so doing, they critiqued a democracy compromised by its racist institutions and created a legacy that "opened the door for subsequent claims for social justice by immigrants and their children, religious minorities, women, workers, and people with disabilities. From voting rights to affirmative action, from fair housing to fair hiring, the 14th Amendment is an enduring and abiding force for social justice in US society." These shared histories of radical critique among Blacks and Mexican Americans helped make it possible for them to view their related but nonidentical struggles as part of the same constellation.[10]

These moments might be thought of as the canvas upon which Walter Mosley paints the lives of his characters in *Devil in a Blue Dress* (1990), the first book we take up, as well as the second turned to thereafter, Luis J. Rodriguez's *Music of the Mill* (2005). Though both novels start out in the 1940s, Mosley's novel, and the film (1995) made from it, is entirely set in the late 1940s, shortly following World War II, while Rodriguez's book chronicles Los Angeles from World War II to the 2000s, focusing on one family, and their intergenerational struggles, in ways that resonate with the making of an increasingly multicultural and multiracial Los Angeles. In his introduction to the novel in the thirtieth anniversary edition of *Devil in a Blue Dress* (2020), Mosley notes that thirty years is a significant amount of time to struggle

with its own history, its own unconscious awareness of race. . . . We've been running for centuries, all of us have . . . entered the eternal tournament rushing to get ahead, to keep up, or to escape the consequences of being poor and black, being white and poor, or simply being the underdog in a system, a nation. . . .

When I wrote *Devil* . . . I wanted to tell a story about Los Angeles that reflected black life and the black contribution to culture within a mirror- darkly that partially reflected the American experience within a shadowy landscape of national shame.[11]

And indeed, Mosley does exactly what he sets out to do. The story's main character, Easy, has returned from World War Two, moved from the South to the West Coast, Los Angeles, specifically, and gotten a job at Champion Aircraft, a job he loses at the beginning of the novel. Easy, subsequently, fresh out of work, takes on a job as a private detective for a Mr. DeWitt Albright, a fixer of sorts, who is seeking to find a young visibly white woman who has vanished into Black Los Angeles, into places that Albright, who is visibly white, cannot go without being noticed. Easy is uneasy with the job, but takes it, so that he might eat and pay the mortgage on his house, that bastion of middle-class existence, which he loves and does not want to lose. And yet as Mosley points out, Easy came from people who

were the first humans in the world to be considered property under the rubric of
pure capitalism. . . . As time has gone . . . women, transgendered people, other
so-called races, and even working-class whites—have begun to understand that
this world wants to own their labor, hollow out their souls, and sell their produce
in bulk to a world that does not know their names.[12]

Here, through Easy, Mosley deftly connects the typically disconnected histories of capitalism and racism that undergird our democratic republic, shaping
the ground on which we all stand, to borrow a phrase from August Wilson,
even as such collocation, the ways in which all life in the United States, if
not the world, is connected, is given little recognition. The very humanity of
these collocated groups has been endangered by this system, in some large
part because of the ways in which it measures success by accumulation
and production, labeling people as product, and by extension, their labor
as product, with little to no acknowledgement that people might be seen as
something else more human and humanizing. Even the legal system, we are
told, is shaped for, and used by, the rich few to control poor people, to keep
them from prospering, running in place, so to speak.[13] Rightly, this sentiment
is echoed by Ralph Ellison, in his short story, "Battle Royal" (1947), which
became the opening chapter of his novel, *Invisible Man* (1952). "Nobody
knew what I was up to and that made me sort of invisible," Rawlins explains.
"People thought that they saw me but what they really saw was an illusion
of me, something that wasn't real." In other words, the "Invisible Man" has
turned a social liability into a professional asset.[14] Even armed with such
knowledge of the deck being stacked against them, still folks migrated seeking better living conditions, knowing that while their lives held some con-
stants, like a stacked legal system, it held a few variables, as well.

One such constant was the American Dream, and the possibility of its
realization in California. If Texas, Arkansas, Mississippi, or Alabama was
not working for you, then maybe better fortune might be had in a place like
Southern California. As Mary Young puts it, "After establishing Los Angeles
as a plantation, Mosley continues the analogy. Like the enslaved Africans
who dreamed of escaping North to freedom, post-World War II African
Americans dreamed of moving to California."[15] As Easy reflected: "People
told stories of how you could eat fruit right off the trees and get enough work
to retire one day. The stories were true for the most part but the truth wasn't
like the dream . . . if you worked every day you still found yourself on the
bottom."[16] And indeed, one can eat fruit right off the trees and, maybe, work
enough to build a nest egg for retirement, but as Easy points out, what one
wants to happen, thinks could or should happen, is often distinct from what
does happen. Working for a living was still a requirement, generally, to get
ahead, and not in any way a guarantee of success.

In fact, Easy is more cynical than this; life was as difficult in Los Angeles as it was in the South, and that work assured you a place at the bottom of the barrel; there is no equivocation in the assertion that after days of hard work the bottom is where you would still be. The only consolation evident here is in remembering your days dreaming about moving west, and, with a little help from a friend, Scotch, in Easy's case, for a minute or two you could feel as though your dreams had taken on material form. He does not stop there, however, when one leaves this dream state for reality, one finds a rather eerie comparison between factory work in the West and work in the South, suggesting a kind of changing same in the material conditions of the working world for workers of color, Black workers in particular, which is that, in Easy's words: "A job in a factory is an awful lot like working on a plantation. . . . The bosses see all the workers like their children. . . . So Benny thought he'd teach me a little something about responsibility because he was the boss and I was the child."[17] The metaphors, or similes, specifically, are striking; working in a factory is like working on a plantation; bosses are like overseers; workers are thought of as or like children, and called boys and girls, as if they were children.

These thoughts are echoed and extended by Mary Young in "Walter Mosley, Detective Fiction and Black Culture" (1998):

> Although Mosley places Easy in this hard-boiled tradition, he adds an extra dimension. The primary difference is that Mosley situates his protagonist squarely within traditional Black culture by using aspects of the oral tradition and the slave narrative. From the folklore identified with these traditions arise two heroic characters: the bad Black man and the trickster.
>
> These Black heroes are different from their hard-boiled counterparts. The trickster as Black hero is not on a quest. He does not want to rescue a damsel in distress nor does he desire to accomplish a noble deed. His one goal, according to Daryl Dance in *Shuckin' and Jivin': Folklore from Contemporary Black Americans*, is to outsmart the man, to humiliate him, to outperform him mentally, verbally, physically . . . or to force him to recognize him and to respect him.
>
> Mosley uses these two heroic figures as he reconstructs post-World War II Los Angeles from an African American perspective. He guides readers through a tangle of after-hours juke joints, corrupt politicians and violence, all filtered through the eyes of "Easy" Rawlins, who comes from the same oral tradition as Zora Neale Hurston. Rawlins says at one point, "He told me a few stories, the kind of tales that we called 'lies' back home in Texas." The use of traditional culture is easily understood since Mosley considers Emancipation a joke and he describes 1940s and 1950s Los Angeles as a gigantic, transformed plantation. Even the factory system is equated with the plantation system.[18]

And so, from this frame, the dream shifts into something akin to a nightmare; shifts from a realm of abundance and the satiation of what one desires, to a realization of a lack, not only of unsatisfied desires, but of unfulfilled needs. Easy daydreams, for want of better words, having been hauled into the police station for questioning again, something that seems to happen regularly, and while locked in an interrogation room alone, and in a growing darkness, he notes: "I was awake but my thinking was like a dream. . . . I saw faces in the darkness; beautiful women and feasts of ham and pie. It's only now that I realize how lonely and hungry I was then."[19]

Dreams suggest a presence of that which is desired but not yet attained. What Easy's dreams ultimately reveal is his loneliness and hunger. The material world provides, instead, journeys to police stations where he is questioned in questionable ways, a house that he cannot afford to keep, or lose; a life of general isolation, with the occasional stolen moment of companionship, and above all, jobs that barely keep him afloat, that are hard to come by, harder to keep, and, aside from the need to survive, not much worth having. Easy works to live, and lives to work, much like a majority of humans do in a world where debt entraps and heavily burdens far too many, and in which far too many workers are understood as, as one of former President Trump's top economic advisors, Kevin Hassett, recently put it, "human capital stock."[20] To be fair, the term has been in circulation for some time among economists, but, no matter where it has been in circulation, or more aptly because it is in common use, even among economists, the dehumanization of people to a term used for store products and other saleable goods, reveals much about how they are experienced and understood.

DeWitt Albright takes these notions farther when in conversation with Easy, who he has hired to find the missing love interest of his boss, when Easy does not deliver and offers Albright his money back. Albright rejects Easy's offer and asserts that he now owns Easy. Not being too hip on the idea of being owned, Easy responds: "I don't belong to anybody," but Albright disagrees, asserting that under capitalism, debt conveys ownership, that all debtors are owned, no matter their race, religion, or creed.[21] One must now confront the role and relationship that capitalism, described here as a form of debt slavery, has to a democratic republic, as is, presumably, the United States, and to the American Dream. Thus far, it seems that the Dream provides a means of acquiring labor, the United States provides a base for capitalism to flourish on the labor of its dehumanized "human capital," who, generally, profit little from their labor, when compared to the profits garnered by their employers. What we are talking about is a kind of bait and switch.

One of Easy's capitalist bosses is the person who fires him from his job at the factory. A second boss is Albright, from whom we receive this treatise on capitalism, and who is at that moment threatening Easy's life for not producing the white girl he was supposed to find. A third boss is Mr. Terrel, a pedophile, protected in his aberrancies by money and political position. And then there is Mr. Todd Carter, who employs Albright, and thus Easy, in finding the white girl that he has a thing for, a white girl, who is visibly white, but not "really" white, a person whose racial ambiguity makes clear the amorphousness of racial categories. Carter is a special kind of white guy, we discover. In speaking of Carter, Easy notes, that Carter had so much money that he did not even think of Easy as human: "It was a strange experience but I had seen it before. . . . He could tell me anything. I could have been a prize dog that he knelt to and hugged when he felt low. It was the worst kind of racism. The fact that he didn't even recognize our difference showed that he didn't care one damn about me."[22]

Here we reach an unprecedented level of dehumanization, the presumption being that the higher up the hierarchy, the harder it is to even consider those down the food chain, as anything other than a food source. Benny, Easy's boss at the factory, thinks of him as a child; Albright thinks of him as property; and Carter, well, Carter does not even think of him as human when he thinks of him at all. In Easy's terms, he might as well as be Carter's prized dog. One must wonder at Carter's love for this woman that Easy and Albright seek, particularly knowing that this woman, Daphne Monet, or Ruby Hanks, the name she was born with, is as Black as she is white.[23] Ruby seems to think that Carter's love is genuine, or at least as genuine as her sense of love, twisted by incest and her place on the color line, allows her to think.[24] She believes that Carter knows her "better than any other man," and this may well be so, given that they share a kind of double-bodied sense of self: As Ruby puts it: "I'm different than you because I'm two people. I'm her *and* I'm me."[25] Effectively, Ruby develops a second personality, Daphne, to deal with her feelings toward their (Daphne's and Ruby's) father; one that saw him as a lover, and the other that saw him as a rapist. Carter also develops a second personality; one who loves a black woman who passes at times for white, and the other who cannot be caught loving a black woman who passes at times for white.

The claim here is not that these are equal degradations, but that they may well be so perceived in the kind of twisted society we have. Mouse, Easy's friend, gets it, but Easy does not. As Easy contemplates the possibility of a life with Daphne, he seems to forget what Carter does not forget, that Daphne has another self, Ruby, a double-life, that he can afford to live on some level. Easy cannot live or afford to live such a double life. He cannot take a walk on the white side of life and come back from it all right, all bright. Daphne, Ruby, and Carter pay a cost, but a different cost, the text seems to say, than Easy will pay. As Mouse says to Easy: "you be thinkin' like white men be thinkin' . . . that what's right fo' them is right fo' you. She look like she white and you think like you white. But brother you don't know that you both poor niggers. And a nigger ain't never gonna be happy 'less you accept what he is."[26] And herein lies the difference. Carter and Ruby can want and have, at least for a time, what is classified as white, and what is classified as not white; Easy can want *but not have* what is classified as white, only what is classified as Black; indeed, whatever he has is by stint of location and proximity, no longer white, but Black. This is knowledge for Mouse that Easy has not yet acquired, wanting, as he does, the Dream, without full recognition that it was never intended for Black people.

Much, in fact, becomes twisted at the intersections of what might well be thought of as the racist, sexist, and classist manifestations of this American Dream, the nightmares that it closets away, hides, generally, from the prying eye. We are sadly, as a people, unapologetic about, if not embracing of, our sexism. For the most part, we either deny that class exists, or we claim that virtually everyone is middle-class, which ironically, does not really exist anymore. Most of us fall into the categories of the Haves and the Have-nots, with a dwindling few in the middle. Our tendency is to think of other places as racist, for example, like Hitler's Nazi Germany, and not of the United States as the place Hitler's Germany drew on for some of its racist ideologies, although they found some of them too extreme.[27] All too often we recognize the differences between groups (Black males versus white males) and the commonalities within them (all Black males are presumably Black), without recognizing the commonalities between groups (Black and white males are still male), and the differences within them (not all white males are alike in any way other than being white). This pattern of classification tends to occlude its other, to hide it from view to our consistent detriment.

This is a pattern that Easy reverses in his look back at his time in World War II. Here, speaking of Jewish brothers-in-law who immigrated to the United States following the horrors of this war, Easy tells us their story, told to him by his acquaintance Jackson. Easy and Jackson are on their way to buy liquor from these Jewish men, which is being used as an excuse to elicit information from them Easy hopes will lead him to Daphne. The brothers-in-law came to Los Angeles from Poland, by way of "Auschwitz; Jews who survived the Nazi camps. . . . Abe . . . saved Johnny from the gas chamber . . . dragged him to the GI station where they applied to emigrate."[28] Jackson has more stories to tell, but Easy doesn't want or need them, having some stories of his own from the same war. Easy had seen the concentration camps and seen Jews who had been held captive in them, and he remembered, and quite possibly could not forget seeing Jews in states of utter desiccation, near death, or soon to be dead. He also could not forget a young malnourished Jewish boy who bonded with another soldier, Vincent, and to whom Vincent fed whatever sweets he had, attempting, one might surmise, not knowing the harm it might do, to bring a little joy to a deeply painful life. Vincent enjoyed those sweets, fell ill, and died the next day, from not being able to ingest the sweets he had been given. Easy notes that Vincent shouldered the blame for this young boy's demise, but Easy cannot help thinking that "those Germans had hurt that poor boy so terribly that he couldn't even take in anything good."[29]

Walter Mosley's poignant description of what some have called the multi-directional memory of the Holocaust, or Shoah, the catastrophe that was the destruction of European Jewry, as well as the Roma, the Slavs, the Russians, and so many others, is paralleled in the Japanese American experience. For while their friends and family were forcibly rounded up and imprisoned within American concentration camps, thousands of Japanese Americans, from Hawaii, and from camps in the continental United States, served in the US Armed Forces and fought against the Axis powers of Japan, Italy, and Germany. In what was perhaps one the supreme ironies of their experience of the war, as Roger Daniel notes, these courageous patriotic young men, helped to liberate the Jews in some of the satellite concentration camps around Dachau, all at a time when their own brethren were incarcerated in con-centration camps in the US, their only crime being that they were Japanese American.[30] Sadly, though surprising to some, during the time of patriotic wartime fervor in the United States, the racism that underlay the stripping of Japanese Americans of their rights were responded to only belatedly, if at all. And so, an important opportunity for the Double V campaign to fight racism at home and fascism abroad was squandered, with horrific and long-term traumatic effects.[31] Among the few who stood up early on, most memorably, along with courageous Japanese Americans themselves were Dorothy Day and the Catholic Worker movement, who immediately denounced and pro-tested this policy, and other iconoclasts such as Louis Adamic and W.E.B. Du Bois, but they were sadly the exception, not the rule.[32] Also, and equally sadly, consider how Black soldiers, like Easy, returning from this war were treated.

This story ends with Easy finding Daphne, Daphne remembering and out-ing Ruby, with a little help from Mouse who remembered Ruby from earlier days when they lived in the same place, Albright dying by Mouse's hand, Easy getting paid enough to keep his house, buy another, and start a business as a private detective. Easy is uneasy as the story ends, for his dreams are built of shifting sands, and he knows it, but his life is still easy enough to keep on living and dreaming. Easy is a pragmatist, as Mary Young notes, and Mouse, too, is as pragmatic as Easy. Mouse recognizes that African Americans cannot succeed playing by the white man's rules. African Americans must develop a different game with different rules. Mouse tells Easy, "you gotta have some-body at yo' back. . . . That's just a lie them white man give 'bout makin' it on they own. They always got they backs covered."[33] One point here is that such a reading belies the notions of radical individualism that so deeply informs one trajectory of the American Dream, that southern historical romance version. Mouse might be insane, and quite possibly sociopathic, but he understands something our American Dreams seem to have hidden from our view, which is that we are not yet, nor have we ever been, in any collective way, free. Thus, as Easy, in Young's terms, "rationalizes Mouse's behavior," he also points out that "he was the only black man I'd ever known who had never been chained in his mind, by the white man. Mouse was brash and wild and free. He might have been insane but any Negro who dared to believe in his own freedom in America had to be mad."[34] Note here that Easy has included himself among those Black men "chained in his mind, by the white man," and that he locates Mouse's insanity, and insanity generally, as the only place where a belief in one's freedom in this country can exist.

A connection between Walter Mosley's *Devil in a Blue Dress* (1990) and Luis Rodriquez's *Music of the Mill* (2005) is brought into view by Malcolm Jones Jr., who closes his review of Mosley's novel with words from Easy Rawlins about the state of Black and Brown relations:

> Best of all is Mosley's main creation, Easy Rawlins, a man as hard-nosed as he needs to be yet still capable of relishing decency when he finds it: "That was back in 1948, before Mexicans and black people started hating each other. Back then, before ancestry had been discovered, a Mexican and a Negro considered themselves the same. That is to say, just another couple of unlucky stiffs left holding the short end of the stick."[35]

This use of Easy's thoughts by Jones Jr. points to a moment and place where a schism developed between these racial and ethnic groups, if not others, whose recognition of shared conditions aided for a time coalition building, and then, we would argue, misguided by dreams of individual advancement over collective action, struggled to find any footing. For this reason, it seems important that this recognition of a shared location, a shared "short end of the stick" situation, prior to, and then into separation, is brought into the open. In focusing on this collocation, Gaye Theresa Johnson asserts that:

> For Blacks and Mexican Americans in Los Angeles in the 1940s and 1950s, the physical and sonic spaces of the city were places of containment and confinement. . . . Yet the tactics of spatial entitlement enabled them to perceive similarities as well as differences, to build political affiliations and alliances grounded in intercultural communication and coalescence in places shaped by struggles for spatial entitlement. I use the spatial metaphor of "constellations of struggle" to trace these activities. Stars in constellations are related to one another because taken together they reveal patterns, but they also have independent existences. The spatial and racial politics of Los Angeles in the 1940s and 1950s created constellations of struggle that tell us a great deal about how alliances and

affiliations coalesce into coalitions, even though participants did not necessarily think of themselves as creators of a common cause.[36]

Johnson arrives at this view from an analysis of the lives and works of two activists influential in the Los Angeles area, namely Charlotta Bass and Luisa Moreno. Moreno, Johnson informs us, also viewed the sites of struggle as extending beyond the geographic and juridical boundaries of the United States.

Alicia Camacho offers a critical understanding of the value of Moreno's contributions to Latina/Latino cultural and political identities, arguing:

> Moreno's vision of relationships of Latinas/Latinos to the "social, economic, and political affiliations" of other aggrieved groups constitutes a keen aware-ness of what David Harvey calls a "cartographic imagination": an understanding of how lives in one place are affected by the unseen actions of distant strang-ers elsewhere. Moreno had personal knowledge of and political experience in many "elsewheres," making every place she worked in significant for its mutual others. This flexible cognitive mapping of relations between places no doubt assisted Moreno in recognizing how Blacks and Latinos in Los Angeles could form relations between races. They did not need uniformity to have unity. They did not need to be identical to share similar identities.[37]

Among the most powerful works to capture key aspects of the increas-ing diversity of Los Angeles is Rodriguez's novel, *Music of the Mill* (2005), which paints a multicultural reality of peoples and social classes in the City of Angels, as a City of Workers, and reflects the "flexible cognitive mapping of relations between places" outlined above. The novel follows the Salcido family through generations of life after their migration to Los Angeles.[38] The book is set, first, in Yaqui country, in northern Mexico, where many Mexicans fought against attempted conquest, forced removal, and extermination, and many worked as slaves in plantations and sugarcane fields in Oaxaca. Procopio Salcido, 18 years of age, is one of them. It is 1943 and Procopio, effectively forced from his home, walks away, eventually ending up doing work in the southern Arizona copper mines, where he meets a young girl of 15, Eladia, of Mayan, Indian, Spanish, and African descent.[39]

When the mine workers go on strike in response to many having been killed or otherwise crushed in the mines, Procopio "becomes a fugitive," hid-ing from the white vigilantes hired by the company to crush the workers. He reaches out to Eladia with thoughts of moving further West, to Los Angeles:

> "I know if I stay here, I'll be killed. But in Los Angeles, I can start over. Find decent work to provide for a wife and family. I know we don't know each other

that well. But I'm leaving and I won't come back. Would you go with me, Eladia? That would make me proud—to be your companion."

"Estas loco!" Eladia quickly responds. . . . "How can I leave. I have family here. They depend on me."

"Listen, I don't know much but I know one thing—you are not happy," Procopio continues. "I saw that the first day we met. You are beautiful, but you have such sad eyes. . . . I'm leaving tomorrow morning. I'm on the first train."

. . . "I wish you hadn't asked me. I hope this is just a dream."[40]

In the end, Eladia agrees and they go to LA to pursue their dreams, running away from the past, hoping for a different and better future, arriving in the "City of Angels as Mr. and Mrs. Procopio Salcido."[41] And they arrive at the very time as the infamous Zoot Suit riots explode, with white serviceman attacking Mexican youth known as *pachucos*, from the barrios, who they also encounter among the copper miner communities in Southern Arizona. Luis Rodriguez outlines the ways in which *pachucos* influenced, and were influenced by, Los Angeles culture and beyond in "The End of the Line: California and the Promise of Street Peace" (2005):

In the 1920s and 1930s, the sons and daughters of Mexican refugees created street organizations and a hybrid culture of youth known as *pachucos* that were the precursors to 1950s rebel youth, 1960s outlaw bikers, 1970s punk rockers and Crips and Bloods, and the pervasive *cholo* gang style that influenced the original Dogtown skaters, Salvadoran immigrants, and subsequent generations of street people.

Unfortunately, in the 1940s, while the U.S. was involved in World War II, *pachucos* became the target of racist white soldiers, sailors, and police in various incidents in L.A., culminating in the Zoot Suit Riots of June 1943. Many more Mexicans came to the state during the war, when jobs became plentiful, as well as in the 1950s to work in the labor-intensive, low-paid farm labor camps, which resulted in major organizing efforts and strikes led by labor leaders such as Cesar Chavez in the 1960s. They also suffered through a number of repatriations—when tens of thousands of Mexicans were deported, including those born on U.S. soil.[42]

Rodriguez locates in California, for many, what might be understood as something like the last frontier, although he offers another and perhaps more pertinent metaphor here when he states:

But California takes the cake. This is due to what I call the "end of the line" syndrome. . . . For many, it is the end of the line—there is nowhere else to go. . . . Most of these people cannot return to their homelands. They make it here or they don't make it anywhere. This is particularly true for poor whites and

African Americans, who came from the South or Midwestern and Eastern cities, and cannot return to the cold, unemployment, and poverty they left behind.

It is also the end of the line in terms of the psyche of the general population. The vast Pacific Ocean forms the western border; you cannot go any further. People become homeless in California; it has more homeless people than any other state. They may appear to be beach homeless or "sunny-day" homeless, but they also suffer, get hungry, and are attacked and despised. It is not good to be homeless in California. . . . Yes, it is colder to be homeless in Chicago or New York City, but these cities have extensive homeless shelters and settlement houses, in contrast to Los Angeles, which has hardly any.[43]

Though driven by the need to escape the violence of racism and the related labor wars, central to the struggle for a common cause was the efforts of these new arrived on behalf of multicolored humanity, driven by the realization of the vast chasm between America's ideals and their continued experience of America's painful and often unspoken dramatically different realities.

By the early 1960s the efforts of the Black Freedom Movement long active in LA had dramatically stepped up its efforts, in the context of a national conversation and activism for freedom and equality. In 1961, Langston Hughes's close friend Arna Bontemps published his *100 Years of Negro Freedom*. The following year, in 1962, Hughes published his own history of the NAACP, *Fight for Freedom*. And the following year, 1963, the noted sociologist and co-author of *The Black Metropolis*, St. Clair Drake, gave The Emancipation Proclamation Centennial Lectures, entitled *The American Dream and the Negro: 100 Years of Freedom?* In these lectures, Drake analyzed the dialectical interplay between nonviolent protest and violent insurrection in the Black freedom struggle from the slave revolts of earlier days to the struggles for Civil Rights of the day. In this series of lectures, Drake is clear: "The American Dream, in its initial form as expressed by The Founding Fathers, most emphatically did *not* include the Negro."[44]

Later that May of 1963, just three months before the March on Washington for Jobs and Freedom, Dr. Martin Luther King Jr. addressed one of the largest Civil Rights demonstrations to ever take place in the U.S., the LA Freedom Rally where some tens of thousands attended. Active on the scene were a host of organizations, including the NAACP, the ACLU, and the Congress on Racial Equality (CORE), pressing up against racist discrimination in housing, schools, and public facilities, and against police brutality, attracting the likes of the Nation of Islam's Malcolm X to the city to work with the movement. Just a few years later, shortly after his famous "Letter from Birmingham Jail," Martin Luther King Jr. returned to Los Angeles, and spoke to over 35,000 persons, calling for freedom "in Birmingham and Los Angeles," saying: "You asked me what Los Angeles can do to help us in Birmingham [Alabama]? The most important thing you can do here is to set Los Angeles free because you have segregation and discrimination here, and police brutality."[45]

The response to King's visit and the increasing visibility and struggles of the Civil Rights movement from Los Angeles to Birmingham culminated in a new level of unity, bringing together some 76 organizations in the United Civil Rights Council (UCRC). The UCRC then led a freedom march in 1963 starting at downtown LA's First African Methodist Episcopal Church—the oldest Black religious institution in Los Angeles going back to 1872, created in part by formerly enslaved African Americans—and ending at the Board of Education. That Summer, James Forman of the Student Nonviolent Coordinating Committee (SNCC) and James Farmer of CORE came to LA and organized a march of over 600 to the Board of Education building, continuing with hunger strikes, student marches, and other protests against the Board's resistance to calls for desegregation, despite it being the law of the land.[46]

In 1964, the movement turned its attention towards blocking efforts, evident in Proposition 14 of the 1964 ballot, to repeal the 1963 Fair Housing Act that banned racist discrimination in property sales. A multiracial coalition organized for Proposition 14's defeat, and Diane C. Fujinio's *Ninsei Radicals: The Feminist Poetics and Transformative Ministry of Mitsuye Yamada and Michael Yasutake* (2020), chronicled some of this coalition's challenges. One major aspect of this challenge was the evolving ideology of the American Dream of home ownership, conjoined to visions of whiteness and white picket fences. So, for example, the California Real Estate Association promoted the idea of the home as a castle, with normative assumptions about the goodness of the patriarchal heterosexual family, in which the man brooks no interference. Opportunities for Asian Americans were predicated on their adherence to opposition or at least tolerance of anti-Black bias. An irony here is of course that Yamada and her family, migrants from Japan to the US, were incarcerated along with other Japanese Americans in internment camps during World War II, and then were socially and culturally coerced to be intolerant of others, as others had been intolerant of them.[47]

Thus, despite the powerful efforts of this multiracial civil rights movement, a white supremacist backlash against Civil Rights during this period gained steam, presaging the later victories of Goldwater, Reagan, and more recently Donald Trump. Despite then California Governor Edmund Brown coming out against Proposition 14, and the Reverend Dr. Martin Luther King Jr. coming out to LA in 1964 to help mobilize against its passage, and for the passage of the Civil Rights Act, only some four months after the passage of the latter in July of 1964, California repealed its fair housing law. This white backlash and the dialectic of racial progress and racist progress is critical to understanding, on the one hand, the dreams deferred that led to the Free Speech Movement which broke out at UC Berkeley that Fall of 1964, with its roots in the Civil Rights struggle, and the Watts explosion in 1965, Ronald Reagan's election as California Governor in 1966, and Nixon's ascension to the Presidency in 1968, not to mention the related rise of George Wallace.[48]

On July 4, 1965, a year after the passage of the Civil Rights Act, none other than Martin Luther King, who had just years earlier evoked the Dream in his famous speech, spoke of how the Dream had so often turned into a nightmare.[49] And as they moved closer together, the prophetic voices of Malcolm X and Reverend King anticipated the eruption of South Los Angeles, Watts. Langston's famous last lines of his poem, "Dream Deferred," "Or does it explode," revealed itself in the Watts Rebellion of August of 1965, set off by a tinderbox of structural racism, massive Black unemployment, failing schools, constant police harassment and brutality. In a retrospective "Beyond the Los Angeles Riots," King noted: "The flames of Watts . . . cast light on the imperfections in the civil rights movement and the tragic shallowness of white racial policy in the explosive ghettos."[50]

Even more so than Berkeley and the Free Speech Movement, which grew out of the Civil Rights struggle in the Bay Area, the Watts Riots were a critical moment in the making of the 1960s. For the uprising exploded for many the myth of the American Dream, where Southern California dreaming was seen as its very embodiment, especially for the young.[51] The uprising demonstrated too that the hopes of some that the Civil Rights Movement in the South would also have some significant impact in the North and elsewhere were chimerical.[52] As Malcolm X once said, in reality, "There's no such thing as a Mason Dixon line. It's America."[53] Mike Davis and Jon Wiener, start out the introduction to their *Set the Night on Fire: L.A. in the Sixties* (2020), with the following arresting statement:

> In August 1965 thousands of young Black people in Watts set fire to the illusion that Los Angeles was a youth paradise. Since the debut of the TV show *77 Sunset Strip* in 1958, followed by the first *Gidget* romance films in 1959 and then the Beach Boys' "Surfin' USA" in 1963, teenagers in the rest of the country had become intoxicated with images of the endless summer that supposedly defined adolescence in Southern California. Edited out of utopia was the existence of a rapidly growing population of more than 1 million people of African, Asian and Mexican ancestry. Their kids were restricted to a handful of beaches; everywhere else, they risked arrest by local cops or beatings by white gangs. . . . If these were truly golden years for white teenagers, their counterparts in South Central and East L.A. faced bleak, ultimately unendurable futures.[54]

Astonishingly, even the existing Black gangs of this time, united in their efforts to drive the police out of the ghetto, underwent a deep process of politicization. Of course, that was a threat that the LAPD and the FBI would not tolerate. The result was the destruction of the Panthers in Los Angeles. This same drama of the destruction of the Panthers played out across the country. In the aftermath of this destruction arose gangs largely shorn of their revolutionary thrust, such as the Crips and the Bloods, becoming increasingly prominent in the 1980s, and providing the undergirding for the 1992 Rebellions some thirty years ago.[55] In *City of Quartz*, Mike Davis tells the tale of the then Human Relations Conference, who despite police opposition, provided a platform for the leaders of LA's Black gangs to be heard, and then, as earlier, demanded decent jobs, housing, community investment and control, and other programs to improve the lives of residents. "It was a bravura demonstration that gang youth, however trapped in their own delusionary spirals of vendetta and self-destruction, clearly understood that they were the children of dreams deferred and defeated equality."[56]

Music of the Mill mirrors the history chronicled above. Procopio gets a job in the emerging steel plants and moves to Florence Street in South Los Angeles, a predominantly Mexican barrio. Immediately, Procopio is introduced to the bitter racist environs within the smoldering steel plants and experiences the same feelings of emasculation and dehumanization that Himes registered in his LA novels, which increases Procopio's compulsion towards a compensatory patriarchal domination within the family. The Salcidos eventually have five boys one after another between 1945 and 1950, Severo, Procopio Jr., Rafael (or Rafas), Juan, and Johnny, and then their only daughter Azucena who arrives in 1952 tragically drowns soon after she is born. Procopio, increasingly consumed by the mill, and devastated at the loss of his daughter, becomes increasingly shut down after her death, present, but essentially absent, leaving Johnny alone with his brothers, all of whom except the oldest beat up on him, as do their friends occasionally. Johnny, ends up getting into trouble with the law, doing time at the California Youth Authority for robbery, and when he finally gets out of jail, he marries a girl from South Central, and manages to get a job where his father works in the steel plant.

Yet in the aftermath of the Watts riots and East Los Angeles uprisings, including the famous high school blowouts and related rebellions, the steel mill has been forced to open to workers of color.[57] Soon enough, Johnny runs into trouble with heads of the KKK contingent there. Johnny also meets radical workers, notably Harley, and his Puerto Rican wife from New York, Nilda. Nilda had formerly been part of the gang, turned political activists for social and racial justice, the Young Lords. These radical activists challenge the racist hierarchy inside and outside of the plant walls. The novel also reveals the inner workings of the delusional racism wrapped up for some in the American Dream, notably the head of the KKK group at the plant, Earl Denton, who hates Blacks and the "dusk-faced, mostly Indian Mexicans" and loves what he sees as the "Great White Way."[58] In the face of the racist assaults inside and outside the plant, in the 1970s, Johnny starts to organize, recruiting, among others, a Black worker named Al, who came up with Los Angeles' legendary Black gangs and now works with the remnants of the Black Panthers. There is intense rivalry in the emerging multiracial coalition, which comes out in one of the organizing meetings. Here, Al lays down his worldview: "Look around you, *brother* . . . You can see the bloods is the only strong group here. We don't need Mexicans; they can get their own selves together. . . . And sure as *hell* don't need white people."[59] At this point, Johnny's father Procopio speaks:

> You say you hate white people? . . . You have no idea what hate is . . . I know one thing—hating people kills you, not them. My father saw thousands of people shot, hung, and tortured during the Mexican revolution. . . . He hated so much that the alcohol that eventually killed him could not break through his stone heart. He hated his wife—my mother, a beautiful and wonderful Indian woman—and he hated us, his own children. . . . Why do we want to keep splitting up the poorest people by color and language, yet we treat all whites like they are as solid as a block of granite. They're not. They don't all agree. They aren't all racist. Some of them, as you know, are as poor as we are. If we unite—all the poor, regardless of color—and we split our enemies up, that's the winning combination.[60]

On the day before the elections the members of the KKK cell meet to talk shop and plan strategy. Denton lets them know of what, for them, is an even more apocalyptic reality, that the consent decree is now going to force the mill to hire women. As Denton relates:

> "You know what this means? Not only do we have to contend with these mud people, now we'll have fucking pussies working right next to us. This is fucked up. This is goddamn communism. Worse than hell."
>
> "Shit, the days of whites, Christians, and men are numbered," Ace says under his breath.[61]

Indeed, women enter the plant: Darlene, a poor white woman whose family hailed from the coal mines of Colorado, who once worked as a stripper and then was on welfare; Carla, a Salvadoran migrant, part of the burgeoning wave of Central Americans coming into California; and Angie, a Chicana from East LA. All experience intense sexism from most of their male co-workers, but not Johnny. In the plant, the women are set up for serious injuries, including the loss of limbs, and almost their lives, by the KKK. And then, the plant announces its closure, and in this loss of industrial jobs, Los Angeles echoes the experiences of cities across the US, as more and more plants migrate to cheaper locations. Johnny, having failed to successfully challenge the plant's old guard, is depressed and disappointed and like so many others at the plant, falls into addiction. To fight this, Johnny runs again on a multiracial slate, this time heading this ticket. They win the election, but it is a Pyrrhic victory given the impending closure of the mill which they fail to stop.

The Salcidos have children, including Chena, or Azucena Salcido. By this time, they have moved to the northeast San Fernando Valley, to a predominantly Mexican community. Chena never works in steel, as her parents told her she would, like Johnny's father before him. Chena, like her parents, knows the score. After having a child and becoming a single mother, she tries to make the best of it, realizing as she does that when the mill died, so too did the community of which it was a larger part: "That's why I've always felt like I'm floating in the world. . . . Like all true Chicanas with our borderless souls and endless migrations, I've had to anchor myself in indigenous traditions, healing, and art."[62] Chena eventually gets hooked up with one of the Salvadoran migrants in Los Angeles. In this context, she tells the story of the discrimination they faced, from Mexican American gangs, and how they started their own gangs to fight back. And though not mentioned in the book, as California racism peaked in the 1990s these very Salvadoran migrants fleeing civil and pursuing the American Dream were arrested and got deported back to nations they hardly knew. So, they created their own networks of familiarity, their gangs, in El Salvador, which soon proliferated across Central America, starting anew a resurgence in people seeking asylum in the United States, to get some distance from the gang violence there, which, ironically, started in the place they wished to come.[63]

As Chena remarks, though, the biggest gang on the block in Los Angeles, was still the Los Angeles Police Department. Here, Chena tells the story of the 1992 riots and uprisings against the beating of Rodney King, the acquittal of the officers responsible, struggles for bilingual education, and the anti-immigrant English Only Proposition 187 initiative, passed but later overturned by the courts.[64] Yet, instead of getting involved with her parents in social movements against racism and police brutality, Chena falls prey to drugs and alcohol, her American dream turning into a nightmare. These life stories are a powerful meditation on what James Baldwin calls the price of the ticket.

At this point her father is dying, from illness likely caused by working at the chemical filled plants for decades. After her father's passing Chena reconciles with her own son, Joaquin, now out of prison, but with whom she kept in touch during his incarceration. Joaquin lays down his truths to his mother noting that today, the realities are inescapably multicultural, involving "even whites. Poor people. That's all what's in here. We may hate each other but damn, we all have to look at the same empty walls with the same futureless eyes." Joaquin sees much value in reaching out to the young ones, this at a time when one of Tupac Shakur's famous songs articulated, "They say there's no hope for the youth. Truth is there ain't no hope for the future," commenting on the skyrocketing numbers of people of color going into prison. They all, Joaquin, Chena, come to recognize in themselves and in each other the desire to change these realities, for the poor and despised everywhere, in their own way, in a new multicultural setting.[65] Here, Rodriguez seeks to remind Angelenos that the City of Angels was once, and still is, in many ways, the City of Workers, while seeking to understand those realities that arise in the city of dreams deferred, an increasingly multicultural and multiracial city, bringing together communities from around the globe.[66]

An example of this increasing complexity are the 1992 uprising and riots, which while often still told in a Black and white frame, their actual reality was inescapably multicultural and therefore what Cornel West calls, multi-contextual.[67] Luis Rodriguez takes up this challenge in his novel, in part, dealing with the signal participation of recent migrants from Central America in the uprising. Yet of particular importance as well is the often-untold story of the relationship between Korean and Black Los Angeles, as well as the emerging Latinx metropolis. Elaine Kim, one of the foremost scholars of Korean-America and Asian American literature, has articulated something that Chester Himes registered in his novels of Los Angeles: the infinite complexities of the individual identities of people often overly simplified through a racist lens. Koreans have a long and complex presence in the US, emanating as they do from one of the world's great civilizations, going back thousands of years. Today, they make up an increasing number of persons in the US, and one of the largest populations of Asian American Los Angeles. Already in the 1920s there were thousands of Koreans in the continental US, mostly in Los Angeles. By the late 1940s they had their own paper, the *Korean Independent*, left-liberal New Dealish in orientation. The paper was openly critical of the American occupation of South Korea and intervention in the Korean revolutionary and civil war.[68] The paper's politics ensured unremitting surveillance from the FBI and the LAPD. Ironically, anti-Japanese racism after Pearl Harbor was targeted too against Koreans. Elaine Kim, who like so many immigrants, wanted to be seen as American remembers being called "chink" and "Jap" and hearing others say Remember Pearl Harbor.[69]

By 1975, there were well over ten thousand Korean Americans born in the US. By the 1980s, with the critical changes in United States immigration in 1965, tens of thousands of Koreans were entering the US every year, fleeing South Korea's United States–sponsored repressive dictatorship. Yet Americans have had a kind of amnesia about the Korean War (roughly 1950–1953), so that while the famous program *MASH* (1972–1983) was set in Korea, young Americans growing up hardly realized it was about that country and war, rather than Vietnam (roughly 1955–1975).[70] By the 1990s, there were tens of thousands of Korean Americans living in Los Angeles. Their depiction as a model minority, their presence in South Los Angeles and the realities of racism and mutual misunderstanding between Korean and African Americans, sometimes led to deadly conflict. In March of 1991, an immigrant Korean female shopkeeper, Soon Ja Du, shot and killed an African American girl, Latasha Harlins, over a $1.79 bottle of orange juice. The case was brought before the courts, and Judge Joyce Karlin gave out an exceptionally light sentence, with no jail time. Especially galling to the Black community and others, was a Pacoima postal worker who got a heavier penalty, a six-month jail sentence for killing a dog, while another Korean immigrant got thirty days in jail for abusing their dog.[71] Such realities set the stage for the explosive anger in what was a multiracial riot and civic uprising. Many have chronicled just how important Latino poverty and participation was in the uprising, in a period of extensive federal disinvestment from the nation's urban areas.[72]

The 1992 protests were primarily against the LAPD, but also tragically involved the looting and burning down of stores throughout Koreatown in Los Angeles, along with random attacks against innocent motorists. There were hundreds of millions of dollars in damage to Korean-owned stores. Many saw pictures of armed Korean Americans seeking to protect their property. Many authors of the collection by Nancy Abelmann and John Lie, *Blue Dreams: Korean Americans and the Los Angeles Riots* (1995), vividly describe the anguish in the community over the riots. Yet, as Bruce Cumings points out: "Rarely if ever did any media pundit point out that the Koreans had bought their stores from African Americans, who had bought them from Jews after the Watts riots a generation earlier; or that Korean merchants were often the poorest segment of Korean business people in the United States, doing a job and providing a service that most others would reject."[73]

Only in 2017 did the film *Gook* come out, which tried to capture with empathy and complexity some of the relationships between Blacks and Korean Americans around the Los Angeles riots. This environment, akin to Hobbesian war of all against all in an increasingly ethicized polity, is poignantly depicted in the Hollywood film and related PBS documentary, *Freedom Writers* (1997, 2019), and *Freedom Writers Diary* (1999).[74] In the Hollywood version of the documentary, after violent fights between students of different ethno-racial backgrounds and a related killing outside the school comes into the classroom in the form of a racist cartoon, we hear Erin Gruwell, played by Hillary Swank, say: "So what you're saying is, if the Latinos weren't here, or the Cambodians or the blacks or the whites or whoever they are, if they weren't here, everything would be better for you, isn't that right?" Erin uses the incident to talk about the Holocaust. One courageous student raised their hand and asked, "What is that?" As Erin was to find out, none of her students had ever heard of the Holocaust but almost all of them had been shot at. Her students were struggling every day just to survive. Erin then realized that she needed to help her students see outside themselves, to understand the roots of hatred, and racism, and bring them together to create a new way forward for all of them. Erin took the students on trips, including to the Museum of Tolerance in Los Angeles, where students met actual survivors, and they began to see each other in a new way. Moreover, the legacy of this movement continues, most recently with the publication of *Dear Freedom Writer: Stories of Hardship and Hope from the Next Generation* (2022), about the coming of age of a new generation of dreams in a global pandemic.

What we witness in the films and related book, *The Freedom Writers Diary*, is an emerging portrait of a multicultural metropolis, and what will be needed in contemporary struggles for personal and social transformation, for human emancipation, and against racism. We also see the challenges that must be overcome to overturn what Jonathan Kozol calls the restoration of apartheid education in the United States.[75] This period was also time of important initiatives throughout the US in general and Los Angeles in particular. These included the Immigrant Workers Freedom Rides, and the 2006 May Day protests for immigrant rights. Here, half a million marched. Subsequently, a million participated in the Great America Strike to emphasize "No One is Illegal" and "We Are America."[76] The sanctuary movement of the 1980s was especially important for the thousands fleeing from United States funded death-squad governments and civil war in Central America. Mario Garcia has written eloquently about this, most recently in his biography *Father Luis Olivares: Faith Politics and the Origins of the Sanctuary Movement in Los Angeles* (2018). Garcia reminds us that so many fleeing to the United States are coming, not so much to pursue their American Dream, but instead to flee the nightmares of their countries, long subjected to US intervention and US support for oligarchic military rule, and from which inspiration for the solidarity movement of the 1980s grew.

Among the most poignant expressions of this sacrifice is the life and journey of Sister Dianna Ortiz, her family hailing in part from former uranium miners in the Southwest, who went on to join the Ursuline nuns, working and teaching in some of the poorest regions of Guatemala. There, Sister Dianna was kidnapped, raped, and tortured before she escaped back to the United States. Her unimaginable experience led her to try and bring attention to those who have experienced torture, and she went on to help found the Torture Abolition and Survivors Support Coalition (TASCC). Sister Dianna Ortiz's powerful memoir, *The Blindfold's Eyes: My Journey from Torture to Truth* (2002), ought to be read by every sentient being who seeks to understand the American Dream, dreams deferred, and how dreams can turn into nightmares.

Yet Sister Dianna's memoir also poignantly expresses the incredible spirit of resilience that had led increasing numbers to search for new dreams of a world without torture, racism, or misogyny, where as Dr. King said, we can provide sustenance for the body, the spirit, and the mind.

Today, Los Angeles and California show the future diversity of America. Yet they also reveal the urgent necessity of overcoming structural legacies of centuries of racism and discrimination, and soaring inequality.[77] In 2021, one of every eight persons in the United States lived in California.[78] And here, in the City of Angels, and LA County, we see the state of the dream and dreams deferred; roughly 8 percent of the population is Black, though 34 percent of this group are homeless. Moreover, this Black population is increasingly diverse, with many recent immigrants coming from Africa and the Caribbean. In fact, the diversity of a significant portion of the racial and ethnic groups currently existent in the world, exists in California. Here in Los Angeles alone, lives the largest population of people of indigenous descent, Asian American descent, and Latin@ descent in the United States, and the nation's largest immigrant population. Some communities in Los Angeles are so large and vibrant, for example, the Iranian diaspora, estimated at anywhere between 500,000 and 600,000 persons, that they now have names such as Tehrangeles, or Little Persia, including a large Sephardic Jewish Iranian population. And then there is Filipinotown, Little Armenia, Little Ethiopia, and Little Eritrea, following earlier iterations, such as America's Chinatowns, Koreatowns, Little Vietnams, and so on.[79] Not surprisingly, California and Los Angeles are the two locations that hold the majority of those roughly 11 million undocumented Americans named Dreamers, who were brought to the US as children, and have been leading the fight for citizenship rights, and thus kept with other Americans from access to the promissory note of the American Dream.[80] It is important to remember too, that many groups have and are composed of multicultural and multiracial individuals. The reality is that many children come from mixed race backgrounds, and many more of us live in "constellations of struggle" with every increasing multicultural, multiracial, and multiethnic interconnection, so here the statistics and our forms of categorization hide more complex realities. As scholars and activists are increasingly bringing to our attention, categorical classifications often miss the realities and complexities of the lived experience of our various isms, including but not limited to racism, sexism, classism, as well as our ways of forming our various identities and identifications.[81]

Perhaps the ethos of this chapter, and of our vision of California, with all its contradictions, from gang capital of the world to the possible capital of the 21st century, in a differently imagined future, is best captured by Luis Rodriguez when he asserts:

California can lead the way to truly healing, redemptive, comprehensive, and community-based efforts to turn street gangs and street violence (including domestic violence) around. It will require great imagination, intense dialogue, effective strategies, and truly liberating and inspiring arts and creative endeavors that will encompass entire communities. It must not be piecemeal, isolated, fractured, or an afterthought.

When it comes to real peace and justice in our streets and in the world, the U.S. has long been poised at a crossroads. Having missed the fork in the road a long time back, it will take an immense overhaul before we can get back on the right track. There is no doubt in my mind that we must do so.[82]

Rodriguez is saying something that is not as complicated as it may seem. Our history, the United States, and the American Dream, has been wrapped up in whiteness; historically, you become white, or as much like whiteness as you can become, to gain access to the opportunities the United States offers. Despite the increasing diversity of this place, it is still framed by a white or non-white binary. It is this binary, among other boundaries, that must be removed before we can realize anything like our potential, as a diverse nation in a diverse world. The price of the ticket to the United States, and to access to the American Dream, cannot be people repackaged in white paper, tied with a white bow. Yet even these bows are failing for more and more.

And a fork in the road suggests the kind of dialectical visions and versions of America and of the American Dream, of which we speak where, on the one hand, there is a dream steeped in the ethos of our southern historical romance, one that elides virtually anything, any place, and anyone unaligned with whiteness, and on the other hand, there is a dream steeped in the ethos of struggle and lived experience, one that embraces or at least struggles to acknowledge, reckon with, and embrace virtually anything, any place, and anyone.

For the sake of greater clarity, let us turn to James Baldwin, speaking in his role as a witness. In his 1985 essay, "The Price of the Ticket," Baldwin writes about the different trajectories of groups in the United States, and the inequalities that have been perpetuated, and the limits of the founders, who believed that "Property was more important—more real—than the possibilities of the human being." And then Baldwin says something even more profound, which he says he learned in church, which is to do your first works over, reexamine everything, to know from *"whence you came,"* something that he continues, "is precisely what the generality of white Americans cannot afford to do."

They come through Ellis Island, where *Giorgio* becomes Joe . . . Goldsmith becomes *Smith or Gold*. . . . So, with a painless change of name, and in the twinkling of an eye, one becomes a white American.

Later, in the midnight hours, the missing identity aches. One can neither assess nor overcome the storm of the middle passage. One is mysteriously shipwrecked forever, in the Great New World. . . .

The Irish middle passage, for but one example, was as foul as my own, and as dishonorable on the part of those responsible for it. But the Irish became white when they got here and began rising in the world, whereas I became black and began sinking.

. . . The price the white American paid for his ticket was to become white—: and, in the main, nothing more than that, or if he was to insist, nothing less. This incredibly limited . . . ambition has choked many a human being to death here: and this, I contend, is because the white American has never accepted the real reasons for his journey. I know very well that my ancestors had no desire to come to this place; but neither did the ancestors of the people who became white and who require of my captivity a song. They require of me a song less to celebrate my captivity than to justify their own."[83]

If we are to sing a new song, as we believe we must do, we will have to turn to some of our greatest explorers of our pasts and possible futures to understand where we came from, and where we are going. The path we have taken to achieve this is through the possibilities of multidirectional memories, with horizontal linkages oriented toward a better future as opposed to the unidirectional zero-sum memories that have largely informed our pasts. Baldwin's invocation of the costs so many have paid for their one-way ticket to the New World, both forcible and nominally voluntary, informed by this enlarged sense of what Benedict Anderson calls *Imagined Communities*, informs our passageway from past to future here. And so, we first turn in our final chapter to our recent past, and the work of August Wilson, Dinaw Mengestu, Imbolo Imbue, and Toni Morrison. Then, in the epilogue, we turn to the incomparable Black feminist Afrofuturist science fiction writer, Octavia E. Butler. For it is to Butler's parables and investigations of past, present, and possible alternative futures that we must finally turn, if there is to be any human future at all.

NOTES

1. There are already existing interrogations of the California Dream, in the literature, from Kevin Starr's Americans and the California Dream series on which we've drawn, as well as two important collections: Ingrid Banks, Gaye Johnson, George Lipsitz, Ula Taylor, Daniel Widener & Clyde Woods, eds., *Black California Dreamin': The Crisis of California's African-American Communities* (University of California, Santa Barbara, Center for Black Studies Research, 2012), and more recently, Christine Bacareza Balance & Lucy Mae San Pablo Burns, eds., *California*

Dreaming: Movement & Place in the Asian American Imaginary (Honolulu: University of Hawai'i Press, & Los Angeles: UCLA Asian American Studies Center, 2020).

2. See Dora Beale Polk, *The Island of California: A History of the Myth* (Nebraska: Bison Books, 1995). See Erwin G. Gudde, *California Place Names: The Origins & Etymology of Current Geographical Names*, 4th edition, Revised & Enlarged by William Bright (Berkeley: University of California Press, 1998). For another recent exploration of the myth, see Paul J. P. Sandul, *California Dreaming: Boosterism, Memory, and Rural Suburbs in the Golden State* (West Virginia University Press, 2014).

3. On the centrality of the frontier myth in American history, see the trilogy of Richard Slotkin, especially *The Fatal Environment: The Myth of the Frontier in the Age of Industrialization, 1800–1890* (Middletown, Connecticut: Wesleyan University Press, 1985).

4. Perry Anderson, "Force and Consent," *New Left Review* 17 (September/October 2002): 24–25. See also the important discussion in Franco Moretti, *Far Country: Scenes from American Culture* (New York: Farrar, Straus, and Giroux, 2019), 91–93.

5. Max Horkheimer and Theodor W. Adorno, *Dialectic of Enlightenment: Philosophical Fragments* (Stanford: Stanford University Press, 2002), 111.

6. See also Lynn M. Hudson, *West of Jim Crow: The Fight Against California's Color Line* (Champaign: University of Illinois Press, 2020).

7. See Jeanne Theoharis, "'Alabama on Avalon': Rethinking the Watts Uprising and the Character of Black Protest in Los Angeles," *The Black Power Movement: Re-thinking the Civil Rights-Black Power Era*, ed., Peniel E. Joseph (New York: Routledge, 2006), 27–54.

8. Gaye Theresa Johnson, Ch. 1, "Luisa Moreno, Charlotta Bass, and the Constellations of Interethnic Working-Class Radicalism," *Spaces of Conflict, Sounds of Solidarity: Music, Race, and Spatial Entitlement in Los Angeles (*Berkeley: University of California Press, 2013), 3.

9. Gaye Theresa Johnson, Ch. 1, "Luisa Moreno, Charlotta Bass, and the Constellations of Interethnic Working-Class Radicalism." *Spaces of Conflict, Sounds of Solidarity: Music, Race, and Spatial Entitlement in Los Angeles* (Berkeley: University of California Press, 2013), 4.

10. Gaye Theresa Johnson, Ch. 1, "Luisa Moreno, Charlotta Bass, and the Constellations of Interethnic Working-Class Radicalism," *Spaces of Conflict, Sounds of Solidarity: Music, Race, and Spatial Entitlement in Los Angeles* (Berkeley: University of California Press, 2013), 9.

11. Walter Mosley, *Devil in a Blue Dress* (New York: Washington Square Press, 2020), viii–ix.

12. Walter Mosley, *Devil in a Blue Dress* (New York, Washington Square Press, 2020), x. For an analysis of related themes on World War II's systems of mass production, consumption, and housing, see Donald Albrecht, *World War II and the American Dream: How Wartime Building Changed a Nation* (Washington, D.C., and Cambridge, MA: National Building Museum and MIT Press, 1995).

13. Walter Mosley, *Devil in a Blue Dress* (New York: Washington Square Press, 2020), 20.

14. Jones Jr., M. 1990. "Down and out in the City of Angels." *Newsweek* 116 (2): 65. https://sandiego.idm.oclc.org/login?url=https://search.ebscohost.com/login.aspx ?direct=true&db=aph&AN=9007091202&site=ehost-live.

15. Mary Young, "Walter Mosley, Detective Fiction and Black Culture," *Journal of Popular Culture* 32, Issue 1 (Summer 1998): 143.

16. Walter Mosley, *Devil in a Blue Dress* (New York: Washington Square Press, 2020), 28.

17. Walter Mosley, *Devil in a Blue Dress* (New York: Washington Square Press, 2020), 64.

18. Mary Young, "Walter Mosley, Detective Fiction and Black Culture," *Journal of Popular Culture* 32, Issue 1 (Summer 1998): 141–150.

19. Walter Mosley, *Devil in a Blue Dress* (New York: Washington Square Press, 2020), 76.

20. See Jeffrey Insko, "Extraction," *The Cambridge Companion to Environmental Humanities*, eds., Jeffrey Jerome Cohen and Stephanie Foote (New York: Cambridge University Press, 2021), 173–174, 183.

21. Walter Mosley, *Devil in a Blue Dress* (New York: Washington Square Press, 2020), 103–104.

22. Walter Mosley, *Devil in a Blue Dress* (New York: Washington Square Press, 2020), 121–122.

23. Walter Mosley, *Devil in a Blue Dress* (New York: Washington Square Press, 2020), 207.

24. Walter Mosley, *Devil in a Blue Dress* (New York: Washington Square Press, 1990), 194–195.

25. Walter Mosley, *Devil in a Blue Dress* (New York: Washington Square Press, 2020), 207.

26. Walter Mosley, *Devil in a Blue Dress* (New York: Washington Square Press, 2020), 209.

27. James Q. Whitman, *Hitler's American Model: The United States and the Making of Nazi Race Law* (New Jersey: Princeton University Press, 2018).

28. Walter Mosley, *Devil in a Blue Dress* (New York: Washington Square Press, 2020), 139–140.

29. Walter Mosley, *Devil in a Blue Dress* (New York: Washington Square Press, 2020), 140. See also Malachi Haim Hacohen, *Jacob & Esau: Jewish European History Between Nation & Empire* (New York: Cambridge University Press, 2019); David Sorkin, *Jewish Emancipation: A History Across Five Centuries* (New Jersey: Princeton University Press, 2019); Christopher R. Browning, *The Origins of the Final Solution* (Lincoln: University of Nebraska Press, & Jerusalem: Yad Vashem, 2004). Michael Rothberg, *Multidirectional Memory* (Stanford: Stanford University Press, 2009); Michael Rothberg, *The Implicated Subject: Beyond Victims & Perpetrators* (Stanford: Stanford University Press, 2019).

30. Roger Daniels, *Prisoners Without Trial: Japanese Americans in World War II* (New York: Hill & Wang, 2004), 64–65.

31. See Ellen M. Eisenberg, *The First to Cry Down Injustice? Western Jews & Japanese Removal During World War II* (Lanham: Lexington Books, 2008).

32. See the section on "Japanese Americans, Dorothy Day & the Catholic Worker," with Matthieu Langlois, in Greg Robinson, *The Unsung Great: Stories of Extraordinary Japanese Americans* (Seattle: University of Washington Press, 2020).

33. Mary Young, "Walter Mosley, Detective Fiction and Black Culture." *The Journal of Popular Culture* 32, Issue 1 (Summer 1998): 147.

34. Mary Young, "Walter Mosley, Detective Fiction and Black Culture." *The Journal of Popular Culture*32, Issue 1 (Summer 1998): 148.

35. M. Jones Jr., 1990. "Down and out in the City of Angels." *Newsweek* 116 (2), 65. https://sandiego.idm.oclc.org/login?url=https://search.ebscohost.com/login.aspx ?direct=true&db=aph&AN=9007091202&site=ehost-live.

36. Gaye Theresa Johnson, *Spaces of Conflict, Sounds of Solidarity: Music, Race, and Spatial Entitlement in Los Angeles* (Berkeley: University of California Press, 2013), 3, 10.

37. Gaye Theresa Johnson, *Spaces of Conflict, Sounds of Solidarity: Music, Race, and Spatial Entitlement in Los Angeles* (Berkeley: University of California Press, 2013), 11–12.

38. Born in El Paso, Texas, Luis's family moved to Watts in Los Angeles when he was two, and then they eventually moved to the San Gabriel Valley.

39. See also Nicole M. Guidotti-Hernandez, *Unspeakable Violence: Remapping U.S. & Mexican National Imaginaries* (Durham: Duke University Press, 2011).

40. Luis J. Rodriguez, *Music of the Mill* (New York: Harper Perennial, 2005), 7.

41. Luis J. Rodriguez, *Music of the Mill* (New York: Harper Perennial, 2005), 9.

42. Luis Rodriguez, "The End of the Line: California and the Promise of Street Peace." *Social Justice* 32, No. 3, 101 (2005): 18. Stable URL: https://www.jstor.org /stable/29768318.

43. Luis Rodriguez, The End of the Line: California and the Promise of Street Peace." *Social Justice* 32, No. 3, 101 (2005): 12–23. Stable URL: https://www.jstor .org/stable/29768318

44. St. Clair Drake, *The American Dream and the Negro: 100 Years of Freedom?* (Chicago, Illinois: The Emancipation Proclamation Centennial Lectures, January-February 1963), 53.

45. Quoted in Jeanne Theoharis, "'Alabama on Avalon': Rethinking the Watts Uprising & the Character of Black Protest in Los Angeles," in *The Black Power Movement: Rethinking the Civil Rights-Black Power Era*, ed., Peniel Joseph (New York: Routledge, 2006), 39.

46. See Jeanne Theoharis, "'Alabama on Avalon': Rethinking the Watts Uprising & the Character of Black Protest in Los Angeles," in *The Black Power Movement: Rethinking the Civil Rights-Black Power Era*, ed., Peniel Joseph (New York: Routledge, 2006), especially 40.

47. Diane C. Fujnio, *Ninsei Radicals: The Feminist Poetics and Transformative Ministry of Mitsuye Yamada and Michael Yasutake* (Seattle: University of Washington Press, 2020), 67–68. See also Charlotte Brooks, *Alien Neighbors, Foreign Friends: Asian Americans, Housing, & the Transformation of Urban California* (University of Chicago Press, 2009). Yamada's experiences deepened her commitment to racial justice and equality, and she became one of the poets features in the prominent collection

and foundation feminist text, *The Bridge Called My Back: Writings by Racial Women of Color* (1981, 2021), edited by Cherrie Moraga and Gloria Anzaldua. Yamada would go on to a life of poetry and activism, including founding the Multicultural Women Writers of Orange County. See also Don Parson, *Making a Better World: Public Housing, the Red Scare, and the Direction of Modern Los Angeles*, with a foreword by Kevin Starr (Minneapolis: University of Minnesota Press, 2005). See also Eric John Abrahamson, *Building Home: Howard A. Ahmanson and the Politics of the American Dream* (Berkeley: University of California Press, 2013). And see too, the very different perspective presented in Paul Adamson and Marty Arbunich, *Eichler: Modernism Rebuilds the American Dream*, with a foreword by Gwendolyn Wright (Salt Lake City: Gibbs Smith, 2002).

48. See Dan T. Carter, *The Politics of Rage* (Baton Rouge: Louisiana State University Press, 2000). See also Mike Davis, *Prisoners of the American Dream* (New York: Verso, 2018).

49. Reverend Dr. Martin Luther King Jr., "The American Dream," Ebenezer Baptist Church, Atlanta, Georgia, July 4, 1965, in *A Knock at Midnight: Inspiration from the Great Sermons of Reverend Martin Luther King, Jr.*, eds., by Clayborn Carson and Peter Holloran (New York: Time Warner, 2000), 85–100. We must mention here that in late March of 2021, Atlanta became the site of the most recent hate crimes massacre against Asian-Americans, the culmination of the resurgence of a year of hate, inspired by former President Trump's racist dubbing of the coronavirus, as the China virus. This violated World Health Organization public health protocols for naming viruses in a way that does not further racism, hatred, and discrimination. For the new diversity in the Atlanta, Georgia suburbs, see an important new voice in fiction, set both in Atlanta and in California by Sanjena Sathian, involving her own powerful meditation on the American Dream, *Gold Diggers: A Novel* (New York: Penguin Press, 2021). See also Sathian's heartfelt reflections on the massacre and its meanings, "After the Atlanta Shootings, All I See is the Fragility of Our Belonging," *Los Angeles Times* (March 18, 2021). See also *New York Times*, "An Uneasy, Brittle Birthright" Alisha Haridasani Gupta, April 3, 2021, C1, 4.

50. Martin Luther King Jr., "Beyond the Los Angeles Riots," *Saturday Review* (November 13, 1965): 33–34, 105. Mike Davis and Jon Wiener, *Set the Night on Fire: L.A. in the Sixties* (New York: Verso, 2020). See also Elizabeth Hinton, *America on Fire: The Untold Story of Police Violence & Black Rebellion Since the 1960s* (New York: Liveright, 2021).

51. Kirse Granat May, *Golden State, Golden Youth: The Image of California in Popular Culture, 1955–1966* (Chapel Hill: University of North Carolina Press, 2002).

52. For an important history of electoral disenfranchisement in the United States, see, among other sources, David A. Bateman, *Disenfranchising Democracy: Constructing the Electorate in the United States, the United Kingdom, and France* (New York: Cambridge University Press, 2018). On the subsequent struggles to overthrow the structures of oligarchical white supremacy in the South, see two critically important works, Charles M. Payne, *I've Got the Light of Freedom: The Organizing Tradition and the Mississippi Freedom Struggle* (Berkeley: University of California Press, 2007), and Robert Mickey, *Paths Out of Dixie: The Democratization of Authoritarian*

Enclaves in America's Deep South, 1944–1972 (Princeton, NJ: Princeton University Press, 2015). See also Davison Douglas, *Jim Crow Moves North: The Battle Over Northern School Segregation, 1865–1954* (New York: Cambridge University Press, 2005). See also the landmark work compiled and edited by Pauli Murray, *States' Laws on Race and* Color, with an introduction by Davison Douglas (University of Georgia Press, 2016), whose signal contributions to the antiracist and feminist movements, not to mention those for gender nonconformity, as part of efforts for human liberation, are now the subject of an important film, *My Name Is Pauli Murray* (2021), as well as a series of important books, including Rosalind Rosenberg, *Jane Crow: The Life of Pauli Murray* (New York: Oxford University Press, 2020). See also Serena Mayeri, *Reasoning from Race: Feminism, Law, and the Civil Rights Revolution* (Cambridge, MA: Harvard University Press, 2011). See also Thomas J. Sugrue, *Sweet Land of Liberty: The Forgotten Struggle for Civil Rights in the North* (New York: Random House, 2009). Brian Purnell, Jeanne Theoharis, and Komozi Woodard, eds., *The Strange Careers of the Jim Crow North: Segregation and Struggle Outside of the South* (New York: New York University Press, 2019).

53. Malcolm X, Speech in Harlem, 1964. Quoted in Jason Sokol, *All Eyes Are Upon Us* (New York: Basic Books, 2014), xix. See also Desmond King and Stephen Tuck, "De-Centering the South: America's Nationwide Supremacist Order After Reconstruction," *Past and Present* 194, Issue 1 (February 2007): 233–253.

54. Mike Davis and Jon Wiener, *Set the Night on Fire: L.A. in the Sixties* (New York: Verso, 2020), 1.

55. For the background, see Mike Davis, *Dead Cities* (New York: New Press, 2002).

56. Mike Davis, *City of Quartz* (London: Verso, 2018), 272.

57. On the background, see Mike Davis & Jon Wiener, *Set the Night on Fire: L.A. in the Sixties* (New York: Verso, 2021), Mario T. Garcia and Sal Castro, *Blowout! Sal Castro & the Chicano Struggle for Educational Justice* (Chapel Hill: University of North Carolina Press, 2011), Carlos Munoz Jr., *Youth, Identity, Power: The Chicano Movement* (New York: Verso, 2007), Rodolfo S. Acuna, *The Making of Chicana/o Studies* (New Jersey: Rutgers University Press, 2011).

58. Luis J. Rodriguez, *Music of the Mill* (New York: Harper Perennial, 2005), 68–69.

59. Luis J. Rodriguez, *Music of the Mill* (New York: Harper Perennial, 2005), 81.

60. Luis J. Rodriguez, *Music of the Mill* (New York: Harper Perennial, 2005), 82–83.

61. Luis J. Rodriguez, *Music of the Mill* (New York: Harper Perennial, 2005), 113.

62. Luis J. Rodriguez, *Music of the Mill* (New York: Harper Perennial, 2005), 207.

63. The classic study is Elana Zilberg, *Spaces of Detention: The Making of a Transnational Gang Crisis Between Los Angeles & San Salvador* (Durham: Duke University Press, 2011).

64. See Zevi Gutfreund, *Speaking American: Language Education and Citizenship in Twentieth Century Los Angeles*, (New York: Oxford University Press, 2020).

65. Luis J. Rodriguez, *Music of the Mill* (New York: Harper Perennial, 2005), 300.

66. See John H.M. Laslett, *Sunshine Was Never Enough: Los Angeles Workers, 1880–2010* (Berkeley: University of California Press, 2012).

67. Cornel West, Point Loma Nazarene, "Writers By the Sea Conference," February 25, 2022.

68. The Elaine Kim quote comes from the epigraph in Chapter 9, "America's Korea," Bruce Cumings, *Korea's Place in the Sun: A Modern History* (New York: W.W. Norton & Co., 2005) 448, and the information above comes largely from this source. See also Young-Key Kim-Renaud, R. Richard Grinker, & Kirk W. Larsen, ed., *Korean American Literature* (Washington, D.C.: George Washington University, 2004). Korea was divided by the US without consultation with Koreans in 1945, having been before then a Japanese colony since Japan's brutal conquest. See Peter Duus, *The Abacus & the Sword: The Japanese Conquest of Korea* (Berkeley: University of California Press, 1998).

69. In sadly similar ways, Sikhs and other South Asians were targeted with violent hate crimes after the terrorist attacks of September 11, 2001, and they were also victimized in yet another mass shooting in April 2021.

70. For the background, see Daniel Ellsberg, *Secrets: A Memoir of Vietnam & the Pentagon Papers* (New York: Penguin 2003), and Neil Sheehan, *A Bright Shining Lie* (New York: Vintage, 1989).

71. See *Los Angeles Times*, "Sentence Ends in Question: Dog Abuser Gets Six Months; Slayer of Black Teen Gets Probation," (Archives) (January 28, 1992). See Bruce Cumings, *Korea's Place in the Sun: A Modern History* (New York: W.W. Norton & Co., 2005), 448–469, and Brenda Stevenson, *The Contested Murder of Latasha Harlins: Justice, Gender, & the Origins of the LA Riots* (New York: Oxford University Press, 2013), from which the information in the preceding paragraphs is largely taken.

72. See Mike Davis, *Dead Cities* (New York: New Press, 2002).

73. Bruce Cumings, *Korea's Place in the Sun* (New York: W.W. Norton & Co., 2005), 463–464.

74. In the introduction to "Magical Urbanism: Latinos Reinvent the US Big City," by Mike Davis, the editors argue that the author "demonstrates that only a class-based movement can avoid the perils of an increasingly ethnicized polity." *New Left Review* 234 (March-April 1999): 2. The image of the war of all against all is famously depicted in Thomas Hobbes, *Leviathan*, 1651, written during the period of the Age of Religious Wars and the English Civil War. See Thomas Hobbes, *Leviathan* (New York: Oxford World Classics, 1996).

75. Jonathan Kozol, *The Shame of the Nation: The Restoration of Apartheid Schooling in America* (New York: Crown, 2006).

76. See Kim Voss and Irene Bloemraad, eds, *Rallying for Immigrant Rights: The Fight for Inclusion in 21st Century America* (Berkeley: University of California Press, 2006). See also Gary Y. Okihiro, *American History Unbound: Asians & Pacific Islanders* (Oakland: University of California Press, 2015), 434.

77. See Deepak Narang Sawhney, ed., *Unmasking L.A.: Third Worlds & the City* (New York: Palgrave, 2002).

78. Public Policy Institute of California, California's Population (March 2021). https://www.ppic.org/publication/californias-population/. For the national trends, see William H. Frey, *Diversity Explosion: How New Radical Demographics are Remaking America* (Washington, D.C.: Brookings, 2018). Manuel Pastor, Jennifer Ito, & Vanessa Carter, *The Next California* (April 18, 2018); Robert J. Sampson, Jared N.

Schachner & Robert D. Mare, "Urban Income Inequality & the Great Recession in Sunbelt Form," *Russell Sage Foundation Journal of the Social Sciences* 3, Issue Number 2, (February 2017): 102–128. Richard A. Walker, *Pictures of a Gone City* (Oakland: PM Press, 2018).

79. Carlene Sobrino Bonnivier, Gerald G. Gubatan & Gregory Villanueva, eds., *Filipinotown: Voices from Los Angeles* (2nd edition, 2014). Arpi Sarafian, *Endless Crossings: Reflections on Armenian Art & Culture in Los Angeles* (Tekeyan Cultural Association, 2019), and her interview with Aris Janigian, and the latter's book on the LA uprising/riots of 1992.

80. These statistics are compiled from a variety of sources, including the US Census, the US Community Survey, the LA Almanac, and USC Dornsife, Center for the Study of Immigration, State of Immigrants in LA County (2020). Interactive Map: The American Dream & Promise Act of 2019, hosted at the USC Dornsife, Equity Research Institute (2021). Sarah Abrevaya Stein & Caroline Luce, *100 Years of Sephardic Los Angeles* (Los Angeles: UCLA Leve Center for Jewish Studies, 2020).

81. Anthony Christian Ocampo, *The Latinos of Asia: How Filipino Americans Break the Rules of Race* (Stanford, CA: Stanford University Press, 2016). Mike Davis, "Magical Urbanism," *New Left Review* 234 (March/April 1999): 3–43, and his book of the same title, (New York: Verso, 2001). Richard Alba & Kenneth Prewitt, Special Editors, *The Annals of the American Academy of Political and Social Science: What Census Data Miss About American Diversity* 677 (May 2018). Victor M. Valle & Rodolfo D. Torres, *Latino Metropolis* (Minneapolis: University of Minnesota Press, 2000).

82. Luis Rodriguez, "The End of the Line: California Gangs and the Promise of Street Peace," *Social Justice* 32, No. 3 (2005): 22. See also James Diego Vigil, *A Rainbow of Gangs: Street Culture in the Mega-City* (Austin: University of Texas Press, 2002).

83. James Baldwin, *Collected Essays* (New York: The Library of America), 841–42. On the centrality of property rights over other rights in the US, see Jennifer Nedelsky, *Private Property & the Limits of American Constitutionalism* (University of Chicago Press, 1990).

Chapter 5

The Beautiful Dreams and Nightmares that America Bears

Here we investigate select works of Dinaw Mengestu, August Wilson, Toni Morrison, and Imbolo Mbue to address, yet again, Hughes' question: What happens to a dream deferred? This question resonates throughout *The Cycle Plays* of August Wilson, written between 1982 and 2005. These plays chronicle the lives of Black people in the United States, from roughly 1900 to 2000. Wilson's sweeping interrogation of Black life is paralleled in many respects by Toni Morrison's work, especially the novel *Paradise* (1997). These works end near the paths where the novels, *The Beautiful Things that Heaven Bears* (2007), by Dinaw Mengestu, and *Behold the Dreamers* (2016) by Imbolo Mbue, begin. Mengestu's text reflects the life of an Ethiopian refugee in Washington D.C., attempting to carve a space out of American Dreams, and Mbue's text looks at the lives of African immigrants from Cameroon, in New York City, working for the family of a Wall Street powerbroker.

Few efforts better articulate the dialectic we seek to encapsulate in our work than Toni Morrison's sweeping genealogy, *Paradise* (1997). *Paradise* focuses on the town of Ruby, and its nearest neighbor, a large house about seventeen miles away. The story ranges from the origins of Ruby in, roughly, the 1870s, to its near demise in the 1970s. The novel moves geographically from the south, with early days in Louisiana and Mississippi, and subsequently to the north, ending in rural Oklahoma.

Ruby is an offshoot of Haven, and Haven, representative of many primarily Black towns that sprang up in the early years of the twentieth century, only to be destroyed, turns out to not live up to its name. Indeed, Haven sounds a lot like the Greenwood neighborhood of Tulsa, Oklahoma, known as Black Wall Street, for its Black people of wealth and self-sufficiency, which was wiped from the map in 1921. Ruby springs to life out of the remnants of Haven, around 1950, in the early days of Civil Rights.

In *Paradise*, Morrison retells American and African American history, much like Ira Berlin does later in *The Making of African America: The Four Great Migrations* (2010), as a history of migrations. Indeed, as the foreword to Michel-Rolph Trouillot's *Silencing the Past: Power & the Production of History* (1995) notes, "The history of the United States is a history of migrations," and then adds, "The true history of the United States is a history of migrations. That history remains to be written," though Morrison and Berlin would soon seek to in part do just that, to tell some true stories of the United States, following the presence of Native Americans, of the subsequent history of the country as a series of ongoing migrations. Berlin goes on to cite the work of Frederick Jackson Taylor, with his myth of the frontier, and then later Oscar Handlin's work on American immigration, where the latter notes: "Once I thought to write a history of the immigrants in America. Then I discovered that the immigrants *were* American history." Yet Berlin rightly goes on to add: "Handlin's appreciation of migration as the master narrative of American history strangely was never extended to African Americans."[1]

Berlin attempts to redress this historical erasure by chronicling the African American or Black experience though what he calls "the four great migrations," the first one being "the transatlantic passage," where West African chiefdoms sold enslaved Africans to Europeans in exchange for guns and supplies, as part of the transatlantic slave trade. The second great migration was the "passage to the interior," and the third was "the passage to the North," or what was known as the Great Black Migration. The fourth great migration is the too little understood story of the vast flows of migration of foreign-born Blacks to the United States after the passage of the 1965 immigration act. Starting slowly but reaching some 900,000 Black immigrants from the Caribbean and 400,000 from Africa in the 1990s, these new arrivals from Africa and the diaspora now totaled over a quarter of the entire Black population of the U.S. Black Americans too is increasingly "becoming an immigrant society."[2] This fourth global great migration we take up later in Dinaw Mengestu's *The Beautiful Things that Heaven* Bears, with the story of Ethiopian migration to the US, and in Imbolo Mbue's *Behold the Dreamers* (2010), chronicling immigrant journeys from Cameroon to the US.

While Berlin chronicles the unique trajectory of those kidnapped in Africa who survived the transatlantic passage and beyond through successive migrations, and Mengestu and Mbue take up the fourth of these migrations, Toni Morrison's strategy in her novel *Paradise* is different, and returns us to that grand African American theme taken up by Bob Marley, of the biblical Old Testament tale of Exodus. Morrison takes the actual historical tale of what were called the Exodusters, those families escaping the dashed hopes and American Dreams that emanated from the violent defeat of Black Reconstruction, into account. As Nell Irvin Painter notes:

The Exodusters came from Tennessee, Texas, Mississippi, and Louisiana. They were Black tenant farmers, freed from slavery only to be made victim of a more insidious bondage: a vicious credit system that kept them in unrelenting poverty; systematic violence aimed at preventing them from exercising their civil rights; the return of Democratic state governments denying them any of the benefits of Reconstruction; and the refusal, by statute and common agreement among white men, to sell or lease land to Black people, land that was basic to any real independence from their former masters and overseers. And so, in the spring of 1879, they fled by the thousands—to the one sure promised land they knew: the Kansas of John Brown, the quintessential free state.[3]

Yet rather than stay true to the actual historical tale, within which as far as we know many of the migrants, who were relatively light-skinned, moved to places like Kansas, and Oklahoma, often going through St. Louis, Missouri, Morrison instead imagines a community where formerly enslaved persons, and in Morrison's tale, of extremely Black rather than light complexion, founded communities and aimed to keep them intact.

Morrison examines the implications of that choice to keep a group intact, and the foundations on which such an act might be shaped. The core foundation of each move, each migration, and each new settlement, is that said foundation is not new, is in fact a reiteration of what forms of community have come before; this is to say that each movement and settlement is founded on some form of virulent containment, exploitation, and exclusion. The resulting internal configuration of this trinity, or what issues from it, is a world in which one has: the owners (white, landed, male generally), and the owned (non-white, without property, non-male generally), or, put in other terms, those who possess, and those who are dispossessed. So, we started with the founding fathers of the United States, from which then issued the founding fathers of Haven, who, in journeying forth freed, at least in theory, from the bonds of slavery, sought to establish along with other freed people places in which they could live, only to find themselves excluded from these new communities because they were too dark, even for other dark people. They continued moving north, finally establishing Haven.

Deacon provides our first glimpse of Haven's history.[4] Against a backdrop of struggle and destruction, Haven functions as a protected space. Tulsa has been bombed.[5] The stock market has crashed.[6] Haven remains secure during and after the last of these events, around 1932, precisely because it exists as a place in which Haven is what it imagines itself to be. As Deacon recalls, "families shared everything, made sure no one was short. . . . Having been refused by the world in 1890 on their journey to Oklahoma, Haven's residents refused each other nothing, were vigilant to any need or shortage."[7] Thus,

Haven unfolds out of rejection and hardship and is formed in and informed by sharing. No one is refused, left short, or disallowed, initially.[8]

Their travel north is in some part prompted by advertisements, invitations really, to join in the construction of Black towns springing up around the 1920s.[9] One advertisement reads "Come prepared or Not at All," and the founders of Haven and Ruby came prepared, to their way of thinking, being intelligent, hardworking, and enterprising. But they were to discover that white and Black people rejected their kind of Blackness. The advertisement proves to be no more than an open invitation to a place that is not, well, open. The historian Mychal Odom calls such a provocation an intentional misrepresentation of inclusivity, a term that may be all too fittingly representative of what the American Dream has become, or has always been. These are the American Nightmares of American Dreams; they are not separate from, but integral parts of each other.

Haven's founders, conceived and nourished by their rejection from place after place, give birth to places similar in distance and difference from the places that gave birth to them. They seek a haven, a safe and protected space, and they build one briefly, that is all too soon destroyed. The wars waged by the free against the enslaved, the wealthy against the impoverished, the white against the black, morph into the "light skinned against black."[10] Differences proliferate, and the fight to bridge differences seems to make little difference. As Pat remarks concerning the founders of Haven and Ruby, including one named Zechariah:

> Oh, they knew there was a difference in the minds of whites, but it had not struck them before that it was of consequence, serious consequence, to Negroes themselves. . . . The sign of racial purity they had taken for granted had become a stain. The scattering that alarmed Zechariah because he believed it would deplete them was now an even more dangerous level of evil, for if they broke apart and were disvalued by the impure, then, certain as death, those ten generations would disturb their children's peace throughout eternity.[11]

Disallowing is the term Ruby's leading members use to capture this process of reiterative differentiation and disconnection. They are rejected during Reconstruction, rejected on the way to Oklahoma, and rejected again after they returned from World War II. As Pat notes, those who returned

> saw what had become of Haven, heard about the missing testicles of other colored soldiers; about medals being torn off by gangs of rednecks and Sons of the Confederacy—and recognized the Disallowing. . . . So, they did it again. . . . They consolidated the 8-rock blood and . . . moved farther west.[12]

Ruby takes its shape from the sign of exclusion, of disallowing, negating the chance that it might open its arms to embrace others. In fact, they now follow an inverse model of the nation's founding fathers choosing Blackness and property as their criteria for inclusion, rather than whiteness and property.

The founding fathers of Haven, twin brothers, primarily identified by the names Coffee and Tea, fell out with each other. The catalyzing event here is that when confronted by white men who threatened them with violence if they did not dance for them, Tea started shuffling, while Coffee stood his ground, taking a bullet in the foot for his blatant disregard of white power, and a metaphorical bullet to the heart from his twin brother.[13] They went their separate ways soon thereafter from Haven, which was no more a Haven, some presumably with Tea, who we lose sight of until the book's end, and others with Coffee. Coffee heads further north, and further consolidates its Blackness, becoming, or seeing itself as being, eight-rock Black, or pure Black.

Coffee and his community then found Ruby, a town named after his progeny, his daughter, and led by his sons, aptly named Deacon and Steward. The bulk of the text follows the town of Ruby. The evidence of its purity is always marked and marred by the desired absence of the always present, not Black enough, other, which, thus, sets up its pure paradise as an open-ended, perpetual war. No wonder then that Morrison's first name for the book, *Paradise*, was war. It is this configuration, along with devotion to the concept of property that sets the groundwork for the town of Ruby's virulent response to the Mansion near it, and its troubled sense of itself, its internal animosity towards and vigilance concerning those aspects of itself that are presumably assimilated, contained, but which are, by their very designation, always already potential sites of disruption.

A crucial element here is the profound intersectional linkages between racism and sexism, involving control over bodies, especially women's bodies, in the history of the United States and in *Paradise*. The Founding Fathers thought of themselves as free white men, and as regards women, as one leading jurist noted, as such, they had "no *political relation* to the *state* any more than an *alien*."[14] In *Women's War: Fighting & Surviving the American Civil War* (2019) Stephanie McCurry writes:

> At the very moment when slavery was permanently destroyed, and the US government moved to incorporate 4 million people of African descent into the nation, it took care to shore up and extend the institution of marriage. An act as radical as emancipation was unthinkable without the anchoring order, yoking men to the responsibilities of husbands, and subjecting women to the authority of particular men. It was virtually a condition of emancipation that slave husbands would assume the responsibility. Slavery had been built into the very foundation of the republic since its inception. In 1865, Republicans abandoned

one kind of property in persons while clinging desperately to another. Freedom
was unimaginable without marriage—a conclusion confirmed by the simultaneous debate over the Thirteenth Amendment.[15]

Thus, as African Americans won rights to freedom and citizenship, women
lost ground in light of "powerful new impediments to any serious reconceptualization of women's political identity and standing in the nation."[16] Not
surprisingly, Ruby's issues are almost always concerns with men and women
who bring into the town what it does not want seen there, or near there:
Roger Best who marries a light (possibly white) woman; the women who
are thought to be safe there, but are more accurately thought of as domesticated; and the women nearby in the Mansion, beyond the control of men,
anywhere. These internal disruptions, or potential disruptions, lead to the
Mansion's evisceration.

The path taken here is intended to show that configurations of community (the concept or ideal) and communities (the ideal solidified, made real)
builds exclusion into itself, here, on the basis of race and sex, overrides key
social institutions, such as family and religion, writes an exclusionary idealized history, idolizes equality as it actualizes inequality, assumes purity as it
obfuscates a necessary impurity, thereby gutting the very dream systemati-
cally and systemically, as it takes shape. Put in other terms, it is always under
construction, because it is always already under deconstruction. In virtually
each moment when some form of paradise is at hand some form of warfare
ensues enhanced within a kind of visceral, surreal dreamscape, or topography.
The first instance of such is of course within the opening scenes of the novel
where the men from Ruby invade the Mansion: "One of them, the youngest,
looks back, forcing himself to see how the dream he is in might go. The shot
woman, lying uncomfortably on marble, waves her fingers at him—or seems
to. So, his dream is doing okay, except for its color. He has never before
dreamed in colors such as these: imperial black sporting a wild swipe of red,
then thick, feverish yellow. Like the clothes of an easily had woman."[17]

Another such moment appears near the novel's end, but is, in cyclical
fashion, another view of the invasion, bringing the book's circularity again
into focus. In this latter instance, we see the aftermath of this event through
the eyes of Reverend Richard Misner and his love interest, Anna, who, having been traveling together elsewhere during the Mansion's invasion, and
troubled upon their return by the explanation given of the disappearance of
its inhabitants, decided to take a look.[18] It was here toward the end of their
examination, upon Misner's return from seeing what was still salvageable
from the Mansion's once extensive, now neglected garden:

It was when he returned, as they stood near the chair . . . that they saw it. Or sensed it, rather, for there was nothing to see. A door, she said later. "No, a window," he said, laughing. "That's the difference between us. You see a door; I see a window."[19]

Yet again, the colors deepen, the shapes sharpen; different visions of the same scene are seen; and sensibilities waver and waft as if blown by a soft wind. We are in something akin to a dreamscape again. What follows in the thoughts of Misner, at the funeral of the child Save-Marie soon after this moment, on the men of Ruby confirms this rendition: "They think they have outwitted the whiteman when in fact they imitate him. . . . How exquisitely human was the wish for permanent happiness, and how thin human imagination became trying to achieve it. . . . How can they hold it together . . . this hard-won heaven defined only by the absence of the unsaved, the unworthy and the strange?"[20] Here where wishes convey dreams, and dreams enfold wishes, Misner reveals what dreams, American Dreams, too often conceal: the thinness of the dream, its lack of substance, which is also perhaps its appeal; it promises us much but offers us, by way of substance or sustenance, very little, which is why it is so often invoked and so seldom revealed as a living non-ethereal thing.

Morrison doesn't leave us entirely in this devastated and devastating state, for when Misner begins to conclude this eulogy, he sees something he has seen before: "Misner repressed a sigh before concluding his remarks with prayer, but when he bowed his head and gazed at the coffin lid he saw the window in the garden, felt it beckon toward another place—neither life nor death—but there, just yonder, shaping thoughts he did not know he had."[21] These thoughts included the idea that Save-Marie's life was so well enfolded in love and care that "the dreams, the visions she had, the journeys she took made her life as compelling, as rich, as valuable as any of ours and probably more blessed," following which, Morrison takes us through that window he saw in the Mansion's garden and recalled in the closing moments of his remarks, to a place where Gigi, one of the Mansion's former residents, meets what appears to be her formerly incarcerated father, with whom she had long since lost touch.[22] Dee Dee (Divine True Love) has taken up (or is continuing) painting, in some living room somewhere, when Pallas True Love, her daughter, with whom she has fallen out over a man, shows up outside with a little fat-legged baby in a knapsack strapped across her chest, "One hand on the knapsack bottom, the other carrying a sword. A sword?"[23] Pallas shows up again, in a bedroom of the house this time, where her and her daughter's contested lover slept, picks up a pair of shoes, and walks out the door, gets into a car, and drives off "into a violet so ultra it broke her heart," bringing the aforementioned surreal topography into view, as well as the presence of a heart that can still be broken.[24] Sally Albright pops up walking the street of a town fairly certain that she has spotted her mother, Mavis, sitting at a table in an inn. Seneca also appears in these closing pages, as does one of the most beautiful and profound scenes ever written.

Paradise (that fictive ideal, that Dream) ends where Paradise (as war, how such an ideal is understood and experienced) begins. In some part, this way of being and seeing ourselves must be what Misner meant when invoking the thinness of human imagination. And yet, still, *Paradise* (the novel) ends, where Paradise begins.[25] A woman, "black as firewood," a color and a substance similar to the 8-rock darkness of Ruby's leading inhabitants, holds the head of a woman with tea brown hair on her lap. A mutual admiration seems expressed in the embrace of the Black women and in the gaze of the woman with tea brown hair. And then there is the younger woman's face infused with the panorama of colors extant in a seashell. The colors named specifically, "wheat, roses, pearl," provoke an image of light pastels of the women that in memory Deacon and Steward hold dear. Emerald eyes bring someone like Consolata into this panorama. This moment is not ambivalent, the scene set in it is. "Going home to be at home" and "coming back to love" that which, and those who, are already, love. What is significant here is her connection, link, and interaction with the Black faced woman framed in blue. What is visible is their adoration for each other in this sea-framed place. They sit among the gleaming sea trash, among the discarded evidence of a surrounding world, both treasure and trash. Piedade's song evokes a solace—an alleviation of grief or anxiety—that they share along with memories they do not have. It speaks of memories not of their making, in but not of their minds, souls, and bodies: of growing together, of shared language and warm bread. Of having a home and of being at home with one's others.

Certainly, some in this tale seek some form of material prosperity, but what Morrison makes clear is that such desires are not of primary concern in the Mansion. What is desired is that ability to grow, or progress, to develop, unimpeded "by social orders which had developed for the benefit of" particular people, instead of for all people.[26] Indeed, one can read this book as a chronicle of impediments that issue out of social orders designed to benefit some and impede others. And this is the story told time and time again by August Wilson in his Cycle Plays, starting with *Jitney* (1979), and ending with *Radio Golf* (2005).

August Wilson graced our lives through his living, physical presence from 1945 to 2005. Born of a Black mother and white father, he lived his life ensconced in Black life, courtesy of being raised primarily by his mother, in the Hill district of Pittsburgh, Pennsylvania. Educated, much like the writer James Baldwin in the school of the public library, having found the traditional educational system provided him inadequate to the task, Wilson ultimately transitioned educationally, artistically, politically, and socially to the Black

Arts and Black Power movements of the 1960s and 1970s, finding a solidi-fying foundation in these movements, and developing relationships with the likes of personages like Amiri Baraka (aka LeRoi Jones), who Wilson cred-ited as one of his greatest influences. Ironically, Baraka's artistic trajectory moved from playwright to poet, while Wilson's artistic trajectory moved from poet to playwright. In her interview with August Wilson, visible in the Poetry Foundation's archives, Ruth Graham shares an edited segment of a conversa-tion she had with Chuck Smith, a longstanding director of Wilson's plays, who rightly notes that: "In a sense, they are both writers for social change, for social justice. There is always an element of social justice in all of August's works. Not so much that it is a protest play, but what you do is you see the situation as it really is, from the eyes of the African American, from an ordi-nary man, an everyman perspective. . . . Baraka . . . he was pretty much in your face with it. August Wilson is not in your face. August Wilson is much more subtle, and it comes at you in a different way."[27]

Consider this theme of a writer portraying whatever situation "as it really is, from the eyes of the African-American, from an ordinary man, an every-man" point of view throughout the remainder of this commentary. Note the connection, if you will, of the African American, with the ordinary man, with every man. Put in different terms, Wilson was concerned to portray the particularities of Black life in terms of the ways in which such particularities share in and are shared by other men, everywhere. This is not to exclude the presence of women and others for whom these designations are inadequate; it is to say that his vision focuses on what he felt he knew best, allowing even then that the most powerful presence across his plays is a woman, Aunt Ester, while also acknowledging that there are far more men than women in his vision, and that other sexes and genders are not readily evident. Within this frame, however, allow us to stress that Wilson's efforts were, in his own words, which he shares in the following interview with Bill Moyers, intent to place the particularities of the Black experience in the then oft heralded frame of universalities which suffused the worlds of art and culture in much of the twentieth century.[28] Moyers asks Wilson how it was possible he could be brought to tears watching the play *Fences*, given that the play articulates the Black experience. The question might be rephrased as, why can I as a white man, with different cultural experiences, be moved by this play about Black life? Wilson responds: "I try to explore in terms of the life I know best those things that are common to all cultures."[29]

Wilson's Cycle Plays are much more than an excavation of Black lives across the decades that constitute the twentieth century. They are also a chronicle of decades of disappointment and despair against the backdrop of racism that permeates Black life within the United States, ensuring limited success in some cases, and no progress in others, always with a ray of hope in the end. Hope is found in the presence of persistence, and this persistence is seen in the undaunted although beleaguered Black presence. Also, we see this persistence in Aunt Ester, that maternal figure who serves as a material, if often ethereal, manifestation of a spiritual connection linking past Black lives to possible futures through its ever-present roughly 300-year presence.

The Cycle Plays chronicle a decade of Black life in the twentieth century, starting with *Gem of the Ocean* (2006), set in 1904, but spanning backwards in time to set sail with Aunt Ester and others in their journey in the holds of slave ships across what Paul Gilroy has called the Black Atlantic. Wilson continues the journey of these characters on land through the Underground Railroad that brought a number of the enslaved from the south to northern states where they could exist within some less restrictive form of enslavement. We know the narrative goes that these formerly enslaved people came north to freedom, but the reality is a bit more complicated than the notion of freedom permits. While many did indeed escape the bondage of legal enslavement, which held sway in the south, they found something layered within their legal freedom in the north, an accompanying social and economic bondage, which left them not actually free. They paid an extraordinary price for the ticket, to use the language of James Baldwin, and found that while they may have been delivered from legal slavery, they were not delivered from the evils of white supremacy and Black subjugation.

Gem of the Ocean, set in the Hill district of Pittsburgh, Pennsylvania, and centered within Aunt Ester's house at 1839 Wylie Avenue (a house number that sparks connections to the Trail of Tears, and the *Amistad* slave revolt of 1839), begins a litany of sorrows and troubles, in the light of some redemptive potential. Here, relying on Octavia Butler's *Parable of the Talents* to frame this redemptive potential, we get a view of such rooted in another biblical assertion, one in which one is told to render unto Caesar the things that are Caesar's, and unto God the things that are God's (Mark 12:17). We find that Caesar, the aptly named local Black authority on the Hill, offers Citizen, newly arrived from Alabama, and seeking the solace he has heard that Aunt Ester can offer, a quarter, and the adage, "I'm gonna see what you do. You turn that twenty-five cents into five dollars and you come and see me and I'll give you a job."[30] Citizen does not want Caesar's money, however; he wants something for the soul, not the pocket, and he may be as aware as we are by this time in the play that both Caesar and the God that Caesar's people created want something in return.

What they discover is that Caesar wants his cut, and his cut may well leave you with less than nothing; as Citizen notes, getting money is much less of a problem than keeping it, although getting money can be a problem too. Citizen says, when Aunt Ester asks him if he has ever had enough money, and his answer is not just no, not right now, but no, always, past, present, and from the looks of it, future. And Citizen ain't just whistling Dixie; he speaks from experience. In his most recent experience, he and a friend went to the local mill seeking work, and find it; Citizen tells Aunt Ester: "They say they was paying two dollars a day but when we got there they say a dollar fifty. Then they say we got to pay two dollars room and board. They sent us over to a place the man say we got to put two dollars on top of that. . . . Come payday they give me three dollars say the rest go on my bill."[31] Add to this equation another two dollars for the landlord, and Citizen walks with a dollar for his work. Assuming payday is once a week, and he worked a full seven days, Citizen earned ten dollars and fifty cents, and walked with one dollar, which in today's numbers amounts to making something like two hundred and eighty dollars, out of which he pockets twenty-eight bucks. That sounds like some pure dogshit, metaphorically speaking, which, it turns out, is not much different than the pure dog shit Solly, another character in the text, our local traveling salesman, is literally, not metaphorically, selling. In fact, to Solly, the pure, as he calls it, is too valuable to him to leave on the porch, so he brings it with him into Aunt Ester's house.[32] As he tells Black Mary, pure dog shit is worth something, "It's pure!" Solly replies, "It's called pure! They got pure collectors all over the world. People been collecting pure for four hundred years. . . . Anybody would steal it. Look here. (pulls some money out of his pocket) Where you think this comes from? It come from this basket of pure. People will kill people over money."[33] And indeed they have done, and they do just that. When pure is as valuable, in both its metaphoric and material forms, if not more valuable, than a person's life, we are all in for some serious trouble. This thought guides the remainder of the play's motion.

As the play closes, we learn that Aunt Ester has been charged with aiding and abetting a criminal, Alfred, aka Two Kings, and Solomon, known also as Solly, who ended up burning down the mill. Caesar shoots and kills Solly. Aunt Ester is in trouble with the law, and Black Mary comes to an instructive realization. Black Mary says to Caesar, who is also her brother, the following:

Caesar I gave you everything. . . . I turned my eyes away. I figured if I didn't see it I couldn't hold fault. If I held fault I couldn't hold on to my love for you. But now you standing in the light and I can't turn away no more. I remember you when you was on the other side of the law. . . . The one selling hoecakes off the back of a wagon. The one that helped Mrs. Robinson and the kids when nobody else would. . . . The one who used to get out of bed to take me to school. The one who believed everybody had the same right to life . . . the same right to whatever there was in life they could find useful. That's my brother. I don't know who you are. But you not my brother.[34]

Notice that the brother on the wrong side of the law, but on the right side of this wrong, cares for others, more than he cares for law or money, shares what little he has from hustling with others, goes out of his way to help his sister; that brother who believes in equity and equality, that brother has gone and been replaced by someone, something, she doesn't know or wish to know as in any way related to her. This division between Caesar and Black Mary, between what is legal and what's right, between being legally free but bound socially and economically, follows us throughout the corpus of Wilson's work, work that says, from beginning to the end, we are in a war here, but that as long as we are in a war, we are still here, we have not been taken over, we have not given in. And we are not yet free. Eli entombs Solly with words that speak eloquently to this subject position:

> They laid him low. Put him in the cold ground. . . . Solly never did find his free-dom. He always believed he was gonna find it. The battlefield is always bloody. Blood here. Blood there. Blood over yonder. Everybody bleeding. Everybody been cut and most of them don't even know it. But they bleeding just the same. It's all you can do sometime just to stand up. Solly stood up and walked.
>
> He lived in truth and he died in truth. He died on the battlefield. You live right you die right.[35]

Part of living right might require some knowledge or clarity about the meaning of the terms upon which we place so much faith, and accord so much weight, without any clear sense of what they mean ideally, but, and perhaps more importantly, what is done with them, how they work, in the material world. Here, in a conversation between Eli, Aunt Ester's gatekeeper or protector, Citizen, and Solly on freedom, we hear the following:

> Solly: The people think they in freedom. That's all my daddy talked about. He died and never did have it. I say I got it but what is it? I'm still trying to find out. It ain't never been nothing but trouble.
>
> Eli: Freedom is what you make it.
>
> Solly: That's what I'm saying. You got to fight to make it mean something. All it mean is you got a long row to hoe and ain't got no plow. Ain't got no seed. Ain't got no mule. What good is freedom if you can't do nothing with it.[36]

Solly, yet again, the voice of reason, asks a question of deep import, not only in the play, but concerning our lives in the United States, and elsewhere. Freedom is not free, we learn. It must be accompanied by some means of achieving something of substance from it, and one must have some way of utilizing it, otherwise it is just an empty word. Here, the parable of the sower from the Bible, Mark 4:3–41, comes to mind, in an intriguing form. This parable, which Octavia Butler takes up in her novel of the same name, and which we approach in the epilogue, concerns what happens to seed sown by a sower. Some end up being eaten by birds, some fall on shallow ground where they cannot take root, some fall among other plants that choke out their life, and some, finally, fall on good soil, where they can find root before they are eaten, grow without being hampered, and produce fruit. If, however, the sower has nothing to sow, no hoe, plow, or mule to help prepare the soil for the seed, one is without the necessary tools to do what is necessary to sow seed in any way that might help ensure one will have something to harvest, and even a harvest worth having. Dreaming of a harvest, much like dreaming of being free, only takes one so far. For the dream, the idea, the ideal to take on some material form of existence requires something more than the dream, idea, or ideal itself; it requires, first, some knowledge about what these concepts mean, "you got to fight to make it mean something," and you have got to have the tools necessary to help that dream bear fruit.

Wilson echoes these themes in the introduction to his play *Fences*, noting:

> Near the turn of the century, the destitute of Europe sprang on the city with tenacious claws and an honest and solid dream. The city devoured them. . . . They city grew. It nourished itself and offered each man a partnership limited only by his talent, his guile, and his willingness and capacity for hard work. For the immigrants of Europe, a dream dared and won true.
>
> The descendants of African slaves were offered no such welcome or participation. They came from places called the Carolinas and the Virginias, Georgia, Alabama, Mississippi, and Tennessee. They came strong, eager, searching. The city rejected them and they fled and settled along the riverbanks and under bridges in shallow, ramshackle houses made of sticks and tar-paper. They collected rags and wood. They sold the use of their muscles and their bodies. They cleaned houses and washed clothes, they shined shoes, and in quiet desperation and vengeful price, they stole, and lived in pursuit of their own dream.[37]

Wilson's tales are tales of survival, tales of attempts to survive. Equally as important, though, is not simply survival, but how we do so and at what cost to our humanity, the human soul. Aunt Ester affirms the importance of this question, in conversation with Citizen, speaking with regard to the man accused of stealing nails from the nearby mill, which Citizen stole. Citizen is charged with apprehending the man, but the man makes a last stand in the river and ends up drowning. In a conversation with Citizen concerning this event, Aunt Ester states, like Solly above, "I'd rather die in truth than to live a lie."[38] And she reiterates, almost verbatim, the following words that we hear from Solly: "If you live right, you die right."[39]

Hope springs from these words. Living right would address numerous ills inflicted on ourselves and others. Living right would create a pattern of good deeds in the world. Hope also springs from the indomitable human spirit, that spirit that moves through us, across time and space, leaving us still standing, year after year, decade after decade, life after life. In the words of Aunt Ester, rebuking Caesar for desecrating her house in coming to arrest her, she tells him: "A man will come and look at the stars. . . . You can shoot him but sooner or later somebody gonna come and stand in the same spot. He's gonna come and stand and *count* the stars. Black Mary put that pot on and bring Mr. Caesar some tea."[40] Magnanimous until the end, and in every way possessed of one simple truth, they were still there, and would be there again.

And yet it is also true, that if you want beans and you plant wheat, or you want corn and you plant beans, you will not most likely get the crop you want. These analogies are meant to suggest that what one desires requires some thought about what one should plant, and no matter what you plant, you might want to give some serious consideration to how, where, and when you plant. This latter consideration, of the ground in which you plant, might be considered analogous to our history and memory, for the future is undoubtedly shaped by the past, is in fact the past revealed, the harvest of a previous planting. August Wilson was assuredly attuned to this way of framing existence, as evident in his speech, "The Ground on Which I Stand" (1996), before the Theatre Communications Group's (TCG) National Conference at Princeton University, which is, in many respects, a manifesto. Here, early on, Wilson remarks: "I have come here today to make a testimony, to talk about the ground on which I stand and all the many grounds on which I and my ancestors have toiled, and the ground of theater on which my fellow artists and I have labored to bring forth its fruits, its daring and its sometimes lacerating, and often healing, truths."[41] Wilson's repeated use of the term, ground, as well as his selection of the terms "toiled" and "labored" to locate his work as issuing from his ancestors, and that work combined as intended to "bring forth its fruits," fitfully carries forward a parable, a story, a metaphor; what makes this statement so riveting is that said fruit is not here the kind of bounty one might normally associate with a harvest. Here, much like what Wilson invokes through Solly, the harvest is of "its daring and its sometimes lacerating, and often healing, truths." This "is the ground of the affirmation of the value of one being, an affirmation of his worth in the face of society's urgent and sometimes profound denial," points on which our book is built, as an excavation of life in the United States that seeks to reveal the profound presence of so much human life, and life wasted, not given the chance the American Dream promises to flourish, that is so often concealed. Wilson asserts that the abuses of human life so evident in Black enslavement, segregation, and the many and varied racist ways in which race has been used:

That this abuse of opportunity and truncation of possibility is continuing and is so pervasive in our society in 1996 says much about who we are and much about the work that is necessary to alter our perceptions of each other and to effect meaningful prosperity for all. The problematic nature of the relationship between white and black for too long led us astray from the fulfillment of our possibilities as a society. We stare at each other across a divide of economics and privilege that has become an encumbrance on black Americans' ability to prosper and on the collective will and spirit of our national purpose.[42]

This latter sentence is a profound summation of Wilson's work, each play in some way offering a means of bridging this divide we stare across, by offering to each of us a way to see ourselves in the characters and stories provided. They also, ironically, tell a story of what is seen, when one looks back, as the side of this divide most heard in our world are those of high social and economic standing; one then gets to look at who looks back, and what, and where, and when, and why.

If we stand on the shores of the Black Atlantic in *Gem of the Ocean*, it may be useful to ask where we stand in Wilson's final play in the cycle, *Radio Golf.* The answer is a different historical moment, with different characters, with what most would see as respectable middle- and upper-class jobs and aspirations, scenes that seem a far cry from the world of *Gem of the Ocean.* The cultural scene moves from one in which jobs are scarce and money is tight, to one in which Black people in the business and political worlds seem to be doing alright. And yet, money, as Aunt Ester put it in *Gem of the Ocean*, is still something people cannot seem to get enough of, and there is still a world in which the line between what is legal and what is right remains contentious. Money problems start *Radio Golf,* and legal problems end it. Aunt Ester's house, the place of sanctuary, is slated by the city and its business leaders for demolition, urban renewal functions as urban removal. In the case of Aunt Ester's house, one of her descendants, originally onboard with its demise, has a change of heart, begins to wonder if what is being lost is worth that which is supposedly being gained, and decides the house is worth keeping after all, to the dismay of those around him, including his business partners, the city officials of Pittsburgh, and even his wife.

Harmond: Here I'll give you twenty-six dollars but we're going to tear down the house. The matter is already settled.

Sterling: That ain't right.

Harmond: Rightly or wrongly we're going to tear down the house.

Sterling: Wait a minute . . . wait a minute . . . say that again. Did I hear that shit right? "Rightly or wrongly" you're going to tear down Mr. Barlow's house. "Rightly or wrongly"? It don't matter to you if it's wrong?

Harmond: I didn't say it didn't matter to me.

Sterling: It's got to matter. If it don't matter then nothing don't work. If nothing don't work than life ain't worth living. See you living in a world where it don't matter. But that's not the world I live in. The world I live in right is right and right don't wrong nobody.[43]

Turns out that Harmond and Old Joe are related. Harmond is the grandson of Caesar Wilks, and, as you may recall, Caesar had a sister named Black Mary, well, a half-sister one might say, as they shared the same father but had different mothers. And the name of their father, Henry Samuels, appears to be the name of Old Joe's grandfather, I say appears because we are never explicitly told. What we see instead is the following exchange between Harmond and Old Joe:

Harmond: My grandfather was named Caesar Wilks and he had a sister named Black Mary. They had different mothers but they had the same father. I know the name of their father. Do you know the name of your Grandfather?

Old Joe: Yeah. But I ain't gonna tell you. But I'll write it down. You write it down, too.

They each write the name on a piece of paper. They recognize that this is one of the important moments of their lives in which everything may change for them. They exchange what they've written. Old Joe waits to find out the truth. Harmond looks at the paper and smiles broadly as he reads:

Harmond: Henry Samuels.

Old Joe looks at the paper in his hand. Harmond goes and wraps Old Joe in his arms. The lights go down on the scene.[44]

Old Joe's mother is Black Mary, and Harmond's grandfather is Black Mary's brother, Caesar. It also seems as though Black Mary took on Aunt Ester's name, and took over the house, continuing its tradition as a sanctuary, upon the former Aunt Ester's demise. Black Mary, the young woman we met in *Gem of the Ocean*, who disowned her brother for killing Solly, for his adherence to what is legal over what is right, dropped her given name, Black Mary, and took on the name of Aunt Ester, Ester Tyler. As Old Joe tells it: "She didn't tell nobody what that was. Now that she is dead I guess it don't matter. When you dead you done. Her birth name was Black Mary." He is right and wrong. For both Harmond and Old Joe, even Old Joe's mother, Black Mary, also, are living embodiments of what and who once was, the living presence of the past in the future's present. Dead does not mean done, does not mean gone, does not mean it does not matter. Old Joe takes on the role of seer, in this respect, the living embodiment of Aunt Ester, when he tells Harmond earlier in the play after Harmond admonishes him to stop painting Aunt Ester's house, an act for which he has been sanctioned, Old Joe responds: "I ain't painting the house. That was yesterday. Today's today. Tomorrow's been following me for a long time. Everywhere I go it follows me. It ain't caught me yet. Today's faster than tomorrow. Some places it's still yesterday."[45] These statements suggest that the future is as much in the past, as the past is in the future. That the present is but a fleeting refrain. And that in each frame, past, present, and future, in the United States, Black people stand and build on untenable soil, on shifting sand; and that the American Dream is yet still deferred, for Black and white people, for Wilson was both, in the United States.

The text *The Beautiful Things That Heaven Bears* (2007) by Dinaw Mengestu offers a fitting tribute to Wilson's work, in that the dreams of its central characters are also deferred. The text, an exquisite and yet melancholy reading, provides a strong critique of the American Dream. Stephanos provides the leading narrative voice in Mengestu's novel. Stephanos is an Ethiopian immigrant that leaves his homeland after his father is killed. What is particularly haunting about the text is that Stephanos has a particularly dislocated and disembodied identity. He is a political refugee that cannot return home, and still, he cannot establish a home with any meaning in this country. He is a ghost at the margins of society. His store serves the other residents that exist, and then disappear, on the fringes of Washington, D.C.

Ironically, the protagonist's longing for a family and a home become the driving force of the novel, yet this desire is unrequited by the novel's end. And though Stephanos lives in an apartment near Logan Circle, the apartment is simply a place where he sleeps; he establishes few relationships with long-time residents. His only friends are other African immigrants that live outside the neighborhood. At the end of the novel, Stephanos abandons his liquor store, and permits residents to loot the store. In doing so, he vacates one of the few spaces where many of the old and new residents would cross paths and interact. Indeed, his existence functions as a metaphor for many immigrants dealing with such changes in their neighborhoods; that is, dealing with the pressures of gentrification, and that of fitting in, in a space that does not, and seemingly cannot be made to, feel like home. Consider the building where his uncle lives. Here he sees a world much like the one he left in Ethiopia:

> Living here is as close to living back home as one can get, which is precisely why I moved out after two years. . . . When I got off the elevator, I was met by a row of open apartment doors, each one guarded by a young woman who . . . stared at me with more apprehension and fear than I've ever been greeted by. I

turned back to the elevator immediately, feeling as if I had intruded onto something sacred, something that I had no right to witness.[46]

Why such apprehension in the presence of other displaced Ethiopians? One
might see such a place as a kind of home away from home, a place where
one is surrounded by others like them where a shared culture, and place of
origin, may bring a sense of belonging. Part of the answer to this question
might be found in the ways in which this new location seems to function as
a kind of ghetto, as in a place to which one's social, economic, and political
circumstances keep one restricted, as in a place to go to, from which you may
never be able to go from. The text is a bit more ambivalent, in that we are told
that these Ethiopians "found to their surprise that they would never leave,"
indicating no clear reason for their never leaving, but the reasons seem clear
nonetheless; this is place much like home, that is not home; one might even
call it a home away from home; but does one leave home, particularly given
the reasons for leaving, in this case war and revolution, and thus instabil-
ity and violence, only to bring home along? Perhaps one brings tokens and
memories, connections to people left behind, but beyond such, leaving a place
behind gets murky. Hence, Stephanos remarks that this building holds "old
lives and relationships transported perfectly intact from Ethiopia," which is
why he leaves. He does not want his old life, he wants a new one, in a place
that promises that a new life can be had.

In considering his choice to strike out beyond the world of Ethiopia in
this apartment complex in Washington, D.C., Stephanos shares the following thoughts: "Sometimes I think of my decision to leave this building as an
escape, while at other times it seems more like an abandonment. . . . When
every eye you catch seems to hold an accusation or question behind it, a
decision has to be made."[47] These thoughts are not simply academic, or theo-
retical, musings. Part of the terror of the complex is the potential presence of
old-world conflicts, in new-world locations, of bringing the strife and dangers
presumably left behind to this new place. Hence, as noted in the earlier passage, of women "guarding" doorways and staring at Stephanos, "with more
apprehension and fear than" he had ever seen, we see a place and a people
still under duress, still, perhaps, suffering a kind of post-traumatic stress, a
place where "every eye you catch seems to hold an accusation or a question."
Stephanos's decision, partly guided by a desire to begin anew, and by being
in a place that promises new beginnings, was to leave as much of the past as
he could in the past. And still, he finds the implementation of this desire problematic, for not only does the apartment complex remind him of Ethiopia, so
too does Washington, D.C. remind him of his home city:

The two cities share a penchant for circular parks and long diagonal roads. . . . I can't help but think of what I'm doing as going home. . . . There is a simple and startling power to that phrase: going back home. There's an implied contradiction, a sense of moving forward and backward at the same time . . . an understanding, perhaps, that what you're returning to can never be the same as what you left.[48]

Poignancy abounds in this passage, in the realization that one can never truly go back home, that even in places that look and feel like home, that one is not yet or ever home, that no matter where one goes, including back to the place one first called home, that that place is gone. As Salman Rushdie remarks in his wonderful short text, *The Wizard of Oz* (1992), on the concept of home in that iconic piece of Americana, the film *The Wizard of Oz* (1939), and the L. Frank Baum book (1900) from which it evolved:

So Oz finally *became* home; the imagined world became the actual world, as it does for us all, because the truth is that once we have left our childhood places and started out to make up our lives, armed only with what we have and what we are, we understand that the real secret of the ruby slippers is not that "there's no place like home," but rather that there is no longer any such place *as* home: except, of course, for the home we make, or the homes that are made for us, in Oz: which is anywhere, and everywhere, except the place from which we began.[49]

Stephanos cannot return home, quite literally, given his status in Ethiopia as an undesirable there; he cannot return home here, in the apartment complex that is largely filled with Ethiopian immigrants in Washington, D.C., or in this city that resembles Addis Ababa. He can't return, even though he thought from time to time that he would: "How long did it take for me to understand that I was never going to return to Ethiopia again? . . . My hallucinations of home became standard. . . . I talked to my mother from across the bus; I walked home with my father across the spare, treeless campus of my northern Virginia community college. . . . I never understood that until right now: that everything went with you."[50] And, indeed, everything does go with you, they just don't always stay with you. As time passes, or you pass it, some things fade. His conversations with now imaginary family members, imaginary in the sense that they exist in his mind, but not in his physical presence as material, rather than immaterial, or spiritual, manifestations. Some aspects of his hallucinations are, however, quite real, as in physical, as in what Stephanos calls "the spare, treeless campus of my northern Virginia community college," a place that is quite real, even as his thoughts concerning it, including it being his community college, are quite imaginary:

Behind me is an ad for the Virginia community college I briefly attended. The school's ad campaign and motto, "Taking You to Where You Want to Be," is splayed across the bottom in gold-letters. . . . Four students—one white, one black, one Asian, one Hispanic—are walking across the lawn, books in arm, smiling at one another. After seventeen years here, I am certain of at least one thing: the liberal idea of America is at its best in advertising.[51]

If, in seventeen years, Stephanos is no closer to this dream, to achieving some semblance of this image of happiness, contentedness, purpose, that presumably comes from reaching where he wants to be, then it would seem reasonable for him to question the accessibility of what the image is advertising. It would seem reasonable to hope and hold out for dreams to become more than paperweights, holding some facets of our lives down on a desk or table somewhere, while serving no other worthwhile purpose, beyond the promise of some form or happiness that never evolves beyond a promise.

If, as Aristotle surmised, the question of whether one has had a happy life could not be answered while one is still alive, then, perhaps, Stephanos's sense of ennui might be taken as premature, as not yet worth investigation. And yet, as our work here should suggest—given the numerous writers and thinkers we cite here who have "shuffled off this mortal coil," to borrow from Shakespeare's *Hamlet*—that Stephanos, and Mengestu, follow an exceedingly long line of people for whom a happy life is and was a dream deferred.[52] It would be nice to have some sense of whether one is happy, or even approaching a state of happiness, while still alive to appreciate it. When asked, what is happiness? Aristotle concludes that happiness can only be attained through living a virtuous life, which signifies that happiness, or its attainment, is contingent on what one does, rather than on what one has or wants, and that what one does must issue from a rationally shaped perspective. That is, virtuous acts derive from rational thought, rather than our presumably baser, irrational impulses. Aristotle queries: "Why then should we not say that he is happy who is active in accordance with complete virtue and is sufficiently equipped with external goods, not for some chance period but throughout a complete life?"[53] Yet who among us "is sufficiently equipped with external goods"? And what are those external goods? And what exactly is their relationship to happiness or moreover, what the Greeks and others called eudaimonia, or human flourishing? As Amartya Sen notes, Aristotle, as in the Sanskrit text of the Indian *Upanishads*, notes that wealth is not simply the good we seek, for it is merely a means to something else.[54] Aristotle also discusses the importance of friendship, as well as health, the development of one's capabilities; and yet, considering these, for too many have these things been in short supply. Friends, sure, many of us probably have a few, but when we bring in wealth, honor, power, good looks, physical strength, ability, and dexterity the numbers of friends melt like ice cream on a hot day. Arguably, well-being, or happiness, is central to concepts such as the so-called American Dream that draws people here in trickles, floods, streams and keeps people here dreaming of reaching happiness, even as many have called this and similar dreams into question for about as long as these questions and quests have likely existed. As ultimately a promise of happiness, or at the very least a promise that one will be free here to fully pursue it, does this Dream still have any cultural relevance in the national and global imagination?

Stephanos is no more or less virtuous than most. His life exists as a reflection of a shared and yet also singular experience. He is, what we often are, as Rob Nixon tells us, citing Maeve Brennan: "travelers in residence"—men and women suspended between continents; suspended, too, between memory and forgetting.[55] And suspended is where Stephanos remains. As the novel draws to its end, we find that Stephanos's attempts at a relationship with a young white woman and her biracial daughter have followed the rest of his tattered and shattered dreams. His life desires are fading in line with the fading of Black and largely poor life in Logan Circle. His unrequited love interest, Judith, returns one last time; her house, next to his apartment, has been burned down. She does not bring her daughter with her to see the ruins, an omission that, perhaps unbeknownst to her, is heartbreaking to Stephanos, on its own, as he has spent much more time with, and become deeply connected to, this young girl, Naomi. Stephanos suggests that Judith rebuild, a suggestion that she rejects, seeing rebuilding as an attempt to recapture an uncapturable past.[56] Judith opts to start over, but that she can consider rebuilding, something Stephanos cannot do, is worth considering.

While Stephanos shows no animosity towards Judith's elevated social and economic status, she comes from money and is a college professor on sabbatical, their differences spark the divide that keeps them apart, and these differences are reflected in Judith's words. Stephanos is stuck in the past, stuck socially and economically; his move to the United States, sparking something like much of a changing same, leaves him as if not more impoverished than when he arrived, some seventeen years ago. It may well indeed be better for both to start over, but she has the means he does not have. Both will indeed start over, but there is nothing to say for either that starting over will yield something better than what they had before. For, despite Judith's reasonably solid social and economic status, she has sought, twice now, socially tenuous situations—the first with a Mauritanian man with whom she has a daughter, and the second with an Ethiopian man, Stephanos, her neighbor and, perhaps, her only friend in this Logan Circle environment—which come at a too often unacceptable cost, even today. And, for Stephanos, starting over simply means starting over with less: no store, no potential love interest and developing friendship, no little girl with and by whom his life has been enriched; no going back home, and no home, really, just a house, an apartment, in which to fade away, or steadily decline, alongside the secondhand furniture he owns. Much like the quote she uses as an epigraph to her book, they will fall away, only to be replaced, their foot tracks in this momentary sojourn together scuffed out, scuffed over, eventually disappearing, effaced. They do not see each other again, but Stephanos takes what pleasure he can from the moment he allows himself to imagine that such a meeting might one day happen. He thinks of a saying he had heard his father say: "A bird stuck between two branches gets bitten on both wings," a saying he then revises, "Father: a man stuck between two worlds lives and dies alone." And when and where and what Stephanos is in this moment is alone, left, sadly, and then again, thankfully, given how little else he has to ground him, except for his imagination. In this moment, he is as clear as a dream can be, that his "store looks more perfect than ever before." He sees it as he wants to see it, not as it is or was. Stephanos sees "a store, one that is neither broken, nor perfect, one that . . . [he is] happy to claim" as his own.[57] A store is his dream store but not the store, which is his, or was his, store, since it is the bank's store, at this point.

And indeed, Stephanos is stuck between two worlds, the old world from which he came, the new world in which he resides, and more aptly at this moment of his life, he is stuck between the world of dreams and that of dreams deferred. Here, he ends this moment of reflection, convinced, in this moment, that his store is perfect, in his heart and mind, even as it is everything other than perfect in the material world; here he sees it as he has "always wanted to see it," clarifying, poignant, heartbreakingly, that it is and has never been what he has always wanted it to be. When he awakes from this dream, he will be confronted with the fullness of his American nightmare, wherein this land of plenty's bounty has been apportioned to a select few, leaving the rest to dream of what we might achieve, given the ways and the means.

Behold the Dreamers (2016), by Imbolo Mbue, begins with a biblical passage, Deuteronomy 8: 7–9. It reads, in part: "For the Lord your God is bringing you into a good land . . . a land where bread will not be scarce and will lack nothing."[58] This opening suggests that the United States of America is a land of plenty, and that land's goodness is available to all there. The title, *Behold the Dreamers,* suggests that this land is what some dream about, and that these dreamers, this time from a little town called Limbe, in Cameroon, in Central or West Africa, are dreaming, what has come to be known as the American Dream. Jende, having immigrated to New York City, has arrived with a work visa, and is waiting on his green card. He is sharing this information with Mr. Clark Edwards, his soon-to-be employer, in the early pages of this story. As Jende waits in Mr. Edwards' office to be interviewed for a position as the Edwards' family chauffeur, he notices the headline of one of the *Wall Street Journal* articles "peeking from beneath sheets of numbers and graphs," which read, "White's Great Hope? Barack Obama and the Dream of a Color-Blind America."[59] Jende is fascinated by what he calls the "young ambitious senator" who ultimately becomes the President of the United States of America.

The primary characters of this novel include: Jende, his wife Neni, Clark Edwards, his wife, and their child, Liomi. We learn that Jende has been in the United States since 2004, and that he has been in the US for three years, setting a majority of the novel in 2007.[60] Neni arrived in the US around 2005, roughly one and a half years after Jende, on a student visa, with their child, Liomi, on a visitor's visa.[61] We first meet Neni shopping with a friend, also an immigrant from Africa, but one that has been in the US for twenty-four years, and one who has found her status in life as impoverished to have gone largely unchanged in her time here, a state of existence for which she feels ashamed, so ashamed, in fact, that she says she tells people she meets that she just got here. Neni and Jende live in Harlem. His reason for staying is clearly expressed in the following passage, where Jende notes that just visiting America was not enough for people like him. They needed to "return home as . . . American passport-bearing conquerors with pockets full of dollars and photos of a happy life. Which is why . . . he was certain he wouldn't see Cameroon until he had claimed his share of the milk, honey, and Liberty flowing in the paradise-for-strivers called America."[62]

There are several aspects of Jende's thought worth further attention. First, the conditions of the place from which he departs, or at least his sense of Cameroon, leaves little room to see any way forward or upward. Reality there overshadows fantasy; what is, or what he sees as being there, does not allow room for dreams of what might be. He has not, however, experienced the United States, and so what might be has no point of comparison yet to what is here. Second, he uses conquest as a dominant metaphor for this journey to the United States; that is, he sees his act of immigration as an act of conquest. Jende does not wish to return to Cameroon without having first conquered the United States, returning to Cameroon with the spoils of war, so to speak: a green card, an American passport, lots of money, "and photos of a happy life."[63] Effectively, these spoils signal access, cash, and a third form of evidence, photos. Of these signs of conquest, the last is the most intriguing for our purposes, for photos offer snapshots of a life, not a life, proof of nothing more than posed, if not composed, moments that certainly say something about a life, but rarely the fullness of it.

We are thinking here of the many ways in this visually dominant age that we sell and are sold dreams, images which rarely morph into reality. Ultimately, we find that when Jende, Neni, and their children do return to Cameroon, one does not imagine them proudly showing pictures of their tiny, roach infested, hothouse-like apartment. It does not seem like they would regale family, friends, and associates in Cameroon with the details of their incredibly busy lives as chauffeur, housekeeper, nanny, dishwasher, and such for long hours with little pay. One does not imagine them sharing that they worked for people like the Clarks with more money than they can fathom anyone having, yet with problems within both households that neither wealth and privilege, or near poverty and decidedly unprivileged lives can keep at bay. Initially, Jende thought seeking asylum in America offered him the best opportunity to stay; this opportunity turned to dust, and ultimately, Jende became too discouraged to stay, anyway. When asked why he wants to live in the U.S. by Clark, Jende responded that in Cameroon, one can only be somebody, if born somebody.[64]

The fact of the matter is that in America, Jende does not become that something that he thinks he can become. He does not conquer, and yet he returns home in the image of a conqueror, having saved a decent enough amount of money to set them up in relative comfort in Cameroon, but the act of doing so came at great cost. In hindsight it becomes clear to him, although Neni most certainly disagrees, that his reality in the United States obliterates his dreams of what is possible here. Neni, however, as mentioned, has not yet lost faith, and returns to Cameroon under duress, seeing still more of the life she wants in the United States, even given their dire circumstances, than she can see for herself and their children, back in Cameroon. This distinction between these two is born in part on their distinct trajectories and life experiences as visibly Black people with divergent social, sexed, and gendered situations. Neni has been attending school seeking to become a pharmacist, and doing rather well, despite numerous roadblocks in her way. She is also savvier than Jende concerning the importance of appearance in the United States and uses this sense of things to blackmail Cindy for about ten thousand dollars to not reveal to the public the unhappiness of the outwardly happy life the Edwards project to the world. That Neni has acquired or at least employed this skill in the United States is telling. She has learned of both a way in which success happens here, and in some sense of its failure, the latter part of this notion twisted, deeply, by what happens to the big corporate finance engine where Clark Edwards works, and from which wealth the Edwards have amassed comes, which is Lehman Brothers.

Beyond and in the fictional world of this novel, Lehman Brothers, once a global financial services firm, roughly fourth in size among such firms in the United States, declared bankruptcy in 2008. Among its various investments, Lehman Brothers held a sizable chunk of the subprime mortgage market, and suffered, as did the many subprime mortgage holders, many visibly Black and brown people among them, when the real estate market crumbled. Lehman Brothers was not alone in its collapse, for given its size, and the tenuous situations of several high finance companies, the millions of lives subject to the vicissitude of things under the sway of these titans of global finance suffered along with them. Many, in fact, seemed to suffer more than these titans, and their key leaders, did. Clark, following the pattern of some leaders we have heard of, apparently joined some of his peers in funneling company funds to escorts, as his home life, long fragile, begins to crumble.

One irony of this scenario is that Jende and Neni, having consumed deeply from the larders of Hollywood television and movies, see some similarities between the lives of the Edwards and that of the central couple in the award-winning film and one of their favorite movies, *American Beauty* (1999), thinking, among other things, that Cindy Edwards and Carolyn Burnham, played by Annette Benning, look alike, and that city life was better than suburban life.[65] That this is the lesson they take from the movie is more than interesting, for the city is at best a backdrop in the movie, and thus more reliant on fantasy, on projection, than the fantasy of suburban life it holds. This reliance on fantasy, or, more aptly, illusion, as a component of human existence is fleshed out rather soundly by Vince, one of the sons of Clark and Cindy in a conversation he has with Jende, while Jende is driving him to the dentist, about the way in which Jende sees and others see America. Having discovered that Vince has left his phone at home, Jende offers to return for it and Vince declines this offer, asserting, that in the absence of his phone, he might be better able to chat with him without interruption, to help Jende understand the lies he had been led to believe about the United States of America:

> Jende chuckled. . . . "I like how you want to help me see things another way, but really the way I see America is good for me."
> "That's exactly the problem! People don't want to open their eyes and see the Truth because the illusion suits them. As long as they're fed whatever lies they want to hear they're happy, because the Truth means nothing to them."[66]

At some point it becomes clear that Clark gets it. When the shit hits the fan, and Clark is clearly covered in shit, he acknowledges that he understands why Vince does not want to follow in his footsteps, in stating that he doesn't want his current status, where the lies have taken him, either. The issue as he sees it is: "not some system. It is us. Each of us. We've got to fix ourselves before we can fix a whole damn country. That's not happening on the street. It's not happening in Washington. It's not happening anywhere!"[67]

Sadly, Clark is right and wrong. Vince does indeed have a point, it is "some system," despite Clark's disparagement of this notion, and it is also us, because the system is us, put in ungrammatical but accurate terms, which is to say our propensity to separate ourselves from the systems we create, support, and sustain is insane, delusional, and yet it is also a delusion we seem to prefer. Systems somehow exist outside of us, and thus also seemingly beyond our control. And while systems certainly exist outside of us, they also simultaneously exist within and between us, which places them within our collective control. Consider it this way: the absence of a country, a street, a Washington, an anywhere, and thus an anyone, means the absence of a system, or the presence of a system that might as well be absent, because what can it do in the absence of a people and a place for it to do what it is there to do?

Vince is also right and wrong, for India offers little distance in a global system from the system he runs from. And Jende's response to Clark, and the conditions of social and economic disaster surrounding him is equally flawed, simultaneously erudite, and unenlightened. As he seeks sleep in these tumultuous days, hoping for better days ahead, unaware in part because he is dreaming, sleepwalking in the light of the sun and moon, not knowing that worse days were on the horizon, unaware that: "More jobs would be lost. . . . Dream homes would not be bought. . . . Dream vacations would not be taken, no matter how many days had been worked in the past year, no matter how respite was needed."[68]

Unaware that his dream, and the dreams of many others, would be deferred or in one calamitous way or another, ended. Here, Imbolo, functioning as a kind of omniscient presence, articulates present iterations of the American Dream, or at least its most common, shared manifestations, what it has become, and, more accurately, what it does not, or did not, provide in that historic juncture. This moment is not the first such moment, however, or the last, and for some in the United States, neither this moment, nor these moments, fittingly encompass the generational deferment plan that best encompasses their relationship to the American Dream. This latter relationship to American dreams seems beyond the reach of Jende's reason, in large part because he is beyond the reach of the memories and histories that might apprise him of such. So too are Vince and Clark beyond the reach of memories and histories; the one person with any relationship to such is Cindy Edwards, whose past life was full of trouble, only to be succeeded by reaching dreamland and finding it full of troublesome things. Jende thinks of their historical moment in the following way, and here, finally, we approach the limitations of his vision. He thinks:

> In many different ways it would be . . . a calamity like the one that had befallen the Egyptians in the Old Testament. The only difference . . . Jende reasoned, was that the Egyptians had been cursed by their own wickedness. They had called an abomination upon their land by worshipping idols and enslaving their fellow humans, all so they could live in splendor. They had chosen riches over righteousness, rapaciousness over justice. The Americans had done no such thing.[69]

Ah, but wait a minute, seriously Jende? The history of America is replete with such things; they, we, do worship idols, money in its myriad forms mostly; we do choose riches over righteousness daily; we have and we have continued to enslave our fellow humans, although we call such actions by different names these days; and those we enslave or encumber with so much of the weight of the world that they struggle to lift their heads often live in squalor so that others might never have to dirty or otherwise mar their faces or hands. Yes, this is the America that Jende does not or does not yet see, and yes, as we are further told, "And yet, all through the land, Willows would weep for the end of many dreams," including, in the end, Jende's American dreams.

Neni is similarly deprived of the knowledge that collective memories and histories can provide. Her American knowledge is shaped, rather, by television shows like *Dallas*, which first aired in 1978, continued for fourteen seasons, and was revamped and released yet again in 2012, and *Dynasty*, which ran from 1981 to 1989. From these shows, Neni had learned that there were malignant people in the United States, but also, she had learned from shows "like *The Fresh Prince of Bel Air* and *The Cosby Show*" that there was an equal opportunity for success in the United States, no matter your race or color. "Even after she'd seen the movies *Boyz in the Hood* and *Do the Right Thing*, she couldn't be swayed or convinced that the kind of black life depicted represented anything but a very small percentage of black life. . . . America, to her, was synonymous with happiness."[70]

Like Jende, Neni misses life, Black and white life (or the presence of any others in it) in the United States, this life having been replaced by select and selected images of it, images that fleshed out a dreamland, rather than a lived or living experience of it. What visions might alter the dream, movies concerning inner city life, for example, even in their highly stylized renditions are all but ignored, as representative of only a small portion of American life, rather than as its larger share. And, sadly, wrongly, Neni assumes that Americans imagined Africa in a similar way, even though most images of Africa that filter through into the United States even today seem to cycle and recycle images of hardship as endemic to instead of a small part of African life. Vince, in conversation with Neni, long distance, as he is in India, speaks to the misinformation that informs and forms us in the United States. When asked why he has such a hard time with America, he replies: "People . . . watch garbage interrupted by messages to buy garbage which will create a desire for more garbage. They . . . order from incredibly horrible corporations that are enslaving their fellow humans and pretty much destroying any chance of children growing up in a world where they can be truly free."[71]

We can and we need to be and do better, and we might start by being clear with ourselves and others about why some dreams do not come true. At least this is one of the requests that Imbolo Mbue puts before us in this novel's

Reader's Guide, the lived experience of immigrants here who see their continuing, seemingly unending, poverty as evidence of some internal deficiency: "I know many people who . . . work hard but barely get by; . . . They wonder what they didn't do right, how come their American dreams haven't come true."[72] Mbue leaves us with something else to ponder, as well, which is not only the need for empathy in our ways of seeing and being with others in the world. As she puts it, she struggled to have any empathy for the Edwards, and for those like them, different from her in virtually every external form we are trained to develop our understandings around. To fully develop these characters, Mbue tells us: "I had to learn to see them as humans. . . . I had to learn that showing empathy doesn't really have anything to do with having similar demographics or backgrounds or lifestyles. It's about a shared humanity."[73] And so, we conclude this moment in our time with a plea for empathy, for the work that developing empathy requires; for a more complete and honest presentation and explication of our memories and histories; for a sense of ourselves as perfectly imperfect beings, with long lists of dreams, too often deferred or denied. And to a sense of the world and the words that acknowledge our shared, relational existence, rather than the re-presentation of select portions of that world and the words we use to see ourselves as separate, distinct, without also always seeing ourselves as in and in relationship to each other we have separated ourselves from.

NOTES

1. Michel-Rolph Trouillot, *Silencing the Past: Power & the Production of History* (Boston: Beacon, 2015), 3. Ira Berlin, *The Making of African America: The Four Great Migrations* (New York: Penguin, 2010). For reflections on alternate ways of storytelling from Native American perspectives, most especially the famous Ghost Dance, in contrast to the myths and mirages of the frontier, see Mike Davis, "'White People are Only a Bad Dream . . . ,'" *Dead Cities* (New York: New Press, 2002), 23–32. Similar visions are revealed too in the film *Hell or High Water* (2016).

2. Ira Belin, *The Making of African America: The Four Great Migrations* (New York: Penguin Books, 2010), 6.

3. Nell Irvin Painter, *Exodusters: Black Migration to Kansas After Reconstruction* (New York: W.W. Norton & Company, 1976), description on back cover.

4. This section is from the fourth chapter of *Paradise*, "Seneca." The term Seneca is the name for the language of and for a member of one of the North American Indian Iroquois tribes.

5. Tulsa's bombing most likely refers to Greenwood being burned to the ground by white racists in 1921. Stated reasons for the burning was a pushback against resistance to the lynching of a black man accused of attacking a white woman, for which

no evidence existed. See Jonathan Z. Larsen's "Tulsa Burning" (1997). https://www
.northtulsa.org/index.php/blog/782-tulsa-burning

6. The stock market booms in 1922 and goes bust in 1929 on "Black Friday," an ironic choice of words.

7. Toni Morrison, *Paradise* (New York: Vintage International, 2014), 108–109. Morrison likely refers to Native American's removal to Oklahoma.

8. I borrow the term "disallowed" from Morrison's use of the term later in *Paradise* to speak of the various instances in which other communities rejected Ruby's founders (194).

9. Toni Morrison, *Paradise* (New York: Vintage, 2014), 13–14.

10. Toni Morrison, *Paradise* (New York: Vintage, 2014), 194.

11. Toni Morrison, *Paradise* (New York: Vintage, 2014), 194.

12. Toni Morrison, *Paradise* (New York: Vintage, 2014), 194.

13. Toni Morrison, *Paradise* (New York: Vintage, 2014), 302–3.

14. Quoted in Linda K. Kerber, *No Constitutional Right to Be Ladies: Women and the Obligations of Citizenship* (New York: Hill & Wang, 1998), 25.

15. Stephanie McCurry, *Women's War: Fighting and Surviving the American Civil War* (Cambridge, MA: The Belknap Press of Harvard University Press, 2019), 118–119.

16. Stephanie McCurry, *Women's War: Fighting & Surviving the American Civil War* (Cambridge, MA: The Belknap Press of Harvard University Press, 2019), 62. See also Linda K. Kerber, "Why Diamonds Are a Girl's Best Friend: Another American Narrative," *Daedalus* (Winter, 2012): 89–100. Even after the passing of women's suffrage in 1920 (allowing, predominantly, white women to vote), "this wasn't accompanied by automatic jury service, since women were seen as servants first to their male husbands, so that when Florida's assistant attorney general was asked why their names were only put down if they volunteered to serve he exclaimed: 'They have to cook the dinners!' Discrimination based on sex or gender only began to be invalidated as such by the Supreme Court in 1971. Kerber goes on to note that "not until 1975 did the U.S. Supreme Court rule that men and women must be eligible for all jury service on the same terms. Only in 1992, after Ruth Bader Ginsburg joined it, did the U.S. Supreme Court rule that peremptory challenges based on gender are impermissible." Linda K. Kerber, "Why Diamonds Are a Girl's Best Friend," *Proceedings of the American Philosophical Society* 153, Number 1 (March 2009): 63–64.

17. Toni Morrison, *Paradise* (New York: Vintage, 2014), 5.

18. Toni Morrison, *Paradise* (New York: Vintage, 2014), 303.

19. Toni Morrison, *Paradise* (New York: Vintage, 2014), 305.

20. Toni Morrison, *Paradise* (New York: Vintage, 2014), 305–6.

21. Toni Morrison, *Paradise* (New York: Vintage, 2014), 307.

22. Toni Morrison, *Paradise* (New York: Vintage, 2014), 309–11.

23. Toni Morrison, *Paradise* (New York: Vintage, 2014), 311.

24. Toni Morrison, *Paradise* (New York: Vintage, 2014), 312.

25. Toni Morrison, *Paradise* (New York: Vintage, 2014), 318.

26. James Truslow Adams, *The Epic of America* (Boston: Little, Brown, & Co., 1931), 404–405.

27. https://www.poetryfoundation.org/articles/70213/on-stage

28. (https://vimeo.com/205463920)

29. August Wilson, Interview with Bill Moyers (1988). https://www.youtube.com/watch?v=PBYedQbzGok.

30. August Wilson, *Gem of the Ocean* (New York: Theatre Communications Group, 2006), 32.

31. August Wilson, *Gem of the Ocean* (New York: Theatre Communications Group, 2006), 22.

32. The view of the ancestors, here, and in the work of Toni Morrison, has important resonances with what Michelle M. Jacob calls *The Auntie Way*, (Whitefish, MT: Anahuy Mentoring, 2020).

33. August Wilson, *Gem of the Ocean* (New York: Theatre Communications Group, 2006), 13.

34. August Wilson, *Gem of the Ocean* (New York: Theatre Communications Group, 2006), 84.

35. August Wilson, *Gem of the Ocean* (New York: Theatre Communications Group, 2006), 79.

36. August Wilson, *Gem of the Ocean* (New York: Theatre Communications Group, 2006), 28.

37. August Wilson, *Fences* (New York: Plume, 1986), xvii.

38. August Wilson, *Gem of the Ocean* (New York: Theatre Communications Group, 2006), 45.

39. August Wilson, *Gem of the Ocean* (New York: Theatre Communications Group, 2006), 45.

40. August Wilson, *Gem of the Ocean* (New York: Theatre Communications Group, 2006), 79.

41. August Wilson, "The Ground on Which I Stand," reprinted in *Callaloo* 20, No. 3, (Summer 1997): 493.

42. August Wilson, "The Ground on Which I Stand," *Callaloo* 20, No. 3, (Summer 1997): 495.

43. August Wilson, *Radio Golf*, reprinted in *American Theatre* 22, Number 9 (November 2005), Act Two, Scene 1: 101.

44. August Wilson, *Radio Golf*, reprinted in *American Theatre* 22, Number 9 (November 2005), Act Two, Scene 3: 104.

45. August Wilson, *Radio Golf*, reprinted in *American Theatre* 22, Number 9 (November 2005), Act 1, Scene 3: 96.

46. Dinaw Mengestu, *The Beautiful Things That Heaven Bears* (New York: Riverhead, 2007), 115–116.

47. Dinaw Mengestu, *The Beautiful Things That Heaven Bears* (New York: Riverhead, 2007), 117.

48. Dinaw Mengestu, *The Beautiful Things That Heaven Bears* (New York: Riverhead, 2007), 174.

49. Salman Rushdie, *The Wizard of Oz* (New York: BFI Film Classics, 1992), 57.

50. Dinaw Mengestu, *The Beautiful Things That Heaven Bears* (New York: Riverhead, 2007), 175–177.

51. Dinaw Mengestu, *The Beautiful Things That Heaven Bears* (New York: Riverhead, 2007), 97–98.

52. William Shakespeare, *The Tragedy of Hamlet Prince of Denmark,* eds., Barbara Mowat and Paul Werstine (Washington, D.C.: Folger Shakespeare Library, n.d.), accessed April 19, 2021. https://shakespeare.folger.edu/shakespeares-works/Hamlet (Act 3, Scene 1).

53. Aristotle, *The Nicomachean Ethics* (New York: Oxford World Classics, 2009), 18.

54. See Amartya Sen, *Development and Freedom* (New York, Anchor: 1999), 13–15.

55. Rob Nixon, "The Beautiful Things That Heaven Bears - Dinaw Mengestu," *New York Times Book Review* (March 25, 2007), 1.

56. Dinaw Mengestu, *The Beautiful Things That Heaven Bears* (New York: Riverhead, 2007), 227–228.

57. Dinaw Mengestu, *The Beautiful Things That Heaven Bears* (New York: Riverhead, 2007), 228.

58. Imbolo Mbue, *Behold the Dreamers* (New York: Random House, 2016), epigraph.

59. Imbolo Mbue, *Behold the Dreamers* (New York: Random House, 2016), 5.

60. Imbolo Mbue, *Behold the Dreamers* (New York: Random House, 2016), 8.

61. Imbolo Mbue, *Behold the Dreamers* (New York: Random House, 2016), 11–12.

62. Imbolo Mbue, *Behold the Dreamers* (New York: Random House, 2016), 19.

63. Imbolo Mbue, *Behold the Dreamers* (New York: Random House, 2016), 19.

64. Imbolo Mbue, *Behold the Dreamers* (New York: Random House, 2016) 39–40.

65. Imbolo Mbue, *Behold the Dreamers* (New York: Random House, 2016), 28.

66. Imbolo Mbue, *Behold the Dreamers* (New York: Random House, 2016), 103–104.

67. Imbolo Mbue, *Behold the Dreamers* (New York: Random House, 2016), 146.

68. Imbolo Mbue, *Behold the Dreamers,* (New York: Random House, 2016), 184.

69. Imbolo Mbue, *Behold the Dreamers* (New York: Random House, 2016), 19.

70. Imbolo Mbue, *Behold the Dreamers* (New York: Random House, 2016), 19.

71. Imbolo Mbue, *Behold the Dreamers* (New York: Random House, 2016), 19.

72. Imbolo Mbue, *Behold the Dreamers* (New York: Random House, 2016), 390.

73. Imbolo Mbue, *Behold the Dreamers* (New York: Random House, 2016), 392–393.

Conclusion

Black to the Future?

In her epic, prescient, and prophetic works on the future, *Parable of the Sower* (1993), and *Parable of the Talents* (1998), projecting existing crises forward, Octavia Butler suggests that whatever future we might have worth having will be on Mars. At least this is where the followers of Lauren Olamina, the protagonist at the center of both novels, head in the final pages of *Parable of the Talents*, the second book of this duology. Octavia Butler's life, from 1947 to 2006, like that of her heroine Lauren, is a testament to perseverance and resilience in the face of adversity. While she was very young, Butler declared to her family her determination to become a writer, despite never having read a word written by a Black person. Butler achieved her ambition and more. She did not, however, so far as we are aware, hold herself up as someone who achieved the American Dream, despite numerous accomplishments and accolades. Instead, Butler kept a steadfast eye on the past as a way of under-standing and projecting, if not predicting, what kind of future this past might bring. Her assessment is dire.

Lauren Olamina, the protagonist of both novels, is raised by her Latinx step-mother and Black father in a small, gated community in the Los Angeles area. Her mother dies from drug abuse, leaving Lauren with the gift of hyperempathy, a gift that through most of these two texts is often considered by others, to be a curse. Effectively, Lauren suffers with those she sees suf-fer. She is not disabled by this ability, and we call it an ability, even though many might well disagree with this assessment. To simplify what is a more complicated story, one day Lauren's brother starts going away and coming back until he eventually turns up dead, and then her father leaves the gated community to go to work, never to return. Soon after, the entire community is overrun, burned to the ground, and Lauren, and two other survivors, head north (conjuring up Frederick Douglass's newspaper, *The North Star*), in search of safer grounds. They band with an increasingly diverse group of others as they travel, including former slaves, thus imagining themselves to be a kind of new Underground Railroad, with slaves determined more than anyone else to fight for their newfound freedom, and ultimately reach a place owned by one of their fellow travelers, Bankole.

Originally from San Diego, Bankole is a doctor, and about forty years older than Lauren, who he eventually marries. They settle on some land Bankole owns in Humboldt County, California, and establish a small collective they call Acorn. *Parable of the Talents* begins in Acorn, or rather with an account of Acorn told by Bankole, and Lauren and Bankole's daughter, Larkin. In this novel, after the election of a Christian fundamentalist demagogue as President who wins election with the slogan "Make America Great Again," Lauren and her followers are again uprooted, Acorn destroyed, and its inhabitants killed or enslaved, and yet they and others, committed to the new religious faith Lauren discovers (as she sees it), called Earthseed, continue until they find some semblance of peace, while never, however, finding safety here on earth. This novel ends with Earthseed going from being guided by movement north via the North Star, to seeking a place among the stars, headed, as have others, to Mars. Lauren, her life nearly over, does not join them, but the seeds she planted, she hopes, Earthseed hopes, will take root there.

There is far more to these novels than this short synopsis provides, but this frame is enough to identify some important points. First, Earthseed members find no safe place here on earth, and hence they reach for the stars, but this reach is not simply or only the continuing quest of some *Star Trek*–like mission; it is not to go where no one has gone before; it is not primarily about seeking new life forms on other planets, if not other galaxies; it is not the imperial mission to conquer the ever-sought new frontier; rather it is an exploration of what we do and have done here; what kinds of seeds we've sown, and where; what kind of crops we've grown, if any, and what we have done with what we have been given. These are the questions that arise from the biblical parables on which these novels are based, and the focus of these novels throughout is not where we are going in terms of some intergalactic journey, but where we are going, as a culture, a civilization or civilizations, a people, on this earth.

It is in this context that we turn towards our final reflections, most especially on Octavia Butler's last novel, *Fledgling*, published in September 2005, soon before the author's death in February 2006, her first and only Black Vampire novel and one that arguably dramatically transformed the genre forever. We are introduced to the protagonist, dramatically, as they wake up in a cave. The novel begins with the following words: "I awoke to darkness," not knowing if it was truly dark in the external world, or if they were blind.[1] As Walter Benjamin might have noted, Butler, like Proust before her, begins her novel with someone awakening.[2] And of course, this conjures up too, James Joyce's "History is a nightmare from which I'm seeking to awake." Or, in our terms, the American Dream.

Here Butler introduces us to a world in which her lead character is overwhelmed: "It hurt to move. It hurt even to breathe." They are aware only of pain and hunger, with the latter eventually blending into the former. Something comes near and our protagonist kills it for food, as "the pain of my hunger won over all . . . other pain."[3] Eventually our protagonist ventures out into the world in the rain, and by this time we understand another crucial aspect of this character's reality, the absence of any memory, about who and what they are, about anything in the past. What is especially fascinating here is the contrast between Octavia Butler's *Fledgling*, with its total absence of memory in the mind of the protagonist, and Toni Morrison's *Paradise*, saturated through and through with memory, a profound contrast, with telling implications for questions of history, memory, and hopes for a different future.

To return to *Fledgling*, when a car on the road approaches, and the driver of the car stops to see if he can provide any assistance, the reader and our protagonist learn that the driver sees before him someone who looks to him like a young girl. It is not so much at this moment that he has any sexual desire for her, it is more so a fear of being caught with someone who appears to be so young, around eleven or twelve in his estimation, who has clearly been in some form of altercation, and injured. Neither of these identifications mean anything to the protagonist, given her lack of memory of anything before waking up in a dark cave.

When the driver, a young man named Wright, asks the protagonist: "Are you all right?" our protagonist thinks, "I heard the words, but at first, they meant nothing at all. They were noise. After a moment, though, they seemed to click into place as language. I understood them. . . . I couldn't remember ever speaking to another person and at first, I wasn't sure I could do it." At this point, we get a sense that our protagonist is endowed with language, and must thus be at least in some part human, given our unique species-specific ability.[4] When Wright sees she is hurt and says he must take her to the hospital, she says no, and then bites him, and drinks some of his blood, which gives immense pleasure to them both and appears to give her some sort of power over him. She befriends Wright and comes to slowly realize that she is part vampire, albeit of a unique kind.[5]

She comes to realize that she needs multiple mates that she can take blood from. She connects to her mates by drinking their blood in what is later described as a kind of mutual symbiosis. Yet she is also driven, in a kind of quest for identity, to find out her history, to find out who she is, here famously echoing the Delphic Oracle, "Know Thyself," who inspired Socrates' lifelong quest and lifelong questioning.[6] In going back to where she woke up, she finds that others are trying to kill her, and also discovers her ethical sensibility in that she meets humans who have been directed by some force unknown to her to try and kill her, which they are unable to reveal to her under obvious duress. She chooses to spare their lives and comes to realize that she "had strong moral beliefs about what was right and what wasn't."[7]

Despite these clues, and even after finding out that she is also pansexual, she tells one of her new symbiont companions: "I have to know who I am . . . and what I am."[8] Finally, in her quest, she meets her father, and finds out that her name is Shori Matthews, that one of her parents is a vampire (these vampires are known as the Ina), and that they had Anglicized their name in the 1950s when the suspicion of foreigners was at its height in the United States.[9] Shori also learns that she is 53, which turns out to be incredibly young for her kind. And that she is the result of a unique genetic experiment given a material reality, something she sensed before. Shori's genes are a fusion of the genes of her vampire father and her Black human mother, an effort to create a vampire with melanin, a "Black" vampire, so to speak, who can move about in daylight.[10] This genetic engineering was sought so they could go out during the day without excessively burning, which they have not been able to do.[11] Shori also finds that someone is trying to exterminate her and her family. In the story, Shori learns that vampires are another species, who also have language, but many other unique abilities humanity does not have, and that though they can copulate with humans, they cannot interbreed. Shori learns with their mutual symbiosis, not only does she need humans but that they will die if taken away from their symbionts, unless they find new ones, and that their symbionts will die, if not linked with another Ina, and even this does not always work. The Ina themselves can live for over 500 years. Shori learns from her father, Iosif, that the relationship between her own family and their humans is termed or thought of as a "mutualistic symbiosis," or "mutualism."[12]

Subsequently, Shori's father and brother are killed, and she finds that while the Ina men are territorially inclined, living separately from females, they are also a largely matriarchal species, with complex gender roles that challenge traditional Western binaries of males and females, husbands and wives, sons and daughters.[13] As the attacks upon her continue, Shori learns that her Ina ancestors come from the Middle East and Europe, noting: "Our earliest writings say that we joined humans around the rivers that would eventually be called the Tigris and Euphrates and that we had scattered north and west into what's now Russia, Ukraine, Romania, Hungary, and those regions."[14] Many of these communities were killed by the Nazis and their local collaborators during World War II, and some later by the Communists after the Russians invaded large parts of Eastern Europe and established client states there, including all of Shori's father's relatives, with two brothers and their father dying in Romania.[15] She also learns that there is another group of Ina, who do not treat symbionts as people, who like to watch them fight and kill each other, and get some sort of perverse sexual pleasure out of this blood sport.[16]

Shori meets a group of Ina, that she had already been told were good, the Gordon family, and had in fact met them earlier before her amnesia. The Gordons have no knowledge of the attacks on her and her family, and they deny that any Ina could have hired humans to kill them. Shori surmises that their rejection of this possibility comes more from wounded pride than rationality or logic.[17] Even so, the Gordons deny the possibility of Ina racism against humanity in general, and Black humanity, in particular; they say that questions of human racism have no meaning for the Ina. They also dismiss the possibilities of feuds among the Ina, saying such things had not happened for more than a thousand years, and such things could not have taken place without Shori's father Iosif and many others knowing these realities.[18]

Nevertheless, and in the context of such willful blindness, after meeting the Gordons, the attacks continue, with human symbionts from Los Angeles hired to kill Shori and others.[19] Slowly but surely, a deadly and pernicious inter-species racism, and racism against Black humanity, are revealed. There are a group of old Ina families called the Silks, residing in Los Angeles County, whose hatred towards Shori and her ancestors is intense. The Silks reject Shori as Ina, because she is not pure Ina, and due to her Blackness. The Silks are the ones, it is revealed, who have coerced other humans from Los Angeles to kill Shori and her family, their allies, and symbionts.[20] Shori is then led to consider the irony that the Silks could not live without humans, yet they see them as little more than domesticated animals. At a Council meeting of Ina families, one of the representatives of the Silk family goes on a tirade about how humans breed and breed, while the Ina breed slowly.[21] The representative goes on to say:

> "Their lives are brief, and without us, riddled with disease and violence. And yet, we need them. We take them into our families, and with our help, they are able to live longer, stay free of disease, and get along with one another. We could not live without them."
> "But we are not them!"
> "We are not them!"[22]

What's extraordinary here is Butler's futuristic exploration of multidirectional memory: the destruction of European Jewry and so many others in the Holocaust.[23] And such an exploration, of one of the most violent periods of European history, ties into contemporary events in Eastern and Central Europe from which Shori's ancestors emanate, in part. For example, in a recent interview with NPR, a former leading Ukrainian official characterized Russia's invasion of the Ukraine in terms of Samuel Huntington's clash of civilizations with democracy and freedom, represented by the West and Ukraine, and "a wild horde coming from Russia."[24]

Such historical tropes harken back to old sentiments of fears of the Asiatic hordes, from the Mongols to the Chinese, discussed earlier, and yet are still here in the context of the new hysteria about China, what then President Trump and others labelled the "Chinese virus" to escape his own incompetence in dealing with COVID-19. Such hateful rhetoric fuels the dramatic increase in hate crimes in the US, particularly against Asian Americans. Yet this ought to come as no surprise. For such racist visions arrayed against Russia, China, Asia, and Asians have deep roots in the US, and globally. For example, as a leading historian of Ukraine underscored, "the Ukrainian 'Occidentalist' tradition has mythologized Russia as an 'Asian' nation."[25] So, we are back, through a circuitous route, to the fear of the Other, both within the "West" and across its borders, as the new white supremacist imaginary sees enemies everywhere, with a key ingredient being some version of the phrase, we are not them, and they are different from us.

Clearly the xenophobic sentiments we see today are recycled elements of a racist worldview, more pernicious because of their reusability and utility. What we see in the aftermath of Russia's invasion of Ukraine, we have seen before in responses to Black Lives Matter, in the anti-Muslim animosities of recent history. Historically, this xenophobia is evident from the Chinese Exclusion Act of 1882 to the explicitly racist Johnson-Reed 1924 Immigration Act—arrayed against Jews, Eastern Europeans, Africans, Asians, and virtually all those considered non-white, non-European, exactly such ideas explicitly championed by the Trump administration while in office![26] To really understand the deep roots of this anti-Asian sentiment, we must turn to some of our most gifted Asian American historians, Gary Y. Okihiro, in *American History Unbound: Asians and Pacific Islanders* (2015); Mae Ngai, in *The Chinese Question: Gold Rushes and Global Politics* (2022); and Erika Lee, in *America for Americans: A History of Xenophobia in the United States* (2021) and *The Making of Asian America* (2022). These historians discuss, in different, albeit complementary ways, the long history of anti-immigrant and anti-Asian xenophobia which is today culminating in increasingly deadly attacks on Asian-Americans across the US, accompanied with a demonization of China, now enemy number one, followed closely in the US by the demonization of Russia and Persia/Iran.[27] The suffering imposed upon our Islamic brothers and sisters, after the September 11, 2001 terrorist attacks, and anyone who seems of Middle Eastern descent, is now increasingly being turned towards Asian Americans, and an endless proliferation of scapegoats, Latinx, Blacks, Jews, and LGBTQ+ people. So, the comments from the former Ukrainian Minister of Infrastructure comes as part of an increasing echo chamber of the global Far Right of the words from *Fledgling*: "But we are not them!"

Octavia Butler's novels, and the histories towards which they gesture, thus are of unparalleled contemporary relevance. They also resonate with Toni Morrison's argument in *The Origins of Others* (2017), regarding how our profound attachment to hierarchy, empire, and "othering" can militate against our possibilities of surviving and thriving.[28] The tragic consequences of the "But we are not them!" world-view has been extensively explored in these texts and in various histories of the modern world.[29] In hindsight it is now becoming clearer and clearer that such events are not simply the reality of our past, but an ominous portent for the future, and the question of whether there will even be a future, unless humanity changes its ways, as Octavia Butler beseeches us to do.

In *Fledgling,* because of her amnesia, Shori and the rest of the Ina share a history but have no shared memories, mirroring our human world. Octavia Butler's Parable Series and *Fledgling,* though ostensibly in the realm of science fiction, perhaps more accurately predicts our current moment and likely trajectory than many others. Therein lies its brilliance: Butler's use of science fiction to helps us confront our current human realities, to try and move forward in a positive direction. Perhaps that is why the *Parable of the Sower* was on both the *Los Angeles Times* and the *New York Times* bestseller lists throughout much of Fall 2020.[30] The description of *Fledgling* on the back cover notes: "Shori now becomes the target of a vast plot to destroy her and her kind. And in the final apocalyptic battle, her survival will depend on whether all humans are bigots—or all bigots are human."

In Marleen S. Barr's "The Allegory of Shori's Cave: Teaching *Fledgling* as the Science Fiction of Racism," which harkens back to Plato's famous metaphor of the cave in *The Republic*, we are shown how Octavia Butler's novel is perfectly primed to teach another lesson expressed in Lauren's Earthseed journal in *Parable of the Sower*:

> Embrace diversity.
> Unite—
> Or be divided,
> robbed,
> rules,
> killed
> By those who see you as prey.
> Embrace diversity
> Or be destroyed.[31]

Moreover, in the Parable series, what is omnipresent is the diversity of humanity on the move, migrating in the attempt to survive. We might think of Butler's futuristic Parable series then as pointing beyond Ira Berlin's "four great migrations" towards a fifth great migration, accompanied by tens of millions of others, a glimpse of the likely exponential increase in such flight, if trends continue, as revealed in Ai Weiwei's *Human Flow* (2017, 2020), though Lauren's quest is towards the stars in general, and towards Mars in particular. But what are they migrating from, and to? The from is easy; from other humans, from war, from insecurity, from catastrophic poverty, racism, xenophobia, endemic violence, and climate change, from the countries destroyed by the great powers, and their regional surrogates, assisted by many other bloody hands. And this leads to Lauren's next great moment of understanding. For in *Parable of the Talents,* Octavia Butler's protagonist, Lauren Olamina, writes in her journal:

> EARTHSEED: THE BOOKS OF THE LIVING
> Beware:
> At war
> Or at peace,
> More people die
> Of unenlightened self-interest
> Than of any other disease.[32]

It is fitting too, that Butler highlights the struggles, especially of young people, for it is they that arguably have the most to lose and gain. There is evidence of a growing awareness among the younger generation of Octavia Butler and her heroine Lauren's words that humanity must embrace diversity or be destroyed. This entails the creation of new relationships with human beings, and the non-human natural world, based upon mutual respect and awareness of our interdependence. The challenge, then, as Butler argued, is how to embrace our diversity and come up with a purpose for the flourishing of humanity and other living things. Lauren's solution, in Earthseed, is to shoot for the stars. Butler sees the importance of a positive common purpose, lest what she fears, may come to pass. As Butler puts it:

> Hunting for scapegoats is always popular in times of serious trouble. So is hunting for the great leader who will restore prosperity and stability. Some people know that's the answer. If they could just find the strong, powerful leader that they need, all would be well. And unhappily for them, they do find such a leader. . . . Because of him, innocent people lose their freedom, lose custody of their children, lose their lives.
>
> Sometimes the only thing more dangerous than frightened, confused, desperate people looking for solutions is frightened, confused, desperate people finding and settling for truly bad solutions.[33]

This message, a hard one in the new age of demagogues, is that of the centrality and complexity of history and change, one that recognizes the presence of the past, while not being imprisoned by this recognition. Exactly this type of rethinking such as done by Butler above was done some 80 years ago by W.E.B. Du Bois in a short article in *Jewish Life*, "The Negro and the Warsaw Ghetto" (1952).

Du Bois recounted his three sojourns to Poland, a land that at times overlapped with, or bordered those in East Central Europe, which Octavia Butler conjured up in *Fledgling*. Here Du Bois told a story about speaking to a friend about the race problem in the US, which at the time he imagined to be the only race problem in the world, and the greatest social problem then existing, only to be told he knew little of such things and was then treated to a discussion of Poles in the German empire. Du Bois notes: "I was astonished; because race problems at the time were to me purely problems of color, and principally of slavery in the United States and near-slavery in Africa." During a later sojourn to Galicia, he encountered more mysteries, the "Jewish problem."[34] And of course, it was Du Bois who famously asked the question: "How does it feel to be a problem?" On his third visit, Du Bois came back to Poland after the tremendous destruction of World War II. Witnessing the scene, Du Bois writes:

> I have seen something of human upheaval in this world: the scream and shots of a race riot in Atlanta; the marching of the Ku Klux Klan; the threat of courts and police; the neglect and destruction of human habitation; but nothing in my wildest imagination was equal to what I saw in Warsaw in 1949. . . . The result of these three visits, and particularly of my view of the Warsaw ghetto, was not so much clearer understanding of the Jewish problem in the modern world as it was a real and more complete understanding of the Negro problem. In the first place, the problem of slavery, emancipation, and caste in the United States was no longer in my mind a separate and unique thing as I had so long conceived it. It was not even solely a matter of color and physical and racial characteristics, which was a particularly hard thing for me to learn, since for a lifetime the color line had been a real and efficient cause of misery. It was not merely a matter of religion. . . . No, the race problem in which I was interested cut across lines of color and physique and belief and status and was a matter of cultural patterns, perverted teaching and human hate and prejudice, which reach all sorts of people and caused endless evil to all men. So that the ghetto of Warsaw helped me to emerge from a certain social provincialism into a broader conception of what the fight against race segregation, religious discrimination and the oppression by wealth had to become if civilization was going to triumph and broaden in the world.[35]

These remarks of Du Bois remind us of one of the central messages of Octavia Butler's *Parable of the Sower*, an urgent message that may help us to grapple with the complexity and rapidity of change today, and to act appropriately to shape the future:

> All that you touch
> You Change.
> All that you Change
> Changes you.
> The only lasting truth
> Is Change.
> God
> Is Change.[36]

The purpose then, of Lauren Olamina's Earthseed religion is to prepare for change, recognize its centrality, and shape change in a positive, not negative direction. Butler's Black survivor, Lauren Olamina, doubted human beings could do this without a common project, and thus for her a unifying force was her religion Earthseed, and reaching towards the stars, with the idea of planting seeds on other planets such as Mars. Such a vision undoubtedly inspired NASA to name its Jezero Crater landing site the Octavia E. Butler Landing site in her honor in 2021.[37] Fittingly, among those working on the mission were persons reflective of beautiful diversity and immigrant dreams. NASA engineer Christina Hernandez, in Pasadena in Los Angeles, wrote in a tweet in Spanish: "They wanted to bury us, but they didn't know we were seeds."[38] The exploits of another NASA engineer from South Asia, an Indian specifically, Vandi Verma, also there in Los Angeles, are chronicled in the *Wall Street Journal* op-ed entitled "The American Dream is Alive on Mars" (2021).[39]

Butler, however, as does her character Lauren Olamina, wants us to do more than seek the American Dream on Mars, wants us to do more than persevere to get there; she wants us to also survive and thrive here. And it is not so much that she sees the American Dream as potentially alive on Mars, any more than it is alive here. It is that, to have anything, any place, worth dreaming about, we must go toward paths not yet taken. To borrow from the poet Robert Frost, we must take "the road less traveled by," if we are to make a difference.[40] And this ought to give us caution. For perhaps the most famous of all NASA scientists is Dr. James Hansen, often called the Paul Revere of global warming and catastrophic climate change. Buoyed by a sense of purpose and what Butler called positive obsession, Hansen felt compelled to speak out about climate change posing an existential threat to life on earth. After all, he felt that since NASA's official mission was "to protect the home planet," he should be empowered as a scientist employed there to carry out the mission he was hired to do. Nevertheless, various administrations told Hansen, in no uncertain terms, to remain silent. He did not. At this very time, NASA's mission of protecting the home planet mysteriously disappeared from NASA's official website, though officials said its disappearance in this context, as part of NASA's official mission, was pure coincidence.[41]

Ironically, as the fantasy of the American Dream recedes here on earth, vanishing for more and more, and humans speed up the destruction of life on earth, humanity continues to look for the American Dream on Mars. But it ought to be said that seen here are very different dreams than those consistent with the southern historical romance we depicted earlier. The dreams we favor embrace diversity and mutualism, as in Langston Hughes' American dream and dreams deferred, Benjamin's sense of the dream in ruins, and alternative dreams of the Americas, writ large.[42]

Octavia Butler's feminist science fiction is an important innovation in this storied tradition, like authors such as Ursula Le Guin, who use the genre to explore our pasts and our possible futures, raising up the question of the past and future as it flashes up at a moment of danger, as a dialectical image.[43] The writers Langston Hughes, Walter Benjamin, and Romare Bearden all saw the possibilities of montage for reconstruction of our past, present, and possible futures. Among Bearden's mediums, like Hughes and Benjamin before him, "was the collage, fusing painting, magazine clippings, old paper and fabric, like a jigsaw puzzle in upheaval. But unlike a puzzle, each piece of a Bearden collage has a meaning and history all its own. Shortly before he died . . . in 1988, Bearden said working with fragments of the past brought them into the now."[44] This is what Langston Hughes's *Montage of a Dream Deferred* and the science fiction of Octavia Butler calls upon us to do, to recognize the fusing together of past, current, and possible alternative futures, as seen through her Black female protagonists, Lauren Olamina and Shori.

So, it ought to come as no surprise that *Fledgling* begins with awakening. For as Walter Benjamin noted in the Arcades Project, it was Marx himself, in 1843, who wrote: "The reform of consciousness consists *solely* in . . . the awakening of the world from its dream about itself."[45] Like Langston Hughes' book-length poem, *Montage of a Dream Deferred*, Benjamin's *Arcades Project: A Dialectical Fairyland* was inspired by "literary montage." Both sought to overcome the fairy tale of progress that was part of capitalist modernity in general, and for Hughes, the American Dream in particular. Here enters Benjamin's notion of the dialectical image:

> The historical index of the images not only says that they belong to a particular time; it says, above all, that they attain to legibility only at a particular time. . . . Every present day is determined by the images that are synchronic with it; each

"now" is the now of a specific recognizability. In it, truth is charged to the bursting point with time. (This point of explosion, and nothing else, is the death of the *intentio*, which thus coincides with the birth of authentic historical time, the time of truth.) It is not that what is past casts light on what is present, or what is present its light on what is past; rather, image is that wherein what has been comes together in a flash with the now to form a constellation. In other words, image is dialectics at a standstill. . . . For while the relation of the present to the past is a purely temporal, continuous one, the relation of what-has-been to the now is dialectical. . . . The image that is read—which is to say, the image in its now of recognizability—bears to the highest degree the imprint of the perilous critical moment.[46]

This notion of critical moments, turning points in human history, was also underscored by perhaps the most famous of radical feminist science fiction classics, *Woman on the Edge of Time* (1976), by Marge Piercy. The book follows the story of a Mexican American woman in Spanish Harlem, caught within the realm of patriarchal and psychiatric power, by being confined in Bellevue Hospital, where she is visited by persons from the future. The unlikely protagonist, Connie, thinks they really must be reaching for the bottom of the barrel, coming to her, though they tell her that it is not the powerful who make revolutions:

"What do you want from me?"

"We could put it: at certain cruxes of history . . . forces are in conflict. Technology is imbalanced. Too few have too much power. Alternate futures are equally or almost equally probable . . . and that affects the . . . shape of time."

" . . . But you exist."

"Maybe. Maybe not. . . . It's not clear. We're struggling to exist."

"I don't understand. . . . "

"You may fail us."

"Me? How?"

"You of your time. You individually may fail to understand us or to struggle in your own life and time. You of your time may struggle altogether. . . . We must fight to come to exist, to remain in existence. That's why we reached you."[47]

Beginning with the steady onrush of crises seen in the Parable series, Butler anticipated today's mad rush to consume the planet's resources with abandon, leaving nothing for more and more of today's current global population of some 8 billion, not to mention future generations. Denying these increasingly apocalyptic realities—as the planet burns and the nuclear arms race imperils most life—ensures that there will be no future, or no future worth having.[48] Most especially, as depicted in *Fledgling*, there are two possibilities available to us, given the vampiric forms of relationality in existence. In one, there is limited or no concern for others, and in the other, there is recognition that we need others, and might care for them, even if that care may be but need not be self-serving. In our current world, we have ruling elites with a vampiric relationship to resources, human and otherwise, that shows little or no care for anything more than consuming everything in their lifetime while leaving nothing for others.[49]

All this fits perfectly with G.E.M. de Ste. Croix's *The Class Struggle in the Ancient Greek World* (1981), in which he speaks of the fate of the Roman empire:

> As I see it, the Roman political system (especially when Greek democracy had been wiped out . . .) facilitated a most intense and ultimately destructive economic exploitation of the great mass of the people, whether slave or free, and it made radical reform impossible. The result was that the propertied class, the men of real wealth, who had deliberately created this system for their own benefit, drained the life-blood from their world and thus destroyed Graeco-Roman civilisation over a large part of the empire. . . . That, I believe, was the principal reason for the decline of Classical civilisation. . . . The very hierarchical political structure of the Roman empire, of course, played an important part; but it was precisely the propertied class as such which in the long run monopolised political power, with the definite purpose of maintaining and increasing its share of the comparatively small surplus which could be extracted from the primary producers. . . . *If I were in search of a metaphor to describe the great and growing concentration of wealth in the hands of the upper classes, . . . I should want to think in terms of something much more purposive and deliberate—perhaps the vampire bat*" [emphasis added].[50]

And just because there is arguably more than one vampire bat of the kind described above, does not make the general point any less relevant.[51] On the other hand, there are the cooperative anarchist ideas of mutual aid—argued for by Kropotkin, and the personalist Christian anarchism of Dorothy Day and the Catholic Worker movement invoked by Pope Francis in his speech to the US Congress in 2015, to cite two examples that focus on mutual sustainability, along with the Pope's invocation of Abraham Lincoln, Martin Luther King Jr., and Thomas Merton.[52] In *Fledgling,* of course, we see the ethic of mutual interdependence and cooperation, shown by Shori, who wakes up in a dark cave. And this is ironic, for Shori goes on to be the most far-seeing of all, while those around her, blinded by racism, turn towards hatred and mutual destruction rather than love and cooperation.

It may be that elements of Rome, reconfigured in a world-systems context, predict much of our likely future, or lack thereof.[53] Or we could choose to remake the world, based on hope for solidarity with others and for the future. Whatever the future will be, or whether there will be a future at all, it is clear that we have to go beyond what we will call, for want of better terms, actually existing capitalism and socialism.[54] Here, as we emphasize, the names are less important than the spirit of love for humanity, with all its faults, for the best parts, to be built upon, to make a better world for all living beings, with a new respect for our relationship with non-human nature, and other human beings.

Historically, the American Dream has had embedded within it profound antinomies, in which the search for Paradise was almost always founded upon the exclusion of some Other, whoever they might be. The 1976 Eagles album caught this brilliantly, in the last song of *Hotel California*, "The Last Resort." All the themes discussed herein, the Dream, its deferment, its contradictions, the nightmare within, all are chronicled in this melancholy tale, most especially with the lines "They call it Paradise I don't know why," going on to note that once you call "someplace Paradise," perhaps any place, you can "Kiss it goodbye.[55] Not surprisingly, echoes of Toni Morrison's *Paradise* are seen here, yet also in critical passages from Walter Benjamin's "Theses on the Philosophy of History" and related mediations therein on Paul Klee's famous *Angelus Novus*.

> My wing is ready for flight.
> *I would like to turn back.*
> If I stayed everliving time,
> I'd still have a little luck.

> —Gerhard Scholem, "Greetings from the Angelus"

There is a picture by Klee called *Angelus Novus*. It shows an angel who seems about to move away from something it stares at. His eyes are wide, his mouth is open, its wings are spread. This is how the angel of history must look. Its face is turned toward the past. Where a chain of events appears before *us*, it sees one single catastrophe, which keeps piling wreckage upon wreckage and hurls it at its feet. The angel would like to stay, awaken the dead, and make whole what has been smashed. But a storm is blowing from Paradise and has got caught in its wings; it is so strong that the angel can no longer close them. The storm drives it irresistibly into the future, to which his back is turned, while the pile of debris before him grows towards the "sky. What we call progress is *this* storm."[56]

The American Dream "is *this* storm." For in the past, and moreover in this current moment, critical parts of this Dream are dangerous, part of ideologies of empire, civilizational conflicts, and more that are hurtling the world headlong towards destruction. In *Outside the Gates of Eden: The Dream of America from Hiroshima to Now* (2014), Peter Hales suggests that the obverse side of the American Dream of the paradise of suburbia, is the nightmare of thermonuclear war. And yet, it is also the case that in addition to the urban dystopias created in the U.S., embedded within the supposed bourgeois suburban utopias, driven by the exclusion of the Other, are versions of Dante's image of hell, for all groups.[57]

Whether the world will end hot (catastrophic global warming) or cold, with nuclear winter, is anyone's guess. But it is not too late, even if it might seem so, to put on the brakes, to get off the train we are on, and make the world anew, through inclusion in the way defined by Dr. Martin Luther King, in his notes for his address to the SCLC Retreat, Frogmore, SC, 67/05/29–31, "To Charter Our Course for the Future":

> Beyond constitutional civil rights to human rights of adequate income and decent housing, quality education. Integration not in a romantic and esthetic sense, which "may easily be a system that merely adds color to a still predominantly white power structure. It must be seen in political terms. Integration in its true dimensions is shared power." . . . Genuine equality calls for "radical redistribution of political and economic power."[58]

As Theodor Adorno expresses it in *Minima Moralia: Reflections from Damaged Life* (1951) in a section entitled "*Mélange*":

> That all men are alike is exactly what society would like to hear. It considers actual or imagined differences as stigmas indicating that not enough has yet been done; that something has still been left outside of its machinery, not quite determined by its totality. The racial difference is raised to an absolute so it can be abolished absolutely, if only in the sense that nothing that is different survives. An emancipated society, on the other hand, would not be a unitary state, but the realization of universality in the reconciliation of differences. To assure the black that he is exactly like the white men, while he obviously is not, is secretly to wrong him still further. He is benevolently humiliated by the application of a standard by which, under the pressure of the system, he must necessarily be found wanting, and to satisfy which would in any case be a doubtful achievement. The spokesmen of unitary tolerance are, accordingly, always ready to turn intolerantly on any group that remains refractory: intransigent enthusiasm for blacks does not exclude outrage at Jewish uncouthness. The melting-pot was introduced by unbridled industrial capitalism. The thought of being cast into it conjures up martyrdom, not democracy.[59]

James Baldwin once wrote that "not everything that is faced can be changed. But nothing can be changed until it is faced."[60] We must face that we have been living in a burning house for some time. This reality must be faced if we are to have any hope of change. In *Parable of the Sower*, always the realist, Butler records the following from Lauren's Earthseed journal:

> In order to rise

From its own ashes
A phoenix
First
Must
Burn.[61]

It is time to ascertain what shape we might take as we attempt to rise, phoenix-like, resurrecting ourselves from the ashes, as we remake ourselves and the world anew, in a different and better way. What a difference that might make. If we only try.

James Truslow Adams began *The Epic of America* with a Prologue, the first section of which is entitled "From Time Immemorial."[62] Benjamin, in *The Arcades Project*, notes that "in the dialectical image, what has been within a particular epoch is always, simultaneously, 'what has been from time immemorial.' As such, however, it is manifest, on each occasion, only to a quite specific epoch—namely, the one in which humanity, rubbing its eyes, recognizes this dream image as such."[63] Yet, ultimately, it is from this dream, the American Dream, including its ostensibly sunny, California Dream version, in which we are all imprisoned, from which we must awake.[64] If we are to survive, that is, much less thrive.

We started this book by framing a revised history, one that included some of the refuse, detritus, or neglected participants in this experiment we call a democratic republic, and we point out how historically and currently that many have been left out in formulations of this country, and in access to the American Dream. We have ranged from the writings of Frederick Douglass, John Brown, Erika Lee, Mai Ngai, Harriet Tubman, W.E.B. Du Bois, Paul Laurence Dunbar, Claude McKay, Ralph Ellison, Richard Wright, Walter Benjamin, Louis Adamic, Romare Bearden, Langston Hughes, Emma Lazarus, Duke Ellington, Luis Rodriguez, Chester Himes, Ward Moore, James Baldwin, August Wilson, Walter Mosley, Toni Morrison, Marge Piercy, Dinaw Mengestu, Imbolo Mbue, to Octavia Butler. Every writer here, eloquently, and in their own unique ways, speaks to us forcefully with a common chorus: you must recognize us or perish with us, for you are us, and we are you, no matter how separate you may think yourself to be. Every writer speaks to the determination of the downtrodden to make a way, to survive, no matter the odds against them. Of poignance as we close are some lines from Dinaw Mengestu's *The Beautiful Things that Heaven Bears* (2006). Here, Joseph and Sepha, both refugees from Ethiopia, living in America, are both struck by the lines from Dante's *Inferno:*

Through a round aperture I saw appear,
Some of the beautiful things that Heaven bears,

Where we came forth, and once more saw the stars.

"Think about it," Joseph says to his friend Sepha, "Dante is finally coming out of hell, and that is what he sees. . . . Hell every day with only glimpses of heaven in between."[65]

As we have seen, some people's idea of heaven is other people's hell, and yet we are all one humanity. Today, we are infinitely divided within the circles of Dante's Inferno. To be sure, the wealthy, powerful, and privileged minority garners some protection from the raging fires that continue to burn across our global landscape, but where will they be without the rest of us? Yet as intimated in the novels of Toni Morrison, this supposed Paradise is a mirage, not reality, as it is premised on relational processes of exploitation and exclusion that define our world today.

On our journey back and forth from ideas of heaven and hell, we have crossed history from the birth of the American Dream out of the matrix of the Americas and the new global system to which it gave birth. We have recorded missed opportunities for a much-needed solidarity in a world that seems to be shattering into a trillion shards. In our rescue operation of voices from the ruins of the past, Langston Hughes is especially unique here, in the expression of a global internationalist vision, beyond the color line, and in the shadow of the Dream, which animated the hopes of many in the US and around the world. We started off by noting that the American Dream lives on because the moment to realize it was missed. Arguably, when we realize it, it will not be needed, or perhaps more importantly, it will not have the draw it has, despite massive amounts of information suggesting its improbability, its lottery-like nature, and even more profound questions about the price of the ticket. We went on to argue that the best place to begin our investigation of the Dream is from the ruins of its alternative futures. Now that we have excavated the past, and turned over the rubble and the ruins, which have consumed so many in the fire, it is up to us to use this history to create the alternative future that has truly been the one less traveled, but which we invite all to take with us, together. For we must all work together to bring the worldwide Jubilee, that so many generations fought to achieve, and in whose memory, we must tirelessly carry on the struggle.

NOTES

1. Octavia Butler, *Fledgling* (New York: Grand Central Publishing, 2005), 1.
2. As Benjamin noted, "Just as Proust begins the story of his life with an awakening, so must every presentation of history begin with awakening; in fact, it should

treat of nothing else. The one, accordingly, deals with awakening from the nineteenth century. . . . The realization of dream elements in the course of waking up is the canon of dialectics. It is paradigmatic for the thinker and binding for the historian. . . . All historical knowledge can be represented in the image of balanced scales, one tray of which is weighted with what has been and the other with knowledge of what is present. Whereas on the first the facts assembled can never be too humble or too numerous, on the second there can be only a few heavy, massive weights . . . [for] history is not simply a science but also and not least a form of remembrance." Walter Benjamin, *The Arcades Project* (Cambridge, MA: The Belknap Press of Harvard University Press, 1999), 464, 468, 471. Our study, in contrast, deals with awakening in the twenty-first.

3. Octavia E. Butler, *Fledgling* (New York: Grand Central Publishing, 2005), 1–2.

4. Octavia E. Butler, *Fledgling* (New York: Grand Central Publishing, 2005), 8. Here, Butler wonderfully dovetails with Noam Chomsky, *What Kind of Creatures Are We?* (New York: Columbia University Press, 2018) and the suggestive notion that we are creatures of language, also fruitfully discussed in Robert Wokler, *Rousseau, the Age of Enlightenment, and Their Legacies*, edited by Bryan Garsten, and with an introduction by Christopher Brooke, especially 214–232 (New Jersey: Princeton University Press, 2012).

5. The *Blade* series of films offers the closest narrative rendition. Blade is a genetically manipulated cross between a white vampiric father and a Black human mother, except he is fully grown, does not have symbiotes, and is set on killing all vampires and their followers, and little about him is empathetic.

6. See also Noam Chomsky, "The Delphic Oracle: Her Message for Today," May 4, 2020. https://www.youtube.com/watch?v=SO3tE7clWhI

7. Octavia E. Butler, *Fledgling* (New York: Grand Central Publishing, 2005), 54. For an intriguing exploration of the origins of human moral sensibility, see John Mikhail, *Elements of Moral Cognition: Rawls' Linguistic Analogy and the Cognitive Science of Moral and Legal Judgment* (New York: Cambridge University Press, 2013). See also, Jonathan Glover, *Humanity: A Moral History of the Twentieth Century* (New Haven: Yale University Press, 2012).

8. Octavia E. Butler, *Fledgling* (New York: Grand Central Publishing, 2005), 57.

9. An analogous recent example was discussed with the passing of former US Secretary of State Madeleine Albright, who found out late in her life that she was Jewish, her parents having converted to Roman Catholicism to try and escape Nazi invaders in Czechoslovakia, where 26 members of her family were murdered by the Nazis in the Holocaust. See Robert D. McFadden, "Madeleine Albright: First Woman to Serve as Secretary of State, Dies at 84," *New York Times* (March 25, 2022).

10. Shori also finds out that her Black mother named her for "a kind of bird—an East African nested nightingale."

11. Octavia E. Butler, *Fledgling* (New York: Grand Central Publishing, 2005), 62–67, 133. We thank Jerry Rafiki Jenkins for sharing his important thoughts with us on melanin in the configuration of questions of race, power, and ethnicity in Octavia Butler's work and beyond. See Jerry Rafiki Jenkins, *The Paradox of Blackness in African American Vampire Fiction* (Ohio State University Press, 2019). See Nina G.

Jablonski, *Skin: A Natural History* (Berkeley: University of California Press, 2013), 65–75; Nina G. Jablonski, *Living Color: The Biological & Social Meaning of Skin Color* (Berkeley: University of California Press, 2012), and Nina G. Jablonski, ed., *The Persistence of Race*, Sun Press, 2020, especially George Chaplin and Nina G. Jablonski, "Semantics in the Philosophy of Race," on the deconstruction of the concept in the section "The Ontological Status of Race as a Biological Fact," 143–154.

12. Octavia E. Butler, *Fledgling* (New York: Grand Central Publishing, 2005), 63, 74–76, 123.

13. Octavia E. Butler, *Fledgling* (New York: Grand Central Publishing, 2005), 104–113. The passages also overlap with the important work of Ifi Amadiume, *Male Daughters, Female Husbands* (London: Zed Press, 2017), as well as that of Catherine Coquery-Vidrovitch, *African Women: A Modern History* (New York: Perseus, 1997), and the comparative anthropologist and sociologist Jack Goody, as well as feminist futuristic science fiction writers from Ursula Le Guin to Marge Piercy.

14. Octavia E. Butler, *Fledgling* (New York: Grand Central, 2005), 188.

15. Octavia E. Butler, *Fledgling* (New York: Grand Central Publishing, 2005), 129–132, 187–188.

16. Octavia E. Butler, *Fledgling* (New York: Grand Central Publishing, 2005),131–132.

17. Octavia E. Butler, *Fledgling* (New York: Grand Central Publishing, 2005), 148.

18. Octavia E. Butler, *Fledgling* (New York: Grand Central Publishing, 2005), 148. Such realities also raise what Noam Chomsky has called Plato's and Orwell's problem, how human beings know so much with so little information, which he takes to be a central question of language, thus seeing it as a biological property of the species, and Orwell's problem, how can humans know so little with so much information, though here of course, the problems are raised regarding the Ina. See Noam Chomsky, "Mental Constructions and Social Reality," in *Knowledge and Language, From Orwell's Problem to Plato's Problem*, 29–58, eds., Eric Reuland and Werner Abraham (Dordrecht: Kluwer Academic Publishers, 1993), and Chomsky's "Force & Opinion," in *Deterring Democracy* (London: Verso, 1991).

19. The concept of willful blindness, or willful ignorance, has gotten some much-needed attention in recent scholarly investigations, yet it is also an old concept evident in the notion of false consciousness, though even this raises the questions of the very construction of preferences by humans through which persons and groups pursue their intended aims, to the extent these exist. See Sarah Lichtenstein and Paul Slovic, ed., *The Construction of Preference* (New York: Cambridge University Press, 2006). See also Daniel Ellsberg, *Risk, Ambiguity, and Decision* (New York: Routledge, 2001).

20. Octavia E. Butler, *Fledgling* (New York: Grand Central Publishing, 2005), 132–133, 137–190.

21. Octavia E. Butler, *Fledgling* (New York: Grand Central Publishing, 2005), 257.

22. Octavia E. Butler, *Fledgling* (New York: Grand Central Publishing, 2005), 292. The parallels here with recent questions of demographic change here and the resurgence of white supremacy, xenophobia, and neofascism across the world are prescient. See also Richard Alba, *The Great Demographic Illusion: Majority, Minority, and the Expanding American Mainstream* (New Jersey: Princeton University Press,

2020). See also *Daedalus*, "Immigration, Nativism, & Race in the United States," Douglas S. Massey, Guest Editor (Spring 2021).

23. See Alex J. Kay, *Empire of Destruction: A History of Nazi Mass Killing* (New Haven: Yale University Press, 2021). See also "Memory and History: On the Poverty of Remembering and Forgetting the Judeocide," Arno J. Mayer, *Why Did the Heavens Not Darken? The Final Solution in History* (London: Verso, 2012), 467–482.

24. National Public Radio (March 19, 2022). https://www.npr.org/2022/03/19 /1087712574/former-ukrainian-minister-of-infrastructure-describes-destruction-in -kyiv.

25. Andrew Wilson, *The Ukrainians* (New Haven: Yale University Press, 2nd edition, 2002), 282. See also Andrew Wilson, *The Ukrainians* (New Haven: Yale University Press, 4th edition, 2015), 279–285.

26. See Mai Ngai, *Impossible Subjects: Illegal Aliens & the Making of Modern America* (New Jersey: Princeton University Press, 2014). See also Gabriel J. Chin and Rose Cuison Villazor, eds., *The Immigration and Nationalization Act of 1965: Legislating a New America* (New York: Cambridge University Press, 2018).

27. See David Barsamian, Evrand Abrahamian, Noam Chomsky, Nader Hashemi, Azadeh Moaveni, and Triti Parsi, *ReTargeting Iran* (San Francisco: City Lights Media, 2020). See also Gary Y. Okihiro, *Third World Studies: Theorizing Liberation* (Durham: Duke University Press, 2016). Contemporary Iran is part of a more ancient civilization, Persia, and often contemporary Iranian Americans will call themselves Persians, in part a response to the racist demonization of Iranians and others from the Middle East, as seen for example in the film *American Sniper* (2014), the highest-grossing Hollywood war film of all time, beating out even *Private Ryan* (1998).

28. Toni Morrison, *The Origins of Others*, with a foreword by Ta-Nehisi Coates (Cambridge, MA: Harvard University Press, 2017). See also Morrison's chapter, "Racism and Fascism," in *The Sources of Self-Regard: Selected Essays, Speeches, & Meditations* (New York: Alfred A. Knopf, 2019), 14–16. This concern dovetails too with the Jewish philosopher and Holocaust survivor Emmanuel Levinas about the need for an ethical relationship with other human beings in general, and specific people particularly. The exclamation of the Ina about overbreeding also related to an old antisemitic racist trope that has recently reemerged. In what is referred to as the replacement theory, an antisemitic vision accuses the Jews, who are seen as controlling the world, of setting out to replace white people with people of color, immigrants, and refugees. This horrific antisemitic conspiracy theory has inspired massacres of Jews in synagogues, including those working to aid refugees and immigrants seeking safety in the US. And of course, this language has also been used especially against the supposed invasion by immigrants, tragically leading to the massacres of Mexicans, Mexican Americans, and members of the Latinx community in El Paso, Texas in recent years. For the voices of the refugees and immigrants themselves, see the recent collection by the Vietnamese American novelist Viet Thanh Nguyen, ed., *The Displaced: Refugee Writers on Refugee Lives* (New York: Abrams Press, 2018), and his edited collection, *The Refugees* (New York: Grove Press, 2017). See Ai Weiwei's 2017 documentary film *Human Flow*, his *Humanity* (New Jersey: Princeton University Press, 2018), and his *Human Flow: Stories from the Global Refugee Crisis* (New

Jersey: Princeton University Press, 2020). See also Dohra Ahmad, ed., *The Penguin Book of Migration Literature* (New York: Penguin Classics, 2019), and her *Rotten English: A Literary Anthology* (New York: W.W. Norton & Co., 2007). See also Martha Minow, *Making All the Difference: Inclusion, Exclusion, and American Law* (Ithaca: Cornell University Press, 1990).

29. See Michael Mann, *Fascists* (New York: Cambridge University Press, 2004), Michael Mann, *The Dark Side of Democracy: Explaining Ethnic Cleansing* (New York: Cambridge University Press, 2005), Michael Mann, *The Sources of Social Power, Volume III*, "The Fascist Alternative, 1918–1945" (New York: Cambridge University Press, 2012), 315–346. See also Jeffrey Veidlinger, *In the Midst of Civilized Europe: The Pogroms of 1918–1921 and the Onset of the Holocaust* (New York: Metropolitan Books, 2022). See also, Ivan T. Berend, *A Century of Populist Demagogues: Eighteen European Portraits, 1918–2018* (Budapest; New York: Central European University Press, 2020). Ray Brandon and Wendy Lower, ed., *The Shoah in Ukraine* (Bloomington: University of Indiana Press, in association with the United States Holocaust Memorial Museum, 2008). Timothy Snyder, *The Reconstruction of Nations* (New Haven: Yale University Press, 2003) and Timothy Snyder, *The Bloodlands: Europe Between Hitler and Stalin* (New York: Basic Books, 2016). See also Martha Minow, *Breaking the Cycles of Hatred: Memory, Law, and Repair* (New Jersey: Princeton University Press, 2002). See also, Martha Minow, *In Brown's Wake* (New York: Oxford University Press, 2010). On the Cold War, see Noam Chomsky, *Deterring Democracy* (New York: Verso, 1991), as well as Christopher Jones, "Protection from One's Friends," *Soviet Strategy and the New Military Thinking*, Derek Leebaert and Timothy Dickinson, eds. (New York: Cambridge University Press, 1992), 100–126. And on the current trajectory and for a new way forward, see John D. Steinbruner, *Principles of Global Security* (Washington, D.C.: Brookings, 2000), and John Steinbruner and Nancy Gallagher, "Prospects for Global Security: Constructive Transformation: An Alternative Vision of Global Security," *Daedalus: Journal of the American Academy of Arts & Sciences*, (Summer 2004), 83–103. See also Matthew Evangelista, *Unarmed Forces: The Transnational Movement to End the Cold War* (Ithaca: Cornell University Press, 1999). See also Randall Caroline Watson Forsberg, *Toward a Theory of Peace: The Role of Moral Beliefs*, edited and with an introduction by Matthew Evangelista and Neta C. Crawford (Ithaca: Cornell University Press, 2019).

30. Mike Sonksen, "'Making the Impossible Possible': Octavia Butler Reimagines Space and Time," *Boom California* (December 9, 2020).

31. Marleen S. Barr, "The Allegory of Shori's Cave: Teaching *Fledgling* as the Science Fiction of Racism," in *Approaches to Teaching the Works of Octavia E. Butler*, ed., Tarshia L. Stanley (New York: Modern Language Association of America, 2019), 124–128. Octavia E. Butler, *Parable of the Sower* (New York: Grand Central Publishing, 2000), 196.

32. Octavia E. Butler, *Parable of the Talents* (New York: Grand Central Publishing, 2000), 80, 412. On the question of the "Enlightenment," see Carlton D. Floyd and Thomas E. Reifer, "What Happens to a Dream Deferred? W.E.B. Du Bois and the Radical Black Enlightenment/Endarkenment," *Socialism and Democracy in W.E.B.*

Du Bois's Life, Thought, and Legacy, Edward Carson, Gerald Horne, and Phillip Luke Sinitiere, eds. (New York: Routledge, 2022): 52–80. For a recent exploration of the issues of the Black Atlantic, important for rethinking the question of Enlightenment and Butler's "unenlightened self-interest," see Adriano Pedrosa and Tomas Toledo, eds., *Afro-Atlantic Histories* (DelMonico Books/Museo de Arte de Sao Paulo, 2021).

33. Octavia Butler, *Parable of the Talents* (New York: Grand Central Publishing, 2000), 412.

34. On Galicia, among other works, see Albert Lichtblau and Michael John, "Jewries in Galicia and Bukovina, in Lemberg and Czernowitz," *Jewries at the Frontier*, eds., Sander L. Gilman and Milton Shain (Urbana: University of Illinois Press, 1999), 29–66, and more recently Frank Golczewski, "Shades of Grey: Reflections on Jewish-Ukrainian and German-Ukrainian Relations in Galicia," in *The Shoah in Ukraine*, 114–155, eds., Ray Brandon and Wendy Lower (Bloomington: University of Indiana Press, in association with the United States Holocaust Memorial Museum, 2008), and Dennis Ougrin and Anastasia Ougrin, O*ne Hundred Years in Galicia* (Cambridge: Cambridge Scholars Publishing, 2020).

35. W.E.B. Du Bois, "The Negro and the Warsaw Ghetto," *Jewish Life* (April 1952): 14–15. See also Harold Brackman, "'A Calamity Almost Beyond Comprehension': Nazi Anti-Semitism and the Holocaust in the Thought of W.E.B. Du Bois," *American Jewish History* 88, Number 1 (March 2000): 53–93. See also George Bornstein, "W.E.B. Du Bois and the Jews: Ethics, Editing, and *The Souls of Black Folk,*" *Textual Cultures* 1, Number 1 (Spring 2006): 64–74. See also W.E.B. Du Bois, *The Souls of Black Folk: A Norton Critical Edition*, eds., Henry Louis Gates Jr. and Terri Hume Oliver (New York: W.W. Norton and Company, 1999). Of course, for a more critical perspective on "civilization," see Stanley Diamond, *In Search of the Primitive*, with a foreword by Eric Wolf (New York: Routledge, 2017). For a profound rethinking of the role of xenophobic nationalism, antisemtism, and the roots of the Holocaust in the period before, during, and after World War I, as well as important reflections on the Armenian genocide, see Laura Engelstein, *Russia in Flames: War, Revolution, Civil War 1914–1921* (New York: Oxford University Press, 2019), especially Chapter 2, "Germans, Jews, Armenians," 53–67. And see also Laura Engelstein, *The Resistible Rise of Antisemitism: Exemplary Cases from Russia, Ukraine, and Poland* (Waltham, Massachusetts: Brandeis University Press, 2020).

36. Octavia Butler, *Parable of the Sower* (New York: Grand Central, 2000), 3.

37. See NASA, "Welcome to Octavia E. Butler Landing" (March 5, 2021). https://www.jpl.nasa.gov/images/pia24483-welcome-to-octavia-e-butler-landing

38. National Public Radio, "NASA Scientist Christina Hernandez, Discusses Her Work on the Mars Rover Perseverance Project" (February 20, 2021). https://www.npr.org/2021/02/21/969886082/nasa-scientist-discusses-her-work-on-the-perseverance-mars-rover-project

39. Tunku Varadarajan, "The American Dream is Alive on Mars," *Wall Street Journal* (February 26, 2021). Delightfully, the rover for which Verma is responsible is named Perseverance, a term dear to Butler's understanding of what it will take for us to survive, on earth or on Mars. And yet a necessary trait for humankind, evident in the amount of work, sweat, and maybe tears that went into the rover's use and

development, which in this form can stand as a monument to human perseverance, should be highlighted in this capacity, as symbolic of substantive effort, ingenuity, and hard work.

40. Robert Frost, "The Road Not Taken." The final lines are as follows:

"Somewhere ages and ages hence:

Two roads diverged in a wood, and I—

I took the one less travelled by,

And that has made all the difference." Taken from Poetry Foundation website (April 18, 2021). Originally published, 1915.

41. See the Union of Concerned Scientists ("NASA Reaches for Muzzle as Renowned Climate Scientist Speaks Out") December 12, 2006. See Andrew C. Revkin, "NASA's Goals Delete Mention of Home Planet," *New York Times* (July 22, 2006).

42. For the possibilities of a new mutualism for the Americas and beyond, see *Noam Chomsky and Voices from North, South, and Central America, New World of Indigenous Resistance* (San Francisco: City Lights Books, 2010), and Jeffery M. Paige, *Indigenous Revolution in Ecuador & Bolivia, 1990–2005* (Tucson: University of Arizona Press, 2020).

43. Ursula K. Le Guin, *The Left Hand of Darkness* (New York: Ace Books, 2010).

44. National Public Radio, "The Art of Romare Bearden: Collages Fuse Essence of Old Harlem, the American South," Romare Bearden and Neda Ulaby (September 14, 2003).

45. Marx, quoted in Walter Benjamin, *The Arcades Project* (Cambridge, MA: The Belknap Press of Harvard University Press, 1999), 456.

46. Walter Benjamin, *The Arcades Project* (Cambridge, MA: The Belknap Press of Harvard University Press, 1999), 462–463. Benjamin goes on to say: "A remark by Ernst Bloch apropos of *The Arcades Project:* 'History displays its Scotland Yard badge.' It was in the context of a conversation in which I was describing how this work—comparable, in method, to the process of splitting the atom—liberates the enormous energies of history that are bound up in the 'once upon a time' of classical historiography. The history that showed things 'as they really were' was the strongest narcotic of the century." See also Rolf Tiedemann, "Dialectics at a Standstill," in Walter Benjamin, *The Arcades Project* (Cambridge, MA: The Belknap Press of Harvard University Press, 1999), 929–945. See also Todd Samuel Presner, *Mobile Modernity: Germans, Jews, Trains* (New York: Columbia University Press, 2007), especially Chapter 1, "Dialectics at a Standstill," 1–30. Eduardo Cadava, in *Words of Light: Theses on the Photography of History* (Princeton, New Jersey: Princeton University Press, 1998), 64, gives a slightly different translation of Benjamin here, writing of "an image is that in which the Then and the Now come together in a flash of lightning, into a constellation."

47. Marge Piercy, *Woman on the Edge of Time* (New York: Ballantine Books, 2016), 212–213. Parts of this passage are quoted in Fredric Jameson, *Archaeologies of the Future* (New York: Verso, 2007), 233.

48. Daniel Ellsberg, *The Doomsday Machine* (New York: Bloomsbury, 2018).

49. In his speech, the Pope also mentioned the important figures of Abraham Lincoln, the Reverend Dr. Martin Luther King Jr., and the monastic writer and critic of war and racism, and activist for peace and justice, Thomas Merton. For a sampling of Merton's powerful work, see *Faith and Violence* (University of Notre Dame, 1968).

50. G.E.M. De Ste. Croix, *The Class Struggle in the Ancient Greek World* (Ithaca: Cornell University Press, 1981), 502–503.

51. Andrei P. Tsygankov's *The Dark Double: US Media, Russia, and the Politics of Values* (New York: Oxford University Press, 2019) chronicles the unidimensional view of the US and USSR, and now Russia, as exemplifying freedom (and thus we would say too, the American Dream), and Russia as the epitome of evil. Such a characterization was perfectly captured by the 2022 PBS *Frontline* documentary *Putin's War*, in which the only empire that appears is Russia's, and the US is depicted as selflessly supporting freedom, including in the Arab Spring, despite this being totally false. See also Tom Reifer, "The 'Arab 1848': Reflections on US Policy & the Power of Nonviolence," Transnational Institute, February 23, 2011. See also Noam Chomsky, *Deterring Democracy* (New York: Verso, 1991). For some important and sophisticated background pieces on the Russian invasion and the Ukraine crisis, see "Interview with Volodomyr Artiuk," *Jacobin* (2022); Volodymyr Ishchenko, "Ukraine's Fractures," *New Left Review* 87, (May/June 2014): 7–35; Noam Chomsky, "US Military Escalation Against Russia Would Have No Victors," *Truthout*, March 1, 2022; Richard Sakwa, *Frontline Ukraine: Crisis in the Borderlands* (London: I.B. Tauris, 2015); William H. Hill, *No Place for Russia* (New York: Columbia University Press, 2018); Paul D'Anieri, *Ukraine and Russia* (New York: Cambridge University Press, 2019); William J. Burns, *The Back Channel* (New York: Random House, 2020); and M.E. Sarotte, *Not One Inch* (New Haven: Yale University Press, 2021), the latter a work of critical importance, though it must be said that Sarotte in her various op-ed pieces hews to the official line that the US made no promise to expand NATO to the East, though this is belied by an overwhelming amount of evidence. See especially the website of the National Security Archive, particularly their important series on NATO expansion. See also the various articles and correspondence by Joshua R. Itzkowitz Shifrinson in *International Security*, as well as, more recently, Marc Trachtenberg, "The United States and the NATO Non-extension Assurances of 1990: New Light on an Old Problem?" *International Security* 45, No. 3 (Winter 2020/21): 162–203.

52. See for example, Thomas Merton, *Conjectures of a Guilty Bystander* (New York: Image Books, 1968).

53. See, Immanuel Wallerstein, *Utopistics: Or, Historical Choices of the Twenty-first Century* (New York: New Press, 1998). For another powerful example, see Kyle Harper, *The Fate of Rome: Climate, Disease, and the End of an Empire* (New York: Harper and Row, 2019) and Mike Davis, *The Monster Enters* (New York: Verso, 2022).

54. On existing capitalism, see Giovanni Arrighi, *The Long Twentieth Century* (New York: Verso, 2010), and Noam Chomsky and Marv Waterstone, *Consequences of Capitalism* (Chicago, IL: Haymarket, 2021). On actually existing capitalism and socialism, see Giovanni Arrighi, "Marxist Century, American Century: The Making & Remaking of the World Labour Movement," *New Left Review* 179 (1990): 29–64; Giovanni Arrighi, "World Income Inequalities & the Future of Socialism," *New Left Review* 189 (1991): 39–66; Giovanni Arrighi, *Adam Smith in Beijing: Lineages of the 21st Century* (New York: Verso, 2009).

55. "The Last Resort," written by Don Henley and Glenn Frey. Copyright 1976 Cass Country Music/Red Cloud Music. All Rights Reserved. These lyrics are taken from: https://www.azlyrics.com/lyrics/eagles/thelastresort-1976.html. For a powerful exploration of these themes, which dovetails with that presented here, see Timothy P. Duane, *Shaping the Sierra: Nature, Culture, and Conflict in the Changing West* (Berkeley: University of California Press, 1999), and John Muir, *My First Summer in the Sierra*, with an introduction by Mike Davis (New York: Modern Library, 2003), and Mike Davis, *Ecology of Fear: Los Angeles and the Imagination of Disaster* (New York: Verso, 2022). Walter Benjamin, *Selected Writings, Volume 4, 1938–1940*, edited by Howard Eiland and Michael W. Jennings (Cambridge, MA: The Belknap Press of Harvard University Press, 2003), 392.

56. Peter Bacon Hales, *Outside the Gates of Eden: The American Dream of America from Hiroshima to Now* (Chicago: University of Chicago Press, 2014). See also Peter Bacon Hales, *Atomic Spaces: Living on the Manhattan Project* (Urbana: University of Illinois Press, 1997). See also Paul N. Edwards, *The Closed World* (Cambridge: MIT, 2007). See also Robert Fishman, *Bourgeois Utopias* (New York: Basic Books, 1997) and Robert M. Fogelson, *Bourgeois Nightmares* (New Haven: Yale University Press, 2005).

57. Dr. Martin Luther King, 67/05/29–31, "To Charter Our Course for the Future," Address to the SCLC Retreat, Frogmore, SC.

58. Theodor Adorno, *Minima Moralia* (New York: Verso, 1989), 102–103. For the background of the famous image of the melting pot, see Israel Zangwill, *From the Ghetto to the Melting Pot: Israel Zangwill's Jewish Plays*, edited, with Introduction and Commentary by Edna Nahshon (Detroit, MI: Wayne State University Press, 2006), and Meri-Jane Rochelson, *a Jew in the Public Arena: The Career of Israel Zangwill* (Detroit, MI: Wayne State University Press, 2008).

59. James Baldwin. "As Much Truth as One Can Bear." *New York Times*, January 14, 1962.

60. Octavia Butler, *Parable of the Sower* (New York: Grand Central Publishing, 2000), 153.

61. James Truslow Adams, *The Epic of America* (Boston: Little, Brown, & Company, 1931), 3–9.

62. Walter Benjamin, *The Arcades Project* (Cambridge, MA: The Belknap Press of Harvard University Press, 1999), 464.

63. In *The Arcades Project* (Cambridge, MA: The Belknap Press of Harvard University Press, 1999: 463–464), Benjamin asks: "Is awakening perhaps the synthesis of dream consciousness (as thesis) and waking consciousness (as antithesis)? Then the

moment of awakening would be identical with the 'now of recognizability,' in which things put on their true—surrealist-face. Thus, in Proust, the importance of staking an entire life on life's supremely dialectical point of rupture: awakening. Proust begins with an evocation of the space of someone waking up." See also Jeff Manza and Clem Brooks, "Prisoners of the American Dream: Americans' Attitudes Towards Taxes and Inequality in a New Gilded Age," 2014. In the Eagles' 1976 title track song, "Hotel California," the following words appear:

> Mirrors on the ceiling,
>
> The pink champagne on ice
>
> And she said "We are all just prisoners here, of our own device"

In these words and in this song, and album, we see all the traditional themes, illusion over reality, the imprisonment in the illusion, the dream, and the gesture towards another way, a fervent hope for a different future.

> Source: Musixmatch Songwriters: Henley Donald Hugh / Frey Glenn Lewis / Felder Don
>
> Hotel California lyrics © Cass County Music, Red Cloud Music, Fingers Music

64. Dinaw Mengestu, *The Beautiful Things That Heaven Bears* (New York: Riverhead Books, 2007), 99–100.

65. Toni Morrison, *Paradise* (New York: Vintage, 2014), xi–xvii.

Bibliography

Abelmann, Nancy, and John Lie, eds. *Blue Dreams: Korean Americans and the Los Angeles Riots*. Cambridge, MA: Harvard University Press, 1997.

Abercrombie, Barbara. *A Year of Writing Dangerously.* Novato, California: New World Library, 2012.

Abrahamson, Eric John. *Building Home: Howard A. Ahmanson and the Politics of the American Dream.* Berkeley: University of California Press, 2013.

Acuna, Rodolfo F. *The Making of Chicana/o Studies.* New Jersey: Rutgers University Press, 2011.

Adamic, Louis. *Dynamite: The Story of Class Violence in America.* San Francisco: AK Press, 2008. First published 1931.

Adamic, Louis. *From Many Lands.* New York: Harper & Brothers, 1939.

Adamic, Louis. *Laughing in the Jungle: An Autobiography of an Immigrant in America,* New York: Harper & Brothers, 1932.

Adamic, Louis. *The Old Alien by the Kitchen Window: Selected Writings.* New York: Modern Times Press, 2022.

Adams, James Truslow. *James Truslow Adams, Select Correspondence*, edited with a Bibliographical Essay by Allan Nevins. New Brunswick: Transaction Publishers, 2012.

Adams, James Truslow. *America's Tragedy.* New York: Charles Scribner's Sons, 1934.

Adams, James Truslow. *The Epic of America.* Boston: Little, Brown, & Company, 1931.

Adamson, Paul, and Marty Arbunich. *Eichler: Modernism Rebuilds the American Dream,* with a foreword by Gwendolyn Wright. Salt Lake City: Gibbs Smith, 2002.

Adorno, Theodor. *Minima Moralia: Reflections from Damaged Life.* London: Verso, 1974, first published 1951.

Adorno, Theodor. *Negative Dialectics.* New York: Continuum, 1981.

Ahmad, Dohra, ed. *The Penguin Book of Migration Literature.* New York: Penguin Classics, 2019.

Ahmad, Dohra, ed. *Rotten English: A Literary Anthology.* New York: W.W. Norton, 2007.

Alba, Richard. *The Great Demographic Illusion: Majority, Minority, and the Expanding American Mainstream.* New Jersey: Princeton University Press, 2020.

Alba, Richard, and Kenneth Prewitt, Special Editors. *The Annals of the American Academy of Political and Social Science: What Census Data Miss About American Diversity*. Volume 677 (May 2018).

Ali, Tariq, "The Legacy of Simon B." *New Left Review* 40 (July/August 2006): 149–160.

Alighieri, Dante. *The Divine Comedy. Volume 1: Inferno. Volume 2: Purgatorio. Volume 3: Paradiso*. Edited and translated by Robert M. Durling. New York: Oxford, 1996, 2003, 2011.

Amadiume, Ifi. *Male Daughters, Female Husbands: Gender & Sex in an African Society*, London: Zed Press, 2017. First published, 1987.

Amnesty International, Angelina Jolie, and Geraldine Van Bueren. *Know Your Rights and Claim Them: A Guide for Youth*. Minneapolis: Zest Books, 2021.

Anderson, Benedict. *Imagined Communities: Reflections on the Origins and Spread of Nationalism*. New York: Verso, 2016.

Anderson, Kurt. *Fantasyland: How America Went Haywire: A 500-Year History*. New York: Random House, 2018.

Anderson, Perry. "Force and Consent." *New Left Review* 17 (September/October 2002): 5–30.

Anderson, Perry. "Fredric Jameson: The Fruits of Time." Hoberg Prize Symposium, 2008. https://www.youtube.com/watch?v=_r4jivgr1MA.

Anderson, Perry. "The Nature and Meaning of the Wars of Hispanic American Liberation." *World Society* Studies, edited by Volker Bornschier and Peter Lengyel, 91–110. Frankfurt: Campus Verlag, 1990.

Anguiano, Dani, and Alastair Gee. *Fire in Paradise: An American Tragedy*. New York: W.W. Norton, 2021.

Appiah, Kwame Anthony, and Henry Louis Gates Jr., ed. *Africana: Arts & Letters: An A-to-Z Reference of Writers, Musicians, & Artists of the African American Experience*. Philadelphia: Running Press, 2004a.

Appiah, Kwame Anthony, and Henry Louis Gates Jr., ed. *Africana: Civil Rights: An A-to-Z Reference of the Movement that Changed America*, Philadelphia: Running Press, 2004b.

Arana, Marie. *Bolivar: American Liberator*. New York: Simon & Schuster, 2013.

Ardizzone, Heidi. "Catching Up with History: Night of the Quarter Moon, the Rhinelander Case, and Interracial Marriage in 1959." *Mixed Race Hollywood*, edited by Mary Beltrán and Camilla Fojas, 87–112. New York University Press, 2008.

Aristotle. *The Nicomachean Ethics*. New York: Oxford World Classics, 2009.

Armitage, David. *The Declaration of Independence: A Global History*. Cambridge, MA: Harvard University Press, 2007.

Arrighi, Giovanni. *Adam Smith in Beijing: Lineages of the 21st Century*. New York: Verso, 2009.

Arrighi, Giovanni. *The Long Twentieth Century: Money, Power and the Origins of Our Times*. 2nd ed. New York: Verso, 2010.

Arrighi, Giovanni. "Marxist Century, American Century: The Making and Remaking of the World Labour Movement." *New Left Review* 179 (January/February 1990): 29–64.

Arrighi, Giovanni. "World Income Inequalities and the Future of Socialism." *New Left Review* 189 (September/October 1991): 39–68.

Arrighi, Giovanni, Terence K. Hopkins, and Immanuel Wallerstein. *Antisystemic Movements*, New York: Verso, 1989.

Arsenault, Raymond. *Freedom Riders: 1961 and the Struggle for Racial Justice.* New York: Oxford University Press, 2006.

Badger, Reid. *A Life in Ragtime: A Biography of James Reese Europe.* New York: Oxford University Press, 1995.

Balance, Christine Bacareza, and Lucy Mae San Pablo Burns, eds. *California Dreaming: Movement and Place in the Asian American Imaginary.* Honolulu: University of Hawai'i Press, and Los Angeles: UCLA Asian American Studies Center, 2020.

Balderrama, Francisco E., and Raymond Rodriguez. *Decade of Betrayal: Mexican Americans in the 1930s.* Albuquerque: University of New Mexico Press, 2006.

Baldwin, Davarian L. *Chicago's New Negroes: Modernity, the Great Migration, and Black Urban Life.* Durham: University of North Carolina Press, 2007.

Baldwin, James. *Another Country.* New York: Vintage, 1993. First published 1960.

Baldwin, James. *Collected Essays.* Edited by Toni Morrison. New York: The Library of America, 1998.

Baldwin, James. "Come Out the Wilderness." In *James Baldwin: Early Novels and Stories,* edited by Toni Morrison, 908–932. New York: The Library of America, 1998. First Published in 1958.

Baldwin, James. "Sonny's Blues," In *Early Stories & Novels,* edited by Toni Morrison, 831–864. New York: Library of America, 1992. First published in 1957.

Baldwin, James. *The Price of the Ticket: Collected Nonfiction, 1948–1985.* New York: St. Martin's Press, 1985.

Balibar, Etienne, and Immanuel Wallerstein, *Race, Nation, Class: Ambiguous Identities.* New York: Verso, 2011. First published, 1991.

Baltzell, E. Digby. *The Protestant Establishment: Aristocracy and Caste in America.* New Haven: Yale University Press, 1964.

Bang, Derrick. *Vince Guaraldi at the Piano.* Jefferson, North Carolina: McFarland & Company, Inc., Publishers, 2012.

Banks, Ingrid, Gaye Johnson, George Lipsitz, Ula Taylor, Daniel Widener, and Clyde Woods, eds. *Black California Dreamin': The Crisis of California's African-American Communities.* University of California, Santa Barbara, Center for Black Studies Research, 2012. https://escholarship.org/uc/item/63g6128j.

Banks, Russell. *Cloudsplitter: A Novel.* New York: Harper Perennial, 1998.

Baraka, Amiri. *Digging: The Afro-American Soul of American Classical Music.* Berkeley: University of California Press, 2009.

Barnett, Randy E., and Evan D. Bernick. *The Original Meaning of the 14th Amendment: Its Letter & Spirit*, with a foreword by James Oakes. Cambridge, MA: The Belknap Press of Harvard University Press, 2021.

Barney, William L. "Rush to Disaster: Secession and the Slaves' Revenge." In *Secession Winter: When the Union Fell Apart*, edited by Robert J. Cook, William L.

Barney, and Elizabeth R. Varon, 20–43. Baltimore: The Johns Hopkins University Press, 2013.

Barr, Juliana. "Borders & Borderlands." In *Why You Can't Teach United States History Without American Indians,* edited by Susan Sleeper-Smith, Juliana Barr, Jean M. O'Brien, Nancy Shoemaker, and Scott Manning Stevens, 9–25. Chapel Hill: University of North Carolina Press, 2015.

Barr, Marleen S. "The Allegory of Shori's Cave." In *Approaches to Teaching the Works of Octavia E.* Butler, edited by Tarshia L. Stanley, 124–128. New York: Modern Language Association, 2019.

Barsamian, David, Evrand Abrahamian, Noam Chomsky, Nader Hashemi, Azadeh Moaveni, and Triti Parsi. *ReTargeting Iran.* San Francisco: City Lights Media, 2020.

Bateman, David A. *Disenfranchising Democracy: Constructing the Electorate in the United States, the United Kingdom, and France.* New York: Cambridge University Press, 2018.

Bateman, David A., Ira Katznelson, and John S. Lapinski. *Southern Nation: Congress and White Supremacy after Reconstruction.* New York and Princeton: Russell Sage Foundation and Princeton University Press, 2018.

Bauer, Jr., William J. "Ghost Dances, Bears, and the Legacies of Genocide in California." *Journal of Genocide Research* 19, Issue Number 1 (March 2017): 137–142.

Bauer, Jr., William J. *California Through Native Eyes: Reclaiming History.* Seattle: University of Washington Press, 2016.

Bearden, Romare. "The Negro Artist's Dilemma." In *The Romare Bearden Reader,* edited by Robert G. O'Meally, 91–98. Durham: Duke University Press, 2019.

Beckert, Sven. *Empire of Cotton: A Global History.* New York: Vintage Books, 2014.

Belich, James. *Replenishing the Earth: The Settler Revolution and the Rise of the Anglo-World, 1783–1939.* New York: Oxford University Press, 2009.

Belich, James. "Exploding Wests: Boom and Bust in Nineteenth Century Settler Societies." In *Natural Experiments of* History, edited by Jared Diamond and James A. Robinson, 53–87. Cambridge, MA: Harvard University Press, 2010.

Beltran, Mary, and Camilla Fojas, "Introduction." In *Mixed Race Hollywood,* edited by Mary Beltrán and Camilla Fojas, 1–20. New York University Press, 2008.

Benbow, Mark E. "Birth of a Quotation: Woodrow Wilson and 'Like Writing History with Lightning.'" *The Journal of the Gilded Age and Progressive Era* 9, No. 4, (October 2010): 509–533.

Benjamin, Walter. *The Writer of Modern Life: Essays on Charles Baudelaire.* Translated by Howard Eiland, Edmund Jephcott, Rodney Livingstone, and Harry Zohn. Edited by Michael W. Jennings. Cambridge, MA: The Belknap Press of Harvard University Press, 2016.

Benjamin, Walter. *The Work of Art in the Age of Its Technological Reproducibility, & Other Writings on Media.* Translated by Edmund Jephcott, Rodney Livingstone, and Howard Eiland. Edited by Michael W. Jennings, Brigid Doherty, and Thomas Y. Levin. Cambridge, MA: The Belknap Press of Harvard University Press, 2008.

Benjamin, Walter. *Selected Writings, Volume 4, 1938–1940.* Edited by Howard Eiland and Michael W. Jennings. Cambridge, MA: The Belknap Press of Harvard University Press, 2003.

Benjamin, Walter. "On the Concept of History." *Selected Writings, Volume 4, 1938–1940,* edited by Howard Eiland and Michael W. Jennings, 389–400. Cambridge, MA: The Belknap Press of Harvard University Press, 2003.

Benjamin, Walter. *The Arcades Project.* Prepared on the Basis of the German Volume Edited by Rolf Tiedemann. Translated by Howard Eiland & Kevin McLaughlin. Cambridge, MA: Harvard University Press, 1999.

Benjamin, Walter. *Charles Baudelaire: A Lyric Poet in the Era of High Capitalism.* Translated by Harry Zohn. London, New York: Verso, 1989.

Benjamin, Walter. *One-Way Street and Other Writings.* Translated by Edmund Jephcott and Kingsley Shorter. London: New Left Books, 1979.

Benjamin, Walter. *Illuminations.* New York: Schocken Books, 1968.

Bennett, Matthew R., et al., "Evidence of Humans in North America During the Last Glacial Maximum." *Science* 373 (September 24, 2021): 1528–1531.

Berend, Ivan. *A Century of Populist Demagogues: Eighteen European Examples.* Budapest: Central European University Press, 2020.

Berlin, Ira. *The Making of African America: The Four Great Migrations.* New York: Penguin, 2010.

Berlin, Ira. *Slaves Without Masters: The Free Negro in the Antebellum South.* New York: New Press, 2007.

Bevilacqua, Kathryne. "History Lessons from *Gone with the Wind.*" *The Mississippi Quarterly* 67, No. 1 (Winter 2014): 99–126.

Blackmon, Douglas A. *Slavery by Another Name: The Re-enslavement of Black Americans from the Civil War to World War II.* New York: Anchor Books, 2008.

Blair, Sara. *Harlem Crossroads: Black Writers and the Photograph in the Twentieth Century.* New Jersey: Princeton University Press, 2007.

Blauner, Bob. *Still the Big News: Racial Oppression in America.* Philadelphia: Temple University Press, 2001.

Blight, David W. *Beyond the Battlefield: Race, Memory, and the American Civil War.* Amherst: University of Massachusetts, 2002.

Blight, David W. *Frederick Douglass's Civil War: Keeping Faith in Jubilee.* Baton Rouge: Louisiana State University Press, 1989.

Blumenthal, Sidney. "The Insurrection is Only the Tip of the Iceberg." *The Guardian,* January 6, 2022. https://www.theguardian.com/commentisfree/2022/jan/06/capitol-attack-coup-attempt-trump-far-right-republicans.

Bolton, Herbert Eugene. "The Epic of Greater America." In *Do the Americas Have a Common History? A Critique of the Bolton Theory,* edited by Lewis Hanke, 67–100. New York: Alfred A. Knopf, 1964.

Bonner, Robert E. "Confederate Racialism and the Anticipation of Nazi Evil." In *The Problem of Evil: Slavery, Freedom, and the Ambiguities of American Reform,* edited by Steven Mintz & John Stauffer, 115–124. Amherst: University of Massachusetts Press, 2007.

Bonnivier, Carlene Sobrino, Gerald G. Gubatan, and Gregory Villanueva, eds. *Filipinotown: Voices from Los Angeles,* 2nd edition. CreateSpace Independent Publishing Platform, 2014.

Bornstein, George. "W.E.B. Du Bois and the Jews: Ethics, Editing, and *The Souls of Black Folk.*" *Textual Cultures* 1, Number 1 (Spring 2006): 64–74.

Bowers, Claude. *The Tragic Era: The Revolution After Lincoln.* New York: Halcyon House, 1929.

Boyer, M. Christine. *The City of Collective Memory: Its Historical Imagery & Architectural Entertainments.* Cambridge, MA: MIT Press, 1994.

Brackman, Harold. "'A Calamity Almost Beyond Comprehension': Nazi Anti-Semitism and the Holocaust in the Thought of W.E.B. Du Bois." *American Jewish History* 88, Number 1 (March 2000): 53–93.

Brady, Owen. "Wright's 'Lawd Today': The American Dream Festering in the Sun." *College Language Association Journal* 22, Number 2 (December 1978): 167–172.

Brandon, Ray, and Wendy Lower, eds., *The Shoah in Ukraine.* Bloomington: University of Indiana Press, in association with the United States Holocaust Memorial Museum, 2008.

Braudel, Fernand. "History and the Social Sciences: The *Longue Duree.*" Translated by Immanuel Wallerstein. *Review: A Journal of the Fernand Braudel Center for the Study of Economies, Historical Systems, & Civilizations* XXXII, Number 2 (2009): 171–204. First published in 1958.

Brilliant, Mark. *The Color of America Has Changed: How Racial Diversity Shaped Civil Rights Reform in California, 1941–1978.* New York: Oxford University Press, 2010.

Brinkley, Alan. *The Publisher: Henry Luce and His American Century.* New York, Vintage, 2011.

Brenner, Rebecca. "Walter Benjamin, Walter Johnson, and Reading Early African-American History 'Against the Grain.'" U.S. Intellectual History Blog, Society for U.S. Intellectual History, July 24, 2018. https://s-usih.org/2018/07/walter-benjamin-walter-johnson-and-reading-early-african-american-history-against-the-grain/.

Briones, Matthew M. *Jim and Jap Crow: A Cultural History of 1940s Interracial America.* New York: Oxford University Press, 2012.

Brooks, Charlotte. *Alien Neighbors, Foreign Friends: Asian Americans, Housing, & the Transformation of Urban California.* University of Chicago Press, 2009.

Brossat, Alain, and Sylvie Klingberg. *Revolutionary Yiddishland: A History of Jewish Radicalism.* New York: Verso, 2017.

Brown, Sterling A. *The Collected Poems of Sterling A. Brown.* Edited by Michael S. Harper, with introductions by Sterling Stuckey and James Weldon Johnson, and a new foreword by Cornelius Eady. Evanston, Illinois: Triquarterly/Northwestern University Press, 2020.

Brown, Thomas J. *Civil War Monuments and the Militarization of America.* Chapel Hill: University of North Carolina Press, 2019.

Brown, Thomas J. *The Public Art of Civil War Commemoration: A Brief History with Documents.* Boston: Bedford/St. Martin's, 2004.

Browning, Christopher R. *The Origins of the Final Solution.* Lincoln: University of Nebraska Press, and Jerusalem: Yad Vashem, 2004.

Buck-Morss, Susan. *The Dialectics of Seeing: Walter Benjamin & the Arcades Project.* Cambridge, MA: MIT Press, 1989.

Burnard, Trevor. *Jamaica in an Age of Revolution.* Pittsburgh: University of Pennsylvania Press, 2020.

Burns, William J. *The Back Channel.* New York: Random House, 2020.

Burton, Orville Vernon, and Armand Derfner. *Justice Deferred: Race and the Supreme Court.* Cambridge, MA: The Belknap Press of Harvard University Press, 2021.

Butler, Octavia E. *Fledgling.* New York: Grand Central Publishing, 2005.

Butler, Octavia E. *Parable of the Sower.* New York: Grand Central Publishing, 2000a.

Butler, Octavia E. *Parable of the Talents.* New York: Grand Central Publishing, 2000b.

Cadava, Eduardo. *Words of Light: Theses on the Photography of History.* New Jersey: Princeton University Press, 1998.

Callaway, Ellen. "Ancient Footprints Could Be Oldest Traces of Humans in the Americas," *Nature* 597 (September 30, 2021): 601–602.

Calloway, Colin G. *One Vast Winter Count: The Native American West before Lewis & Clark.* University of Nebraska Press, 2003.

Camus, Albert. *The Plague.* New York: Knopf, 1991. First published in English, 1948.

Campbell, Mary Schmidt. *An American Odyssey: The Life and Work of Romare Bearden.* New York: Oxford University Press, 2018.

Carey, Brycchan. *From Peace to Freedom: Quaker Rhetoric & the Birth of American Antislavery, 1657–1761.* New Haven: Yale University Press, 2012.

Carle, David. *Introduction to Fire in California.* 2nd ed. Oakland, CA: University of California Press, 2021.

Caro, Robert. *Master of the Senate: The Years of Lyndon Johnson.* New York: Vintage, 2003.

Carter, Dan T. *The Politics of Rage.* 2nd ed. Baton Rouge: Louisiana State University Press, 2000.

Case, Anne, and Angus Deaton. *Deaths of Despair and the Future of Capitalism.* New Jersey: Princeton University Press, 2021.

Castells, Manuel. *Networks of Outrage and Hope: Social Movements in the Internet Age.* 2nd ed. New York: Polity, 2015.

Castells, Manuel. *Communication Power.* 2nd ed. New York: Oxford University Press, 2013.

Chacon, Justin Akers, and Mike Davis. *No One is Illegal: Fighting Racism & State Violence on the U.S.-Mexico Border.* 2nd ed. Chicago: Haymarket, 2018.

Chadwick, Bruce. *The Reel Civil War: Mythmaking in American Film.* New York: Vintage Books, 2001.

Chan, Sucheng. *The Bittersweet Soil: The Chinese in California Agriculture.* Berkeley: University of California Press, 1987.

Chang, Gordon H. *Ghosts of Gold Mountain: The Epic Story of the Chinese Who Built the Transcontinental Railroad.* Boston: Mariner Books, 2019.

Chaplin, George, and Nina G. Jablonski. "Semantics in the Philosophy of Race." In *The Persistence of Race*, edited by Nina G. Jablonski, 143–154. Westerly, Rhode Island: Sun Press, 2020.

Chetty, Raj, "Achieving the American Dream Shouldn't Be a Coin Flip." Walter Family Foundation, April 27, 2021. https://www.waltonfamilyfoundation.org/stories/k-12-education/achieving-the-american-dream-shouldnt-be-a-coin-flip.

Chetty, Raj, et al. "The Fading American Dream: Trends in Absolute Income Mobility Since 1940." *Science* 356, Issue 6336 (April 28, 2017): 398–406.

Chin, Gabriel J., and Rose Cuison Villazor, eds. *The Immigration and Nationality Act of 1965: Legislating a New America*, with a foreword by Cruz Reynoso. New York: Cambridge University Press, 2015.

Christian, Henry A., "Louis Adamic and the American Dream." *Journal of General Education* 27, Number 23 (Summer 1975): 113–123.

Chomsky, Noam. *American Power & the New Mandarins: Historical & Political Essays*. New York: Vintage, 1969.

Chomsky, Noam. *Deterring Democracy*. London: Verso, 1991.

Chomsky, Noam. "Mental Constructions and Social Reality." In *Knowledge & Language, From Orwell's Problem to Plato's Problem*, edited by Eric Reuland and Werner Abraham, 29–58. Dordrecht: Kluwer Academic Publishers, 1993.

Chomsky, Noam. *Requiem for the American Dream*. New York: Seven Stories Press, 2017.

Chomsky, Noam. "The Delphic Oracle: Her Message for Today." May 4, 2020. https://www.youtube.com/watch?v=SO3tE7clWhI.

Chomsky, Noam. "US Military Escalation Against Russia Would Have No Victors." *Truthout*, March 1, 2022. https://truthout.org/articles/noam-chomsky-us-military-escalation-against-russia-would-have-no-victors/.

Chomsky, Noam. *What Kind of Creatures Are We?* New York: Columbia University Press, 2018.

Chomsky, Noam, and Tom Reifer, "Language, the Liberal Arts, and the Challenges of the 21st Century," Knapp Chair of Liberal Arts Lecture/Discussion. University of San Diego, Humanities Center. March 22, 2021. https://www.youtube.com/watch?v=I4tX0d3FNxQ.

Chomsky Noam, and Marv Waterstone. *Consequences of Capitalism: Manufacturing Discontent and Resistance*. Chicago, IL: Haymarket, 2021.

Chotiner, Isaac. "Learning from the Failure of Reconstruction." *New Yorker* (January 13, 2021). https://www.newyorker.com/news/q-and-a/learning-from-the-failure-of-reconstruction.

Churchwell, Sarah. "Moonlight and magnolias: The fictions that sustained the American South." *New Statesman.* (August 2015): 21–27.

Clayton, Lawrence A. *Bartolome de Las Casas and the Conquest of the Americas.* New York: Wiley-Blackwell, 2011.

Clayton, Lawrence A. *Bartolome de Las Casas: A Biography.* New York: Cambridge University Press, 2012.

Cobb, William Jelali. *To the Break of Dawn: A Freestyle on the Hip Hop Aesthetic.* New York: New York University Press, 2008.

Cohen, Lizabeth, *Making a New Deal: Industrial Workers in Chicago*. 2nd ed. New York: Cambridge University Press, 2014.

Cohen, Margaret. "Benjamin's Phantasmagoria: The Arcades Project." In *The Cambridge Companion to Walter* Benjamin, edited by David S. Ferris, 199–220. New York: Cambridge University Press, 2004.

Cohen, Margaret. *Profane Illumination: Walter Benjamin & the Paris of Surrealist Revolution*. Berkeley: University of California Press, 1993.

Columbia Law School. "American's Knowledge of the Constitution: A Columbia Law School Survey." May 2002. http://www2.law.columbia.edu/news/surveys/survey_constitution/.

Cook, Robert J. *Civil War Memories: Contesting the Past in the United States Since 1865*. Baltimore: Johns Hopkins University Press, 2017.

Cooper, Marianne. "The Downsizing of the American Dream." October 2, 2015. https://www.theatlantic.com/business/archive/2015/10/american-dreams/408535/.

Corngold, Stanley. "Introduction." In Franz Kafka, *The Metamorphosis*, translated and edited by Stanley Corngold, xi–xliii. New York: Modern Library, 2013.

Coquery-Vidrovitch, Catherine. *African Women: A Modern History*. New York: Perseus, 1997.

Cox, Karen L. *Dixie's Daughters: The United Daughters of the Confederacy and the Preservation of Confederate Culture*. 2nd ed. Tallahassee, Florida: University Press of Florida, 2019.

Crosby, Alfred. *Ecological Imperialism: The Biological Expansion of Europe, 900–1900*. 2nd ed. New York: Cambridge University Press, 2015.

Cullen, Jim. "Twilight's Gleaming: The American Dream and the Ends of Republics." In *The American Dream in the 21st* Century, edited by Sandra J. Hanson and John Kenneth White, 17–26. Philadelphia: Temple University Press, 2011.

Cumings, Bruce. *Korea's Place in the Sun: A Modern History*. New York: W.W. Norton, 2005.

Daedalus: Journal of the American Academy of the Arts & Sciences. "Immigration, Nativism, & Race in the United States." Douglas S. Massey, Guest Editor (Spring 2021). https://www.amacad.org/daedalus/immigration-nativism-race-united-states.

Daniels, Roger. *Prisoners Without Trial: Japanese Americans in World War II*. New York: Hill and Wang, 2004.

Daniels, Roger. "Words Do Matter: A Note on Inappropriate Terminology and the Incarceration of Japanese Americans." In *Nikkei in the Pacific Northwest: Japanese Americans and Japanese Canadians in the Twentieth* Century, edited by Louis Fiset and Gail M. Nomura, 190–214. Seattle: University of Washington Press, 2005.

Davis, Mike. "Star-Spangled Leviathan: A History of American Nationalism, Volume One: 1763–1900." nd. Manuscript in the author's possession.

Davis, Mike. *The Monster Enters*. New York: Verso, 2022a.

Davis, Mike. *Ecology of Fear: Los Angeles and the Imagination of Disaster*. New York: Verso, 2022b.

Davis, Mike. "Planet on a Precipice: Histories & Futures of the Environmental Emergency." University of Massachusetts at Amherst Department of History, 2020–2021 Feinberg Series (October 7, 2020).

Davis, Mike. *Prisoners of the American Dream: Politics and Economy in the History of the U.S. Working Class*. New York: Verso, 2018a. First published, 1986.

Davis, Mike. *City of Quartz: Excavating the Future in Los Angeles*. London: Verso, 2018b.

Davis, Mike. "A Tale of Two Wildfires: Devastation Highlights California's Stark Divide." *The Guardian* (December 5, 2018). https://www.theguardian.com/us-news/2018/dec/04/california-wildfires-paradise-malibu-wealth-class.

Davis, Mike. "Biogeography as Destiny." *Capitalism, Nature, Socialism: A Journal of Socialist Ecology* 8 (2), Issue 30 (June 1997): 63–68.

Davis, Mike. *Dead Cities: And Other Tales*. New York: New Press, 2002.

Davis, Mike. "Marx's Lost Theory: The Politics of Nationalism in 1848." *New Left Review* 93 (May/June 2015): 45–65.

Davis, Mike. "Ward Moore's Freedom Ride." *Science Fiction Studies* 38, Part 3 (November 2011): 385–392.

Davis, Mike, "Who Will Build the Ark?" *New Left Review* 61 (January/February 2010): 29–45.

Davis, Mike. *Magical Urbanism: Latinos Reinvent the US Big City*. New York: Verso, 2001.

Davis, Mike. "Magical Urbanism: Latinos Reinvent the US Big City." *New Left Review* 234 (March/April 1999): 3–43.

de la Fuente, Alejandro, and George Reid Andrews, eds. *Afro-Latin American Studies: An Introduction*. New York: Cambridge University Press, 2018.

de Onis, Jose. "The Americas of Herbert E. Bolton." *The Americas* XII, Washington (1955): 157–168.

de Ste. Croix, G.E.M. *The Class Struggle in the Ancient Greek World: From the Archaic Age to the Arab Conquests*. Ithaca: Cornell University Press, 1981.

Denning, Michael. *The Cultural Front: The Laboring of American Culture in the Twentieth Century*. 2nd ed. New York: Verso, 2010.

Diamond, Stanley. *In Search of the Primitive*. Foreword by Eric Wolf. New York: Routledge, 2017.

Dierksheide, Christa. *Amelioration and Empire: Progress and Slavery in the Plantation Americas*. Charlottesville: University of Virginia Press, 2014.

DiMaggio, Anthony. *Rising Fascism in America: It Can Happen Here*. New York: Routledge, 2021.

Dixon, Melvin. *Ride Out the Wilderness: Geography and Identity in African American Literature*. Urbana: University of Illinois Press, 1987.

Domhoff, G. William, and Michael J. Webber. *Class Power in the New Deal: Corporate Moderates, Southern Democrats, and the Liberal-Labor Coalition*. Stanford: Stanford University Press, 2011.

Douglas, Davison. *Jim Crow Moves North: The Battle Over Northern School Segregation, 1865–1954*. New York: Cambridge University Press, 2005.

Douglass, Frederick. "The Color Line." In *The Portable Frederick Douglass*, edited by John Stauffer and Henry Louis Gates Jr., 501–512. New York: Penguin, 2016. First published June 1881.

Douglass, Frederick. "Composite Nation." Speech to the Colored National Labor Union Founding Convention, 1869. https://www.blackpast.org/african-american -history/1869-frederick-douglass-describes-composite-nation/

Douglass, Frederick. "Lecture on Pictures," Boston's Tremont Temple, December 3, 1861. In *Picturing Frederick Douglass: An Illustrated History of the Nineteenth Century's Most Photographed* American, edited by John Stauffer, Zoe Trod, and Celeste-Marie Bernier, with an epilogue by Henry Louis Gates Jr., and an afterword by Kenneth B. Morris Jr., 126–141. New York: W.W. Norton, 2015.

Dower, John W. *Race & Power in the Pacific War.* New York: Pantheon, 1987.

Drake, St. Clair. *The American Dream and the Negro: 100 Years of Freedom?* The Emancipation Proclamation Centennial Lectures, January-February. Chicago, Illinois: Roosevelt University, 1963.

Draper, Matt. "Vince Guaraldi: The Man Behind the Music of Peanuts." 2017. https: //www.youtube.com/watch?v=i9mnL6QGebs.

Drescher, Seymour. *Abolition: A History of Slavery & Antislavery.* New York: Cambridge University Press, 2009.

Drinnon, Richard. *Facing West: The Metaphysics of Indian Hating & Empire Building.* New York: Schocken, 1990.

Du Bois, W.E.B. *Black Lives 1900: W.E.B. Du Bois at the Paris Exposition.* London: Redstone Press, 2019.

Du Bois, W.E.B. *Black Reconstruction: An Essay Towards the Part Which Black Folks Played in the Attempt to Reconstruct Democracy in America, 1860–1880.* Edited by Eric Foner and Henry Louis Gates Jr. New York: Library of America, 2021. First published 1935.

Du Bois, W.E.B. *The Souls of Black Folk*, with "The Talented Tenth," and "The Souls of White Folk." New York: Penguin Classics 150th Anniversary Edition, 1868–2018. With an introduction by Ibram X. Kendi. New York: Penguin Books, 2018.

Du Bois, W.E.B. *Writings.* New York: Library of America, 1986.

Du Bois, W.E.B. "The Negro and the Warsaw Ghetto." *Jewish Life* (April 1952): 14–15.

Duane, Timothy P. *Shaping the Sierra: Nature, Culture, and Conflict in the Changing West.* Berkeley: University of California Press, 1999.

Dudden, Faye E. *Fighting Chance: The Struggle Over Woman Suffrage & Black Suffrage in Reconstruction America.* New York: Oxford University Press, 2011.

Dudziak, Mary L. *Cold War Civil Rights: Race and the Image of American Democracy.* New Jersey: Princeton University Press, 2000.

Dunbar, Paul Laurence. *The Sport of the Gods & Other Essential Writings.* Edited and with an introduction by Shelley Fisher Fishkin and David Bradley. New York: The Modern Library Classics, 2005.

Dunbar, Paul Laurence. "The Colored Soldiers." Reprinted in *Lyrics of Lowly Life* (Lit2Go Edition). Retrieved February 26, 2021, from https://etc.usf.edu/lit2go/187 /lyrics-of-lowly-life/3691/the-colored-soldiers/. Originally published 1913.

Dunbar-Ortiz, Roxanne. *Growing Up Okie*. With a foreword by Mike Davis. Norman: University of Oklahoma Press, 2006.

Dunkerley, James. *Dreaming of Freedom in the Americas: Four Minds & a Name*. Institute for the Study of the Americas, Inaugural Lecture, School of Advanced Studies, University of London, 2004. https://core.ac.uk/download/pdf/72471.pdf.

Dunkerley, James. *Americana: The Americas in the World, around 1850*. New York: Verso, 2000.

Dunkerley, James. *Power in the Isthmus: A Political History of Modern Central America*. New York: Verso, 1988.

Dussel, Enrique. *The Invention of the Americas: Eclipse of "the Other" and the Myth of Modernity*. Translated by Michael D. Barber. London: Continuum International Publishing Group, 1995.

Duus, Peter. *The Abacus and the Sword: The Japanese Conquest of Korea*. Berkeley: University of California Press, 1998.

DuVal, Kathleen. *Independence Lost: Lives on the Edge of the American Revolution*. New York: Random House, 2016.

Early, Gerald. "How Innocence Became Cool: Vince Guaraldi, *Peanuts*, & How Jazz Momentarily Captured Childhood." In *The Peanuts Papers: Writers & Cartoonists on Charlie Brown, Snoopy & the Gang, and the Meaning of* Life, edited by Andrew Blauner, 197–212. New York: A Special Publication of the Library of America, 2019.

Early, Gerald, and Ingrid Monson. "Why Jazz Still Matters." *Daedalus: "Why Jazz Still Matters?"* (Spring 2019): 5–12.

Early, Gerald, "Jazz and American Literature." In *The Oxford Companion to* Jazz, edited by Bill Kirchner, 734–744. New York: Oxford University Press, 2000.

Edwards, Laura F. *A Legal History of the Civil War and Reconstruction: A Nation of Rights*. New York: Cambridge University Press, 2015.

Edwards, Paul N. *The Closed World*. Cambridge: MIT, 2007.

Egerton, Douglas R. *The Wars of Reconstruction: The Brief, Violent History of America's Most Progressive Era*. New York: Bloomsbury, 2014.

Egerton, Douglas R. *Thunder at the Gates: The Black Civil War Regiments that Redeemed America*. New York: Basic Books, 2016.

Ehrenreich, Barbara. *The Hearts of Men: American Dreams and the Flight from Commitment*. New York: Anchor, 1983.

Eiland, Howard, and Kevin McLaughlin. "Translators' Foreword." In Walter Benjamin, *The Arcades* Project, translated by Howard Eiland and Kevin McLaughlin, ix–xiv. Cambridge, MA: Harvard University Press, 1999.

Eisenberg, Ellen M. *The First to Cry Down Injustice? Western Jews & Japanese Removal During World War II*. Lanham: Lexington Books, 2008.

Elam, Jr., Harry J. *The Past as Present in the Drama of August Wilson*. University of Michigan Press, 2004.

Elder, Robert. *Calhoun: American Heretic*. New York: Basic Books, 2021.

Ellington, Duke. "We Too, Sing 'America.'" In *The Duke Ellington Reader*, edited by Mark Tucker, 146–148. New York: Oxford University Press, 1993.

Ellington, Duke. "Interview in Los Angeles: On *Jump for Joy*, Opera, and Dissonance as a 'Way of Life.'" In *The Duke Ellington Reader*, edited by Mark Tucker, 148–151. New York: Oxford University Press, 1993.

Elliot, J.H. *Empires of the Atlantic World: Britain and Spain in America 1492–1830.* New Haven: Yale University Press, 2006.

Elliot, J. H. *Do the Americas Have a Common History?* Providence, Rhode Island: The John Carter Brown Library, 1998.

Ellison, Ralph. *Invisible Man.* New York: Vintage, 1995. First published 1952.

Ellison, Ralph. *Living With Music: Ralph Ellison's Jazz Writings.* Edited and with an introduction by Robert G. O'Meally. New York: Modern Library, 2002.

Ellison, Ralph. *The Collected Essays of Ralph Ellison.* Edited and with an introduction by John F. Callahan. New York: Modern Classics Library, 2003.

Ellison, Ralph. "Richard Wright's Blues." In *The Collected Essays of Ralph Ellison*, edited and with an introduction by John F. Callahan, 128–144. New York: The Modern Classics Library, 2003.

Ellsberg, Daniel. *Risk, Ambiguity, and Decision.* New York: Routledge, 2001.

Ellsberg, Daniel. *Secrets: A Memoir of Vietnam and the Pentagon Papers.* New York: Penguin, 2003.

Ellsberg, Daniel. *The Doomsday Machine.* New York: Bloomsbury, 2018.

Engelstein, Laura. *The Resistible Rise of Antisemitism: Exemplary Cases from Russia, Ukraine, and Poland.* Waltham, Massachusetts: Brandeis University Press, 2020.

Enyeart, John P. *Death to Fascism: Louis Adamic's Fight for Democracy.* University of Illinois Press, 2019.

Eltis, David, and David Richardson. *Atlas of Transatlantic Slave Trade,* with a foreword by David Brion Davis and an afterword by David W. Blight. New Haven: Yale University Press, 2015.

Evangelista, Matthew. *Unarmed Forces: The Transnational Movement to End the Cold War.* Ithaca: Cornell University Press, 1999.

Farhang, Sean, and Ira Katznelson. "The Southern Imposition: Congress and Labor in the New Deal and Fair Deal." *Studies in American Political Development* 19 (Spring 2005): 1–30.

Felstiner, John. *Paul Celan: Poet, Survivor, Jew.* New Haven: Yale University Press, 1995.

Fernández-Armesto, Felipe. *The Americas: A Hemispheric History.* New York: The Modern Library, 2003.

Fick, Thomas H. "Toni Morrison's 'Allegory of the Cave': Movies, Consumption, and Platonic Realism in *The Bluest Eye.*" *Journal of the Midwest Modern Language Association* 22, No. 1 (Spring, 1989) 12, Midwest Modern Language Association. Stable URL: https://www.jstor.org/stable/1315270.

Fields, Barbara. "Slavery, Race, and Ideology in the United States of America." *New Left Review* 181 (May/June 1990): 95–118.

Fields, Karen E., and Barbara J. Fields. *Racecraft: The Soul of Inequality in American Life.* New York: Verso, 2012.

Finkelman, Paul. *Supreme Injustice: Slavery in the Nation's Highest Court.* Cambridge, MA: Harvard University Press, 2018.

Fishman, Robert. *Bourgeois Utopias: The Rise and Fall of Suburbia.* New York: Basic Books, 1997.

Fitz, Caitlin. *Our Sister Republics: The United States in an Age of American Revolutions.* New York: Liveright, 2016.

Floyd, Carlton D., and Thomas E. Reifer. "What Happens to a Dream Deferred? W.E.B. Du Bois and the Radical Black Enlightenment/Endarkenment." *Socialism and Democracy.* Guest Co-editors Edward Carson, Gerald Horne, and Phillip Luke Sinitiere, Volume 32, No. 3 (November 2018): 52–80.

Floyd, Carlton D., and Thomas E. Reifer. "What Happens to a Dream Deferred? W.E.B. Du Bois and the Radical Balck Enlightenment/Endarkenment." *Socialism & Democracy in W.E.B. Du Bois's Life, Thought, & Legacy.* New York: Taylor & Francis, 2022, 52–80.

Fogelson, Robert M. *Bourgeois Nightmares: Suburbia, 1870–1930.* New Haven: Yale University Press, 2005.

Foner, Eric. *Free Soil, Free Labor, Free Men: The Ideology of the Republican Party Before the Civil War.* New York: Oxford University Press, 1995.

Foner, Eric. *Reconstruction: America's Unfinished Revolution, 1863–1877.* 2nd ed. New York: Harper Perennial, 2014.

Foner, Eric. *The Fiery Trial: Abraham Lincoln & American Slavery.* New York: W.W. Norton, 2010.

Foner, Eric. *The Second Founding: How the Civil War and Reconstruction Remade the Constitution.* New York: W.W. Norton, 2019.

Fones-Wolf, Elizabeth A. *Selling Free Enterprise: The Business Assault on Labor and Liberalism, 1945–1960.* Urbana: University of Illinois Press, 1994.

Fones-Wolf, Elizabeth, and Ken Fones-Wolf. "'Termites in the Temple': Fundamentalism and Anti-Liberal Politics in the Post-World War II South." *Religion & American Culture: A Journal of Interpretation* 28, Issue 2 (2018): 167–205.

Fones-Wolf, Elizabeth, and Ken Fones-Wolf. *Struggle for the Soul of the Postwar South: White Evangelical Protestants and Operation Dixie.* University of Illinois, 2015.

Foreman, P. Gabrielle, Jim Casey, and Sarah Lynn Patterson. *The Colored Conventions Movement: Black Organizing in the Nineteenth Century.* Chapel Hill: University of North Carolina Press, 2021.

Foreman, P. Gabrielle, and Labanya Mookerjee. "Computing in the Dark: Spreadsheets, Data Collection and Digital Humanities' Racist Inheritance." *Always Already Computational: Library Collections as Data.* National Forum Position Statements. (March 2017): 11–13.

Forsberg, Randall Caroline Watson. *Toward a Theory of Peace: The Role of Moral Beliefs.* Edited and with an introduction by Matthew Evangelista and Neta C. Crawford. Ithaca: Cornell University Press, 2019.

Foster, Gaines M. "Guilt Over Slavery: A Historiographical Analysis." *Journal of Southern History* 56 (November 1990): 665–694.

Fox, Cybelle. *Three Worlds of Relief: Immigration and the American Welfare State from the Progressive Era to the New Deal.* New Jersey: Princeton University Press, 2012.

Franklin, Ruth. "A Word, A Corpse: How Paul Celan Reconceived Language for a Post-Holocaust World." *New Yorker* (November 23, 2020): 71–75.

Fraser, Nancy. "On Justice: Lessons from Plato, Rawls and Ishiguro." *New Left Review* 74 (March/April 2012): 41–51.

Frederickson, Kari. *Deep South Dynasty: The Bankheads of Alabama.* Tuscaloosa: University of Alabama Press, 2022.

Frederickson, Kari. *The Dixiecrat Revolt and the End of the Solid South, 1932–1968.* Chapel Hill: University of North Carolina Press, 2001.

Freedom Writers with Erin Gruwell. *The Freedom Writers Diary. Dear Freedom Writer: Stories of Hardship and Hope from the Next Generation.* New York: Crown Publishing, a division of Random House, 2022.

Freedom Writers with Erin Gruwell. *The Freedom Writers Diary*, 20th Anniversary Edition, with new Journal Entries and a New Afterword by Erin Gruwell. New York: Broadway Books, Crown Publishing, a division of Random House, Tolerance Education Foundation, Fall 2019.

Frey, William H. *Diversity Explosion: How New Radical Demographics are Remaking America.* 2nd ed. Washington, D.C.: Brookings, 2018.

Frisby, David. *Fragments of Modernity.* Cambridge, MA: The MIT Press, 1986.

Fujnio, Diane C. *Ninsei Radicals: The Feminist Poetics and Transformative Ministry of Mitsuye Yamada and Michael Yasutake.* Seattle: University of Washington Press, 2020.

Galeano, Eduardo. *Memory of Fire Trilogy, I: Genesis; II: Faces & Masks; III: Century of the Wind.* New York: Pantheon, 1987, 1987, 1988.

Gallagher, Catherine. *Telling it Like it Wasn't: The Counterfactual Imagination in History & Fiction.* University of Chicago Press, 2018.

Garcia, Mario T., and Sal Castro. *Blowout! Sal Castro and the Chicano Struggle for Educational Justice.* Chapel Hill: University of North Carolina Press, 2011.

Garcia, Mario T. *Father Luis Olivaries: Faith Politics & the Origins of the Sanctuary Movement in Los Angeles.* Chapel Hill: University of North Carolina Press, 2018.

Gates, Jr., Henry Louis. *Stony the Road: Reconstruction, White Supremacy, and the Rise of Jim Crow.* New York: Penguin Press, 2019.

Geggus, David. "The Louisiana Purchase and the Haitian Revolution." In *The Haitian Revolution & the Early United States,* 117–129. Edited by Elizabeth Maddock Dillon and Michael Drexler. Philadelphia: University of Pennsylvania Press, 2016.

Gelfort, Blanche H. "'Gone with the Wind' and the Impossibilities of Fiction." *The Southern Literary Journal* 13, No. 1 (Fall, 1980): 3–31.

Ghosh, Peter. *Max Weber and "The Protestant Ethic": Twin Histories.* New York: Oxford University Press, 2017.

Gilmour, Glenda Elizabeth. *Romare Bearden and the Homeland of His Imagination.* Chapel Hill: University of North Carolina, 2022.

Gilroy, Paul. *The Black Atlantic: Modernity and Double Consciousness.* Cambridge, MA: Harvard University Press, 1993.

Ginsburg, Michal. "Visualizing *Les Miserables*." https://lesmiserables.mla.hcommons.org/.

Ginzburg, Carlo. "Latitude, Slaves and the Bible: An Experiment in Microhistory." *Critical Inquiry* 31 (Spring 2005): 665–683.

Glaude Jr., Eddie. *Exodus: Religion, Race and Nation in Early Nineteenth-Century Black America*. Chicago: University of Chicago Press, 2000.

Gleijeses, Piero. *America's Road to Empire: Foreign Policy from Independence to World War I*. New York: Bloomsbury Academic, 2021.

Gleijeses, Piero. "Napoleon, Jefferson, and the Louisiana Purchase." *The International History Review* 39, Number 2 (2017): 237–255.

Gleijeses, Piero. *The Cuban Drumbeat*. London: Seagull Books, 2009.

Gleijeses, Piero. "The Limits of Sympathy: The United States and the Independence of Spanish America." *Journal of Latin American Studies* 24, Number 3 (October 1992): 481–505.

Gleijeses, Piero. "Haiti's Contribution to the Independence of Spanish America: A Forgotten Chapter." *Revista/Review Interamericana* (Winter 1979): 511–528.

Glenn, Evelyn Nakano. *Unequal Freedom: How Race and Gender Shaped American Citizenship and Labor*. Cambridge, MA: Harvard University Press, 2004.

Glover, Jonathan. *Humanity: A Moral History of the Twentieth Century*. 2nd ed. New Haven: Yale University Press, 2012.

Glymph, Thavolia. *The Women's Fight: The Civil War's Battles for Home, Freedom, and Nation*. Chapel Hill: University of North Carolina Press, 2020.

Golczewski, Frank. "Shades of Grey: Reflections on Jewish-Ukrainian and German-Ukrainian Relations in Galicia." In *The Shoah in Ukraine*, edited by Ray Brandon and Wendy Lower, 114–155. Bloomington: University of Indiana Press, in association with the United States Holocaust Memorial Museum, 2008.

Goldfield, Michael. *The Southern Key: Class, Race, and Radicalism in the 1930s and 1940s*. New York: Oxford University Press, 2020.

Goluboff, Risa. *The Lost Promise of Civil Rights*. Cambridge, MA: Harvard University Press, 2010.

Gomez, Nicolas Wey. *The Tropics of Empire: Why Columbus Sailed South to the Indies*. Cambridge, MA: MIT Press, 2006.

Goody, Jack, *Logic of Writing and the Organization of Society*. New York: Cambridge University Press, 1986.

Goody, Jack, *Interface Between the Written and the Oral*. New York: Cambridge University Press, 1987.

Gordon, Bruce. *Calvin*. New Haven: Yale University Press, 2009.

Gordon, Linda, and Gary Y. Okihiro, eds. *Impounded: Dorothea Lange and the Censored Images of Japanese American Internment*. New York: W.W. Norton, 2006.

Gordon, Linda. *Pitied but Not Entitled: Single Mothers and the History of Welfare, 1890–1935*. Cambridge, MA: Harvard University Press, 1998.

Gordon, Linda. "Welfare Reform: A History Lesson." *Dissent* (Summer 1994): 323–328.

Gosse, Van. *The First Reconstruction: Black Politics in America from the Revolution to the Civil War*. University of North Carolina Press, 2021.

Gramsci, Antonio. *Subaltern Social Groups: A Critical Edition of Prison Notebook 25*. Edited and translated by Joseph A. Buttigieg and Marcus E. Green. New York: Columbia University Press, 2021.

Gramsci, Antonio. *The Prison Notebooks, Volume I-III*. Edited and translated by Joseph A. Buttigieg. New York: Columbia University Press, 2011.

Greenough, Sarah. *Tell it With Pride: The 54th Massachusetts Regiment and Augustus Saint-Gaudens's Shaw Memorial*. New Haven: Yale University Press, 2013.

Gregory, James N. *The Southern Diaspora: How the Great Migrations of Black and White Southerners Transformed America*. Durham: University of North Carolina Press, 2005.

Griffin, Farah Jasmine. *Read Until You Understand: The Profound Wisdom of Black Life and Literature*. New York: W.W. Norton & Co., 2022.

Griffin, Farah Jasmine. *"Who set you flowin?" The African-American Migration Narrative*. New York: Oxford University Press, 1996.

Griffith, Barbara S. *The Crisis of American Labor: Operation Dixie and the Defeat of the CIO*. Philadelphia: Temple University Press, 1988.

Gudde, Erwin G. *California Place Names: The Origins and Etymology of Current Geographical Names*. 4th edition. Revised and enlarged by William Bright. Berkeley: University of California Press, 1998.

Guerin-Gonzalez, Camille. *Mexican Workers and the American Dream: Immigration, Repatriation, and California Farm Labor*. New Jersey: Rutgers University Press, 1994.

Guidotti-Hernandez, Nicole M. *Unspeakable Violence: Remapping U.S. and Mexican National Imaginaries*. Durham: Duke University Press, 2011.

Gutfreund, Zevi. *Speaking American: Language Education and Citizenship in Twentieth Century Los Angeles*. New York: Oxford University Press, 2020.

Gutierrez, Gustavo. *Las Casas: In Search of the Poor of Jesus Christ*. Maryknoll, New York: Orbis Books, 1993.

Guyatt, Nicholas. *Providence and the Invention of the United States, 1607–1876*. New York: Cambridge University Press, 2007.

Haag, John. *"Gone with the Wind* in Nazi Germany." *The Georgia Historical Quarterly* 73, Number 2 (Summer 1989): 278–279.

Hacohen, Malachi Haim. *Jacob & Esau: Jewish European History Between Nation and Empire*. New York: Cambridge University Press, 2019.

Hahn, Steven, *The Political Worlds of Slavery and Freedom*. Cambridge, MA: Harvard University Press, 2009.

Hahn, Steven. *A Nation Under Our Feet: Black Political Struggles in the Rural South from Slavery to the Great Migration*. Cambridge, MA: The Belknap Press of Harvard University Press, 2004.

Hales, Peter Bacon. *Atomic Spaces: Living on the Manhattan Project*. Urbana: University of Illinois Press, 1997.

Hales, Peter. *Industry and Ideology: I.G., Farben in the Nazi Era.* 2nd edition. New York: Cambridge University Press, 2000.

Hales, Peter Bacon. *Outside the Gates of Eden: The American Dream of America from Hiroshima to Now*. Chicago: University of Chicago Press, 2014.

Halevi, Ilan. *History of the Jews.* London: Zed Press, 1987.

Hamilton, Alexander, James Madison, and John Jay. *The Federalist Papers.* New York: Mentor Book, 1961. First published, 1788.

Hammond, John Craig. "Mastery over Slaves, Sovereignty over Slavery: James Monroe, Virginia, and the Missouri Crisis." In *Revolutionary Prophecies: The Founders and America's Future,* edited by Robert M.S. McDonald and Peter S. Onuf, 194–222. Charlottesville: University of Virginia Press, 2021.

Hammond, John Craig. "President, Planter, Politician: James Monroe, the Missouri Crisis, and the Politics of Slavery." *Journal of American History* 105, Issue Number 4, (March 2019): 843–867.

Hanebrink, Paul. *A Specter Haunting Europe: The Myth of Judeo-Bolshevism.* Cambridge, MA: The Belknap Press of Harvard University Press, 2018.

Hanke, Lewis. *All Mankind is One: A Study of the Disputation Between Bartolome de Las Casas and Juan Gines de Sepulveda in 1550 on the Intellectual and Religious Capacity of the American Indians.* De Kalb: Northern Illinois University Press, 1974.

Hanke, Lewis. *Do the Americas Have a Common History? A Critique of the Bolton Theory.* New York: Alfred A. Knopf, 1964.

Hanke, Lewis. *The Spanish Struggle for Justice in the Conquest of America.* Dallas: Southern Methodist University Press, 2002.

Hanson, Sandra L., and John Kenneth White, eds. *The American Dream in the 21st Century.* Philadelphia: Temple University Press, 2011.

Harper, Kyle. *The Fate of Rome: Climate, Disease, and the End of an Empire.* New York: Harper and Row, 2019.

Harshav, Benjamin. *Marc Chagall: The Lost Jewish World.* Milan, Italy, 2006.

Harshav, Benjamin. *Marc Chagall & His Times: A Documentary Narrative.* Stanford, CA: Stanford University Press, 2003.

Hartz, Louis. *The Founding of the New Societies: Studies in the Histories of the United States, Latin America, South Africa, Canada, and Australia.* New York: Harcourt, Brace and World, 1964.

Heersink, Bosi, and Jeffery A. Jenkins. *Republican Party Politics & the American South, 1965–1968. New* York: Cambridge University Press, 2020.

Heffernan, Margaret. *Willful Blindness: Why We Ignore the Obvious at Our Peril.* New York, Bloomsbury, 2012.

Herbert, Keith. *Cornerstone of the Confederacy: Alexander Stephens and the Speech that Defined the Lost Cause.* Knoxville, Tennessee: University of Tennessee Press, 2021.

Hernandez, Tim A. *Manana Means Heaven.* Tucson: University of Arizona, 2016.

Hernandez, Tim A. "Author Interview: Tim Z. Hernandez Talks About New Novel, Kerouac's 'Mexican Girl.'" National Public Radio (Central California), August 27, 2013. https://www.kvpr.org/post/author-interview-tim-z-hernandez-talks-about -new-novel-kerouacs-mexican-girl#stream/0.

Hertwig, Ralph, and Christoph Engel, eds. *Deliberate Ignorance: Choosing Not to Know.* Cambridge, MA and London, England: Massachusetts Institute of Technology and the Frankfurt Institute of Advanced Studies, 2020.

Higham, John. *Send These to Me: Urban Immigrants in America.* 2nd ed. Baltimore: Johns Hopkins University Press, 1984.

Hill, William H. *No Place for Russia.* New York: Columbia University Press, 2018.

Himes, Chester. *The Quality of Hurt: The Early Years, The Autobiography of Chester Himes.* New York: Paragon, 1971.

Himes, Chester. *The Lonely Crusade.* Da Capo Press, 1997. 2nd edition. Originally published 1947.

Himes, Chester. *If He Hollers Let Him Go: A Novel.* New York: Da Capo Press, 2002. Originally published 1945.

Hinderaker, Eric. *Boston's Massacre.* Cambridge, MA: The Belknap Press of Harvard University Press, 2017.

Hinderaker, Eric, and Peter C. Mancall. *At the Edge of Empire: The Backcountry in British North America.* Baltimore: Johns Hopkins University Press, 2003.

Hinton, Elizabeth. *America on Fire: The Untold Story of Police Violence & Black Rebellion Since the 1960s.* New York: Liveright, 2021.

Hirabayashi, Lane Ryo. "Incarceration." In *Keywords for Asian American Studies,* edited by Cathy J. Schlund-Vials, Linda Trinh Vo, and K. Scott Wong, 133–138. New York: New York University Press, 2015.

Hittman, Michael. *Wovoka and the Ghost Dance.* Edited by Don Lynch. Lincoln: University of Nebraska Press, 1990.

Hobbes, Thomas. *Leviathan.* New York: Oxford World Classics, 1996.

Holden, Vanessa M. *Surviving Southampton: African American Women and Resistance in Nat Turner's Community.* Champaign, Illinois: University of Illinois Press, 2021.

Holzer, Harold, and Norton Garfinkle. *A Just and Generous Nation: Abraham Lincoln and the Fight for American Opportunity.* New York: Basic Books, 2015.

Holzer, Harold, and Thomas A. Horrocks, eds. *The Annotated Lincoln.* Cambridge, MA: The Belknap Press of Harvard University Press, 2016.

Horkheimer, Max, and Theodor W. Adorno. *Dialectic of Enlightenment: Philosophical Fragments.* Edited by Gunzelin Schmid Noerr. Translated by Edmund Jephcott. Stanford: Stanford University Press, 2002. First published 1944.

Horowitz, Roger. *"Negro and White, Unite and Fight!" A Social History of Industrial Unionism in Meatpacking, 1930–90.* Urbana, Illinois: University of Illinois Press, 1990.

Horton, Lois E. *Harriet Tubman and the Fight for Freedom: A Brief History with Documents.* The Bedford Series in History & Culture. Boston: Bedford/St. Martin's, 2013.

Huang, Nian-Sheng, and Carla Mulford. "Benjamin Franklin and the American Dream." In *The Cambridge Companion to Benjamin Franklin,* edited by Carla Mulford, 146–158. New York: Cambridge University Press, 2009.

Hudson, Lynn M. *West of Jim Crow: The Fight Against California's Color Line.* Champaign: University of Illinois Press, 2020.

Huggins, Nathan Irvin. *Harlem Renaissance.* New York: Oxford University Press, 2007. Updated edition, with a foreword by Arnold Rampersad. Originally published in 1971.

Hughes, Langston. "Democracy and Me." Speech Made at the Public Session of the Third American Writers' Congress, Carnegie Hall, New York City, June 1939. In Langston Hughes, *Collected Works of Langston Hughes: Volume 9, Essays on Art, Race, Politics & World* Affairs, edited with an introduction by Christopher C.D. Sampis, 203–206. University of Missouri Press, 2002.

Hughes, Langston. *The Collected Works of Langston Hughes: Volume 2: The Poems, 1941–1950*. Edited with an introduction by Arnold Rampersad. Columbia: University of Missouri Press, 2001.

Hughes, Langston. "One-Way Ticket." In *The Collected Works of Langston Hughes: Volume 2: The Poems, 1941–1950*. Edited with an introduction by Arnold Rampersad, 153–220. Columbia: University of Missouri Press, 2001. Originally published 1949.

Hughes, Langston. *Poems*. Selected and edited by David Roessel. Everyman's Library Pocket Poets. New York: Alfred A. Knopf, 1999.

Hughes, Langston, *The Panther and the Lash*. New York: Vintage Classics edition, 1992. First published 1967.

Hughes, Langston. *Montage of a Dream Deferred*. New York: Henry Holt, 1951.

Hughes, Langston. *One-Way Ticket*. Illustrated by Jacob Lawrence. New York: Knopf, 1949.

Hughes, Langston. *The Big Sea*. New York: Hill and Wang, 1940.

Hurston, Zora Neale. *Their Eyes Were Watching God*. New York: Harper Perennial, 1937.

Hurtado, Albert L. *Herbert Eugene Bolton: Historian of the American Borderlands*. Berkeley: University of California Press, 2012.

Hutchinson, Sikivu. "White Picket Fences, White Innocence." *The Journal of Religious Ethics* 42, No. 4 (December 2014): 612–639. https://www.jstor.org/stable /24586116.

Insko, Jeffrey. "Extraction." *The Cambridge Companion to Environmental Humanities*, edited by Jeffrey Jerome Cohen and Stephanie Foote, 170–184. New York: Cambridge University Press, 2021.

Isenberg, Andrew C., ed. *The California Gold Rush: A Brief History with Documents*. Boston: Bedford/St. Martin's, 2018.

Isenberg, Andrew C. *The Destruction of the Bison: An Environmental History, 1750–1920*. New York: Cambridge University Press, 2000.

Iton, Richard. *Solidarity Blues: Race, Culture, and the American Left*. Chapel Hill: University of North Carolina Press, 2000.

Iyire, Akia. *Power and Culture: The Japanese-American War, 1941–1945*. Cambridge, MA: Harvard University Press, 1982.

Jablonski, Nina G. *Living Color: The Biological & Social Meaning of Skin Color*. Berkeley: University of California Press, 2012.

Jablonski, Nina G. *Skin: A Natural History*. 2nd edition. Berkeley: University of California Press, 2013.

Jablonski, Nina G., ed. *The Persistence of Race*. Cleveland Heights, Ohio: Sun Press, 2020.

Jackson, Lawrence P. *Chester B. Himes: A Biography*. New York: W.W. Norton, 2017.

Jacob, Michelle M. *The Auntie Way: Stories Celebrating Kindness, Fierceness, & Creativity.* Anahuy Mentoring, LLC, Whitefish, MT, 2020.

Jacobson, Matthew Frye, *Whiteness of a Different Color: European Immigrants and the Alchemy of Race.* Cambridge, MA: Harvard University Press, 1999.

James, C. L. R. *The Black Jacobins.* 2nd edition. New York: Vintage, 1989.

James, Winston. *Claude McKay.* New York: Columbia University Press, 2022.

James, Winston. *Holding Aloft the Banner of Ethiopia: Caribbean Radicalism in Early Twentieth-Century America.* New York: Verso, 2020.

James, Winston. *The Struggles of John Brown Russwurm: The Life and Writings of a Pan-Africanist Pioneer, 1799–1851.* New York: New York University Press, 2010.

Jameson, Fredric. *Archaeologies of the Future: The Desire Called Utopia and Other Science Fictions.* New York: Verso, 2007.

Jameson, Fredric. *Valences of the Dialectic.* New York: Verso, 2010.

Jameson, Fredric. *The Political Unconscious: Narrative as a Socially Symbolic Act.* Ithaca, New York: Cornell University Press, 1981.

Jarrett, Gene Andrew. *Paul Laurence Dunbar: The Life and Times of a Caged Bird.* New Jersey: Princeton University Press, 2022.

Jefferson, Thomas. Thomas Jefferson to John Nicolas Demeunier, 26 June 1786. https://founders.archives.gov/documents/Jefferson/01-10-02-0001-0006.

Jemison, N. K., *How Long 'Til Black Future Month: Stories.* London: Orbit Books, 2018.

Jenkins, Jerry Rafiki. *The Paradox of Blackness in African American Vampire Fiction.* Columbus, Ohio: Ohio State University Press, 2019.

Johnson, Gaye Theresa. *Spaces of Conflict, Sounds of Solidarity: Music, Race, and Spatial Entitlement in Los Angeles.* Berkeley: University of California Press, 2013.

Johnson, James Weldon. *Black Manhattan.* With a foreword by Zadie Smith. New York: Ig Publishing, 2021. First published 1930.

Johnson, James Weldon. *Writings.* New York: Library of America, 2004.

Johnson, Walter, with Robin D.G. Kelley. *Boston Review: Forum 1: Race, Capitalism, Justice.* Cambridge, MA, 2017.

Johnson, Walter. *River of Dark Dreams: Slavery and Empire in the Cotton Kingdom.* Cambridge, MA: The Belknap Press of Harvard University Press, 2013.

Jones, Christopher. "Protection from One's Friends." In *Soviet Strategy and the New Military* Thinking, edited by Derek Leebaert and Timothy Dickinson, 100–126. New York: Cambridge University Press, 1992.

Jones, LeRoi (Amiri Baraka). *Blues People: The Negro Experience in White America and the Music that Developed from It.* With a new introduction. New York: Harper Perennial, 2002. First published, 1963.

Jones Jr., M. "Down and out in the City of Angels." *Newsweek* 116, 2 (1990): 65. https://sandiego.idm.oclc.org/login?url=https://search.ebscohost.com/login.aspx?direct=true&db=aph&AN=9007091202&site=ehost-live.

Jones, Martha S. *Birthright Citizens: A History of Race & Rights in Antebellum America.* New York: Cambridge University Press, 2018.

Jordan, Hillary. *Mudbound.* Chapel Hill: Algonquin Books, 2008.

Joyce, James. *Ulysses: The 1922 Text.* New York: Oxford World Classics, 1998.

Kachun, Mitch. *First Martyr of Liberty: Crispus Attucks in American Memory.* New York: Oxford University Press, 2017.

Kanter, Stefan. "Horatio Alger: The Moral of the Story." *City Journal (*Autumn 2000). https://www.city-journal.org/html/horatio-alger-moral-story-11933.html.

Karp, Matthew. "The Mass Politics of Antislavery." *Catalyst* 3, No. 2 (Summer 2019). https://catalyst-journal.com/2019/10/the-mass-politics-of-antislavery

Karp, Matthew, "The People's Revolution of 1856: Antislavery Populism, National Politics, and the Emergence of the Republican Party." *The Journal of the Civil War Era* 9, No. 4 (December 2019): 524–545.

Karuka, Manu. *Empire's Tracks: Indigenous Nations, Chinese Workers, and the Transcontinental Railroad*, Oakland: University of California Press, 2019.

Kay, Alex J. *Empire of Destruction: A History of Nazi Mass Killing.* New Haven: Yale University Press, 2021.

Kay, Alex J. "'The Purpose of the Russian Campaign Is the Decimation of the Slavic Population by Thirty Million': The Radicalization of German Food Policy in Early 1941." In *Nazi Policy on the Eastern Front, 1941: Total War, Genocide, and Radicalization*, edited by Alex J. Kay, Jeff Rutherford, and David Stahel, 101–129. Rochester, New York: University of Rochester Press, 2012.

Katznelson, Ira. *Fear Itself: The New Deal and the Origins of Our Time*. New York: Liveright, 2013.

Katznelson, Ira, and Quinn Murray. "Was the South Pivotal? Situated Partisanship and Policy Coalitions During the New Deal and Fair Deal." *The Journal of Politics* 74, No. 2 (March 2012): 604–620.

Keefe, Patrick Radden. *Empire of Pain: The Secret History of the Sackler Dynasty.* New York: Doubleday, 2021.

Keith, Leanna. *When it Was Grand: The Radical Republican History of the Civil War.* New York: Hill and Wang, 2020.

Kerber, Linda K. "Why Diamonds Are a Girl's Best Friend: Another American Narrative." *Daedalus* (Winter 2012): 89–100.

Kerber, Linda K. "Why Diamonds Really Are a Girl's Best Friend." *Proceedings of the American Philosophical Society* 153, Number 1 (March 2009): 56–66.

Kerber, Linda K. *No Constitutional Right to Be Ladies: Women and the Obligations of Citizenship*. New York: Hill & Wang, 1999.

Kerber, Linda K. *Women of the Republic: Intellect and Ideology in Revolutionary America*. Chapel Hill: University of North Carolina Press, 1980.

Kendi, Ibram X. *Stamped from the Beginning.* New York: Bold Type Books, 2017.

Kerouac, Jack. *Road Novels, 1957–1960*. New York: Library of America, 2007.

Kerouac, Jack. "The Mexican Girl." *The Paris Review*, Issue 11 (1955). https://www.theparisreview.org/fiction/4990/the-mexican-girl-jack-kerouac

Key Jr., V.O. *Southern Politics in State and Nation.* Knoxville: University of Tennessee Press, 2006.

Kimmage, Michael. "The Politics of the American Dream, 1980 to 2008." In *The American Dream in the 21st* Century, edited by Sandra L. Hanson and John Kenneth White, 27–40. Philadelphia: Temple University Press, 2011.

King, Desmond, and Stephen Tuck. "De-Centering the South: America's Nationwide Supremacist Order After Reconstruction." *Past and Present* 194, Issue 1 (February 2007): 233–253.

King, Jr., Martin Luther. "Beyond the Los Angeles Riots." *Saturday Review* (November 13, 1965): 33–34, 105.

King Jr., Reverend Dr. Martin Luther. "I Have a Dream." Audio Speech, March on Washington for Jobs and Freedom, August 28, 1963. The Martin Luther King Jr. Research and Education Institute, Stanford University. https://kinginstitute.stanford.edu/king-papers/documents/i-have-dream-address-delivered-march-washington-jobs-and-freedom.

King Jr., Reverend Dr. Martin Luther. *Letter from Birmingham Jail*. UK: Penguin, 2018. First published 1964.

King Jr., Reverend Dr. Martin Luther. "The American Dream." Ebenezer Baptist Church, Atlanta, Georgia, July 4, 1965. In *A Knock at Midnight: Inspiration from the Great Sermons of Reverend Martin Luther King, Jr.,* edited by Clayborn Carson & Peter Holloran, 85–100. New York: Time Warner, 2000.

King Jr., Reverend Dr. Martin Luther. King, 67/05/29–31, "To Charter Our Course for the Future." Address to the SCLC Retreat, Frogmore, SC. Unpublished notes in author's possession.

King Jr., Reverend Dr. Martin Luther. *Where Do We Go from Here: Chaos or Community?* New York: Bantam, 1967.

Klarman, Michael J. *The Framers' Coup: The Making of the United States Constitution*. New York: Oxford University Press, 2016.

Klinker, Philip A., with Rogers M. Smith. *The Unsteady March: The Rise & Decline of Racial Equality in America*. University of Chicago Press, 1994.

Kock, Alexander, Chris Brierly, Mark M. Maslin, and Simon L. Lewis. "Earth System Impacts of the European Arrival and Great Dying in the Americas after 1492." *Quaternary Science Reviews* 207 (2019): 13–36.

Kozol, Jonathan. *The Shame of the Nation: The Restoration of Apartheid Schooling in America*. New York: Crown, 2006.

Kundera, Milan. *The Book of Laughter and Forgetting*. New York: Harper Perennial, 1999. First published in English, 1980.

Kutzinski, Vera M. *The Worlds of Langston Hughes: Modernism and Translation in the Americas*. Ithaca: Cornell University Press, 2012.

Lamott, Anne. *Bird by Bird: Some Instructions on Writing and Life*. New York: Anchor, 1995.

Lange, Dorothea, and Paul Taylor. *An American Exodus: A Record of Human Erosion.* Paris: Editions Jean-Michel Place, 1999. First published 1939.

Lantigua, David M. *Infidels and Empires in a New World Order: Early Modern Spanish Contributions to International Legal Thought.* New York: Cambridge University Press, 2020.

Larsen, Jonathan. "Tulsa Burning." 1997 https://www.northtulsa.org/index.php/blog/782-tulsa-burning

Laslett, John H.M. *Sunshine Was Never Enough: Los Angeles Workers, 1880–2010*. Berkeley: University of California Press, 2012.

Latimer, Quinn. "Kalifornientraumen: Bertolt Brecht's Los Angeles Poems and Other Sunstruck German Spectres." *East of Borneo*. October 13, 2010. https://eastofborneo.org/articles/kalifornientraumen-bertolt-brechts-los-angeles-poems-and-other-sunstruck-germanic-specters/.

Le Guin, Ursula K. *The Left Hand of Darkness*. New York: Ace Books, 2010.

Le Guin, Ursula K. *The Wind's Twelve Quarters*. New York: Harper Perennial, 2004.

Lee, Josephine D., ed. *Oxford Encyclopedia of Asian American Literature & Culture*. Volumes I–III. New York: Oxford University Press, 2020.

Lee, Julia H. "Comparative African American and Asian American Literary Studies." In Josephine D. Lee, ed., *Oxford Encyclopedia of Asian American Literature & Culture*, edited by Josephine D. Lee. Volumes I, II, III. New York: Oxford University Press, 2020. https://oxfordre.com/literature/view/10.1093/acrefore/9780190201098.001.0001/acrefore-9780190201098-e-836

Leiter, Andrew. *Documenting the American South. Thomas Dixon Jr.: Conflicts in History and Literature.* The University of North Carolina at Chapel Hill. https://docsouth.unc.edu/southlit/dixon_intro.html#titles_by_author.

Lemay, J.A. Leo. "Franklin's Autobiography and the American Dream." In *Benjamin Franklin's Autobiography: A Norton Critical* Edition, edited by J.A. Leo Lemay and P.M. Zall, 349–360. New York: W.W. Norton & Co., 1986.

Levi, Primo. *The Drowned and the Saved*. New York: Simon & Schuster, 1988.

Levi, Primo. *Survival in Auschwitz*. New York: Touchstone, 1993. This book originally appeared in English with the title *If This is a Man*, in 1958.

Levine, Robert. *The Lives of Frederick Douglass*. Cambridge, MA: Harvard University Press, 2016.

Lew-Williams, Beth. *Violence, Exclusion, and the Making of the Alien in America*. Cambridge, MA: Harvard University Press, 2018.

Lichtblau, Albert, and Michael John. "Jewries in Galicia and Bukovina, in Lemberg and Czernowitz: Two Divergent Examples of Jewish Communities in the Far East of the Austro-Hungarian Monarchy." In *Jewries at the Frontier: Accommodation, Identity, Conflict*, edited by Sander L. Gilman and Milton Shain, 29–66. Urbana: University of Illinois Press, 1999.

Lichtenstein, Sarah, and Paul Slovic, eds., *The Construction of Preference.* New York: Cambridge University Press, 2006.

Lincoln, Abraham. *Lincoln's Speeches*. Edited with an introduction by Allen C. Guelzo. New York: Penguin Books, 2012.

Lincoln, Abraham. "Preliminary Emancipation Proclamation." September 22, 1862. In *The Emancipation Proclamation: A Brief History in Documents*, Michael Vorenberg, 59–61. New York: Bedford/St. Martin's, 2010.

Lincoln, Abraham. "Speech on the *Dred Scott* Decision at Springfield, Illinois." June 26, 1857. In *The Annotated* Lincoln, edited by Harold Holzer and Thomas A. Horrocks, 187–200. Cambridge, MA: The Belknap Press of Harvard University Press, 2016.

Litwak, Leon. *North of Slavery: The Negro in the Free States, 1790–1860*. University of Chicago Press, 1965.

Liu, Eric. *A Chinaman's Chance: One Family's Journey and the Chinese American Dream.* New York: Public Affairs, 2014.

Looney, Dennis. *Freedom Readers: The African-American Reception of Dante Alighieri and the Divine Comedy.* Notre Dame, Indiana: University of Notre Dame Press, 2011.

Los Angeles Almanac. "Asian Ethnic Origin, Los Angeles County. 2010 Census and 2018 Census Estimates, 2021." http://www.laalmanac.com/population/po16.php

Los Angeles Times. "Sentence Ends in Question: Dog Abuser Gets Six Months; Slayer of Black Teen Gets Probation." (Archives). January 28, 1992. https://www.latimes.com/archives/la-xpm-1992-01-28-me-765-story.html.

Loewen, James W. "Dreaming in Black and White." In *The American Dream in the 21st* Century, edited by Sandra L. Hanson and John Kenneth White, 59–76. Philadelphia: Temple University Press, 2011.

Loewen, James W. *Lies Across America: What Our Historic Sites Get Wrong.* New York: New Press, 2019.

Luban, David. *Legal Modernism.* Ann Arbor, MI: University of Michigan, 1994.

Lukacs, Georg. *History and Class Consciousness.* Cambridge, MA: MIT, 1972.

Lynch, John. *Simon Bolivar: A Life.* New Haven: Yale University Press, 2006.

Magubane, Bernard. *The Making of a Racist State: British Imperialism and the Union of South Africa, 1875–1910.* New Jersey: Africa World Press, 1996.

Maier, Charles. *Among Empires: American Ascendancy and its Predecessors.* Cambridge, MA: Harvard University Press, 2006.

Mann, Michael. *Fascists.* New York: Cambridge University Press, 2004.

Mann, Michael. *The Dark Side of Democracy: Explaining Ethnic Cleansing.* New York: Cambridge University Press, 2005.

Mann, Michael. *The Sources of Social Power, Volume 3: Global Empires and Revolution, 1890–1945.* New York: Cambridge University Press, 2012.

Manning, Chandra. *Troubled Refuge: Struggling for Freedom in the Civil War.* New York: Alfred A. Knopf, 2016.

Manza, Jeff, and Clem Brooks. "Prisoners of the American Dream: Americans' Attitudes Towards Taxes and Inequality in a New Gilded Age." October 2014. Unpublished Manuscript in the Author's Possession.

Marable, Manning. *Race, Reform, and Rebellion: The Second Reconstruction in Black America.* University Press of Mississippi, 1991.

Marchand, Roland. *Advertising the American Dream.* Berkeley: University of California Press, 1985.

Margolies, Edward, and Michel Fabre. *The Several Lives of Chester Himes.* Jackson: University Press of Mississippi, 1997.

Marx, Karl. *Selected Writings.* Edited by David McLellan. New York: Oxford University Press, 2000.

Marx, Karl. "Review." (January/February 1850). *Marx and Engels Collected Works, Volume 10.* London: 1978: 265–266.

Marx, Karl. *Capital, Volume 1.* New York: Penguin, 1992.

Masur, Kate. *An Example for All the Land: Emancipation and the Struggle for Equality in Washington, D.C.* Chapel Hill: University of North Carolina Press, 2010.

Masur, Kate. *Until Justice Be Done: America's First Civil Rights Movement, from the Revolution to Reconstruction.* New York: W.W. Norton, 2021.

Maxwell, Angie, and Todd Shields. *The Long Southern Strategy: How Chasing White Votes in the South Changed American Politics.* New York: Oxford University Press, 2019.

Maxwell, Angie, and Todd G. Shields, eds. *Unlocking V.O. Key Jr: "Southern Politics" for the Twenty-First Century.* University of Arkansas Press, 2011.

May, Kirse Granat. *Golden State, Golden Youth: The Image of California in Popular Culture, 1955–1966.* Chapel Hill: University of North Carolina Press, 2002.

Mayer, Arno J. *Why did the Heavens Not Darken: The "Final Solution" in History.* 2nd ed. New York: Verso Books, 2012.

Mayer, Henry. *All on Fire: William Lloyd Garrison and American Slavery.* New York: St. Martins, 1998.

Mayeri, Serena. *Reasoning from Race: Feminism, Law, and the Civil Rights Revolution.* Cambridge, MA: Harvard University Press, 2011.

Mbue, Imbolo. *Behold the Dreamers.* New York: Random House, 2016.

McCurry, Stephanie. *Women's War: Fighting & Surviving the American Civil War.* Cambridge, MA: The Belknap Press of Harvard University Press, 2019.

McDowell, Edwin. "Gone with the Wind Best Seller Again at 50." *New York Times.* June 24, 1986.

McKay, Claude. *Romance in Marseille.* Edited and with an Introduction by Gary Edward Holcomb and William J. Maxwell. New York: Penguin Classics, 2020.

McPherson, James M. "Russell Banks, *Cloudsplitter* (1998); Russell Banks's Fictional Portrait of John Brown; 'In Response to James McPherson's Reading of *Cloudsplitter*,' By Russell Banks." In *Novel History: Historians & Novelists Confront America's Past (and Each Other)*, edited by Mark C. Carnes, 61–76. New York: Simon and Schuster 2001.

McPherson, James M. *What They Fought For, 1861–1865.* New York: Anchor Books, 1995.

McPherson, James M. *For Cause and Comrades: Why Men Fought in the Civil War.* New York: Oxford University Press, 1997.

McPherson, James M. *The Negro's Civil War: How American Blacks Felt and Acted During the War for the Union.* New York: Vintage, 2003.

McWilliams, Carey. *Factories in the Field: The Story of Migratory Farm Labor in California.* Berkeley: University of California Press, 2000. First published 1939.

McWilliams, Carey. *Louis Adamic and Shadow-America.* Los Angeles: Arthur Whipple, 1935.

Meltzer, David J. *First Peoples in a New World: Populating Ice Age America.* 2nd ed. New York: Cambridge University Press, 2021.

Mengestu, Dinaw. *The Beautiful Things That Heaven Bears.* New York: Riverhead, 2007.

Merton, Thomas. *Conjectures of a Guilty Bystander.* New York: Image Books, 1968a.

Merton, Thomas. *Faith and Violence: Christian Teaching and Christian Practice.* University of Notre Dame, 1968b.

Meyer, Lois, and Benjamin Maldonado Alvarado. *New World of Indigenous Resistance: Noam Chomsky and Voices from North, South, and Central America.* San Francisco: City Lights, 2010.

Mickey, Robert. *Paths Out of Dixie: The Democratization of Authoritarian Enclaves in America's Deep South, 1944–1972.* New Jersey: Princeton University Press, 2015.

Mikhail, John. *Elements of Moral Cognition: Rawls' Linguistic Analogy and the Cognitive Science of Moral and Legal Judgment.* New York: Cambridge University Press, 2013.

Miller, Stuart Creighton. *"Benevolent Assimilation": The American Conquest of the Philippines, 1899–1903.* New Haven: Yale University Press, 1992.

Miller, Stuart Creighton. *The Unwelcome Immigrant: The American Image of the Chinese, 1785–1882.* Berkeley: University of California Press, 1969.

Miller, W. Jason. *Langston Hughes.* London: Reaktion Books, 2020.

Miller, W. Jason. *Origins of the Dream: Hughes's Poetry and King's Rhetoric.* Gainesville: University of Florida Press, 2015.

Mills, Charles. "White Ignorance." In *Race and Epistemologies of Ignorance,* edited by Shannon Sullivan and Nancy Tuana, 11–38. Albany: State University of New York Press, 2007.

Mills, Charles. "White Ignorance." In *Agnotology: The Making & Unmaking of Ignorance,* edited by Robert N. Proctor and Londa Schiebinger, 230–249. Stanford: Stanford University Press, 2008.

Minow, Martha. *Breaking the Cycles of Hatred: Memory, Law, and Repair.* New Jersey: Princeton University Press, 2002.

Minow, Martha. *In Brown's Wake: Legacies of America's Educational Landmark.* New York: Oxford University Press, 2010.

Minow, Martha. *Making All the Difference: Inclusion, Exclusion, and American Law.* Ithaca: Cornell University Press, 1990.

Mitchell, Margaret. *Gone with the Wind.* New York: Macmillan, Anniversary Edition 1961. First published 1936.

Mooney, James. *The Ghost Dance Religion and the Sioux Outbreak of 1890.* Lincoln, Nebraska: University of Nebraska Press, 1991.

Moore, Ward. *Bring the Jubilee.* New York: Garrar, Strauss, and Young Inc., with Ballantine Books, 1953.

Moore, Ward. "Bring the Jubilee." *The Magazine of Fantasy & Science Fiction* 3, Number 7 (November 1952): 24–112.

Moraga, Cherrie, and Gloria Anzaldua. *The Bridge Called My Back: Writings by Racial Women of Color.* New York: SUNY Press, 2021. First published in 1981.

Moretti, Franco. *Far Country: Scenes from American Culture.* New York: Picador, 2019.

Moretti, Franco. *Signs Taken for Wonders: Essays in the Sociology of Literary Forms.* 2nd ed. New York: Verso, 1993.

Morrison, Toni. "Abrupt Stops and Unexpected Liquidity: The Aesthetics of Romare Bearden." In *The Romare Bearden Reader,* edited by Robert G. O'Meally, 178–184. Durham: Duke University Press, 2019.

Morrison, Toni. *The Source of Self-Regard: Selected Essays, Speeches, Meditations.* New York: Alfred A. Knopf, 2019.

Morrison, Toni. "Racism and Fascism." In *The Source of Self-Regard: Selected Essays, Speeches, Meditations*, 14–16.

Morrison, Toni. *The Origin of Others*. With a foreword by Ta-Nehisi Coates. Cambridge, MA: Harvard University Press, 2017.

Morrison, Toni. *Paradise*. 2nd edition, with a new foreword. New York: Vintage International, 2014. First published 1997.

Morrison, Toni. *Playing in the Dark: Whiteness and the Literary Imagination*. Cambridge, MA: Harvard University Press, 1992.

Morrison, Toni. *Jazz*. New York: Knopf, 1992.

Morrison, Toni. "Life in His Language." In *James Baldwin: The Legacy*, edited by Quincy Troupe, 75–78. New York: Simon and Schuster, 1990.

Morrison, Toni. *Beloved*. New York: Knopf, 1987.

Morrison, Toni. "The Site of Memory." In *Inventing the Truth: The Art and Craft of Memoir*, edited by William Zinsser, 83–102. Boston; New York: Houghton Mifflin, 1995.

Morrison, Toni. *The Bluest Eye*. Plume: New York, 1970.

Mosley, Walter. *Devil in a Blue Dress*. 30th anniversary edition, with a new introduction by the author. New York: Washington Square Press, 2020. First published 1990.

Muir, John. *My First Summer in the Sierra*. With an introduction by Mike Davis. New York: Modern Library, 2003.

Mulford, Carla. *Benjamin Franklin and the Ends of Empire*. New York: Oxford University Press, 2019.

Munoz, Jr., Carlos. *Youth, Identity, Power: The Chicano Movement*. 2nd ed. New York: Verso, 2007.

Nafisi, Azar. *Read Dangerously: The Subversive Power of Literature in Troubled Times*. New York: Dey Street, 2022.

NASA. "Welcome to Octavia E. Butler Landing." March 5, 2021. https://www.nasa.gov/image-feature/jpl/welcome-to-octavia-e-butler-landing.

National Park Service. "Paul Laurence Dunbar's Life Story." Dayton Aviation Heritage. Updated February 5, 2018. https://www.nps.gov/daav/learn/historyculture/paullaurencedunbarslifestory.htm.

National Public Radio. "NASA Scientist Christina Hernandez Discusses Her Work on the Mars Rover Perseverance Project." February 20, 2021. https://www.npr.org/2021/02/21/969886082/nasa-scientist-discusses-her-work-on-the-perseverance-mars-rover-project.

National Public Radio. "Henry Louis Gates Jr. Points to Reconstruction as the Genesis of White Supremacy." April 3, 2019. https://www.npr.org/2019/04/03/709094399/henry-louis-gates-jr-points-to-reconstruction-as-the-genesis-of-white-supremacy.

National Public Radio. "How 'Franklin,' the Black 'Peanuts' Character Was Born." November 6, 2015. https://www.npr.org/sections/codeswitch/2015/11/06/454930010/how-franklin-the-black-peanuts-character-was-born.

National Public Radio. "America's Forgotten History of Mexican-American 'Repatriation.'" September 10, 2015. https://www.npr.org/2015/09/10/439114563/americas-forgotten-history-of-mexican-american-repatriation.

National Public Radio. "'Watch Nights,' A New Year's Celebration of Emancipation." December 23, 2012. https://www.npr.org/2012/12/29/167905308/watch-nights -honor-emancipation-proclamations-anniversary#:~:text='Watch%20Nights %2C'%20A%20New%20Year's%20Celebration%20Of%20Emancipation%20On ,Lincoln's%20actions%20to%20end%20slavery.

National Public Radio. "The Art of Romare Bearden: Collages Fuse Essence of Old Harlem, the American South." Romare Bearden and Neda Ulaby. September 14, 2003. https://www.npr.org/templates/story/story.php?storyId=1428038.

Nature. "Controversial Cave Discoveries Suggest Human Beings Reached the Americas Much Earlier Than Thought." Colin Barras. July 22, 2020. https://www .nature.com/articles/d41586-020-02190-y.

Nedelsky, Jennifer. *Private Property and the Limits of American Constitutionalism: The Madison Framework and Its Legacy.* University of Chicago Press, 1990.

Neiman, Susan. *Learning from the Germans: Race and the Memory of Evil.* 2nd edition. New York: Picador, 2020.

Nelson, Bruce. *Divided We Stand: American Workers and the Struggle for Black Equality.* New Jersey: Princeton University Press, 2001.

Nevins, Allan. *James Truslow Adams: Historian of the American Dream.* University of Illinois Press, 1970.

New York Times. "Ancient Footprints Push Back Date of Human Arrival in the Americas: Human Footprints Found in the Americas are about 23,000 Years Old, a Study Reported, Suggesting That People May Have Arrived Long Before the Ice Age's Glaciers Melted." Carl Zimmer. September 23, 2021. https://www.nytimes .com/2021/09/23/science/ancient-footprints-ice-age.html

New York Times. "An Uneasy, Brittle Birthright: Americans of South Asian Descent Grapple with Belonging in Sanjena Sathian's Novel." Alisha Haridasani Gupta, April 3, 2021, C1, 4.

New York Times. "The Racism Behind Women's Suffrage." Brent Staples. Sunday, July 29, 2018: p. A8.

New York Times. "NASA's Goals Delete Mention of Home Planet." Andrew C. Revkin. July 22, 2006. https://www.nytimes.com/2006/07/22/science/22nasa.html ?ex=1311220800&en=74c926c8939e58e0&ei=5088&partner=rssnyt&emc=rss.

New York Times. "For 280 Tribes, a Protest on the Plains." Jack Healy. September 11, 2016. https://www.nytimes.com/interactive/2016/09/12/us/12tribes.html.

New Yorker. "In Cleveland, The American Dream Melts Away." July 22, 2016. https: //www.newyorker.com/news/news-desk/in-cleveland-the-american-dream-melts -away

Ngai, Mae. *The Chinese Question: Gold Rushes and Global Politics.* New York: W.W. Norton and Company, 2021.

Ngai, Mae. "Chinese Gold Miners and the 'Chinese Question' in Nineteenth-Century California and Victoria." *The Journal of American History* 101, Number 4, 2015: 1082–1105.

Ngai, Mae. *Impossible Subjects: Illegal Aliens and the Making of Modern America.* 2nd ed. New Jersey: Princeton University Press, 2014.

Nguyen, Viet Thanh, ed. *The Displaced: Refugee Writers on Refugee Lives*. New York: Abrams Press, 2018.

Nguyen, Viet Thanh. *The Refugees*. New York: Grove Press, 2017.

Nixon, Rob. "The Beautiful Things That Heaven Bears - Dinaw Mengestu." *New York Times Book Review*. March 25, 2007.

Nussbaum, Martha. *Cultivating Humanity*. Cambridge, MA: Harvard University Press, 1998.

O'Connor, Stephen. *Thomas Jefferson Dreams of Sally Hemmings: A Novel*. New York: Penguin, 2016.

O'Meally, Robert G. *Antagonistic Cooperation: Jazz, Collage, Fiction, and the Shaping of African American Culture*. New York: Columbia University Press, 2022.

O'Meally, Robert G., ed. *The Romare Bearden Reader*. Durham: Duke University Press, 2019.

O'Meally, Robert. *The Jazz Cadence of American Culture*. New York: Columbia University Press, 1998.

Oakes, James. *Freedom National: The Destruction of Slavery in the United States, 1861–1865*. New York: W.W. Norton, 2014.

Oakes, Stephen B. *The Fires of Jubilee: Nat Turner's Fierce Rebellion*. New York: Harper Perennial, 2016.

Obama, Barack. *Dreams from My Father*. New York: Times Books, 1995.

Ocampo, Anthony Christian. *The Latinos of Asia: How Filipino Americans Break the Rules of Race*. Stanford: Stanford University Press, 2016.

Okihiro, Gary Y. *American History Unbound: Asians & Pacific Islanders*. Oakland: University of California Press, 2015.

Okihiro, Gary Y. *Third World Studies: Theorizing Liberation*. Durham: Duke University Press, 2016.

Omi, Michael, and Howard Winant. *Racial Formation in the United States*. 3rd edition. New York: Routledge, 2014.

Onuf, Peter S. "The Empire of Liberty: Land of the Free and Home of the Slave." In *The World of the Revolutionary American Republic: Land, Labor, and the Conflict for a Continent*, edited by Andrew Shankman, 195–217. New York: Routledge, 2014.

Organization for Economic Cooperation and Development (OECD). *Social Justice in the EU and OECD, Index Report 2019*. Thorsten Hellmann, Pia Schmidt, and Sascha Matthias Heller, OECD, 2019.

Organization for Economic Cooperation and Development. *A Broken Social Elevator?* OECD, 2018.

Organization for Economic Cooperation and Development. *Social Justice in the OECD—How Do the Member States Compare?* OECD, 2011.

Orique, David, OP. *To Heaven or to Hell: Bartolome de Las Casas's Confesionario*. University Park, PA: Pennsylvania State University Press, 2018.

Ortiz, Erik. "Racial violence and a pandemic: How the Red Summer of 1919 relates to 2020." June 21, 2020. https://www.nbcnews.com/news/us-news/racial-violence-pandemic-how-red-summer-1919-relates-2020-n1231499.

Ortiz, Sister Dianna, with Patricia Davis. *The Blindfold's Eyes: My Journey from Torture to Truth*. Maryknoll, New York: Orbis Books, 2002.

Ougrin, Dennis, and Anastasia Ougrin. *One Hundred Years in Galicia.* Cambridge: Cambridge Scholars Publishing, 2020.

Paige, Jeffery M. *Indigenous Revolution in Ecuador & Bolivia, 1990–2005.* Tucson: University of Arizona Press, 2020.

Paige, Jeffery M. *Coffee and Power: Revolution and the Rise of Democracy in Central America*. Cambridge, MA: Harvard University Press, 1998.

Painter, Nell Irvin. *Creating Black Americans: African-American History and Its Meanings, 1619 to the Present.* New York: Oxford University Press, 2006.

Palmie, Stephan. *Wizards and Scientists: Explorations in Afro-Cuban Modernity & Tradition*. Duke University Press, 2002.

Parker, Stephen. *Bertolt Brecht: A Literary Life*. New York: Bloomsbury, 2014.

Parkinson, Robert G. *The Common Cause: Creating Race and Nation in the American Revolution*. Chapel Hill: University of North Carolina Press, 2016.

Parson, Don. *Making a Better World: Public Housing, the Red Scare, and the Direction of Modern Los Angeles.* With a foreword by Kevin Starr. Minneapolis: University of Minnesota Press, 2005.

Parten, Bennett. "'Blow Ye Trumpet, Blow': The Idea of Jubilee in Slavery and Freedom." *The Journal of the Civil War Era* 10, Number 3 (September 2020): 298–318.

Pastor, Manuel, Jennifer Ito, and Vanessa Carter. *The Next California: Demography, Inequality & Our Future*. Othering & Belonging Institute. April 18, 2018. https://belonging.berkeley.edu/next-california.

Patterson, Orlando. *Freedom: Freedom in the Making of Western Culture*. New York: Basic Books, 1991.

Payne, Charles M. *I've Got the Light of Freedom: The Organizing Tradition and the Mississippi Freedom Struggle*. Berkeley: University of California Press, 2007.

Pedrosa, Adriano, and Tomas Toledo, eds., *Afro-Atlantic Histories.* DelMonico Books/Museo de Arte de Sao Paulo, 2021.

Pennington, Jr., Kenneth J. "Bartolome de Las Casas and the Tradition of Medieval Law." *Church History* 39, No. 2, June 1970: 149–161.

Pensky, Max. *Melancholy Dialectics: Walter Benjamin and the Play of Mourning*. 2nd ed. University of Massachusetts Press, 2001.

Perry, Jeffrey B. *Hubert Harrison: The Struggle for Equality, 1918–1927.* New York: Columbia University Press, 2021.

Perry, Jeffrey B. *Hubert Harrison: The Voice of Harlem Radicalism, 1883–1918.* New York: Columbia University Press, 2011.

Pew Research Center. "What Caused the Civil War." Russell Heimlich. May 18, 2011. https://www.pewresearch.org/fact-tank/2011/05/18/what-caused-the-civil-war/

Piercy, Marge. *Woman on the Edge of Time: A Novel*. 40th anniversary edition, with a new introduction by the author. New York: Ballantine Books, 2016. First published 1976.

Pieterse, Jan Nederveen. "Slavery and the Triangle of Emancipation." *Race and Class* 20, No. 2 (1988): 1–22.

Piketty, Thomas. *Capital and Ideology.* Cambridge, MA: The Belknap Press of Harvard University Press, 2020.

Piketty, Thomas. *Capital in the Twenty-first Century*. Cambridge, MA: Belknap Press of Harvard University Press, 2014.

Polk, Dora Beale. *The Island of California: A History of the Myth*. Nebraska: Bison Books, 1995.

Portes, Alejandro, and Ruben G. Rumbaut. *Immigrant America: A Portrait.* Fourth Edition, revised, updated, and expanded. Oakland: University of California Press, 2014.

Porpora, Douglas V. *How Holocausts Happen: The United States in Central America.* Philadelphia: Temple University Press, 1992.

Portes, Alejandro, and Rueben G. Rumbaut. *Immigrant America: A Portrait*. 4th edition. Berkeley: University of California Press, 2014.

Porzucki, Nina. "A Novelist Finds 'The Mexican Girl,' from Jack Kerouac's *On the Road*." In *The World.* November 28–29, 2013. https://www.pri.org/stories/2013-11 -28/novelist-finds-mexican-girl-jack-kerouacs-book-road.

Powell, General Colin L. "Foreword: Hope and Glory: The Monument to Colonel Robert Gould Shaw and the Fifty-fourth Massachusetts Regiment." In *Hope & Glory: Essays on the Legacy of the 54th Massachusetts Regiment*, edited by Martin H. Blatt, Thomas J. Brown, and Donald Yacovone, xv–xx. Amherst and Boston: University of Massachusetts Press, in association with the Massachusetts Historical Society, 2001.

Prescott, Laurence E. "'Yo tambien soy America': Latin American Receptions of Langston Hughes's American Dream." In *Critical Insights: Langston Hughes*, edited by R. Baxter Miller, 255–274. Ipswich, MA: Salem Press, 2013.

Presner, Todd Samuel. *Mobile Modernity: Germans, Jews, Trains.* New York: Columbia University Press, 2007.

Prince, K. Stephen. *Radical Reconstruction: A Brief History with Documents.* Boston: Bedford/St. Martin's, 2016.

Public Policy Institute of California, California's Population. March 2021. https:// www.ppic.org/publication/californias-population/.

Purnell, Brian, Jeanne Theoharis, and Komozi Woodard, eds. *The Strange Careers of the Jim Crow North: Segregation and Struggle Outside of the South.* New York: New York University Press, 2019.

Pyne, Stephen. *The Pyrocene: How We Created an Age of Fire & What Comes Next.* Oakland, CA: University of California Press, 2022.

Quijano, Anibal, and Immanuel Wallerstein. "Americanity as a Concept, or the Americas in the Modern World-System." *International Social Science Journal* (1992): 549–557.

Radway, Janice A. *Reading the Romance: Women, Patriarchy, and Popular Literature.* Chapel Hill: University of North Carolina Press.

Rampersad, Arnold. *The Life of Langston Hughes: Volume I: 1902–1941, I, Too, Sing America.* New York: Oxford University Press, 2002a.

Rampersad, Arnold. *The Life of Langston Hughes: Volume II: 1941–1967, I Dream a World.* New York: Oxford University Press, 2002b.

Rana, Aziz. *The Two Faces of American Freedom.* Cambridge, MA: Harvard University Press, 2010.

Reider, Jonathan. *Gospel of Freedom: Martin Luther King, Jr.'s Letter from Birmingham Jail and the Struggle that Changed a Nation.* New York: Bloomsbury, 2013.

Reifer, Tom. "The 'Arab 1848': Reflections on US Policy & the Power of Nonviolence." Transnational Institute, February 23, 2011. https://www.tni.org/files /Arab1848_0.pdf

Reifer, Tom. "The Battle for the Future Has Already Begun: The Reassertion of Race, Space and Place in World-Systems Geographies and Anti-Systemic Cartographies," edited by Christian Suter and Christopher Chase-Dunn, 129–153. Berlin: Verlag, World Society Studies, 2014.

Reifer, Tom. "The Reassertion of Race, Space and Punishment's Place in Urban Sociology and Critical Criminology." *Environment & Planning D: Society & Space* 31 (April 2013): 372–380.

Reuland, Eric, and Werner Abraham. *Knowledge & Language, From Orwell's Problem to Plato's Problem.* Dordrecht: Kluwer Academic Publishers, 1993.

Ricoeur, Paul. *Memory, History, Forgetting.* Chicago: University of Chicago Press, 2004.

Richardson, Alissa V. *Bearing Witness While Black: African Americans, Smartphones, & the New Protest #Journalism.* New York: Oxford University Press, 2020.

Richardson, Heather Cox. *To Make Men Free: A History of the Republican Party.* 2nd ed. New York: Basic Books, 2021.

Richardson, Heather Cox. *How the South Won the Civil War: Oligarchy, Democracy, & the Continuing Fight for the Soul of America.* New York: Oxford University Press, 2020.

Roberts-Miller, Patricia. *Fanatical Schemes: Proslavery Rhetoric and the Tragedy of Consensus.* Tuscaloosa: University of Alabama Press, 2009.

Robinson, Cedric J. *Black Marxism: The Making of the Black Radical Tradition.* 3rd edition. Chapel Hill: University of North Carolina Press, 2021.

Robinson, Greg. *The Unsung Great: Stories of Extraordinary Japanese Americans.* Seattle: University of Washington Press, 2020.

Rochelson, Meri-Jane. *A Jew in the Public Arena: The Career of Israel Zangwill.* Detroit, MI: Wayne State University Press, 2008.

Rodriguez, Luis. *Music of the Mill: A Novel.* New York: Harper Perennial, 2005.

Rodriguez, Luis. "The End of the Line: California and the Promise of Street Peace." *Social Justice* 32, No. 3 (2005): 12–23. https://www.jstor.org/stable/29768318.

Roediger, David R. "Radical Culture Without Surrealism." *Socialist Review* 28, Issue 1/2 (2001): 74–88.

Roediger, David R. "Introduction." In *Black on White: Black Writers on What it Means to Be White,* edited by David R. Roediger, 1–28. New York: Schocken Books, 1998.

Roediger, David R. *Working Toward Whiteness.* New York: Basic Books, 2018

Rosales, Steven. *Soldados Razos at War.* University of Arizona Press, 2018.

Rosemont, Franklin, and Robin D.G. Kelley, eds. *Black, Brown & Beige: Surrealist Writings from Africa and the Diaspora.* University of Texas Press, 2010.

Rosenberg, Rosalind. *Jane Crow: The Life of Pauli Murray.* New York: Oxford University Press, 2020.

Rothberg, Michael. *Multidirectional Memory: Remembering the Holocaust in the Age of Decolonization.* Stanford: Stanford University Press, 2009.

Rothberg, Michael. *The Implicated Subject: Beyond Victims and Perpetrators.* Stanford: Stanford University Press, 2019.

Rousseau, Jean-Jacques. *Discourse on Inequality.* A New Translation by Franklin Philip. New York: Oxford World Classics, 1994.

Rohrbough, Malcolm J. "'We Will Make Our Fortunes—No Doubt of It': The Worldwide Rush to California," 55–70. In *Riches for All: The California Gold Rush and the World,* ed., Kenneth N. Owens (Lincoln: University of Nebraska Press, 2002).

Rudd, Jeremy B. "Why Do We Think That Inflation Expectations Matter for Inflation? (And Should We?)." Finance and Economics Discussion Series 2021-062. Washington: Board of Governors of the Federal Reserve System, 2021. https://doi.org/10.17016/FEDSW.2021.062.

Rushdie, Salman. *The Wizard of Oz.* New York: BFI Film Classics, 1992.

Said, Edward W. *Culture and Imperialism.* New York: Vintage, 1993.

Sakwa, Richard. *Frontline Ukraine: Crisis in the Borderlands.* London: I.B. Tauris, 2015.

Sampson, Robert J. *Great American City: Chicago and the Enduring Neighborhood Effect.* Chicago: University of Chicago Press, 2013.

Sampson, Robert J., Jared N. Schachner, and Robert D. Mare. "Urban Income Inequality & the Great Recession in Sunbelt Form: Disentangling Individual Level & Neighborhood-Level Change in Los Angeles." *Russell Sage Foundation Journal of the Social Sciences* 3, Issue Number 2 (February 2017): 102–128.

Sandmeyer, Elmer Clarence. *The Anti-Chinese Movement in California.* With a foreword and supplementary bibliographies by Roger Daniels. University of Illinois, 1991. First published 1939.

Sandul, Paul J. P. *California Dreaming: Boosterism, Memory, and Rural Suburbs in the Golden State.* West Virginia University Press, 2014.

Sarafian, Arpi. *Endless Crossings: Reflections on Armenian Art and Culture in Los Angeles.* Tekeyan Cultural Association, 2019.

Sarafian, Arpi. "Interview with Aris Janigian," *The Armenian Mirror-Spectator.* January 30, 2020. https://mirrorspectator.com/2020/01/30/interview-author-arpi-sarafian-discusses-new-book-with-aris-janigian/.

Sarotte, M.E. *Not One Inch: America, Russia, and the Making of the Post-Cold War Stalemate.* New Haven: Yale University Press, 2021.

Sarra, Janis, and Sara L. Wade. *Predatory Lending and the Destruction of the African-American Dream.* New York: Cambridge University Press, 2020.

Sathian, Sanjena. *Gold Diggers: A Novel.* New York: Penguin Press, 2021a.

Sathian, Sanjena. "After the Atlanta Shootings, All I See is the Fragility of Our Belonging." *Los Angeles Times.* March 18, 2021b. https://www.latimes

.com/entertainment-arts/books/story/2021-03-18/sanjena-sathian-after-the-atlanta-shooting-all-i-see-is-the-fragility-of-my-belonging.

Savage, Kirk. *Standing Soldiers, Kneeling Slaves: Race, War, and Monument in Nineteenth Century America.* Princeton: Princeton University Press, 2019.

Sawhney, Deepak Narang, ed. *Unmasking L.A.: Third Worlds and the City.* New York: Palgrave, 2002.

Saxton, Alexander. *The Indispensable Enemy: Labor and the Anti-Chinese Movement in California.* 2nd ed. Berkeley: University of California Press, 1995. First published 1971.

Schickler, Eric. *Racial Realignment: The Transformation of American Liberalism.* New Jersey: Princeton University Press, 2016.

Scholem, Gershom. *Greetings from Angelus: Poems.* New York: Archipelago Books, 2017.

Schomburg Center for Research in Black Culture. *Unsung: Unheralded Narratives of Slavery and Abolition.* Edited and with an introduction by Michelle D. Commander, and with a foreword by Kevin Young, 2021.

Schor, Esther. *Emma Lazarus.* New York: Schocken, 2017.

Schoultz, Lars. *That Infernal Little Republic: The United States & the Cuban Revolution.* Chapel Hill: University of North Carolina Press, 2009.

Scott, Peter Dale. *Coming to Jakarta: A Poem About Terror.* San Francisco: New Directions, 1988.

Seed, Patricia. "Are These Not Also Men? The Indians' Humanity and Capacity for Spanish Civilization," *Journal of Latin American Studies* 24, No. 3 (October 1993): 629–652.

Sellers, Charles. *The Market Revolution: Jacksonian America, 1815–1846.* New York: Oxford University Press, 1991.

Sellers, Jr., Charles Grier, ed. *The Southerner as American.* New York: E.P. Dutton, 1966.

Sellers, Jr., Charles Grier. "The Travail of Slavery." In *The Southerner as American,* edited by Charles Grier Sellers Jr., 40–71. New York: E.P. Dutton, 1966.

Sen, Amartya. *Development as Freedom.* New York: Anchor, 1999.

Shakespeare, William. *The Tragedy of Hamlet Prince of Denmark.* Edited by Barbara Mowat and Paul Werstine. Washington, D.C.: Folger Shakespeare Library, n.d., accessed April 19, 2021. https://shakespeare.folger.edu/shakespeares-works/Hamlet (Act 3, Scene 1).

Sheehan, Neil. *A Bright Shining Lie: John Paul Vann and America in Vietnam.* New York: Vintage, 1989.

Sherman, Jennifer. *Dividing Paradise: Rural Inequality and the Diminishing American Dream.* Oakland, CA: University of California Press, 2021.

Sides, John, Michael Tesler, and Lynn Vavreck. *Identity Crisis: The 2016 Presidential Campaign and the Battle for the Meaning of America.* 2nd edition. New Jersey: Princeton University Press, 2019.

Simpson, Brooks D., ed. *Reconstruction: Voices from America's First Great Struggle for Racial Equality.* New York: Library of America, 2018.

Sinha, Manisha. *The Slave's Cause: A History of Abolition.* New Haven: Yale University Press, 2017.

Sleeper-Smith, Susan, Juliana Barr, Jean M. O'Brien, Nancy Shoemaker, and Scott Manning Stevens. *Why You Can't Teach United States History Without Native Americans.* Chapel Hill: University of North Carolina Press, 2015.

Slotkin, Richard. *The Fatal Environment: The Myth of the Frontier in the Age of Industrialization, 1800–1890.* Middletown: Wesleyan University Press, 1985.

Slotkin, Richard. *Lost Battalions: The Great War and the Crisis of American Nationality.* New York: Henry Holt and Company, 1995.

Slotkin, Richard. *The Long Road to Antietam: How the Civil War Became a Revolution.* New York: Liveright, 2012.

Smith, Betty. *A Tree Grows in Brooklyn.* New York: Harper Perennial, 2006. First published 1943.

Smith, John David, and J. Vincent Lowery, eds., *The Dunning School: Historians, Race, and the Meaning of Reconstruction.* With a foreword by Eric Foner. Lexington: University Press of Kentucky, 2013.

Snyder, Timothy. *Black Earth: The Holocaust as History and Warning.* New York: Tim Duggan Books, 2015.

Snyder, Timothy. *The Reconstruction of Nations.* New Haven: Yale University Press, 2003.

Snyder, Timothy. *The Bloodlands: Europe Between Hitler and Stalin.* New York: Basic Books, 2016.

Sokol, Jason. *All Eyes Are Upon Us.* New York: Basic Books, 2014.

Solnit, Rebecca. *Storming the Gates of Paradise: Landscapes for Politics.* Berkeley: University of California Press, 2007.

Sonksen, Mike. "'Making the Impossible Possible': Octavia Butler Reimagines Space and Time." *Boom California* (December 9, 2020). https://boomcalifornia.org/2020/12/09/making-the-impossible-possible-octavia-butler-reimagines-space-and-time/

Sorkin, David. *Jewish Emancipation: A History Across Five Centuries.* New Jersey: Princeton University Press, 2019.

Squires, Gregory D., ed. *The Fight for Fair Housing: Causes, Complications, & Future Implications of the 1968 Federal Fair Housing Act.* New York: Routledge, 2017.

Stanley, Tarshia L., ed., *Approaches to Teaching the Works of Octavia E. Butler.* New York: Modern Language Association of America, 2019.

Starr, Kevin. *Endangered Dreams: The Great Depression in California.* New York: Oxford University Press, 1996.

Stauffer, John, Zoe Trod, and Celeste-Marie Bernier. *Picturing Frederick Douglass: An Illustrated History of the Nineteenth Century's Most Photographed American.* With an epilogue by Henry Louis Gates Jr. and an afterword by Kenneth B. Morris Jr. New York: W.W. Norton, 2015.

Stauffer, John, and Zoe Trod, eds. *The Tribunal: Responses to John Brown & the Harpers Ferry Raid.* Cambridge, MA: The Belknap Press of Harvard University Press, 2012a.

Stauffer, John, and Zoe Trod. "Introduction: The Meaning & Significance of John Brown." In *The Tribunal: Responses to John Brown & the Harpers Ferry* Raid, edited by John Stauffer and Zoe Trod, xix–lix. Cambridge, MA: The Belknap Press of Harvard University Press, 2012b.

Steers, Jr., Edward. *Lincoln's Assassination.* Carbondale: Southern Illinois University Press, 2014.

Steers, Jr., Edward. "Why Was Lincoln Murdered?" In *1865: America Makes War and Peace in Lincoln's Final Year,* edited by Harold Holzer and Sara Vaughn Gabbard, 81–100. Carbondale: Southern Illinois University Press, 2015.

Stein, Sarah Abrevaya, and Caroline Luce. *100 Years of Sephardic Los Angeles.* Los Angeles: UCLA Leve Center for Jewish Studies, 2020. https://levecenter.ucla.edu /ucla-sephardic-initiative/.

Steinbeck, John. *In Dubious Battle.* New York: Penguin Classics, 2006. First published 1936.

Steinbeck, John. *The Grapes of Wrath.* New York: Penguin Classics, 2006. First published 1939.

Steinbruner, John, and Nancy Gallagher. "Prospects for Global Security: Constructive Transformation: An Alternative Vision of Global Security." *Daedalus: Journal of the American Academy of Arts and Sciences.* (Summer 2004): 83–103.

Stepan-Norris, Judith, and Maurice Zeitlin. *Left Out: Reds and America's Industrial Unions.* New York: Cambridge University Press, 2003.

Stevenson, Brenda. *The Contested Murder of Latasha Harlins: Justice, Gender, and the Origins of the LA Riots.* New York: Oxford University Press, 2013.

Stewart, Jeffrey C. *The New Negro: The Life of Alain Locke.* New York: Oxford University Press, 2018.

Stokes, Melvyn. *D.W. Griffith's Birth of a Nation: A History of the Most Controversial Picture of All Time.* New York: Oxford University Press, 2008.

Sugrue, Thomas J. *Sweet Land of Liberty: The Forgotten Struggle for Civil Rights in the North.* New York: Random House, 2009.

Takaki, Ronald. *Double Victory: A Multicultural History of America in World War II.* Boston: Little, Brown, 2000.

Taylor, Alan. *American Revolutions: A Continental History, 1750–1804.* New York: W.W. Norton, 2016.

Terrault, Lisa. *The Myth of Seneca Falls: Memory and the Women's Suffrage Movement, 1848–1898.* Durham: University of North Carolina Press, 2014.

Thernborn, Goran. "Inequality and Democracy." *New Left Review* 129 (May/June 2021): 5–28.

Theoharis, Jeanne. "'Alabama on Avalon': Rethinking the Watts Uprising and the Character of Black Protest in Los Angeles." In *The Black Power Movement: Rethinking the Civil Rights-Black Power* Era, edited by Peniel Joseph, 27–54. New York: Routledge, 2006.

Thoreau, Henry David. *Walden.* Edited with an introduction and notes by Stephen Fender. New York: Oxford World Classics, 2008. First published 1854.

Thunberg, Greta. *No One is Too Small to Make a Difference.* New York: Penguin Books, 2021.

Tiedemann, Rolf. "Dialectics at a Standstill." In Walter Benjamin, *The Arcades Project,* translated by Howard Eiland and Kevin McLaughlin, and prepared on the basis of the German Volume Edited by Rolf Tiedemann, 929–945. Cambridge, MA: The Belknap Press of Harvard University Press, 1999.

Todorov, Tzvetan. *The Conquest of America*. New York: Harper Perennial, 1984.

Tomlins, Christopher. *Freedom Bound: Law, Labor, and Civic Identity in Colonizing America, 1580–1865*. New York: Cambridge University Press, 2010.

Tomlins, Chistopher. *In the Matter of Nat Turner: A Speculative History*. Princeton, New Jersey: Princeton University Press, 2022.

Trachtenberg, Marc. "The United States and the NATO Non-extension Assurances of 1990: New Light on an Old Problem?" *International Security* 45, No. 3 (Winter 2020/21): 162–203.

Trefousse, Hans L. *The Radical Republicans: Lincoln's Vanguard for Racial Justice*. Baton Rouge: Louisiana State University Press, 1968.

Trombley, Laura Skandera, and Ann Ryan, "Mark Twain and Critical Race Theory." *Inside Higher Ed*, October 7, 2021.

Trouillot, Michel-Rolph. *Silencing the Past: Power and the Production of History*. 2nd ed. Boston: Beacon Press, 2015.

Trouillot, Michel-Rolph. *Trouillot Remixed: The Michel-Rolph Trouillot Reader*. Edited by Yarimar Bonilla, Greg Bekcett, and Mayanthi L. Fernando. Durham: Duke Univeristy Press, 2021.

Trouillot, Michel-Rolph. "The North Atlantic Universals." In *The Modern World-System in the Longue Duree*, edited by Immanuel Wallerstein, 229–238. New York: Routledge, 2015.

Troupe, Quincy, ed. *James Baldwin: The Legacy*. New York: Simon & Schuster, 1990.

Tsygankov, Andrei P. *The Dark Double: US Media, Russia, and the Politics of Values*. New York: Oxford University Press, 2019.

Tucker, Mark, ed. *The Duke Ellington Reader*. New York: Oxford University Press, 1993.

Union of Concerned Scientists. "NASA Reaches for Muzzle as Renowned Climate Scientist Speaks Out." December 12, 2006. https://www.ucsusa.org/resources/nasa-reaches-muzzle-renowned-climate-scientist-speaks-out.

USC Dornsife Center for the Study of Immigrant Integration. *State of Immigrants in LA County*. January 2020. https://dornsife.usc.edu/assets/sites/731/docs/SOILA_full_report_v19.pdf.

USC Dornsife Equity Research Institute, 2021. Interactive Map: The American Dream and Promise Act of 2019. https://dornsife.usc.edu/csii/map-dream-and-promise-act/.

USC Dornsife Center for the Study of Immigration. State of Immigrants in LA County 2020. https://dornsife.usc.edu/csii/state-of-immigrants-la.

Valelly, Richard M. *The Two Reconstructions: The Struggle for Black Enfranchisement*. Chicago: University of Chicago Press, 2004.

Valle, Victor M., and Rodolfo D. Torres. *Latino Metropolis*. Minneapolis: University of Minnesota Press, 2000.

van Wagtendonk, Jan W. et al. *Fire in California's Ecosystems*. 2nd ed. Oakland: University of California Press, 2018.

Veidlinger, Jeffrey. *In the Midst of Civilized Europe: The Pogroms of 1918–1921 and the Onset of the Holocaust.* New York: Metropolitan Books, 2022.

Vice News. "The American Dream Melts at the Republican National Convention." July 20, 2016. https://www.vice.com/en/article/qkwq4x/watch-the-american-dream -melt-before-your-eyes

Vigil, James Diego. *A Rainbow of Gangs: Street Culture in the Mega-City.* Austin: University of Texas Press, 2002.

Voss, Kim, and Irene Bloemraad, eds. *Rallying for Immigrant Rights: The Fight for Inclusion in 21st Century America.* Berkeley: University of California Press, 2006.

Walcott, Derek. *White Egrets.* New York: Farrar, Straus, and Giroux, 2010.

Wald, Alan M. *Exiles from a Future Time: The Forging of the Mid-Twentieth Century Literary Left.* Chapel Hill: University of North Carolina Press, 2002.

Waldstreicher, David. *Runaway America: Benjamin Franklin, Slavery, and the American Revolution.* New York: Hill & Wang, 2005.

Walker, Charles F. *The Tupac Amaru Rebellion.* Cambridge, MA: The Belknap Press of Harvard University Press, 2014.

Walker, Charles F., and Liz Clarke. *Witness to the Age of Revolution: The Odyssey of Juan Bautista Tupac Amaru.* New York: Oxford University Press, 2020.

Walker, Richard A. *Pictures of a Gone City: Tech and the Dark Side of Prosperity in the San Francisco Bay Area.* Oakland: PM Press, 2018.

Wall Street Journal. "The American Dream is Alive on Mars." Tunka Varadarajan, February 26, 2021.

Wallace, Mike. *Greater Gotham: A History of New York City From 1898 to 1919.* New York: Oxford University Press, 2017.

Wallerstein, Immanuel. "Braudel on the *Longue Duree*: Problems of Conceptual Translation." *Review* XXXII, Number 2 (2009): 155–170.

Wallerstein, Immanuel. *European Universalism: The Rhetoric of Power.* New York: New Press, 2006.

Wallerstein, Immanuel. *The Decline of American Power.* New York: New Press, 2003.

Wallerstein, Immanuel. *The Modern World-System: Capitalist Agriculture and the Origins of the European World-Economy in the Sixteenth Century.* San Diego: Academic Press, 1974.

Wallerstein, Immanuel. *The Modern World-System III: The Second Era of the Great Expansion of the Capitalist World-Economy.* Berkeley: University of California Press, 2011.

Wallerstein, Immanuel. *Utopistics: Or, Historical Choices of the Twenty-first Century.* New York: New Press, 1998.

Walter, Barbara F. *How Civil Wars Start: And How to Stop Them.* New York: Crown Books, 2022.

Warren, Louis S. *God's Red Son: The Ghost Dance Religion and the Making of Modern America.* New York: Basic Books, 2017.

Wasserstrom, Jeffrey. "Here's Why Xi Jinping's 'Chinese Dream' Differs Radically from the American Dream." *Time Magazine.* October 29, 2015.

Weber, Devra. *Dark Sweat, White Gold: California Farm Workers, Cotton, and the New Deal.* Berkeley: University of California Press, 1994.

Weber, Max. *Charisma and Disenchantment: The Vocation Lectures.* Edited by Paul Reitter and Chad Wellmon. New York: New York Review of Books, 2020.

Weber, Max. *The Protestant Ethic and the Spirit of Capitalism.* London and New York: Routledge, 1992. First published 1905.

Weiwei, Ai. *Human Flow: Stories from the Global Refugee Crisis.* New Jersey: Princeton University Press, 2020.

Weiwei, Ai. *Humanity.* New Jersey: Princeton University Press, 2018.

Werner, Craig H. "Chicago Renaissance." In *The Oxford Companion to African American Literature*, edited by William L. Andrews, Frances Smith Foster, and Trudier Harris, with a foreword by Henry Louis Gates Jr., 132–133. New York: Oxford University Press, 1997.

West, Cornel. "W.E.B. Du Bois: An Interpretation." In *Africana: Civil Rights: An A-to-Z Reference of the Movement that Changed America*, edited by Kwame Anthony Appiah and Henry Louis Gates Jr., 432–458. Philadelphia: Running Press, 2004b.

White, Hayden. *The Content of the Form: Narrative Discourse and Historical Representation.* Baltimore: The Johns Hopkins University Press, 1987.

White, Jr., Ronald C. "Abraham Lincoln's Sermon on the Mount: The Second Inaugural." In *1865: America Makes War and Peace in Lincoln's Final Year*, edited by Harold Holzer and Sara Vaughn Gabbard, 52–65. Carbondale: Southern Illinois University Press, 2015.

Whitman, James Q. *Hitler's American Model: The United States & the Making of Nazi Race Law.* New Jersey: Princeton University Press, 2017.

Widener, Daniel. *Black Arts West: Culture & Struggle in Postwar Los Angeles.* Durham: Duke University Press, 2010.

Widener, Daniel. "'Perhaps the Japanese are to Be Thanked': Asia, Asian America, and the Construction of Black California." *Positions: East Asia Cultures Critique* 11, Number 1, Spring 2003: 135–181.

Widmer, Ted. "Opinion: The Capitol Takeover That Wasn't: In 1861, a pro-Southern mob wanted to block the tallying of electoral votes for Lincoln. So did some congressmen." *New York Times.* January 8, 2021.

Widmer, Ted. *Lincoln on the Verge: Thirteen Days to Washington.* New York: Simon and Schuster, 2020.

Wiecek, William M. "*Somerset:* Lord Manfield and the Legitimacy of Slavery in the Anglo-American World," *University of Chicago Law Review* 42 (1975): 84–146.

Wiecek, William M. *The Sources of Antislavery Constitutionalism in America, 1760–1848.* Ithaca: Cornell University Press, 1977.

Wilentz, Sean. "Forging an Early Black Politics." *New York Review of Books* (July 1, 2021): 42–44.

Wilkerson, Isabel. *Caste: The Origins of Our Discontents.* New York: Random House, 2021.

Williams, Linda Faye. *The Constraint of Race: Legacies of White Skin Privilege in America.* Philadelphia: Pennsylvania State University Press, 2003.

Williams, Raymond. *Problems in Materialism and Culture.* New York: Verso, 1997.

Wilson, Andrew. *The Ukrainians.* 4th ed. New Haven: Yale University Press, 2015.

Wilson, Andrew. *The Ukrainians.* 2nd edition. New Haven: Yale University Press, 2002.

Wilson, August. "Bearden: Black Life on Its Own Terms." In *The Romare Bearden Reader*, edited by Robert G. O'Meally, 175–177. Durham: Duke University Press, 2019.

Wilson, August. *Fences.* New York: Plume, 1986.

Wilson, August. *Radio Golf.* Reprinted in *American Theatre* 22, Number 9, November 2005: 88–108.

Wilson, August. *Gem of the Ocean.* New York: Theatre Communications Group, 2003, 2006.

Wilson, August. "The Ground on Which I Stand." 11th Annual Biennial Theatre Communications Group National Conference. Princeton University, Princeton, New Jersey. June 26, 1996. https://www.americantheatre.org/2016/06/20/the-ground-on-which-i-stand/.

Wilson, Emily. "Introduction." *The Odyssey*, translated by Emily Wilson, 1–79. New York: W.W. Norton & Company, 2018.

Wise, Steven M. *Though the Heavens May Fall: The Landmark Trial That Led to the End of Human Slavery.* Lebanon, IN: De Capo Press, 2006.

Wokler, Robert. *Rousseau, the Age of Enlightenment, and Their Legacies,* edited by Bryan Garsten, and with an introduction by Christopher Brooke. New Jersey: Princeton University Press, 2012.

Wolf, Eric. *Europe and the Peoples Without History.* 2nd ed. Berkeley: University of California Press, 2010.

Woods, Clyde. *Development Arrested: The Blues and Plantation Power in the Mississippi Delta.* With an introduction by Ruth Wilson Gilmore. New York: Verso, 2017a.

Woods, Clyde. *Development Drowned & Reborn: The Blues & Bourbon Restorations in Post-Katrina New Orleans.* Edited by Jordan T. Camp & Laura Pulido. Athens, Georgia: University of Georgia Press, 2017b.

Wright, Richard. "Introduction." In St. Clair Drake & Horace R. Cayton, *Black Metropolis: A Study of Negro Life in a Northern City,* xvii–xxxiv. New York: Harcourt, Brace, and Company, 1945.

Wright, Richard. *Richard Wright, Early Works.* Edited by Arnold Rampersad. New York: The Library of America, 1991.

Wright, Richard. *Native Son.* New York: Harper Perennial Classics, 2005. First published 1940.

YIVO Encyclopedia of the Jews of Eastern Europe. https://yivoencyclopedia.org/.

Young, Kevin. *The Grey Album: On the Blackness of Blackness.* Minneapolis, Minnesota: Grey Wolf Press, 2012.

Young, Kevin. "Introduction: The Difficult Miracle." In *African American Poetry: 250 Years of Struggle and Song, A Library of America Anthology,* edited by Kevin Young, xxxix–lx. New York: Library of America, 2020.

Young, Kevin. "Foreword." *Unsung: Unheralded Narratives of American Slavery and Abolition,* edited by the Schomburg Center for Research in Black Culture, xi–xvi. New York: Penguin, 2021.

Young, Mary. "Walter Mosley, Detective Fiction and Black Culture." *The Journal of Popular Culture* (2004): 141–150.

Young-Bruel, Elisabeth. *Childism: Confronting Prejudice Against Children.* New Haven and London: Yale University Press, 2012.

Young-Key, Kim-Renaud, R. Richard Grinker, and Kirk W. Larsen, ed. *Korean American Literature.* Washington, D.C.: George Washington University, 2004. https://www2.gwu.edu/~sigur/assets/docs/scap/SCAP20-KoreanWriters.pdf.

Yung, Judy. *The Chinese Exclusion Act and Angel Island.* New York: Bedfords/Saint Martin's, 2018.

Zangwill, Israel. *From the Ghetto to the Melting Pot: Israel Zangwill's Jewish Plays.* Edited with introduction and commentary by Edna Nahshon. Detroit, MI: Wayne State University Press, 2006.

Zilberg, Elana. *Spaces of Detention: The Making of a Transnational Gang Crisis Between Los Angeles & San Salvador.* Durham: Duke University Press, 2011.

Zingales, Luigi, "Who Killed Horatio Alger?" *City Journal* (Autumn 2011). https://www.city-journal.org/html/who-killed-horatio-alger-13413.html.

Zunz, Oliver. *The Changing Face of Inequality.* Chicago, Illinois: University of Chicago Press, 2000.

DISCOGRAPHY

Chapman, Tracy. "Mountains of Things." *Tracy Chapman.* 1988.

Eagles. "Hotel California." *Hotel California.* 1976.

Eagles. "The Last Resort." *Hotel California.* 1976.

Lady Gaga. "Always Remember Us This Way." Soundtrack, *A Star is Born*, Bradley Cooper and Lady Gaga, 2018.

Marley, Bob. *Exodus.* 1977.

Marsalis, Branford, Quartet. *Romare Bearden Revealed.* Jazz Album. New York, New York, 2013.

Springsteen, Bruce. *The Ghost of Tom Joad.* 1995.

FILMOGRAPHY

Césaire, Aimé, *Aimé Césaire: Une Parole Pour Le XXIeme Siecle/A Voice for the 21st Century*, California Newsreel, 1994/2006.

Chi, Alex, and James Y. Yi *Gook.* 2017.

Burns, Ken. *Dust Bowl.* PBS, 2012.

Chomsky, Noam. *Requiem for the American Dream.* 2016.

Eastwood, Clint, et al. *American Sniper.* 2014.

LaGravanese, Richard. *Freedom Writers.* 2007.

Lazin, Lauren. *Tupac, Resurrection.* 2003.

Mackenzie, Davis. *Hell or High Water.* 2016.

McMahon, Talleah Bridges. *My Name is Pauli Murray*. 2021.
Mendes, Sam. *American Beauty*. 1999.
Nolan, Christopher. *Interstellar*. 2014.
PBS. *Putin's War*. 2022.
PBS. *Freedom Writers: Stories from the Heart*. 2019.
Sloan, Cle Bone. *Bastards of the Party*. 2005.
Snipes, Wesley. *Blade* (film series, 1998, 2002, 2004).
Spielberg, Steven, et al. *Saving Private Ryan*. 1998.
Weiwei, Ai. *Human Flow*. 2017.

Index

"The Colored Soldiers" (Dunbar): freedom in, 81–82; heroism in, 80–81; on massacres, 81; memory in, 79; sacrifice in, 78, 82–83; on solidarity, 79

Columbus, Christopher, 35–36

Common Ground, 104

concentration camps, 174–75

Congress of Industrial Organizations (CIO), 124; failure of, 141–42; limits of, 125–26; Operation Dixie by, 140–41

consumer society, 7

Convention of People of Color, 45

COVID-19, 194n50, 236

Cullen, Jim, 16–17, 40

Cultural Front, 118, 138

Culture and Imperialism (Said), 4

Cumings, Bruce, 186

The Cycle Plays (Wilson, A.), 22–23, 199; freedom in, 210; hope in, 207–8, 211–12; persistence in, 207–8; social justice in, 207; social order impediments in, 206; survival in, 211. *See also Fences; Gem of the Ocean; Radio Golf*

Dante's Inferno, 246–47

Davis, David Brion, 41

Davis, Mike, 7, 117, 134–35, 140; on CIO, 141–42; on gangs, 182; "Ward Moore's Freedom Ride" by, 143–44; on Watts, 181

Day, Dorothy, 175

Declaration of Independence, 42; egalitarianism in, 43; interpretations of, 54

democracy, 15

Democratic Party, 90

Denning, Michael, 118, 127–28

de Ste. Croix, G.E.M., 243

Devil in a Blue Dress (Mosley), 169; collocated groups in, 170; concentration camps in, 174–75; dehumanization in, 173; double-life in, 173–74; dreams in, 172; freedom lacking in, 175–76; similes in, 171; Young, M., on, 170–72, 175–76

Dialectic of Enlightenment (Adorno & Horkheimer), 63, 134–35, 166

diasporas, 10

Discourse on Inequality (Rousseau), 7

Disney, 14–15

Dixiecrats, 144, 162n92

Dixon, Thomas, Jr., 94–95

Double V campaign, 140, 175

Douglas, Aaron, 120

Douglas, Stephen, 57

Douglass, Frederick, 10; on Brown, J., 55–56, 72n93; on Chinese immigrants, 49

Drake, St. Clair, 45, 179

Dream. *See* American Dream

Dreamers, 188

dream interpretation, 3–4

Dreams of My Father (Obama), 16

Dred Scott vs. Sanford (1857), 13, 40, 56

Drescher, Seymour, 64n14

Du Bois, W.E.B., 12; on abolitionist movement, 44, 52; accomplishments of, 92; on the Black problem, 239; against internment, 126; "The Negro and the Warsaw Ghetto" by, 239–40; *The Souls of Black Folk* by, 92, 115. *See also Black Reconstruction*

Dunbar, Paul Laurence, 60, 78; acclaim for, 92; invisibility of, 87; "Robert Gould Shaw" by, 84–85; "To the South, on Its New Slavery" by, 85. *See also* "The Colored Soldiers"

Dust Bowl, 129

Eagles, 22; "Hotel California" by, 256n64; "The Last Resort" by, 165–66, 244

economists, 3–4, 24n5

Eisenhower, Dwight, 144

Ellington, Duke, 139–40

Elliot, John H., 46

About the Authors

Dr. **Thomas Ehrlich Reifer** is professor of sociology and affiliated faculty in Asian studies, ethnic studies, and Latin American studies at the University of San Diego, an associate fellow of the Transnational Institute (Amsterdam), an official Freedom Writers teacher, and one of the authors, with Giovanni Arrighi and Beverly Silver, of *Chaos and Governance in the Modern World System* (University of Minnesota, 1999), *Dear Freedom Writer: Stories of Hardship and Hope from the Next Generation* (New York: Random House, 2022), The Freedom Writers with Erin Gruwell, and has written for publications such as the *Cambridge Dictionary of Sociology* (2006), the *International Encyclopedia of the Social Sciences, Journal of World-Systems Research, New Left Review*, and *Society and Space*.

Dr. **Carlton D. Floyd** is associate professor of English, affiliated faculty in women's and gender studies, a former associate provost for inclusion and diversity, and cofounder of the Center for Inclusion and Diversity at the University of San Diego. He is coauthor with Dr. Reifer of "What Happens to a Dream Deferred? W.E.B. Du Bois and the Radical Black Enlightenment/ Endarkenment," *Socialism & Democracy in W.E.B. Du Bois's Life, Thought, and Legacy*, eds., Edward Carson, Gerald Horne, & Phillip Luke Sinitiere, New York: Taylor and Francis, 2022; "Terrorism, the International, and the American Dream: A Dialectical Fairy Tale," "*Relaciones Internacionales*: Special Issue on Rethinking Terrorism from the International" (2016); and "Politics, Poetry and Prose: W.E.B. Du Bois, *Black Reconstruction*, and the Origins of Our Times," ed., Phillip Luke Sinitiere, *No Deed but Memory: Forging American Freedom in W.E.B. Du Bois's Twilight Years*, University Press of Mississippi, forthcoming.

www.ingramcontent.com/pod-product-compliance
Lightning Source LLC
Chambersburg PA
CBHW022301280326
41932CB00010B/942

* 9 7 8 1 7 9 3 6 3 4 1 3 9 *